VOLUME ONE
Comfort From

Meditations

For Such a Time as This

OLD TESTAMENT

NORTHWESTERN PUBLISHING HOUSE
Milwaukee, Wisconsin

Northwestern Publishing House
1250 N. 113th St., Milwaukee, WI 53226-3284
© 2010 by Northwestern Publishing House
Published 2010
Printed in the United States of America
ISBN 978-0-8100-2285-0

CONTENTS

Comfort for Troubled Lives

Faith Looks to the Future

Lessons from the School of Faith

Living in Security

Conversations with God

Tests of Faith

Hold Fast to the Word

This Is Our Father's World

This Is Our Wonderful God

EDITOR'S PREFACE

For Such a Time as This. The title of this three volume set of devotions comes from a thought that Mordecai brought to Queen Esther's attention during days of trial and tribulation for the Old Testament people of God. "For such a time as this," Mordecai suggested, God had placed Esther in a position of honor and influence so she could bring God's promised help to God's people (Esther 4:14).

For Such a Time as This. Days of trial and tribulation are no strangers to God's people today. Trials and troubles challenge us, spiritual enemies beset us, fiery trials scorch our faith, our own frailty and mortality frightens us, tragic losses mount, guilt plagues our consciences, personal problems put us on the verge of despair, and sometimes even daily life seems difficult and discouraging.

For Such a Time as This. In times such as these Christians of all ages have turned to God in prayer seeking his help, his promised deliverance, his comfort. They have turned to his Word to find what he has to say to them, and for the past thirty-three years *Meditations* has helped to lead Christians to that comfort of God's Word. Comfort in the fact that God knows who we are, where we are, what we are. Comfort in that God knows the story of our lives and has seen to it through Jesus Christ that it has a happy ending. Comfort in that Jesus has promised to guide us through every trouble, even through the valley of the shadow of death, until we safely stand with him at God's right hand.

For Such a Time as This. Now 300 of those messages of comfort have been selected for inclusion in these three volumes. Each volume contains 100 devotions based on texts chosen from the Gospels, the Epistles, and the Old Testament. Pastor Henry Paustian of Watertown, Wisconsin read through some 12,045 devotions and selected the best of these comfort meditations. Minor changes have been made in some of the original devotions to bring them into line with current procedures. All Scripture quotations and citations are from the NIV; capitalization and punctuation principles reflect current style; titles now are solely the themes of individual devotions instead of a weekly series.

For Such a time as This. Note that on the cover the letters "h-i-s" in the word **this** are printed in another color. That was done to remind all of us that no matter in what situation we may find ourselves, this is still **his,** God's time, that our lives and the events in our lives happen not by chance but under the providential direction of our Father in heaven. As the cover illustration further indicates, we are always safe in his hands.

May the reader find God's comfort in these devotions.

Lyle Albrecht

Do you not know? Have you not heard? The LORD is the everlasting God, the Creator of the ends of the earth. He will not grow tired or weary, and his understanding no one can fathom. He gives strength to the weary and increases the power of the weak. Even youths grow tired and weary, and young men stumble and fall; but those who hope in the LORD will renew their strength. They will soar on wings like eagles; they will run and not grow weary, they will walk and not be faint. (Isaiah 40:28-31)

GOD PROVIDES STRENGTH FOR EACH DAY

"**G**od is not dead, nor doth he sleep," said the poet. God does not even get tired, the Prophet Isaiah adds in these words of our text. God is not dead, so we may enjoy living in our Father's world. God does not sleep, so we can lie down and rest in peace. He does not even get tired, so we can relax and let him run the universe!

He is strong and has strength to share. He will always provide today's strength for today's burdens and today's efforts. Do not try to take tomorrow's tensions and work, frustrations and anxiety, suffering and temptation today. Your God has not yet equipped you for tomorrow. You *can* cope today with today's load, for He is at your side, bearing you up. Tomorrow you will be able to cope with tomorrow's problems, because tomorrow He will give you the strength for that day.

Athletic coaches like to say: "When the going gets tough, the tough get going." Isaiah speaks of a time when even the tough might not be able to go any further, a time when "Even the youths shall faint

and be weary, and the young men shall utterly fall." By his prophet the Lord assures us here that even when the youngest and toughest and strongest can neither keep going nor get going, then those who trust in him will receive new strength from him. The Apostle Paul wrote of the experiences he had undergone for the Gospel's sake. They were experiences that only a tough man could take and they would have stopped a man who lacked commitment. He wrote: "Though outwardly we are wasting away, yet inwardly we are being renewed day by day. When our outward life seems to be a struggle which we are losing, then God renews us inwardly. He comes in Word and Sacrament, in answer to prayer, as the gracious Father of his world. He helps and renews and bears us up on eagle's wings.

The athletic coach tells his young men to reach down into themselves for reserves of strength and energy. The prophet invites us here to reach up to the LORD for a supply of his strength. He has it to spare and to share.

Almighty Father, give us each day the strength for that day. Amen.

"When my life was ebbing away, I remembered you, LORD." (Jonah 2:7)

DO HEROES FAINT?

Heroes and heroines never quit! The more exhausted their bodies become, the more they seek within themselves for reserve strength. The body just won't give up because the spirit and mind push it to continue on. Observe the prize-fighter in the late rounds of the fight. Observe the farmer straining to clear the hay-field before the threatening storm arrives. This is the stuff of which heroes are made.

Jonah nearly quit. He just about gave up. The situation looked bleak. The waters of the sea surrounded him and closed in on him. Death seemed to encircle him, growing closer and closer with each breath. Any hope for escape dimmed with the passing moments. He was down in the dumps, giving up, fainting in his heart and soul. And what added to the feeling of weakness was the fact that he knew very well he had brought this whole situation upon himself.

But Jonah did not quit. He found new hope and strength. It was not in some inherent power which he suddenly remembered that he possessed. "I remembered the LORD," Jonah tells us. The faith in his Lord which filled his heart reminded him that he had a strength outside of himself, a strength he could look to and call on to sustain him and see him through his dilemma. Oh, how this remembering lifted up his heart and soul with new courage and strength! His faith prevented his fainting into despair.

Remember the Lord! What good and sound encouragement for us when we feel faint. "I can't do it," is the frustration every heart feels at times. It may be in times of danger. It may be at times of physical exhaustion or times of worry. It may be when our sins weigh heavily on us. Remember the Lord! He has paid for those sins. He has carried the burden for us. In our Lord Jesus we have the blessed invitation from God, "Cast your cares on the LORD, and he will sustain you" (Psalm 55:22).

Remember the Lord! His strength is made perfect in us when we are most weak in body or soul. Even if our outward man, our body, grows weak under the stresses of life or the burdens of old age, we faint not because "inwardly we are being renewed day by day" (2 Corinthians 4:16). It is nourished and strengthened by God's mighty Word. Remember the Lord, and faint not!

Lord, help me remember you to find strength when I feel faint. Amen.

(The LORD) hath sent me ... to proclaim the year of the LORD's favor and the day of vengeance of our God, to comfort all who mourn, and provide for those who grieve in Zion—to bestow on them a crown of beauty instead of ashes, the oil of gladness instead of mourning, and a garment of praise instead of a spirit of despair. (Isaiah 61:2,3)

THE FORTIFIER

"**I** will praise the Lord no matter what happens" (Psalm 34:1-LB). Would you give such unconditional praise to God? Could you ever say that? Do you praise the Lord even though you have poor health, are in serious financial difficulties or have family problems? It is almost unbelievable that a sensible person would make such a statement.

And yet David did. And David was no stranger to troubles. He not only had the Philistines after him because he killed Goliath; he also had to contend with the envy and hatred of King Saul. King Saul tried to kill him on several occasions, pursued him mercilessly, so that David had no peace. David lost several children— one a baby, the others when grown.

David was also no stranger to temptation and sin. He fell into the sins of pride, adultery, lying and murder—to name just a few. Read 1 and 2 Samuel if you are interested in more details of the life of this saint-sinner King of Israel.

How could he under the circumstances of his life say, "I will praise the LORD no matter what happens"? How was David able to rise above sin and sorrow to victory and greatness?

The answer is in today's text. It points out that Jesus is the Fortifier. To fortify means to strengthen. If you find yourself weak and helpless, in need of strength and aid, then turn to Jesus. We do not find strength in ourselves, nor in the world, but in Jesus Christ. We mourn over our sin, our guilt and our mistakes. Jesus forgives our sin, removes our guilt, corrects our mistakes and gives us the ability to cope with life and death and eternity.

David was very realistic in his faith. He wrote in Psalm 34: 18,19: "The LORD is close to those whose hearts are breaking; he rescues those who are humbly sorry for their sins. The good man does not escape all troubles—he has them too. But the LORD helps him in each and every one" (LB). Believe and rejoice in Jesus your Fortifier!

Jesus, thank you for the faith and strength to cope with life. Amen.

If the LORD had not been on our side—let Israel say—if the LORD had not been on our side when men attacked us, when their anger flared against us, they would have swallowed us alive; the flood would have engulfed us, the torrent would have swept over us, the raging waters would have swept us away. Praise be to the LORD, who has not let us be torn by their teeth. We have escaped like a bird out of the fowler's snare; the snare has been broken, and we have escaped. Our help is in the name of the LORD, the Maker of heaven and earth. (Psalm 124)

OUR ONLY HOPE AND HELP

"I just don't know where to turn any more for help." Has this feeling ever crept into your heart? Have you ever felt that there was no help for you and your particular problem? Next time Satan puts this feeling into your heart, say confidently with the writer of Psalm 124, "Our help is in the name of the LORD."

The children of Israel had faced great difficulties and powerful enemies. The psalmist compares these to wild beasts ready to devour them, to a flood of waters about to engulf them and to a snare with the noose tightening around them. He confesses, "If it had not been the LORD who was on our side," we would have been overwhelmed. We were lost, hopelessly lost. But we found help with the Lord. Yes, "our help is in the name of the LORD, the Maker of heaven and earth."

The Lord is your only hope and help. When you feel that your spiritual enemies, the devil, the world and your flesh are about to devour you; when you feel that the floodwaters of doubt and uncertainty are about to drown you; when you feel that the very noose of unbelief is tightening around you, then remember: "our help is in the name of the LORD."

And if you wonder whether he is able to help, remember that he made heaven and earth. With him all things are possible. There is no problem so great that he can not solve it for you. There is no enemy so strong that he cannot defeat him. Even the greatest enemy of all, Satan, is not too strong for him. Christ has overcome the devil and the world, and he will help you overcome the temptations of your flesh.

So there is never cause for a Christian to doubt or to despair. Rather, when the minister reminds him in church every Sunday: "Our help is in the name of the LORD," he will express his confidence and trust by responding, "Who made heaven and earth."

Who trusts in God, a strong abode In heaven and earth possesses;
Who looks in love to Christ above, No fear his heart oppresses.
In Thee alone, dear Lord, we own Sweet hope and consolation,
Our Shield from foes, our Balm for woes, Our great and sure Salvation.
                                                            Amen.

Therefore we will not fear, though the earth give way and the mountains fall into the heart of the sea, though its waters roar and foam and the mountains quake with their surging. (Psalm 46:2,3)

DON'T BE AFRAID!

To feel helpless is frightening. To fear for one's life is terrible. This psalm reminds us of such feelings in a striking way: the ground giving way beneath our feet, massive mountains quaking and toppling around us, plunging into the deepest part of the sea as the waters crash and roll together with earth-shattering force. The natural catastrophes of earth—earthquakes, tornadoes, floods, etc. remind us of how easily earthly security can give way to overwhelming disaster.

Even in an otherwise peaceful world, trouble may come—a severe accident, an illness, the loss of a family member or the loss of our job or home. On our own we are vulnerable and helpless in the face of evil. With dangers and trouble all around us, what hope can the Bible offer?

In this world we will have trouble. But in Christ we have a way through the evils of life, through its troubles and trials. God is our refuge and strength. Even when we walk through the valley of the shadow of death, we fear no evil, for our Good Shepherd is with us, leading the way. His word sets our hearts at ease as we entrust ourselves and all things into his almighty care. His grace restores our lives.

We can best cope with hard times by walking with Jesus every day. We draw courage and comfort from his Word. We call for his help in prayer. We learn to share our burdens with Christian friends, and in turn help and encourage others. Together as a church and on our own as individuals, we lay down every care at our Father's throne of grace.

How often God's angels told believers in the past, "Fear not! Don't be afraid!" God is our refuge. The Holy Spirit who first brought us to trust in Jesus preserves our faith through God's Word and sacraments. This heavenly assurance of peace with God sets us free from the shame and frustrations of sin. It moves us to trust fearlessly in God even in the midst of trouble. For we know that all things work together for the good of those who love God. We fix our eyes on Jesus, through whom we have become citizens of an eternal home which will never be lost or destroyed.

Even when the end of this world arrives, and the earth gives way to the fire of the judgment, we need not fear. For out of its destruction, we will arise with joy to live with our faithful Savior forever.

Thank you, Lord, for delivering me from every evil. Amen.

They cried to you and were saved; in you they trusted and were not disappointed. (Psalm 22:5)

WHERE IS YOUR GOD?

Disappointments, failures, tragedies make life hard, trying and bitter. Does God really care when we are in trouble? "Where is your God?" says the man of the world as misfortune and sorrow heap themselves on believers.

Trials and troubles seem to tumble in from all sides, making life difficult and discouraging. At times even the sinful heart of the Christian anxiously asks, "Where is God? Has he forgotten me?"

As the believer stands at the deathbed of a dear child and then at the grave, the thought surges through the mind: Does God really love me? As the Christian has one prop after another pulled out from under him, he asks: Has God turned from me?

See all the misery, loneliness, distress and destruction in the world! And sometimes it seems as though the Christian gets a double portion of it all. Does God care? Is he really my God?

"Where is your God?" There he hangs on Calvary's cross, dying because he cares. There Jesus shed his blood because he loves us and does not want us to perish. If God did not spare his own Son, but gave him into death to make us heirs of life eternal, then he certainly does care as we go through life. He will not leave us hopeless or helpless. Underneath are the everlasting arms of God, which will not let us fall.

When it comes right down to it, we really deserve nothing good at all from God. We deserve "nothing but punishment," as we confess every Sunday. Nevertheless, he abundantly pardons us through Christ. Jesus' blood blots out even the foulest deed. There is peace, hope and joy in Christ crucified. God will not accuse us or close the door on us, but will finally deliver our souls from death and hell.

So we can live joyfully through each day, knowing that our God will sustain us. We are not stumbling along on an aimless road, but in a direction that God wills to take us for our good. So we can sleep in safety each night under the shadow of his wings. The Lord is the Keeper of our body and the Lover of our souls. And he is the Ruler of the universe. We will never be disappointed for having put our trust in him.

Dearest Savior, teach me to appreciate your sacrifice on the cross. Remove all thoughts of rebellion and dissatisfaction from my heart and help me confess that your will is wiser than mine. In every problem, let your presence calm my spirit. Help me to know and to understand that you love me with an everlasting love. Amen.

But those who hope in the LORD will renew their strength. They will soar on wings like eagles; they will run and not grow weary, they will walk and not be faint. (Isaiah 40:31)

IN HIM WE SHALL OVERCOME

The problems that faced Israel in Isaiah's day were very much like those we face today. There was tension between nations with the ever-present possibility of war. The influence of pagan religion was disturbing Israel. Economic, social, political and religious differences are equally disruptive today. Include also the personal difficulties of making a living, trying to stay healthy and out of trouble, and putting forth all the emotional energy needed to stay on good terms with family, neighbors and fellow workers. Add up all the trying and difficult problems of life, and you have all the ingredients for being really tired—dead tired. It is no wonder that many people seek escape at some weekend retreat. Some divert their attention from worries through sports activities. Others may seek escape in drugs and alcohol.

Sad to say, most people tend to look in the wrong direction for relief from the sin-included tensions of life. That is why tensions are growing, not lessening. Isaiah has a solution for this sorry situation. He promises that those who wait upon the Lord, that is, those who believe in God's power to deliver us from any and all difficulty, shall be blessed with renewed strength. He uses an illustration from nature to picture God's help. As effortlessly as an eagle spreads its wings and lets currents of air lift it up to lofty heights, so the believer will be lifted up above all his problems, especially the problems of sin. He who trusts in God's salvation in Christ will "run" through life and not be weary. He will walk the walk of life with all its responsibilities and tensions and not grow faint.

Does all this sound too good to be true? Not to the Christian who has learned with St. Paul that he can do all things through Christ, who strengthens him. For that reason it is a distinct privilege and pleasure for us to go to church to worship our God and Savior, to sing of his blessings and to praise his holy name. And we eagerly listen to his Gospel, which assures us that in Christ God has cleansed us of our sin; in Christ we have overcome death and damnation.

Thy Word doth deeply move the heart,
Thy Word doth perfect health impart,
Thy Word my soul with joy doth bless,
Thy Word brings peace and happiness. Amen.

But now, this is what the LORD says—he who created you, O Jacob, he who formed you, O Israel: "Fear not, for I have redeemed you; I have summoned you by name; you are mine. When you pass through the waters, I will be with you; and when you pass through the rivers, they will not sweep over you. When you walk through the fire, you will not be burned; the flames will not set you ablaze. (Isaiah 43:1,2)

THE PROTECTED LIFE

Famous persons and public officials are not the only people exposed to danger. Every one of us faces the possibility of injury, sickness and death. When we Christians experience such things in our lives, we may be troubled as to whether the Lord really is protecting us. Luther says in the explanation to the First Article that God is "defending me against all danger, and guarding and protecting me from all evil." If the Lord is at our side, how can evil happen to us?

This is not a new question. It was often asked by the people of Israel. Many of the psalms raise questions about the Lord's care and concern for his people. What was God's answer to Israel? What is his answer to us?

Public figures often have their body guards. Candidates for the presidency are protected by the secret service. Yet we know from experience that there is no foolproof protection. If someone is really determined to hurt or harm another person, he will at times be successful despite all protective efforts.

The words of Isaiah in our text are addressed to the people of Israel who are suffering in the Babylonian captivity. This is a word from the Lord to a nation created, redeemed and called by him. This is a word from the Lord to people who belong totally to him.

What is his promise? He does not say they will not go through any "waters" or walk through any "fire." Water and fire are symbols of the dangers and evil surrounding people. Fire is often used as a symbol for punishment and destruction. The Lord does allow trouble to come to us. We are exposed to dangers, to injury, to sickness, to death.

Yet the Lord protects us by bringing us through these dangers and troubles. He brings us through the deep waters of earthly trials and tribulations. The Lord says to his own dear children, "I will be with you. You will not drown in the deep waters. You will not be scorched by the fire." With the Lord walking at our side, we will reach the goal of our journey unharmed.

Gracious Savior, comfort me with the assurance that you will be with me in all danger, trouble and sickness. Amen.

Yours, O LORD, is the greatness and the power and the glory and the majesty and the splendor, for everything in heaven and earth is yours. (1 Chronicles 29:11)

THE COMFORT OF GOD'S POWER

A "weather rock" hangs by a rope from a tripod along a road on Washington Island in Lake Michigan. A sign is tacked up next to the "weather rock." It tells how to use the rock to tell the weather. If the rock is wet, it is raining. If the rock feels cold, it is cold. If the rock is white, it is snowing. The sign continues on and on and at the end it reads, "The wonderful thing about this 'weather rock' is that it is not affected by the weather." The implication is that we human beings are unlike the rock. We are affected by the weather and by our environment and by all of God's creation.

Because we in this world are affected by cold and heat, prosperity and disaster, these words of 1 Chronicles are so comforting: "Everything in heaven and earth is yours." God is the creator of all things. Everything that is exists with his knowledge and by his creation. Because God loves us, all things created are for our good.

But sin has corrupted all things. Sin has ruined the goodness of God's creation. But sin has not destroyed God's love for all people. "For God so loved the world that he gave his one and only Son, that whoever believes in him shall not perish but have eternal life" (John 3:16).

God loves us. He cares for us. He knows that we are not "weather rocks" unaffected by the storms and troubles of this life. Therefore God gives us his promises found in his Word: "In all things God works for the good of those who love him" (Romans 8:28). "He who did not spare his own Son, but gave him up for us all—how will he not also, along with him graciously give us all things?" (Romans 8:32)

These are the promises of the almighty God who created all things and who governs all things. He loves us. We praise our almighty God for the comfort of his power which he uses out of love for our eternal good. "Yours, O LORD, is the greatness and the power and the glory and the majesty and the splendor, for everything in heaven and earth is yours."

O Lord, since all things are yours, protect us in this sinful world in your love and mercy by your great power. Amen.

Abraham fell facedown; he laughed and said to himself, "Will a son be born to a man a hundred years old? Will Sarah bear a child at the age of ninety?" (Genesis 17:17) Sarah . . . bore a son . . . at the very time God had promised him. . . . Sarah said, "God has brought me laughter, and everyone who hears about this will laugh with me." (Genesis 21:2,6)

REASSURANCE FOR DOUBTING HEARTS

This laughter of Sarah and Abraham is the same joy and happiness that lives in our hearts when we know that God's promises are sure and that his promises apply to us. We rejoice when we finally come to see that even during our times of trouble and doubt God was with us to take care of things and make them work out for our good.

This joy and laughter are a response that comes from a faith that has just been uplifted by God's repeated promises and their fulfillment. In Abraham's case his faith came to rejoice in God's promises even before their fulfillment. Sarah's joy was complete when she saw that God truly did bring to pass everything he had promised.

We can also laugh with Sarah when we recognize that this whole story can serve to reassure our doubting hearts. It can move us to reason, "If God was faithful to his promise to Abraham and Sarah, will he not also be faithful to the promises he has made to us in his Word?"

Here God performed a mighty miracle to keep the promise of the Savior. He had promised the Savior of the world was to come from the family of Abraham and Isaac. If Isaac had not been born, that family line would have ended and along with it the promise of a Savior. If it took a miracle to bring this important child to these two old people, then God would provide the miracle.

If 2,000 years later it would take a miracle for Jesus to be born of a virgin, then God would provide another miracle. If it would even be necessary for God to leave heaven to come to earth to save mankind, then this is what God would do. He did, and Jesus who is God came to earth for our salvation.

Jesus is the reason we can laugh and sing for joy. Jesus is the reason the fear of death and hell has been replaced with joy and hope. God let nothing stop him from bringing the Savior into the world. Let us rejoice in our Savior. He wishes the laughter of faith to be found in our home.

I will greatly rejoice in the Lord, my soul shall be joyful in my God, for he hath clothed me with garments of salvation, he hath covered with the robe of righteousness. Amen.

For men are not cast off by the LORD forever. Though he brings grief, he will show compassion, so great is his unfailing love. (Lamentations 3:31,32)

GOD'S TIME IS THE BEST TIME

"How long will this suffering continue?" This is a question which many a Christian has asked during periods of severe testing. And yet his very suffering can serve as a source of real comfort to him. Scripture makes this point repeatedly. The Bible is lined with comforting passages which become especially precious to those who are experiencing the chastening rod of God. Job, for example, who endured afflictions far greater than any we will ever have to bear, was comforted by the knowledge that, "When he has tested me, I will come forth as gold" (Job 23:10). The Apostle Paul, who experienced numerous tribulations himself, encourages us to "rejoice in our sufferings," because "suffering produces perseverance; perseverance, character; and character, hope" (Romans 5:3,4).

So leave everything up to the Lord! His time is the best time when it comes to bestowing blessings of joy as well as blessings of affliction.

The psalmist writes, "Out of the depths I cry to you, O LORD; O LORD, hear my voice. Let your ears be attentive to my cry for mercy. If you, O LORD, kept a record of sins, O LORD, who could stand? But with you there is forgiveness; therefore you are feared. I wait for the LORD, my soul waits, and in his word I put my hope. My soul waits for the LORD more than watchmen wait for the morning, more than watchmen wait for the morning. O Israel, put your hope in the LORD, for with the LORD is unfailing love and with him is full redemption. He himself will redeem Israel from all their sins" (Psalm 130).

When we remember that the Lord "will have compassion according to the multitude of his mercies," our thoughts include, but also soar above, the many temporal blessings which we sinners receive from him in this world of sin. We fix our gaze upon the compassionate Christ, who bestows eternal blessings on those who are oppressed by sin and guilt —for he has removed our sin and guilt and the cause of all suffering. In him we have conquered sin and death and Satan and hell.

When we are reminded by the theme for today that "God's time is the best time," how can we forget that best "time" of all, the "fullness of the time" when God sent forth his Son to redeem the world! The redemptive work of this Son of God makes it easy for us to endure the tribulations of life on earth, for we look ahead in confident faith to the endless bliss of heaven!

To you, O God and Savior, we give all praise and honor. Amen.

Who has understood the mind of the LORD, or instructed him as his counselor? Whom did the LORD consult to enlighten him, and who taught him the right way? Who was it that taught him knowledge or showed him the path of understanding? (Isaiah 40:13,14)

QUESTIONING GOD'S WAYS

"**L**ord, sometimes I just don't understand you. Just when our income is already strained, the washing machine breaks down. When I could be teaching Sunday school, this illness keeps me in bed. You have promised what is best for me, but, Lord, this is hard to understand." Does this sound like us at times? Often because we do not understand God's ways, we are tempted to doubt the wisdom of God's dealings with us. There are many things we don't understand about God.

Job, an Old Testament believer, found himself questioning God's way of doing things. Job was suffering a prolonged hardship when his questioning of God's wisdom began. Emphatically God asked Job, "Where were you when I laid the earth's foundation? Tell me, if you understand" (Job 38:4). Job was unable to respond. God thus taught him the truth of the words, "For my thoughts are not your thoughts, neither are your ways my ways," declares the LORD (Isaiah 55:8).

The text of today's meditation is a similar reminder from God when we begin to question the wisdom of his dealings with us. We are asked, "Who has directed the Spirit of the Lord? Who was his counselor? Who taught him justice, knowledge, understanding?" The answer: No one. The lesson: God's wisdom, knowledge, understanding and his way of doing things are supreme. The heroes and heroines of faith didn't always understand God's will for their lives. But they trusted his wisdom, his knowledge, his judgment and his foresight. With a childlike faith they learned that "God moves in a mysterious way, his wonders to perform."

There will be times when we just don't understand God's will for our lives or his ways of dealing with a loved one. It is at such moments that we will be comforted by remembering how his wisdom far excels ours. In time, like Joseph, we will discover that even the most perplexing and disastrous events can become a source of blessings from God—from a loving God, who knew in advance the result.

Dear Lord, forgive us for doubting your wisdom and your manner of dealing with us. May the knowledge that you know all things be a comfort to us. Teach us to pray, "Lord, I don't understand, but I do believe." We thank you for the blessings you have bestowed upon us, especially faith in Jesus Christ as our Savior. Amen.

I will not die but live, and will proclaim what the LORD has done. The LORD has chastened me severely, but he has not given me over to death. (Psalm 118:17,18)

IF A MAN DIES, WILL HE LIVE AGAIN?

In the midst of life we are in death. As we see people, the young and the old, one by one leave the land of the living, there arises the question, "If a man dies, shall he live again?"

Yes, says Jesus. But even more. The resurrection day of Jesus Christ makes me sure that I shall not die, but live.

I shall not die eternally. Eternal death, the fearful wages of sin, with all its hellish torments, has lost its power over believers. Christ has abolished it. He has brought life and immortality to light. Jesus said of himself: "I am the Resurrection and the Life." He proved that claim. Not only did he raise Lazarus from the dead and restore life to him, he also laid down his life for our sins and took it up again to confirm his words as true.

This is the same Jesus who says to us: "Because I live, you shall live also." "He who believes in me will live, even though he dies; and whoever lives and believes in me will never die."

Of course, the prospect of physical death faces all of us. Our body will then corrupt in the grave. But we shall rise from the dead. Christ will fashion our vile body like unto his glorious body, and we shall see him as he is, for we shall be like him and live with him eternally in his home of glory.

This is our resurrection hope, glorious, comforting and sure. As death and the grave could not hold Jesus, so it cannot hold those who die trusting in him. Christ is the first fruits of them that slept. The full resurrection harvest of all believers will follow when Christ comes again at the last day.

This hope which we have in Christ, however, has meaning for us during this life as well. With this sure hope of life in Christ, we do not despair under adversity and affliction. God may indeed let trials, afflictions, pain and suffering come upon us. We know, however, why he does this. In his love he is only chastening us, for whom the Lord loves, he chastens. He wants to correct us when we sin, so that we are not condemned with the world. He wants to exercise our faith in humble trust and patience, and draw our eyes upward to that untroubled life he has prepared for us in heaven.

Therefore, even as he chastens us, we are confident that he has not given us over to death, that we should suffer eternally. With unshaken faith in our risen Savior, we will go on to declare the works of the Lord and praise him for the marvels of his mercy both here in time and hereafter in eternity.

**Abide with us; with heav'nly gladness
Illumine, Lord, our darkest day;
And when we weep in pain and sadness,
Be Thou our Solace, Strength, and Stay.
Tell of Thy woe, Thy vict'ry won,
When Thou didst pray: "Thy will be done." Amen.**

So the two women went on until they came to Bethlehem. When they arrived in Bethlehem, the whole town was stirred because of them, and the women exclaimed, "Can this be Naomi?" "Don't call me Naomi," she told them. "Call me Mara, because the Almighty has made my life very bitter. I went away full, but the LORD has brought me back empty. Why call me Naomi? The LORD has afflicted me; the Almighty has brought misfortune upon me." (Ruth 1:19-21)

LOOKING TO A HAPPY ENDING

Why do some of God's children seem to have such unhappy and miserable lives? A good person to ask would be Naomi, mother-in-law of Ruth. Remember her story.

There was a severe famine in Israel. Naomi, her husband Elimelech, and their two sons were forced to leave their home in Bethlehem and immigrate to the country of Moab across the Jordan River. But this new land did not give the family the happiness it sought. Elimelech died very soon. The rest of the family still stayed in Moab. His two sons married Moabite women, Ruth and Orpah. Then unexpectedly the two sons also died.

Ten years after leaving Bethlehem, Noami returned. She left with an empty stomach; she returned with an empty heart. She left with a husband and two sons; she returned with a daughter-in-law. And she was a Moabite. Her old friends hardly recognized sad Naomi. No wonder she told them, "Don't call me Naomi (Gracious). Call me Mara (Bitter)."

We can readily understand Naomi's bitterness. All she could see at her homecoming was her past suffering and sorrow. She had lost her husband and sons. Their life in Moab was a failure. She was destitute. It seemed like even God was against her.

But we know how the story turned out. We can read ahead and find out that Ruth becomes a greater blessing to her mother-in-law than a dozen sons. We know that in time Naomi would hold in her arms a grandson. He was destined to be the grandfather of great King David and the ancestor of David's greater Son, the Savior Jesus Christ. However Naomi could see none of this at her return.

As with Naomi, God in his all-knowing wisdom does not allow us to look into our future either. So then it is not surprising that sometimes we too are inclined to bitterness. When we look backward at deaths in the family, loss of a job, failure in school or rejection by a loved one, it becomes rather easy to blame God.

We can only look at the past, God knows the future. Our heavenly Father already knows the story of our life. And he has seen to it that through Jesus Christ it has a happy ending—in heaven.

Gracious God, remove all bitterness and fill me with your love. Amen.

14

I know that my Redeemer lives, and that in the end he will stand upon the earth. And after my skin has been destroyed, yet in my flesh I will see God; I myself will see him with my own eyes—I, and not another. How my heart yearns within me! (Job 19: 25-27)

FAITH THAT LOOKS TO THE FUTURE

Job was sure he was dying. He was in agony. His strength had completely left him. All hope of recovery was gone. What was left? Job's only comfort was the living hope of the resurrection.

There is nothing that helps a Christian through difficult days more than meditating on the resurrection. Christ is risen, and so we too shall rise. It's a glorious future that awaits us in heaven. That sunbeam of eternity can pierce through any gloom and misery which weigh us down now.

The thing that's so remarkable about Job was that he could express so clearly the same hope we have. Even though he lived hundreds of years before Christ rose from the dead, he could see with eyes of faith his living Redeemer standing on the earth at the last day.

With those same spiritual eyes he could see himself in front of the Savior, looking at him with his own eyes, his bones once more clothed with flesh, ready to hear the blessed invitation of Christ: "Come, you who are blessed by my Father; take your inheritance, the kingdom prepared for you since the creation of the world" (Matthew 25:34).

That faith which Job had is the same faith we need when everything seems to fall apart. When death itself appears to be at the door, it is our hope of the life to come with Christ that sustains us. A faith which looks to the future can say with Paul, "I consider that our present sufferings are not worth comparing with the glory that will be revealed in us" (Romans 8:18).

Can we see that glory? Can we look beyond the grave with Job to the day when our bodies will be raised and made like Christ's own glorious body? Can we fix our vision on the day when we will see the Lord with those same eyes that so often see only misery and suffering on this earth? Job conquered all with his triumphant faith in the resurrection. We can too.

Dear Lord, let me see your Son on the glorious day of the resurrection and hear his invitation to the blessings of heaven. Amen.

The LORD blessed the latter part of Job's life more than the first. (Job 42:1,2)

STORM CLOUDS ON THE ROAD TO HEAVEN

The air is never so fresh and full of zest as after the storm. The air is cool, the atmosphere clear and the sun is radiant. That's true after the spiritual storms that strike us also pass. After coming to the brink of despair on account of illness, financial reverses or spiritual depression, the Lord blesses us more at the end than at the beginning as he did Job.

After hiding his face behind the black clouds of suffering, once more God lets the sunshine of his love flood over us and we are overwhelmed with the consciousness of the goodness of the Lord. The person who was oppressed with an overpowering sense of guilt and sinfulness suddenly realizes that it's really true that where sin abounded, grace abounds much more.

Job's suffering had an end. Job once had been the greatest man in the east. Now we read that the Lord blessed him with twice as much as he had in the first place. Job saw that the Lord had not cast him away forever but rather had purified him like fine gold, so that the glory of his faith shone brighter at the end than at the beginning.

Our trials and sufferings will also have an end. All Christians may say with confidence, "Even though I walk through the valley of the shadow of death, I will fear no evil, for you are with me; your rod and your staff, they comfort me." The road on which the Lord leads us is still the road to heaven. Job, Noah, Abraham, Jacob, Joseph, Moses and David all passed through dark days of trial, but all basked again in the Lord's favor. We can look back on past difficulties in our lives and must confess that the Lord has delivered us from them all.

Finally, after the trials of this life have passed and our faith like Job's shall have triumphed by the power of the Holy Spirit, we have the sure promise of God's Word: "He will wipe every tear from their eyes. There will be no more death or mourning or crying or pain, for the old order of things has passed away" (Revelation 21:4).

Surely, our end will also be greater than anything we have ever experienced up until now. "You have heard of Job's perseverance and have seen what the Lord finally brought about. The Lord is full of compassion and mercy" (James 5:11). Follow Job, then, in patient suffering to the abundant blessing which inevitably follows.

Lord, deliver us from all evil and finally for Jesus' sake receive us into the eternal happiness of heaven. Amen.

Rejoice greatly, O Daughter of Zion! Shout, Daughter of Jerusalem! See, your king comes to you. (Zechariah 9:9)

JOY IN THE MIDST OF PROBLEMS

At the time Zechariah wrote these words, there was little to rejoice about. The people of Judah had recently returned from captivity in Babylon. Work on the Temple had been halted by Samaritan opposition. The Jews had fallen into disfavor with the ruling Persian monarchs. God's people had become spiritually lethargic. To rouse his people to action and also to comfort them, the Lord sent the prophets Zechariah and Haggai. In the midst of Judah's gloom, Zechariah cried out, "Rejoice! Your king comes to you." God would send his Son to rescue them. This was cause for rejoicing.

The people of Jesus' day also lived in depressing times. They were under the domination of the Roman government. Tax collectors overcharged them and made their lives miserable. The religious leaders of the day misled and oppressed the people. Yet, in the midst of this gloom Christ brought joy. When he was born on Christmas, the angels filled the fields of Bethlehem with their songs of joy. God's Son had become flesh. This was a cause for rejoicing. When the aged Simeon beheld the Christchild, he joyfully praised the Lord.

Wherever Jesus went, he brought joy into the lives of sinners. Whether they were publicans, like Zacchaeus or Matthew, or the woman taken in adultery or the blind Bartimaeus, Jesus brought joy into their lives. The joy he brought was not a mere surface emotion that soon left them. Rather, Jesus brought joy based on the forgiveness of sins and the certainty of eternal life.

In our day, people also live in depressing circumstances. People have financial problems, health problems, marital problems and a host of other problems. People may be victimized by crime, unemployed, or socially disadvantaged. We all point to a number of things that are perplexing to us. But whatever problems we may have, we still have every reason to be happy and filled with joy. Jesus came to save us from death and hell. We are the children of God through faith in him. Our King made it possible for us to reign with him in heaven. We shall live forever in the presence of our King before his throne. There is no greater joy than this.

"Hosanna in the highest!" That ancient song we sing,
For Christ is our Redeemer, the Lord of heaven our King.
Oh, may we ever praise Him with heart and life and voice
And in His blissful presence eternally rejoice! Amen.

The LORD their God will save them on that day as the flock of his people. (Zechariah 9:16)

THE GOOD SHEPHERD LEADS US HOME

Sheep are very helpless animals. They are not intelligent. They cannot outwit their enemies. They do not have sharp hoofs to ward off an enemy's attack. They do not have sharp teeth to tear at the flesh of an attacking animal. They do not have great speed to outrun predators. They really have only one means of defense, and that is the shepherd. If it were not for the faithful shepherd, the sheep would soon perish.

It is no coincidence that Scripture frequently compares us with sheep. We, too, are helpless. In and of ourselves we cannot stand against the attacks of the devil, the world and our own sinful flesh. If it were not for the constant care of our Lord we also would perish.

It is with good reason that Jesus is called "the Good Shepherd." The prophet Ezekiel foretold the fact that the shepherd of God's people would be a king descended from the line of David (Ezekiel 34:23,24). Zechariah prophesied that this shepherd would be struck down (13:7), sold for 30 pieces of silver (11:12) and pierced through (12:10). All of this coincides with the words of Jesus, "I am the Good Shepherd. The Good Shepherd lays down his life for the sheep" (John 10:11). Jesus not only cares for his flock's physical needs, he has taken care of their greatest need— the need for forgiveness. He did this by his death on the cross and resurrection from the dead.

Though his lifeless body was in the grave for a brief time, Jesus rose from the dead triumphant on the third day. We, the members of his flock, have assurance that he lives to preserve us as his own until we stand with him in heaven. There the glorious vision of St. John will be fulfilled, "For the Lamb at the center of the throne will be their shepherd; he will lead them to springs of living water. And God will wipe away every tear from their eyes" (Revelation 7:17).

When we become frightened by the troubles in our lives and our own frailty, let us turn our eyes to our King, our Good Shepherd. He says to us, "My sheep listen to my voice; I know them, and they follow me. I give them eternal life, and they shall never perish; no one can snatch them out of my hand" (John 10:29).

The Lord my Shepherd is,
I shall be well supplied.
Since He is mine and I am His,
What can I want beside? Amen.

On that day the LORD will shield those who live in Jerusalem, so that the feeblest among them will be like David. (Zechariah 12:8)

STRENGTH FOR GOD'S PEOPLE

There are times, places and conditions that cause us to feel helpless, hopeless and powerless. In such circumstances the very thought of having enough strength to meet and overcome those things which make us feel feeble is beautiful. To be the possessor of an infallible promise which guarantees a time of strength fills us with joy, hope and peace. How one yearns to be so blessed at such times.

The people of God at Zechariah's time were in a most difficult and discouraging situation. There seemed to be no light in the darkness which was settling on them. They seemed to have no future. Everything seemed hopeless. They needed some inspiration. They needed some hope.

In our text God sets before his people that which they needed so desperately. He urges them not to look so much at themselves and their troubles but to lift up their eyes and look to the wonderful blessings in the day of the Messiah. That day would come. Its fulfillment would be total bliss and perfection in heaven.

There the salvation of God would completely fill God's people and strengthen them. Then all weakness would be gone. The most feeble would be royalty like David, the great king. Each of God's people would then be crowned with everlasting glory, honor and power. No matter how discouraging or hopeless things might seem, God's people were to take heart. God's promise of the day of the Messiah was true. He would come and give to his people the glory of heaven.

Such a message is vital for us of today also. There are so many things that trouble us, so many that confront us, so many dangers which threaten and worry us. Sometimes we all feel that we cannot go on and that we have no hope, no future. We become worried, afraid and feeble. At such times we need to listen to God speak through Zechariah of the coming eternal day of royal majesty and glory.

Through Christ this day is yours and mine now. We need to lift up our eyes to see our glorious future and by faith to walk onward in joy, strength, hope and peace. God in love pledged that day would come. God's Son lived, died and rose that it would be ours by faith in him. Therefore, people of God, listen to your God and be strengthened. Lift up your eyes and be encouraged. Walk onward in faith as those who are royalty and who will be like David in heaven.

Lord, let the spirit of David be ours in life, his glory be ours in death. Amen.

"And you will go out and leap like calves released from the stall. Then you will trample down the wicked; they will be ashes under the soles of your feet on the day when I do these things," says the LORD Almighty." (Malachi 4:2,3)

AWAITING THE DAY OF VICTORY

If you've ever lived on a farm or visited one at the right time, you probably have seen one of the most amusing things that can happen there. In the winter, the young cattle are put in barns to protect them from the bitter cold outside. They stay there until spring comes when they are let loose into the pasture. The moment the doors and gates are opened, those young calves take off for the wide open spaces like a bunch of clowns. They kick their heels high in the air and dance in circles. They act as if they were the happiest creatures God ever made.

In our passage for today, Malachi compares the joy of those who believe in Christ as their personal Savior from sin, death and hell, to the joy of those released calves. Even while living here on earth, we have already experienced that joy. It's the deep happiness that comes from knowing that our souls are secure for eternity—safe in the hands of Jesus our Lord. But that joy has only just begun.

Everything is not perfect yet. Being a believer and follower of Jesus is not *all* sunshine and roses.

We find that we are continually plagued by enemies—there is that unbelieving person who regularly pokes fun at our faithfulness to the Lord. There is the old evil Foe himself, Satan, who is always trying to tempt us to sin, and succeeding far too often. And there is one final enemy—death. These enemies are terrifying—and powerful. Who are we to cope with them?

But God promises us in this passage that these enemies shall one day be totally put down. They will be as powerless on the great day of the Lord as the dirt we walk on.

The Lord has already won the victory. When Jesus rose from the dead on Easter morning, he gave us visible proof that he had the power to conquer all our enemies—even death.

We have a share in that victory through faith in Christ as our Savior. For us it's only a matter of time until we sit at the victory table with our Lord in heaven. When judgment day comes, we will experience firsthand what it means to have absolutely perfect happiness and joy forevermore. That day may be very soon.

Alleluia! Alleluia! Alleluia! The strife is o'er, the battle done; now be the song of praise begun. Alleluia!

"The Redeemer will come to Zion, to those in Jacob who repent of their sins," declares the LORD. (Isaiah 59:20)

THE MEANING OF CHRIST'S VICTORY FOR US

What comfort to know we will surely obtain the glory which Jesus won for us. Clinging to that Victor we can exult in a world of strife. If God is for us—and Calvary's cross shows he is—who can be against us?

But can our conscience exult, recalling our rebellion against him? The blood of Jesus Christ, God's Son, cleanses us from all sin. Our sins are completely removed.

Can the legions of hell overcome us? The Redeemer came and he destroyed Satan's power forever. That's final!

Can our evil nature triumph over us? The unbreakable Word shows us that, "if anybody does sin, we have one who speaks to the Father in our defense—Jesus Christ, the Righteous One" (1 John 2:1). He has washed all our scarlet guilt white as snow, and made it spotless as fleecy wool.

Can affliction gain supremacy over us? Paul challenges, "Who shall separate us from the love of Christ? Shall trouble or hardship or persecution or famine or nakedness or danger or sword?" (Romans 8:35)

Because what seem losses to us come as proof of God's love, we can battle disaster and cry out, "No, in all these things we are more than conquerors through him who loved us" (Romans 8:37).

More than conquerors of sin.

More than conquerors of evil thoughts.

More than conquerors of the hostile world.

More than conquerors of temptations.

More than conquerors of doubt.

More than conquerors of death.

We can challenge, "Where, O death, is your victory? Where, O death, is your sting?" (1 Corinthians 15:55)

We have won with Christ. He is the Savior of all. He stands at our side. He meets every need. He has defeated every enemy of our soul once and for all.

Let us build our hope on him. As truly as he is the Son of God, victory is ours. We will face enemies, of course. Yet, with Jesus we will not fight alone. He will help us overcome and obtain the victory.

Jesus, stand at my side every minute of every day to assure me of redemption through your precious blood. Then whatever comes on life's battlefield, I will win with you. Amen.

For the LORD watches over the way of the righteous, but the way of the wicked will perish. (Psalm 1:6)

TRUE JOY HERE—TRUE JOY HEREAFTER

Fellow Christian, be happy! God knows you! He knows the way of the righteous. God laid out the way for us. He called us to it by his Gospel. His Spirit enlightened us to faith with his gifts. He keeps us in that way. "We are God's workmanship, created in Christ Jesus to do good works, which God prepared in advance for us to do" (Ephesians 2:10). How clearly Jesus points to that evidence of God's work in the lives of the righteous. He shows how they walked the way of faith and performed the good works ordained for them.

Be happy even if at times you feel that God doesn't know. You have the privilege to talk things over with him in prayer. Tell him your troubles or your needs at these times. Mary and Martha did that when their brother was ill. They informed Jesus, "Lord, the one you love is sick." They felt: If Jesus knows, he will do what is best and right. They were happy to let it go at that. Remember, even when the way of the righteous is rocky and thorny, be happy. God knows the way he leads. He has numbered the very hairs of your head, and you will not lose a single one without his knowledge.

Be happy. God assures you that everything upon your way will work together for your good. He leads you so that in the end he may invite you to come to his right hand and inherit the kingdom prepared for you from the foundation of the world. He will make you a king! He will greet you and say, "Here is your palace; it is prepared just for you."

Senior citizen, you say you feel forsaken at times? Be happy! You are never alone. He is with you and knows you so well that he calls you by your name. When the time is right, he will ask you to come to him.

Teen-ager, you are suffering ridicule for Christ? Be happy! You are not standing alone; Jesus knows your stand and confession. He is with you and will see you through to victory. He will confess you before his Father.

You who are away from home, in service, in school. Do you feel that the world is against you? Are temptations powerful? God has not forsaken you. He knows. Cling to him in faith, and you will be happy to all eternity.

To Christians everywhere God says, "I know you, you are mine own. Though sin and Satan seek to fell you, rejoice! Your home is with the blest."

Jesus, in mercy bring us
To that dear land of rest.
Who art, with God the Father
And Spirit, ever blest. Amen.

Therefore my heart is glad and my tongue rejoices; my body also will rest secure, because you will not abandon me to the grave. (Psalm 16:9,10)

SAFE EVEN IN DEATH

There is no greater reason for fear and insecurity than the fear of death. Today that fear has been increased by the threat of nuclear war. Every time we hear of the death of a relative or friend, we are reminded of the certainty of our own death. Even if we are young, we never know whether or not today is our last day on earth. It is certainly inevitable and even proper that we have fear of death. Death is not natural. It is a result of the curse of sin. Death is the tearing apart of body and soul, which God created to be together. Death is an enemy to be defeated and overcome. Indeed, death is the last and most terrible enemy which we must confront.

But thanks be to God, we cannot be defeated even by this terrible enemy. Because Christ has defeated Satan, sin and death, death cannot destroy us. Death cannot separate us from God and his love. Even in death our body and soul will be kept safe until they are united again on the day of resurrection. Both body and soul will be kept safe, but in different ways.

When we die, our soul returns to God, its creator. The souls of unbelievers go to hell to await judgment, but the souls of the believers are taken to heaven to be kept safe in the presence of God. Scripture does not give us much information about what the souls in heaven feel or experience between death and the day of resurrection, but we know that they are safe and enjoying a peaceful rest with God.

Although our body decays and returns to the ground from which it was created, we can speak of the death of the body as a sleep. The point of the comparison is that when we lie down to sleep at night we expect to wake up in the morning. When we place a lifeless body in the grave, we do so with the confidence that Jesus will wake that body to life on the day of resurrection. With his almighty power he will be able to restore that body no matter how it has dissolved or has been scattered in the meantime. Since we have this knowledge, not even the fear of death can overwhelm us.

Lord, let at last Thine angels come,
To Abram's bosom bear me home,
That I may die unfearing;
And in its narrow chamber keep
My body safe in peaceful sleep
Until Thy reappearing. Amen.

Into your hands I commit my spirit; redeem me, O LORD, the God of truth. (Psalm 31:5)

SAFE IN GOD'S HANDS

With Thee, Lord, have I cast my lot;
O faithful God, forsake me not,
To Thee my soul commending.
Lord, be my Stay, Lead Thou the way
Now and when life is ending.

(TLH 524:6)

The words of our psalm verse and those of our hymn stanza are quite familiar to us, particularly these words of prayer: "Into your hands I commit my spirit"; for so spoke our Redeemer as he closed his life on the cross.

Many of the noblest saints of God have died with these same words upon their lips. When Johann Huss was on his way to the stake, there was stuck on his head a paper cap scrawled over with the picture of the devil; but he said with sure, calm faith: "Father, into your hands I commit my spirit!"

These words show us the manner in which death can and should be met by all of God's children. We may meet the king of terrors with confidence, with profound repose, for he is a vanquished enemy whose sting has been removed. Note well, that which gives us the confidence to pray: "Father, into your hands I commit my spirit," is this word and assurance of faith: "Redeem me, O Lord God of truth!"

Those who rest in the redemption of Christ are people who can confidently commit themselves body and soul into the hands of God. They know they are safe because they know they are saved. They cling to his promise: "Fear not, for I have redeemed you; I have summoned you by name; you are mine." They know they are secure for all eternity. They say with Paul: "The Spirit himself testifies with our spirit that we are God's children. Now if we are children, then we are heirs—heirs of God and co-heirs with Christ, if indeed we share in his sufferings in order that we may also share in his glory" (Romans 8:16,17). The future shall be one of perfect beauty and blessedness.

But should we use those words only in death? Should we not be committed to the hands of our father every day of our life? Should not every day be a day of self-surrender? Should not our being, our body, our soul, our all be committed to him who has asked us in his love: "Commit your way to the LORD; trust in him and he will do this." That surrender will mean safety and security, blessing and bliss for every day.

"So be it," then I say
With all my heart each day.
We, too, dear Lord, adore Thee,
We sing for joy before Thee.
Guide us while here we wander
Until we praise Thee yonder. Amen.

When the LORD brought back the captives to Zion, we were like men who dreamed. Our mouths were filled with laughter, our tongues with songs of joy. Then it was said among the nations, "The LORD has done great things for them." The LORD has done great things for us, and we are filled with joy. (Psalm 126:1-3)

HOME AT LAST

A scene in New York Harbor affects the feelings of Americans returning from far corners of the globe. Travelers have said that, as they caught sight of the Statue of Liberty, they were overcome with emotion. That lofty torch told of freedoms they had seen in no other land. The sight stirred their hearts and brought forth tears of joy.

God's people are like this. Our text describes the feelings of Old Testament people returning from captivity to their beloved Jerusalem. It was too good to be true! As captives in a far-off land, they had dreamed of this moment. For years the older ones had tried to remember the hills of Jerusalem. Children had heard stories of the homeland they had never seen. Their minds had pictured the old Temple, since destroyed, with its sacrifices, prayers and worship. How they longed to be back there.

Finally it came true. At last they were home. It was like a splendid dream. How good God was to bring them to these delightful scenes. As the longtime exiles trod the holy ground of their fathers, they laughed and shouted and joined their neighbors in grateful songs. They were home! God had brought them home.

Are we not exiles today? While we, as Christians, have our hearts fixed on things of heaven, yet we live in this world, this "Babylon" of sin, grief and death. This captivity is troublesome. It makes the believer in Jesus long for deliverance. And in due time, God has promised, the deliverance will come. When we are escorted by the angels into heaven, we will see an eternal homeland that is beyond our fondest dreams. We will understand fully why it was that Jesus was willing to have "laid on him the iniquity of us all." Jesus died under our sins that his believers might share with him the grand joys of heaven.

These joys are beyond description. When the believer passes through the black but harmless curtain of death and first lays eyes on heaven, he will think he is dreaming. He will wonder how such joys can exist. He will see, as he never fully saw on earth, the immense value of Jesus' blood and death. It was truly a great price which brought sinners the glories of heaven. He will never cease to marvel that these glories are all his, and for no works of his own. Yes, the world had once laughed at the Christian. But now it will be his turn to break into the joyous laughter and singing of eternity. His Lord will have brought him home at last.

Comfort us, O God, with your promises of heavenly joy. Give us patient hearts to bear ridicule and temptation as we await heaven, and even now let us laugh and sing that we have forgiveness in Jesus Christ. Amen.

God is our refuge and strength, an ever-present help in trouble. Therefore we will not fear, though the earth give way and the mountains fall into the heart of the sea, though its waters roar and foam and the mountains quake with their surging. Selah. (Psalm 46:1-3)

GOD IS A VERY PRESENT HELP

When Luther was about to appear before the church council at Worms, he prayed thus: "O God, Almighty God everlasting! How dreadful is the world! Behold how its mouth opens to swallow me up, and how small is my faith in Thee! . . . Oh! The weakness of the flesh and the power of Satan! If I am to depend upon any strength of this world—all is over. . . . The knell is struck. . . . O God! O Thou my God! Help me against all the wisdom of this world. Forsake me not, for the sake of Thy well-beloved Son, Jesus Christ, my defense, my buckler, and my stronghold."

While Luther sang with confidence, "We tremble not, we fear no ill," he always did so with full knowledge of how weak he was. He recognized his need for strengthening from the Lord, who "surrounds his people, as the mountains surround Jerusalem" (Psalm 125:2).

In the history of the old covenant men had been granted visions to bring out this fact that God rings his people with defense in every danger. The army of Benhadad, king of Syria, came and stood around Dothan, the city in which the man of God Elisha lived. He sought to get rid of the prophet, who had proved to be such a thorn in the flesh for him and his people. A great host of horses and chariots came by night and surrounded the city. It was most terrifying to the servant of Elisha when, upon rising that morning, he beheld that very imposing army around the entire city. He rushed in to his master and said, "Oh, my lord, what shall we do?" "Don't be afraid," the prophet answered. "Those who are with us are more than those who are with them."

Elisha had the confidence that the Lord gives. But since the servant still lacked it, Elisha prayed, "O Lord, open his eyes so he may see." The Lord opened the eyes of the young man, and he saw the mountain full of horses and chariots of fire round about Elisha. God is a very present help, if men will only see him!

With might of ours can naught be done,
Soon were our loss effected;
But for us fights the Valiant One,
Whom God Himself elected.
Ask ye, Who is this? Jesus Christ it is,
Of Sabaoth Lord,
And there's none other God;
He holds the field forever.

(LH 262:2)

O Lord, who gives power to the faint and increases strength to those who have no might, help us, who are your children by faith in your Son, to know assuredly that no evil will befall us and that no plague can come nigh our dwelling. Amen.

The LORD . . . keep you; (Numbers 6:24)

KEPT IN HIS CARE

Now I lay me down to sleep;
I pray the Lord my soul to keep.
If I should die before I wake,
Take me to heaven for Jesus' sake.

We wonder how many thousands of children have learned that verse as their first bedtime prayer. And it's a good prayer. It reminds children, and their parents, that the Lord will keep them. They are in his care. The word translated "keep" in the Aaronic blessing says the same thing. Sometimes the Hebrew word is translated "guard" or "watch over." When God keeps us that is what he is doing—guarding us and watching over us.

Even when we are asleep, God is taking care of us. As one of the psalms says, "He who watches over you . . . will neither slumber nor sleep." In addition to his personal care, our loving God also uses his angels to keep us. Another psalm states this truth: "He will command his angels concerning you to guard you in all your ways."

What greater confidence could we ask for? The almighty God and his powerful angels are keeping us day and night. Many times without our realizing it they are keeping us from death or disaster on the highway. They keep us safe at home, at school and at work. More importantly, the Lord keeps us spiritually. Through his Word he keeps our faith alive and prevents us from falling into unbelief and eternal death.

This doesn't mean that we never have any troubles or heartaches. God says we can expect that while we live in this world. But because we are kept in his care, we know that everything is working together for our eternal good.

So even in the darkest hour we can be sure that God is keeping us. Even in the hour of death we know that he will keep us from falling away and will take us to heaven for Jesus' sake.

Because God is so good to us, there is something we will want to do for him. To show our love for him we will want to keep his commandments. That's our way of saying, "Thanks, Lord, for keeping me in your care!"

Hold Thou Thy Cross before my closing eyes,
Shine through the gloom, and point me to the skies.
Heaven's morning breaks, and earth's vain shadows flee;
In life, in death, O Lord, abide with me! Amen.

Then we your people, the sheep of your pasture, will praise you forever; from generation to generation we will recount your praise. (Psalm 79:13)

OUR TENDER SHEPHERD'S CARE

The shepherd guides his sheep along a narrow, stony path. Ever so often a sheep strays from the path to be brought back by a smarting blow of the shepherd's staff. Another straggles behind and would be lost, did not his shepherd poke him along. One slips off the mountain path and is caught on a ledge. The shepherd tenderly hauls him to safety with the crook of his staff. Even when the flock reaches the grass-covered slope of the valley, some are not satisfied, but stray from the rest only to expose themselves to the clutches of wild animals. These the shepherd seeks out, rescues and many a time nurses back to health. He is not content unless he can bring each one back to the safety of the fold.

We are such sheep of our Good Shepherd. Having made us his own through his holy, precious blood and innocent suffering and death, he leads us gently along the narrow and often forbidding pathway of life. Though we hesitate to follow, his voice continues to call and encourage, and to keep us from becoming lost. When we straggle behind, when we choose a more inviting byway of the world, when we stumble and fall into sin, his voice lovingly calls us back. At times his rod strikes very hard, but no matter from what depths of despair we cry out, we hear the voice of him who promises: "I will never leave you or forsake you." "Come, follow me!" We are delivered from all the hurts of sin by him who came to heal the broken-hearted and bind up their wounds. Our repentance and faith are always and continually answered by his Shepherd's care.

"So we your people and sheep of your pasture will praise you forever." In the same breath that we penitently pray with the psalmist: "Oh, do not hold against us our former iniquities," we are able to thank him for his goodness. He is so close to us with his saving Word that forgiveness and help are assured. So deep and heartfelt should be our gratitude that it cannot be kept hidden. As it has come down to us through the ages of our Lord's eternal grace, so is it ours to share from one generation to the next: "From generation to generation we will recount your praise."

O faithful Savior, we praise you for tenderly watching over your sheep; keep your eyes upon us when we are in danger of growing secure and careless; make us to see the weakness and helplessness of the flesh, and warn us to watch and pray that we may not put our trust in ourselves, but in fervent prayer call on you for help. Amen.

Since you are my rock and my fortress, for the sake of your name lead and guide me. (Psalm 31:3)

ONE PLUS GOD!

Thou art my Strength,
my Shield, my Rock,
My Fortress that withstands each shock,
My Help, my Life, my Treasure.
Whate'er the rod, Thou art my God;
Naught can resist Thy pleasure.

(TLH 524:4)

No matter how great the danger or how mighty the foe, "if God be for us, who can be against us?" This truth is also expressed by the hymn stanza above. We *are* surrounded by fearsome foes and deadly dangers. We must not be unmindful of the fact that our "enemy the devil prowls around like a roaring lion looking for someone to devour." Make no mistake about it— he is a powerful foe. He comes with signs and lying wonders. He, too, could turn the Egyptian sorcerers' rods into serpents; he, too, could change Egypt's water into blood; he, too, could call up Samuel's spirit against Saul. He caused the hounding and harassment of David, and he causes the same for us. It is his evil will and counsel that seeks to hinder and hamper the good will of God. He is truly the old evil Foe!

Powerful he is, but not all-powerful. When he pitted his strength against God in heaven, he was defeated and cast out into hell. Now, God is our God, and when we say with David: "You are my God," we are saying that he is our Strength, our Fortress, our Help, our Life, our Treasure, our Shield and our Rock.

You may be only one; you may be all alone; you may be forsaken by all others; yet you are a majority with God. Surely, David experienced this truth in a most extraordinary way, when God sent him out to battle against the giant Goliath. Humanly speaking, David didn't have a ghost of a chance; but he was not alone; God's promise was behind him! One plus God is always a majority!

Paul Gerhardt has said it for us:

If God Himself be for me,
I may a host defy;
For when I pray, before me
My foes, confounded, fly.
If Christ, my Head and Master,
Befriend me from above,
What foe or what disaster
Can drive me from His love?

(TLH 528:1)

Why are we often so quick to forget and so slow to remember the power and promise of our God? Why are our fears so large and our faith so little? Why not build and bolster our faith with the power of his Word and rest securely and serenely on his promises? Is it mere idle talk when God says: "Commit your way to the LORD; trust in him and he will do this"? No; our trust shall ever be: "Thou art my rock and my fortress." "What'er the rod, Thou art my God; naught can resist thy pleasure."

I am trusting Thee for power;
Thine can never fail.
Words which Thou Thyself shalt give me
Must prevail. Amen.

But the men who had gone up with him said, "We can't attack those people; they are stronger than we are." And they spread among the Israelites a bad report about the land they had explored. They said, "The land we explored devours those living in it. All the people we saw there are of great size. We saw the Nephilim there (the descendants of Anak come from the Nephilim). We seemed like grasshoppers in our own eyes, and we looked the same to them." (Numbers 13:31-33)

THE FEAR OF FAILURE

It was a golden moment for the children of Israel. It was a time to take advantage of one of the opportunities the Lord was placing before them. After a long journey through the desert they had now come to the Promised Land. In obedience to a command of the Lord they sent spies to scout the land.

The resulting report was partly favorable. It spoke of a fruitful country; it pictured a land flowing with milk and honey. But the report was also partly unfavorable. A majority of the scouts emphasized the fortified town and formidable enemies they had seen; they were afraid.

They were afraid in spite of the Lord's promise to them. As Joshua and Caleb stated in a minority report, "If the Lord is pleased with us, he will lead us into that land. . . . The Lord is with us. Do not be afraid of them" (Numbers 14:8,9).

The problem that the majority of the scouts thought confronted them in the land of Canaan reflects a problem that frequently arises in the lives of all Christians. The fear of failure looms large.

To be sure, Christians are to count the cost before they embark on some venture. But that cost is to be counted in the light of the Lord's will. If we are confident that we are doing his will, then the fear of possible problems and fear that we might not succeed should not deter us. If we rely entirely on ourselves, we have a right to be fearful of the outcome. But if we are doing what the Lord wishes, then we can be assured that he will be with us in what we do.

This does not eliminate the possibility of problems, but it does remove the threat of failure. Troubles may well arise, but the final, *eternal* result will be success—even if, for the time being, we experience what appears to be nothing but pure failure and frustration. When Christ is with us, there are no ultimate failures or tragedies. Knowing that, let us move forward in faith and work during the daylight the Lord has given to us.

O Lord, give us the courage to take advantage of the opportunities that you place before us, and not to shrink in fear of failure. Amen.

And Abram said, "You have given me no children; so a servant in my household will be my heir." Then the word of the LORD came to him: "This man will not be your heir, but a son coming from your own body will be your heir." He took him outside and said, "Look up at the heavens and count the stars—if indeed you can count them." Then he said to him, "So shall your offspring be." (Genesis 15:3-5)

COUNT YOUR BLESSINGS

Astronomers have long ago given up trying to count the stars. With entire galaxies thought to be still undiscovered, who can say how many stars there are? Counting the stars is an impossibility. It must be put into the same category as walking on the ceiling, burning water on the stove or lifting oneself up by his own bootstraps. It cannot be done.

What then could Abram hope to accomplish by trying to count the stars? For one thing, he might begin to see how wrong he was. Today when a person has made an error of judgment, we say that he was "off by a mile." Abram was off more than that. How badly he had miscalculated his future! How foolish he was to doubt God's promise and God's ability! He had begun to doubt that God was able to give him one offspring, but God was going to give him as many as the stars. Therefore as he counted the stars, the sheer multitude of those stars was a gentle reminder to Abram how far wrong he had been in doubting God.

But every one of those twinkling stars also represented a blessing from God to Abram. In counting the stars, Abram was at the same time counting his blessings from God. Every star was a sign of God's love and faithfulness. God would keep his word. He would give Abram offspring as numerous as the stars, just as he had promised.

Today the stars still twinkle in the heavens to remind us how wrong anyone would be who doubted God. Just as the rainbow stands in the heavens as an assurance of God's faithfulness, so the stars are witnesses of that same great faithfulness. When we see the stars and think of Abram's blessings, we might also think of our own blessings. Our blessings too are as numerous as the stars.

Take time out this evening. If weather permits, go outside and count the stars. Count your blessings if you can. What a wonderful God we have! How great and how good! What God is able to give, man cannot count—blessings as many as the stars.

Thank you, Lord, for all your blessings to me. They are as many as the stars. Thank you especially for my Savior. Amen.

"Yet I reserve seven thousand in Israel—all whose knees have not bowed down to Baal and all whose mouths have not kissed him." (1 Kings 19:18)

WE ARE NOT ALONE

Loneliness is a problem which everyone faces at sometime in their life. It has been known to lead a person to drink, to commit suicide, to have an extramarital affair, to even lose one's sanity. It might even be safe to say that loneliness leads to no good, because it so often leads to despair.

Despair can be unbearable. The devil would have us believe that we are all alone because of our sins. He plants thoughts in our minds such as: "God can't possibly forgive you for that. Don't listen to all that bunk about not having to do anything to make up for your shortcomings. You can work it out yourself." This kind of thinking led Martin Luther to try to work out his own peace with God. In the process he nearly killed himself.Our sinful minds can also come up with ideas about despair. "What's the use of living, no one loves me!" "I can't have this baby now; it will destroy my career." Elijah, prophet of God, was just as good at despairing as we are. "I am the only one left; take my life," he told God.

Certainly each of us has problems. They may seem unbearable, and we just cannot cope with them. As Christians, however, we have been given a joy that is greater than any of the problems we have now or ever will have. Our joy is found in our Savior who has rescued us from the clutches of sin by his death on the cross. He has rescued us from the power of death by his resurrection. He continues to rescue us every day from problems, despair and temptation by being with us. Through his Word he continues to come to us with the reassurance that we are not alone in our fight against sin, death and the devil. The sweet message of his gospel turns our sorrow over sin into joy and expectation. The hope of heaven is ours.

This hope of heaven is something we have in common with our fellow Christians. Just as the Lord needed to remind Elijah that the church still existed, so we too need to hear that we are not alone. We have fellow sufferers in Christ. God's Word and his church will endure forever.

Thank you, Lord Jesus, for coming to this earth to share in our suffering. Keep the joys of heaven before us at all times, lest we allow sin to lead us to despair. Amen.

The LORD will watch over your coming and going both now and forevermore. (Psalm 121:8)

BLESS OUR GOING OUT WE PRAY

How has everything gone so far today? Did it turn out just as you expected it would? Or were there some surprises? Some disappointments? Did you please God in all your thoughts and desires, your words and deeds? Or did you sin?

However things went for you this day, you've made it through only because God walked with you. He provided for all your needs. He preserved and protected you in all your ways. He blessed your coming into today, your journey through it, and now also your going out of it.

As Christians we surely know that we have good reason to be thankful for each day of our lives. Because of our sinfulness, we have deserved nothing good from God. It is only because of Jesus, our Savior, that God has been with us and blessed us so bountifully. It is because of God's mercy in Christ that we were not consumed by his anger. He has rather granted us his peace and love, pardon and protection.

At the end of each day, each week, and at the end of our lives, we can fall asleep and rest in peace. God has preserved our coming in and will also preserve our going out according to his promises. By faith in Christ I know that he has forgiven me all my sins and will graciously keep me this night. Into his hands, I can commend my body and soul and all things. His holy angels will be with me that the wicked Foe may have no power over me.

We have walked with God today. We entered it in his name, bringing him our sorrows and needs, our worries and sins. He has met us right here through his living Word and bestowed upon us all the blessings of salvation. What faith and joy, courage and strength are ours in Jesus Christ.

May we spend every day and every week walking with God in worship and prayer. Then he will indeed bless us and keep us. He will make his face shine upon us and be gracious unto us. He will lift up his countenance upon us and give us peace.

Bless our going out, we pray, bless our entrance in like measure; bless our bread, O Lord, each day, bless our toil, our rest, our pleasure; bless us when we reach death's portal, bless us then with life immortal. Amen.

As the deer pants for streams of water, so my soul pants for you, O God. My soul thirsts for God, for the living God. When can I go and meet with God? My tears have been my food day and night, while men say to me all day long, "Where is your God?" These things I remember as I pour out my soul: how I used to go with the multitude, leading the procession to the house of God, with shouts of joy and thanksgiving among the festive throng. Why are you downcast, O my soul? Why so disturbed within me? Put your hope in God, for I will yet praise him, my Savior and my God. (Psalm 42:1-5)

THE CRY OF THE SOUL HOMESICK FOR GOD

Have you ever been homesick? There are those who make fun of this sickness as though it were a mere childish weakness. But men with really broad shoulders have this sickness.

The author whom God inspired to write Psalm 42 was homesick. His homesickness, however, had this peculiarity that he was depressed, not because of his absence from home, but because of his absence from God's house and from fellow worshipers in that house. The son of Korah who wrote this psalm appears to have been in exile with David at the time when the king had to flee before his son Absalom. So he found himself surrounded by heathen people who constantly made fun of him because of his religion. They were always trying to make a fool out of him because of his childlike trust in his God. How this man would have loved to run away from the taunting unbelievers and again enjoy religious services with God's people! But at the moment that privilege was not his. That made him homesick.

Have you ever been homesick for God and for the church service? If you have been in a situation where you could not enjoy your accustomed church service, then you will have had this homesickness. Christians simply cannot escape such homesickness for God and for his house. For every soul that knows God feels its need for him very keenly. Where there is no feeling or real need for God, there Christianity has ceased to exist. Only God can give that spiritual life which is known as Christianity, and only God can sustain it. He does so through his Word and sacraments. The Christian realizes that when he is cut off from the Word and sacrament, his Christianity is in danger. For that reason he experiences the pangs of homesickness when he cannot enjoy the Means of Grace regularly in the public service.

Most of us are not cut off from public worship. Do we cherish this blessing?

Heavenly Father, graciously give us hearts that would be homesick for you and your house if we lacked the privilege of regular worship there. We ask this in Jesus' name. Amen.

Can a mother forget the baby at her breast and have no compassion on the child she has borne? (Isaiah 49:15)

GOD'S GRACIOUS CONCERN FOR HIS PEOPLE

The people of God in Isaiah's time had questioned God's concern for his chosen ones. Likewise, in the hour of despair when our faith becomes weak, we are in need of God's strengthening Word of assurance. Though it may seem to us that we are forgotten and forsaken, yet God would have us put such thoughts out of mind by asking us to contemplate the question, "Can a mother forget the baby at her breast and have no compassion on the child she has borne?"

Luther, in his commentary on this text, presents some beautiful thoughts for our consideration: "The love of a mother's heart cannot forget its child. This is unnatural. A woman would be ready to go through fire for her children. So you see how hard women labor in cherishing, feeding and watching. To this emotion God compares himself, as if to say, 'I will not forsake you, because I am your mother. I cannot desert you.' In that word there is comprised the example of a woman, and from it we derive our consolation."

The second question that God asks his children as he puts their faith to the test is, "Can a mother . . .

have no compassion on the child she has borne?" The word "compassion" in this text suggests a very close tie—like that which exists between a mother and her beloved son. She is ready to make sacrifices for her son even though they may not be noticed or appreciated. She is willing to forgive him when he has done wrong. She is willing to forget ingratitude. She is ready to show mercy even when the son's behavior causes feelings of frustration and disappointment.

Our God here uses the example of what is most likely the greatest of human loves—that of a mother for her infant child. Yet even this love will change because of sinful human nature. The daily papers regularly carry the news of parents abandoning or abusing their children. Usually the children are not to blame.

Our heavenly Father is not like a human parent. Because of our sin he could abandon us to a fate worse than death—eternal death. Instead he sent his Son to take our punishment and die our death. For Jesus' sake God forgives us all our sins. He is most graciously concerned about our eternal welfare.

Lord God, heavenly Father, continue to manifest your love and forgiveness to us. We believe that your love is greater than that of any mother, for you gave your Son for our salvation. Amen.

The LORD has done this, and it is marvelous in our eyes. This is the day the LORD has made; let us rejoice and be glad in it. (Psalm 118:23,24)

A DAY NOT TO BE FORGOTTEN

Whenever we have experienced a day of special significance or joy, it is not easily forgotten. We never really tire of thinking about it or talking of it. It is even more so with this day which the Lord has made, the day of our Lord's triumphant resurrection from the dead. When we truly realize the tremendous significance of that day for the Lord Jesus and for ourselves, we understand that this day is not one to be soon forgotten.

The blessings of Easter are meant for us to enjoy each day of our lives. This day, then, ought to remain great and marvelous in our eyes at all times.

Certainly, we then will never tire of hearing the message of what God has done for us in raising Jesus from the dead. God wants us to live each day with faith in the risen Christ and with the eternal hope that he has made sure for us. Each day we have work to do for our Lord; there are new problems in life to face and overcome, new responsibilities to carry out.

Let Easter give constant strength, courage and confidence to our faith. It reminds us that we have a risen and living Lord who cares for us, who provides for all our needs, who helps us do all things, who lives to forgive our sins daily and bless us with peace in our hearts.

When we may have the sad duty to stand at the open grave of a believing loved one, let us again remember this day which the Lord has made, this day of our Lord's victory over death and the grave. Our tears will dry as we hear him say to us: "For the perishable must clothe itself with the imperishable, and the mortal with immortality."

Scripture reminds us that we were buried with Christ by baptism into death, that like as he was raised up from the dead by the glory of the Father, even so we should walk in newness of life. We were once dead in sin and under Satan's tyranny. But Christ has redeemed us from all that. He paid the price. We have risen with him to a new life. Let the day of Easter remain marvelous in our eyes in this way, too, that we walk in a new life. Let us daily crucify the flesh with its affections and lusts, growing in love, and all good works, living under Christ in his kingdom, and rejoicing in hope.

Finally, when we ourselves must go down to the grave, let us hold firmly the hand of our victorious Savior. Our hearts will then be comforted, knowing that we shall ever be with the Lord.

Grant me grace, O blessed Savior,
And Thy Holy Spirit send
That my walk and my behavior
May be pleasing to the end;
That I may not fall again
Into Death's grim pit and pain,
Whence by grace Thou hast retrieved me
And from which Thou hast relieved me. Amen.

"This is what the LORD says—your Redeemer, who formed you in the womb: 'I am the LORD, who has made all things, who alone stretched out the heavens, who spread out the earth by myself.' " (Isaiah 44:24)

OUR LIFE IS SECURE FOR ETERNITY

Life is such a struggle. We never know from one moment to the next what to expect. Of one thing we Christians can be sure, and that is that, "We must go through many hardships to enter the kingdom of God" (Acts 14:22). Satan would have a field day with this truth. He causes our sinful nature to focus on the "hardships." Our old Adam doesn't like hardships. It likes ease and pleasure. Satan likes to whisper in our ears, "See, God wants you to suffer."

This is when we need God's reminder that he is our Redeemer. He called us to be his own people even before the world itself was formed. Having been made and redeemed by God himself, we can answer Satan's objection with, "hardships, yes, to enter God's kingdom."

Trials and tribulations will come our way. It often seems as though we Christians have more trials than anyone else. Yet God has prepared for us an eternity of glory. With such a prospect before us we can see our trials as only temporary, and as means by which God readies us for heaven.

God also reminds us of his almighty power. By his power he made all things. What we can see, as well as what we cannot see, came into existence when God said, "Let there be!" The wondrous heavens above and the beautiful earth beneath exist because God made them and preserves them. God also emphasizes that he did this alone.

This almighty God is the God who loves us with an everlasting love. He sent his only-begotten Son "that whoever believes in him shall not perish but have eternal life."

He forgives us all our sins, creating in us faith which trusts in Jesus alone as Lord and Savior. He made us what we are. We are his sheep and lambs, who rest in his almighty, loving hands.

"If God is for us, who can be against us? He who did not spare his own Son, but gave him up for us all —how will he not also, along with him, graciously give us all things?" (Romans 8:31-32) Having redeemed us by Jesus' death, he lets us know that our lives are secure for eternity by Jesus' resurrection.

Lord God, by your almighty power graciously keep us secure from all harm and danger unto eternal life, for Jesus' sake. Amen.

"Have I not commanded you? Be strong and courageous. Do not be terrified; do not be discouraged, for the LORD your God will be with you wherever you go." (Joshua 1:9)

GO WITH GOD

Once before the children of Israel had been up to the Promised Land. Fear had kept them out. Yes, it was a land flowing with milk and honey. But there were difficulties in taking it. The people who lived there were very strong, and their cities were protected with stout walls. So the children of Israel were afraid to try to go in. God had promised that he would give them the land, but they were not willing to take him at his word. Theirs was a fear born of unbelief.

Unbelief still produces fear. Unbelief can paralyze our mission program if we are afraid to go out and possess the land for Christ. We may find all kinds of excuses for not carrying out God's commands, but the real reason is usually fear and unbelief.

That's why God still tells us in his Word, "Be strong and courageous. Do not be terrified; do not be discouraged, for the Lord your God will be with you wherever you go." The Lord takes care of us as we walk! He is our Good Shepherd, defending us with his strong rod, and guiding us with his staff. He is our Comforter and Protector in the valley of death. Wherever we go in faith, we can also go with confidence because he goes with us!

"Go with God, then." This was the message given to Joshua and the people of Israel. This is the message for us. Young people can "go with God," as they plan their education, their work and their life. Parents can "go with God" through all the difficulties along life's way. And those who are approaching the end of their journey can "go with God" even through death's dark valley.

God gave the land to Joshua and the faithful people of Israel. The forbidding walls of Jericho crumbled before the blast of their trumpets. The inhabitants of the land fled in fear before the army of God's people. "The Lord is with them and he fights for them," they cried.

Go with God and your goal is assured, a God-pleasing life here on earth and a glorious crown of life in heaven! Fear him, and you will have nothing else to fear, as he says,

"Fear not, I am with thee,
  oh, be not dismayed;
For I am thy God and
  will still give thee aid;
I'll strengthen thee, help thee,
  and cause thee to stand,
Upheld by My righteous,
  omnipotent hand!"

Lord, be with me, and I shall not be afraid! Amen.

The LORD . . . give you peace. (Numbers 6:26)

A LASTING PEACE

Just what is this peace God gives us? There is a little story which, I believe, precisely illustrates the peace of God. The story tells of an artist who was asked to paint a picture that would visualize the idea of peace. The artist painted a roaring waterfall with a large tree hanging over it. On a limb of that tree, bending over the churning waters and almost touched by the rising spray, a sparrow calmly sat on her nest. Amid the roar and danger of the waterfall, the tiny bird was at peace.

That is a picture of our peace from God. Like that bird, we are surrounded by danger and troubles. But in the middle of all life's turmoil the Lord gives us peace. We are at rest.

Jesus assures us, "Peace I leave with you; my peace I give you. Do not let your hearts be troubled and do not be afraid." Our hearts are at peace. We know that the almighty God loves us. We know that life's dangers can bring us no lasting harm. We know that the joys of heaven lie ahead. This is the peace, lasting peace, God leaves us.

It is not a peace that comes naturally. We had been God's enemies—at war with him, rebelling against his every command. But our sins have been washed away in the blood of Christ. The Holy Spirit has brought us to faith in Christ as our Savior. St. Paul put it this way, "Since we have been justified through faith, we have peace with God through our Lord Jesus Christ."

There's something else special about this peace. It's for each of us. Throughout the Aaronic blessing the original Hebrew language uses the singular for "you." God's peace is not just for "you" as a large group of people. It's for "you" as a priceless individual. You may be a parent or a child. You might live alone or in barracks or a dormitory with hundreds of other people. You might be a man or woman, black or white, living in America or across the seas. It doesn't matter; you can still have peace. God's peace is for you!

That means, of course, that others can also enjoy it. Share the peace you have. Confess your Savior. With your gifts and prayers support God's missionaries—those messengers of life and peace.

**Grant us Thy peace throughout our earthly life,
Our Balm in sorrow and our Stay in strife;
Then, when Thy voice shall bid our conflict cease,
Call us, O Lord, to Thine eternal peace. Amen.**

**"In those days Judah will be saved and Jerusalem will live in safety."
(Jeremiah 33:16)**

THE CHRISTIAN'S SAFETY NET

A construction company in charge of building a bridge across a rather large body of water discovered that by putting a net below the men working on the steel girders of the bridge the efficiency and attitude of the workers rose dramatically. Just knowing that there was a net below to keep them from drowning gave the men a confidence and sense of security that they just couldn't have without it.

The sufferings and death of our Lord Jesus Christ have the same effect on us spiritually. God told the children of Israel that when the promised Messiah, the righteous Branch from David's line, would come, Judah would be saved and Jerusalem would live in safety. God was not simply referring to a time of earthly peace for Israel during the years that Jesus walked on this earth. He was referring to that peace which surpasses all understanding. That peace comes from a knowledge of the forgiveness of all our sins in Christ. By shedding his holy, precious blood on the cross and suffering its pain and torment, Jesus paid in full the penalty for all our sins. Because of Jesus' death on the cross we do not have to fear death. We do not have to fear judgment day, for neither death nor hell can harm us. Because of Jesus' death on the cross for our sins there is peace once more between God and man.

The knowledge of forgiveness in Christ, the knowledge that come what may, we are safe from eternal death and damnation, gives us as believers in Christ a peace, a confidence and a sense of security that sickness or sorrow, hardship or trouble, pain or even death cannot shake. The Apostle Paul states it so beautifully, "For I am convinced that neither death nor life, neither angels nor demons, neither the present nor the future, nor any powers, neither height nor depth, nor anything else in all creation, will be able to separate us from the love of God that is in Christ Jesus our Lord."

Peace in our hearts, confidence to face any situation in life, and a sure hope of eternal life in heaven some day are the "net" results of Jesus' suffering and death on the cross. May the cross of Jesus Christ be ever before our eyes throughout our life.

O loving Father, may the cross of Christ calm all our fears and give us peace and hope all the days of our life here on earth. Amen.

Though the fig tree does not bud and there are no grapes on the vines, though the olive crop fails and the fields produce no food, though there are no sheep in the pen and no cattle in the stalls, yet I will rejoice in the Lord, I will be joyful in God my Savior. (Habakkuk 3:17,18)

JOY WHEN YOU'RE DOWN AND OUT

"Good morning," said the man as he passed the stranger on the sidewalk. To his surprise the stranger turned and said, "I have never had a bad morning." "May you always be so fortunate," he replied. "I have never been unfortunate," the stranger said. "Then may you always be so happy." To that the stranger replied, "I've never been unhappy."

There probably are few people in the world who would answer as that stranger did—and fewer still who would think he was telling the truth. The prophet Habakkuk, however, seems to be speaking in this euphoric way in our devotional text. And he means what he says, because he knows the Lord is in charge and that all things serve the Lord's purpose. Habakkuk can say in his prayer that no matter what happens he will be joyful in the Lord.

Habakkuk paints a picture of perhaps the most desperate situation which people in Bible times could possibly envision. If there were no figs, grapes, olives, grain or domestic animals—items which were the very staples of life—it would be most difficult to survive.

When droughts came, people feared just such a thing. Apart from capture and death at the hands of their enemies they could imagine nothing worse.

Even if he were to be in such a desperate situation, Habakkuk says he would still rejoice in the Lord. Why? The words of Paul to the Romans, chapter 8, give the answer, "If God is for us who can be against us?" With God on our side we are never at a loss. The situation may seem desperate, even totally hopeless, but he who loved us so much that he sent his Son to die for our sins will take care of us and give us all we need.

Perhaps we will never experience a situation so desperate as that which Habakkuk describes, but sometimes money may be scarce, it may even be difficult to put food on the table. Even then we can rejoice in God our Savior, in whom we have forgiveness and eternal life in heaven. No one can ever take that away from us, and having that, we have everything—including the assurance that he will take adequate care of us during our life on earth.

Heavenly Father, you have taken care of our greatest need, our need for forgiveness and salvation in Jesus our Savior. Strengthen us in our convictions that you will take care of our other needs as well. Help us to rejoice in all circumstances. Amen.

Let the sea resound, and everything in it, the world, and all who live in it. Let the rivers clap their hands, let the mountains sing together for joy. (Psalm 98:7,8)

NOTHING BUT JOY AND THE SOUNDS OF JOY

I t is difficult for us to visualize a life without sorrows, pains, tears and death. These are man's common experience here, and not man's only, but of all creatures since the fall into sin. Groaning and travail or anguish—how familiar! But how tragic, too, for those who believe that it is the only world that ever shall be!

It is precisely from the curse over this world that a gracious God has redeemed us. For those who accept this redemption and trust the precious promises of God there is a great comfort. They foresee by faith the new heaven and earth which God has prepared for them. In this new heaven and earth there is nothing but joy and the sounds of joy. The whole environment in this new life reflects and echoes the songs of praise and joy of God's redeemed people: The sea roars or thunders, the rivers clap their hands, the mountains sing together for joy.

Truly, "you have made known to me the path of life; you will fill me with joy in your presence, with eternal pleasures at your right hand."

Even in this life, in the hour of worship, as we hear God speak to us and so reveal his love again and again; as we are assured of forgiveness, peace and an inheritance with the saints in light, we have some small foretaste of the glorious reign of the Savior in the next world. We sense, and in a small way begin to understand and appreciate, the joys that shall be ours.

How this prospect of the eternal reign of Christ and the bliss it brings us stirs up feelings of hope and confidence! Though we may face sorrows and troubles here, they are eased and made light by him who calls us to himself to give us rest. Indeed, the sufferings of this present time are not worthy to be compared with the glory which shall be revealed in us.

With these wonderful and sure promises of God before us, with glimpses of the good things God has prepared for them that love him, we will hold fast in faith to the Savior Jesus Christ and patiently await the day that brings us nothing but joy.

Lord God, let us live and die in peace, for our eyes have seen your salvation in Christ, your Son and our Redeemer. Amen.

Praise the LORD, O my soul; all my inmost being, praise his holy name. Praise the LORD, O my soul, and forget not all his benefits—who forgives all your sins and heals all your diseases, who redeems your life from the pit and crowns you with love and compassion, who satisfies your desires with good things so that your youth is renewed like the eagle's. (Psalm 103:1-5)

PRAISE THE LORD, O MY SOUL

Soar like an eagle! Who can soar like an eagle? The true Christian can! For he has been born again to a "lively hope" through the Gospel of God.

In olden times the eagle had a reputation for quick recovery and the ability to make a fresh start, with energy, wings and feathers renewed. And such also is the rebirth which the Holy Spirit accomplishes in God's people. That is why their jubilation and thanksgiving are not a sometime thing, but a way of life. "Praise the Lord, O my soul!"

Outside of Christ it is hard to think of life as a celebration of God's benefits. For the eye of reason surveys the ruin of human nature caused by the Fall: everywhere there is greed and strife, disease and death. Yes, even within ourselves we sense the corruption and weakness which come from sin. Deep in their hearts all men tremble at the ripening judgment of God the Holy One!

What, then, is different about the Christian, that his heart alone brims over with praise to the Holy One? Nothing but the exceeding charity of God in Christ. For through Jesus Christ God has bought our lives back from damnation and eternal death. God has satisfied his justice with that one precious death upon Calvary's cross—there need be no more. The Christian lives in this truth.

Now if God's love is the great, active reality in my heart, then all of life wears a new face. There is healing when I need it and ask for it, in order that I may live and praise the works of the Lord. There are good gifts at every turn: parents, spouse, family, friends, food, shelter, the air, the earth, the land I love. Even hardship and heartache become forms of grace when I think about God's tender care. And at the last, the crown of eternal life! "Praise the Lord, O my soul, and forget not all his benefits!"

I will sing my Maker's praises
And in Him most joyful be,
For in all things I see traces
Of His tender love to me. . . .
All things else have but their day,
God's great love abides for aye. Amen.

You will go out in joy and be led forth in peace; the mountains and hills will burst into song before you, and all the trees of the field will clap their hands. (Isaiah 55:12)

FOLLOWING WHERE GOD LEADS

The final blessing of the Christian faith is to depart from this world in peace and to enter into everlasting glory. Christ makes our death a glorious victory rather than a final defeat. From that moment on our joy is complete.

The whole Bible prepares us for that moment of triumph. When Adam and Eve left the Garden of Eden, they took God's gracious promise of redemption with them. The blessings that they lost in Eden would ultimately be restored to them when they would leave this sin-infected world. The Exodus from Egypt reminds us how God will deliver us from the bondage of sin and bring us into the heavenly land of promise. We find the same reassurance in the return of the Jews from 70 years of exile in Babylon. Jesus promises, "I am going there to prepare a place for you. And if I go and prepare a place for you, I will come back and take you to be with me" (John 14:2,3). So we know where we are going as we follow Jesus.

There will be no perfect outward joy or peace along the way. We can expect trouble and sorrow as long as we live in this world. We will experience our share of uncertainty and doubt, disappointment and failure. If we follow Jesus, we may expect the same kind of treatment as he received from this world. With the help of God, however, we can learn to rejoice even in our tribulations. We have God's promise that he will make all things work together for our good.

We are at peace with God through faith in Christ Jesus. Nothing destroys inner peace like a guilty conscience. As we do our best to follow the guidance of God's Word day by day, our consciences remain clear. As we daily receive God's forgiveness for our many misdeeds, we are at peace with God.

As we go on our way hand in hand with Jesus, as we faithfully follow his instructions, we need not worry at all. We are not responsible for the way that things finally turn out; he is. Our only duty is to follow and to obey. He assures us that we will finally reach the perfect joy and peace of our heavenly home.

In our final moment of triumph we may pray with pious Simeon:

Sovereign Lord, as you have promised, you now dismiss your servant in peace. For my eyes have seen your salvation, which you have prepared in the sight of all people. Amen.

Even to your old age and gray hairs I am he, I am he who will sustain you. I have made you and I will carry you; I will sustain you and I will rescue you. (Isaiah 46:4)

OUR ONE AND ONLY SOURCE OF SECURITY

Many people in the world to- day are desperately search- ing for security—security from the cradle to the grave. In their minds, if they could find the right combination of material blessings, such as the perfect job with high pay and a solid retirement plan, they would never need to worry again. If they would only look around them and consider what has happened to others like them who have placed their trust and sought their security in the things of this world! There is no lasting security in the material things of life.

What these worldly minded people are doing is little different from what God's ancient people, Israel, had done. Israel turned away from God and sought security, peace of mind, in things of this world. People today make money, a good position, earthly goods, their gods. They are thus caught up in various forms of idolatry. But their search for security in such false gods of this world is useless and vain.

In our portion of God's Word, the Lord reminds Israel that he is their one and only source of true security. He reminds them of the loving care he has shown them in the past, saying, "I have made and I will carry you; even I will sustain . . . you." It is the Lord God of Israel who had created them and had cared for them in their youth. He is the One who was providing for them now and would continue to do so even unto their old age. "Even to your old age . . . I am he," is God's assurance.

What God is saying here applies also to us. He is our faithful God who has provided for us in the past, is doing so now, and will continue to provide for us all the days of our life. Our faithful God provides all the security we need in this world. He also provides for our eternal life. This is what he means when he says in the final words of our text, ". . . and (I) will rescue you."

The psalmist, by God's inspiration, reassures us of these same wondrous blessings, saying, "The Lord will watch over your coming and going both now and forevermore" (Psalm 121:8). Our faithful God is our God from eternity to eternity.

Lord, we thank you for your promises to preserve us for evermore for Jesus' sake. Amen.

In you our fathers put their trust; they trusted and you delivered them. (Psalm 22:4)

WHOM DO YOU TRUST?

We can't live without trust. Marriage is a relationship based on mutual trust. Children trust and depend on their parents. Patients who submit to surgery rely on the doctor's skilled hands.

But on earth our confidence is often misplaced, often disappointed. We trust our physical strength, yet illness lays us low. We build our assets with investments, and then a recession comes to threaten our security. We trust friends with secrets only to find their hearts are false and that they use their tongues against us. We trust our own opinions, only to find that they often don't square with facts.

Our ideals lie shattered, our goals unattained, our ambitions unfulfilled. In the end we find that self-reliance is able to produce nothing but depression and despair.

The psalmist reminds us to redirect our trust and to focus our attention on God, who alone is trustworthy. We can rely on him because we have proof that he has acted mightily for us. In Jesus Christ God assumed the burden of our broken nature and canceled out the charge of sin. By his death and resurrection Jesus demonstrated that the God of power is the God of love who is "for us." He is the same powerful God who again and again delivered his people down through the ages.

On earth there is no sure and snappy cure for all that ails us. There is no insurance policy that will protect us against illness and death. Neither does God tell us in his Word that we will have a heaven on earth. Our calling as Christians is not to sit back and drink in the pleasures of this world, but to toil and labor while it is day—to seek the welfare of Christ's kingdom. This is not without suffering and trouble. We are still sinners living in a world that is under God's curse. But he has promised his presence even in the middle of toil and trouble, crisis and calamity. He sustains us through sorrow and strengthens us through strife with a grace that is sufficient for us. He protects us and delivers us from all that would harm us or rob us of our salvation. And in the end he will bring us into heaven, where we will find our eternal rest and joy in him.

Lord God, you have always proved faithful to your promises in the past. Our fathers will agree that you have blessed them in every way. We know from your Word that you will fulfill all your promises to us now and in the future. Keep us safe in the hollow of your hand, for the sake of your Son, Jesus Christ. We have put our trust in you. Amen.

And the LORD commanded the fish, and it vomited Jonah onto dry land. (Jonah 2:10)

DO HEROES NEED HELP?

"I had a lot of help along the way." True heroes in whatever walk of life will gladly admit to this. They will readily speak of the help given to them by a father or mother, a teacher, a coach, a husband or wife, or a friend. How many an award of achievement has not been accepted accompanied by the words, "I would like to recognize and thank those who helped me."

As Jonah lay on the dry land along the seashore, he might well have sighed within his heart, "I would like to recognize and thank him who helped me." Jonah had not done a thing to help himself. But help came. It came from God. The Lord, who controls all things in his creation, told that large fish to spit Jonah out, and out came Jonah. All of nature bows to the mighty commands of its Creator. Neither did Jonah have to do the rest on his own. There was no distance to shore he still had to swim. He was placed directly and safely on dry land. Jonah did nothing but trust his Lord. And the Lord helped!

"I'll do it myself," is often the contention of the little child learning the skills of life. And often frustration results because he has not yet learned the value of needing and accepting help. Needing help, accepting help, and recognizing help with appreciation after it is given are not signs of weakness. This is wisdom and experience showing up. In the Christian, it is also evidence of faith.

"My help comes from the LORD, the Maker of heaven and earth" (Psalm 121:2). How ready, willing and happy we are to admit this at all times, even as we do in the service each time we go to God's house. We look to our past with all of its ups and downs, its sicknesses and worries, its sorrows and heartaches, and its joys and accomplishments; and, behold, we made it through them all.

As people of faith, by the grace of God, we are not at all ashamed to admit, in fact, we declare it loudly, "I had a lot of help along the way." God was our help in the past. And that gives foundation to our confidence that he will continue to be our help in the days to come. Correctly, we look to the future with the words, "The Lord is my helper; I will not be afraid. What can man do to me?" (Hebrews 13:6) That is not a cry of weakness. That is a hero talking—a hero of faith.

Dear Father, even as you have helped me in the past, graciously help me in the days to come. Amen.

Then you will call, and the LORD will answer; you will cry for help, and he will say: "Here am I." (Isaiah 58:9)

THE BLESSED PRIVILEGE OF PRAYER

"What a privilege to carry ev'rything to God in prayer!" The words of the familiar hymn express well the importance which Christians attach to prayer. It is a wonderful privilege that we are able to speak to God in prayer. It is a privilege to be able to call upon him and to know that he will answer. It is a privilege to be able to cry to him in time of need and to know that he will respond with an almighty, "Here I am."

People often forget that prayer is a privilege granted only to believers. Only the repentant have access to God through prayer. No one else has that privilege—not the person who refuses to admit his sins, nor the person who depends on himself for salvation, nor the Buddhist, nor the Hindu, nor anyone who looks for salvation elsewhere than in the life and death of Jesus.

Failure to repent closes the door in Jesus' face. We must remember that a closed door does not allow passage in or out. Not only does the closed door of the unrepentant heart shut Jesus out, that same door prevents a person from going to the Father in prayer.

Failure to repent can only be called a tragedy. It deprives a person of all the blessings of salvation. That person is without the privilege of prayer. That person has shut the door to God's saving presence.

What a privilege prayer is for us! How wonderful to have access to the Lord! A long line of believers can be called upon to testify to the power of prayer. Moses requested, "I beseech Thee," and God answered his request. Samuel sought God's help against the Philistines. Help was provided. Elijah prayed for fire on Mt. Carmel. Fire poured down from heaven. The mighty power of a prayer-answering God is the only explanation for Daniel's deliverance from the lions' den. While in the fish's belly, Jonah repented and called upon the Lord. The Lord rescued him. Peter was released from prison at the request of Christians who prayed without ceasing.

If prayer was an exercised privilege in the lives of Moses, Samuel, Elijah, Daniel, Jonah, Peter and countless others, prayer can be an equally blessed privilege in our lives as repentant and believing Christians.

Lord, give me a repentant heart and hear and answer my prayers for Jesus' sake. Amen.

Abraham remained standing before the LORD. Then Abraham spoke up . . . "I have been so bold as to speak to the LORD, though I am nothing but dust and ashes." (Genesis 18:22,27)

GREAT AND SMALL, TAKE THEM ALL TO THE LORD

"There is a time for everything, and a season for every activity under heaven . . . a time to be silent and a time to speak" (Ecclesiastes 3:1,7). There are times when we stand silent before the Lord. We want him to speak to us. It may be at church or at home. When God speaks to us in his Word it is time to listen. What God has to tell us is important.

There are other times when we have the need to speak to our Father in heaven. It makes sense to go to him in prayer. His power has no limits. His love knows no bounds. Whatever our burden, we can turn it over to the One who is willing to carry it for us. We can place on his shoulders those concerns which are so small we hesitate to bring them up.

And what about big problems? God will solve them too—not only our worries about physical health or earthly losses, but also our concerns about sin, the weakness of our faith, our hot-and-cold attitude toward his Word and sacraments.

Our problems great and small we take to the Lord in prayer. Abraham here serves as a fine example for us.

Abraham's words above, "I am nothing but dust and ashes," are well spoken. The words express humility. They remind us that we who are sinners, blind, dead and enemies of God by nature need to approach him on our knees. We are never disappointed when we plead for mercy. It is through our Savior that we have access to God. Jesus Christ has redeemed us from all sins, from death and from the power of the devil. Therefore we can come boldly to the Lord and make our requests known to him.

Yes, we approach God humbly, boldly and fully persuaded that he will hear and answer us. The Apostle Paul says reassuringly, "He who did not spare his own Son, but gave him up for us all—how will he not also, along with him, graciously give us all things?"

"There is . . . a time to be silent and a time to speak." Now that God has spoken to us in his Word, let us bow our heads and speak to him in prayer.

Heavenly Father, we treasure our conversations with you. Continue to speak to us in your Word. Hear and answer our prayers for Jesus' sake. Amen.

Then we cried out to the LORD, the God of our Fathers, and the LORD heard our voice and saw our misery, toil and oppression. (Deuteronomy 26:7)

GOD HEARS AND SEES HIS PEOPLE

It must have seemed to the people of Israel that God had forsaken them. Year after year their misery continued. The forced, hard labor never lightened. The number of Hebrew baby boys dumped into the Nile River grew by the month. During that long period, "The Israelites groaned in their slavery and cried out, and their cry for help because of their slavery went up to God" (Exodus 2:23).

The people must have thought, "Doesn't God hear us? Doesn't he see what we are suffering?" Unknown to them, God was already at work to answer their prayers. Moses tells us, "God heard their groaning and he remembered his covenant with Abraham, with Isaac and with Jacob. So God looked on the Israelites and was concerned about them."

Note what moved God to answer their prayer. It was not that they were such good people. Rather it was God's own promise made to their fathers Abraham, Isaac and Jacob. To abandon Israel to misery and oppression in Egypt would be breaking his own promise. This God could not do, and so he planned Israel's deliverance.

God's answer to Israel's prayers did not come immediately. God saved Moses from death in the Nile and had him trained in the Pharaoh's palace for forty years. When Moses killed the Egyptian slavemaster, he chose the wrong time and the wrong way to deliver Israel. He had to flee and live in Midian. Finally when Moses was eighty, God brought him back to Egypt to deliver Israel.

When we cry to God for help in time of need or misery, he does not always answer our prayer right away. But God sees and hears us just as surely as he did Israel and for the same reason. Not because we are such good people who deserve to have our prayers answered, but because he has made us his people by the death of his Son for us. Not to answer our prayers would be a denial of his own promise to be with us and help us.

Like Moses we must learn not to try to force the how or the when. All we need to know is that he sees and hears. Therefore, we are also sure that he is working out his answer for us in the way and at the time which his wisdom knows is best.

Lord, because you love me in your Son, I know that you see my troubles and hear my prayers. Help me patiently await your answers in the way and at the time your mercy chooses. Amen.

"In those days and at that time I will make a righteous Branch sprout from David's line." (Jeremiah 33:15)

IN GOD'S OWN TIME

Perhaps some of us remember the name Rudy Vallee. He was an extremely popular crooner in the days of megaphones and raccoon coats. One of his hit songs was entitled "My Time Is Your Time."

The song and the singer may no longer be popular, but the idea that "my time is your time" certainly is — especially when it comes to God's fulfilling his promises to us or answering our prayers. So often people think that their time must be God's time, so that when they want something done, God had better comply with their time schedule.

But our time is not necessarily God's time. For example, God says in our text, "In those days and at that time I will make a righteous Branch sprout from David's line." No doubt Adam and Eve looked for the promised "seed of the woman" soon after God talked with them in the garden of Eden after their fall into sin. Abraham, Isaac, Jacob and all of the children of Israel looked for and longed for the fulfillment of that promise. But the Savior did not come until that time and those days when God in his infinite wisdom felt it was right. And that several thousand years after Adam and Eve or the patriarchs.

Unlike sinful, limited human beings God sees the history of the world as well as the history of our lives in one panoramic view. With wisdom that often goes beyond our understanding, he maps and measures things out so that his eternal will may be done. He does things in his own good time and in his own wise way. His time and his way often may not coincide with our desires or expectations at all.

We need to remember that when it comes to God's promise to hear and answer our prayers. We may pray for something like the recovery from an illness or a special blessing from God or a change in our life, and expect the answer immediately. God promises that he will hear and answer every prayer brought to him in Jesus' name. But when and how he answers them, we must leave up to his infinite wisdom. Concerning the coming of the promised Savior Galatians 4:4 states: "But when the fulness of the time was come, God sent forth his Son" (KJV). So when the time is right in God's eyes, he will answer our prayers and fulfill his promises. Let us with patience and complete trust in the wisdom of our God bring our prayers before his throne. We know that God declares, "My time is not your time."

Dear heavenly Father, help us to understand that your time is not our time, and give us patience to await your answer to our prayers. Amen.

How long, O LORD, must I call for help, but you do not listen? Or cry out to you, "Violence!" but you do not save? (Habakkuk 1:2)

HELP US IN OUR DAY OF TROUBLE

Many of us feel it and have said it, "God does not answer my prayers." The day of trouble comes upon us, and we pray. We ask God to remove our trouble and give us happy days. We become frustrated because our trouble remains, and we seem to face only gloom. Is it true that God does not hear me? Is it true that he helps others but has no concern for me?

Habakkuk and other believers in his day felt this way. The powerful and wealthy abused the weak and poor. Life was unfair and difficult for the majority of the people. Why did not God help when the believers called upon him in prayer? Didn't he see, hear or care?

Is there an answer to such questions? There most surely is. Through faith in Jesus Christ we are God's forgiven and saved children. Our Father hears our prayers. However, he does not comply with our wishes or commands as to how and when our prayers are to be answered. Rather we are to acknowledge his wisdom, trust his love, and submit to his good and gracious will. The Apostle John tells us, "This is the confidence we have in approaching God: that if we ask anything according to his will, he hears us." He has promised to give us strength for carrying our burdens and to make all things work together for our good. He will remove our troubles if and when it is best for us.

God is not lying when he commands and promises, "Call upon me in the day of trouble: I will deliver you, and you will honor me." If we pray to the true God with confidence, he hears and answers every prayer. He gave his only Son to suffer and die and earn our salvation. He will also help us with our lesser needs.

Christians daily pray to God in the name of our Lord Jesus Christ. He wants us to pray to him as we face this life's frustrations. He hears the prayers of his believers. He will help us in frustration, trouble and terror.

Father, help us in our day of trouble. Answer our prayers in your best way and at your best time. We ask this in Jesus' name. Amen.

In my distress I called to the LORD; I cried to my God for help. From his temple he heard my voice; my cry came before him, into his ears. (Psalm 18:6)

PRAYER IN A TRAGIC HOUR

This beautiful psalm directs our hearts to prayer in time of tragedy. In the extremity of Jesus' suffering his nation had rejected him, his Father in heaven had forsaken him, and yet he cried out, "Father, into your hands I commit my spirit." The Father in heaven heard the prayer of his beloved Son and sustained him in the awesome task of saving the world. In his tragic hour Christ prayed.

The Bible is filled with examples of prayer. All of the great people of faith prayed. They prayed in time of distress as well as at other times. "Prayer is the Christian's vital breath."

Our tragic hours are nothing when compared to those which Christ spent as he bore the weight of the sins of the world. Nonetheless, our trials and afflictions represent difficulties for us. Particularly does Satan like to whisper to us amidst our troubles, "See, God doesn't really love you after all. Doesn't this problem prove it?" If ever anyone could have felt forsaken of God, it was Christ. But what did he do? He prayed.

Is some besetting sin getting you down? Is some illness continuing without relief? Is sorrow filling your heart at the loss of a loved one? Take it to the Lord in prayer. He commanded us to pray and has promised to hear us. And having taken it to the Lord in prayer, you will learn to say with Job of old, "Though he slay me, yet will I hope in him." With the psalmist we will say, "The LORD is near to all who call on him, to all who call on him in truth. He fulfills the desires of those who fear him; he hears their cry and saves them."

Surely in these latter days of sore distress we all have reason enough to fall upon our knees before our God. Let us pray boldly and confidently knowing that "The prayer of a righteous man is powerful and effective." It is God's desire to bless us and he himself has bid us to pray. "Let us then approach the throne of grace with confidence, so that we may receive mercy and find grace to help us in our time of need."

Lord, show me what I have to do;
Every hour my strength renew.
Let me live a life of faith;
Let me die Thy people's death. Amen.

Yet you brought me out of the womb; you made me trust in you even at my mother's breast. From birth I was cast upon you; from my mother's womb you have been my God. Do not be far from me, for trouble is near and there is no one to help. (Psalm 22:9-11)

NOT MY WILL, BUT YOURS BE DONE

One of the most difficult prayers to pray is the one which Jesus uttered in Gethsemane: "Not my will, but yours be done." When we have some plan or hope which is very dear to us, it is extremely difficult for us to give it up. We may even feel resentful or bitter that God doesn't see the matter our way.

Jesus, the Lamb of God, had prayed: "My Father, if it is possible, may this cup be taken from me." The prospect of the agony and the pain he would have to endure was almost unendurable. But it could not be any other way! Paying for the sins of the world demanded the sacrifice of the Lamb of God.

Thank God, that in the midst of this desperate situation the Savior still clung to God in faith. As he considered his earthly life, he realized that he had a special position in God's plans for men. From his birth on God had already marked him for special service. That God had led him to the cross had changed nothing. That, too, was part of the eternal plan to save sinners. Thus he trusted that, in spite of being forsaken, he was still an object of great concern to his Father. Even though rebuffed by God, he still sought to remain close to God and recognized him as his only Helper. When he gave up the spirit, it was with the confidence that God was still backing him. For he said, "Father, into your hands I commit my spirit."

Jesus was sure that God's will was a good and gracious will. We have the same conviction as we ponder the death of Christ. Although no life, no work, could have come to a more ignominious or disastrous end than that of our Savior, yet we know that it was not a disaster. That's why we sing: "In the cross of Christ I glory." Christ was faithful to the end. In this Christ was not only our Savior but also our model.

When the answer to our prayers is different than we expect, when the goal we pursue escapes our grasp, it's not really the end of the world. We have the confidence that God has something in mind for us which is wiser and more beneficial—if we too are faithful to the end, as the Savior was.

What God ordains is always good; His will abideth holy.
As He directs my life for me, I follow meek and lowly.
My God indeed in every need Doth well know how to shield me;
To Him, then, I will yield me. Amen.

Turn your ear to me, come quickly to my rescue; be my rock of refuge, a strong fortress to save me.(Psalm 31:2)

HEAR ME AND HASTEN TO HELP

Bow down Thy gracious ear to me
And hear my cries and prayers to Thee,
Haste Thee for my protection;
For woes and fear Surround me here.
Help me in mine affliction.

(TLH 524:2)

The vitality of the Bible is indestructible. No condition or circumstance of human life ever comes but the Bible has a word to meet it exactly. Every word of the Thirty-First Psalm shows us that troubles do come to the children of God. God's people are not exempt from blighting burdens, searing sorrows, perplexing problems, and distressing discouragements. Afflictions and adversities, temptations and trials, bitter experiences and painful sufferings are the lot of God's children.

These things are not due, as some say, to sin on the Christian's part. When you turn to the Word of God, it is perfectly clear on this point. There you hear God say: "The Lord disciplines those he loves." "In this world," says Jesus, "you will have trouble." This is one of the most expressive words in the Bible. But he goes on to add the all-conquering promise: "But take heart! I have overcome the world."

Yes, troubles do come. But we need not give way to despair. We have God and his Word on which we can lean, in which we can trust for help and deliverance. There is a German proverb which says: "Need teaches us to pray." And pray we can, and shall, as David did: "Turn your ear to me"—give attention to my prayer, for you promised: "He will call upon me, and I will answer him; I will be with him in trouble, I will deliver him and honor him." Yes, God knows, God hears, God answers *every* prayer of a believing child of his.

"Come quickly to my rescue." David's need was great and urgent. Enemies were all about him, threatening to crush him. So it sometimes is with us. The unholy three—the devil, the world and the flesh—are always at us with temptations, trials, hatred, ridicule, persecution. And this is not all; there are afflictions that help to make up the cross laid upon us. But we need not fear. We have God's promise: "Call upon me in the day of trouble; I will deliver you, and you will honor me." So we pray:

In God, my faithful God,
I trust when dark my road;
Tho' many woes o'ertake me,
Yet He will not forsake me.
His love it is doth send them
And, when 'tis best, will end them

"So be it," then I say
With all my heart each day.
We, too, dear Lord, adore Thee,
We sing for joy before Thee.
Guide us while here we wander
Until we praise Thee yonder. Amen.

Cast your cares (burden-KJV) on the LORD and he will sustain you; he will never let the righteous fall. (Psalm 55:22)

INVITATION TO PRAYER

"**B**urden" is a heavy word, one of those words which sounds like its meaning. The weight of the problem can be felt even as the word is spoken. As we consider what we ought to do in the hour of need, we hear the advice of the psalmist that we are to seek the help of the Lord.

Seeking help is a regular part of our lives. As differing needs arise, we seek help from those who are able to grant it. The medical doctor cares for our physical ailments, the lawyer unwinds our legal entanglements, the mechanic solves our automotive dilemmas, and so forth. Only the foolish seek no help from the proper source when it is readily available. Only the foolish would seek help for their bodies from a mechanic or for their car from a doctor. Help from the wrong source is no help at all.

As we Christians go through life, there is one common source of help for us in any problem, one individual who can be approached whatever our need. That special source of help is our God. He can and will guide us in every undertaking, as he has promised.

But there is another side to God's invitation. If we do not bring our problems to him in faith, if we continue to worry or fret in the face of problems in spite of his invitation, then we are actually showing a lack of confidence in him and his promise. Even the best Christian is guilty of this weakness from time to time. We have to remember that God didn't say "sometimes" he would help, "sometimes" he would be available, or that he is available only for large burdens. Every problem, every care should be brought to him for help. Not to do so is a vote of "no confidence" in his offer.

In this 55th Psalm, as in so many of them, the psalmist speaks of his enemy. As we pray these same psalms, we understand that enemy to be Satan and the temptations and trials that he sets before us. In the face of all such, we are told simply to "cast your cares on the Lord." All of Scripture is filled with the message of God's love for sinners, his gift of forgiveness and eternal life, his offer to guide and protect each of us on the road to our eternal joy. How simple it is to relax with our cares given over to God, to sing his praises without hindrance from worry or care.

Almighty God, help me to see the joy of giving all my burden of care over to you at your invitation. Amen.

He will call upon me, and I will answer him; I will be with him in trouble, I will deliver him and honor him. (Psalm 91:15)

GOD'S PROMISE TO ANSWER PRAYER

You and I live in a world of change. Governments rise and fall; cities grow and then crumble into dust, clothes you wore just last year are relegated to the rag bag before they are worn out, simply because they are out of style. We see it also in the people around us. We are born, we live and grow, and then we die. Truly, as the hymn writer says: "Change and decay in all around I see."

In view of this it is a comfort to the Christian to know that there are still some things that do not change and never will. In the book of the Prophet Malachi God says, "I am the Lord, I change not." Yes, God never changes. And because God never changes, his Word never changes. It is still the same for all people everywhere. Our salvation in Jesus Christ is firm and sure. Also, because God never changes, his promises never do. When God makes a promise, we can be absolutely sure that he will keep it. There is nothing more certain than that.

Just think of how God has kept his promises to the saints down through history. God made this promise: "He will call upon Me, and I will answer him." So God-fearing Hannah prayed for children, and a son was born. Elijah called out to God before the prophets of Baal on Mt. Carmel, and heaven rained fire to receive the sacrifice. Hezekiah called on the Lord, and the power of Syria died in the night. Elisha reached out to the Lord of Hosts, and chariots and horsemen of fire filled the mountain. Daniel turned to the Lord in prayer, and the angel closed the mouths of the lions. The church at Jerusalem prayed, and St. Peter marched out of prison.

Perhaps there is some trouble that lies heavy on our heart this very day. Do we need some spiritual gift? Is it the Holy Spirit? Is it an increase of faith or of knowledge? Is it the assurance of pardon, peace or eternal salvation? Whatever it is, let us cast our burden upon the Lord. Let us remember the unchanging promise that God has made to us: "He will call upon me, and I will answer him: I will be with him in trouble." That is a promise God made to us. We can be sure that it will never change.

Lord, place into my hands this sword of assurance and strength that you will always keep your word. Amen.

Who forgives all your sins and heals all your diseases, who redeems your life from the pit and crowns you with love and compassion, who satisfies your desires with good things so that your youth is renewed like the eagle's. (Psalm 103:3-5)

PRAY WITH THANKFUL HEARTS

Have you seen choir singers who looked sad when they sang the most joyful music? Pity the director! He hears grumbling about rehearsals. He knows the jealousy one singer might have toward another. He may even have contributed to his choir's bad attitude by recruiting singers with no better inducements than "We need your strong voice," or "We're short an alto."

In our text, David is recruiting a choir. But see how he does it! There must be no reluctance in this choir, no halfhearted singing. The "singers" are to be all the parts of himself— his soul, heart, body, strength, mouth. To his "singers" David says, "Now let us bless the Lord, all that is within me!"

Why this singing? First of all, David says to himself, "Because the Lord heals all your diseases."

When a broken arm knits together, it's because God gives human bones the ability to mend themselves. When surgeon and medicine combine to relieve suffering, it's because God willed it. That's why Christians bless him.

He has redeemed my life from destruction. Many times, often without my knowing it, God has spared me from accidents and injury. But the deepest pit from which he pulled me up is the fiery abyss of hell. It cost him something—his own Son and his Son's blood. Therefore, choir-within-myself, bless his name!

God has "crowned" me with love and compassion. He wants me to know that I wear, like a richly jeweled crown upon my head, all the daily blessings that flow out of His devoted heart. Wearing my gift-crown, I bow before the Giver's throne and praise his name.

Daily God gives me what my body needs. Not spoiled food, poison or the "defiled bread" of Ezekiel's day, but good things does God place into my mouth. An eagle symbolizes strength. A golden eagle has the strength to carry a fawn or collie to its nest. All its life the eagle appears young and powerful. So God renews me, refreshing me both spiritually and bodily.

Gladly I salute such goodness. Choir-of-all-my-being, joyfully sing to God's gracious name!

I bless you for your loving-kindness towards me, O Triune God, especially for redeeming me through the precious blood of Christ. Amen.

My God, my God, why have you forsaken me? Why are you so far from saving me, so far from the words of my groaning? O my God, I cry out by day, but you do not answer, by night, and am not silent. Yet you are enthroned as the Holy One; you are the praise of Israel. In you our fathers put their trust; they trusted and you delivered them. They cried to you and were saved; in you they trusted and were not disappointed. But I am a worm and not a man, scorned by men and despised by the people. (Psalm 22:1-6)

ACCEPTED BECAUSE HE WAS REJECTED

How comforting it is for us in a time of grief or trouble to be able to turn to our gracious Lord in prayer! How reassuring it is for us, when everything seems to go wrong, to know what a Friend we have in Jesus! This has been the experience of the people of God of all times. Even before David's time the "fathers" trusted in God, and they were delivered. They were not confounded.

But what a different situation confronted the Lamb of God, Jesus Christ! He is treated like a worm. Men despise him and reproach him. They treat him as less than human. How arrogantly his enemies strut up and down before his cross and cruelly mock him! Friend and foe alike are a source of agony and suffering to him.

So he applies the time-tested solution of turning to God. But even this avenue is closed to him. God has forsaken him too. He asks plaintively why this should be, but in his heart of hearts he knows. It is because he is "the Lamb of God, who takes away the sin of the world." As the Lamb of God, he must die. He must become a Substitute for all sinners. He must die the death we should have died. He must be separated from God and forsaken by him, although it is we who should have been. This is the depth of his love, that he was willing to endure this for our sake!

Because he was forsaken by God, we need not fear that God will forsake us. Because he was refused by the heavenly Father in his search for help, we are accepted by this same Father. Now our prayers in the name of the Lamb of God find ready acceptance and a proper answer.

O Christ, Lamb of God, you have taken away the sin of the world; have mercy on us and grant us your peace. Many times we have felt driven into a corner, but none of our problems can ever equal yours. Let your great love for us increase our love for you. Fill us with a measure of the courage and strength with which you suffered such great rejection that we may not lose heart, nor murmur, nor complain. Make us patient and enduring for your name's sake. Amen.

See, I have refined you, though not as silver; I have tested you in the furnace of affliction. (Isaiah 48:10)

IN GRACE GOD SHAPES OUR LIVES

How would we describe our daily living? Would we be able to say that we are the masters of our own lives and destinies? We would like to be able to plot out for ourselves our entire life. In it we would place the things that we feel would be good for us. A student may decide to enter a certain type of school to prepare for a profession or trade. A young couple may put off marriage to a later date in order to be free to do what they want without being encumbered by family obligations. A husband and wife may want to build up for themselves a little nest egg so that they will be able to purchase the things they deem necessary.

Note that, in all such planning, little thought may be given to the fact that we really are not the masters of our destiny. There is One who rules our lives. And we soon see how little we are able to carry out everything that we had planned for ourselves.

We may have thought we were planning for our benefit, but God saw it to be otherwise. God had his own plans. When we wanted to do one thing with our life, God did something else. God has refined us in the furnace of affliction, which burns but does not destroy.

It is a marvel to watch workmen start just with the raw material and from that progress slowly and patiently to fashion an object of beauty. In their own way they subject the material they work with to certain stresses and strains. It may appear as if they were destroying the material. However, in the end they have made an object of great value.

So the Lord makes and fashions us into something of great value: from that which is tainted with sin and apart from the Lord, to that which has been set aside for the glory and honor of God. He cleanses us by the blood of Jesus Christ, his Son. With the Gospel he calls us to faith in the Savior, Jesus. God continues to refine us, sanctifying and keeping us in the true faith for time and for eternity. God allows certain crosses and trials to enter our lives in order to strengthen our faith and to keep us as his special people.

Lord of grace, refine our faith and keep us in your love as your people. Amen.

Why have you made me your target? Have I become a burden to you? Why do you not pardon my offenses and forgive my sins? (Job 7:20,21)

WHY ME?

Why? That is the question that comes immediately to the minds of even the most faithful in times of great suffering or tribulation. "Why me?" asks the man stricken with cancer, or the wife who has just lost her husband and has to bring up four children alone. Even the strongest Christians are likely to lift their eyes to heaven and ask, "Why, Lord?" if they lose their home in a tornado or by fire.

Even Job, whose patience is proverbial, had to carry his plaintive query to the throne of heaven itself. He was trying to comprehend the mysterious workings of God as he deals with his saints on earth. Why Lord, why? Maybe I'm wrong; maybe I'm not forgiven. Why don't you pardon my transgression and take away mine iniquity?

Job knew the promise of forgiveness through the Redeemer who would come. But he just didn't feel forgiven. He couldn't comprehend why a gracious and loving God would afflict the very person who believed in him and who constantly tried to do his will.

Job was finally forced to these conclusions: either he was no child of God, and he knew that wasn't true; or God must act arbitrarily without regard to the state of the person whom he afflicts, and that answer didn't satisfy either. Thus, throughout the book, Job continued to ask why. He constantly wished that the Almighty himself would explain to him the reason behind such unbearable suffering.

When problems of suffering wear us down, we, too, often demand to look into the innermost recesses of the mind of God. We also want everything to be explained to us. We cry out "Why?" and sometimes feel that God must be punishing us.

Like Job, we have to learn to bear with patience our afflictions and not doubt that "in all things God works for the good of those who love him." We need to see that it is the love of a Father that chastens us and purifies our love for him. We need to see that nothing can separate us from the love of God, which is in Christ Jesus our Lord.

Job never received a direct answer to all his questions, but he was led to see that the Lord is gracious after all. We, too, will someday see the purpose of all God does with us, if not here, certainly in heaven. Let us trust him, then, rather than speculate about why.

Lord, give me a heart that accepts all things with patience. Amen.

Then the LORD said to Satan, "Have you considered my servant Job? There is no one on earth like him; he is blameless and upright, a man who fears God and shuns evil. And he still maintains his integrity, though you incited me against him to ruin him without any reason." (Job 2:3)

TRIALS—PUNISHMENT OR OPPORTUNITY?

"**W**ho sinned, this man or his parents, that he was born blind?" the disciples asked Jesus one day. They were under the common impression that when misfortune strikes, when everything goes wrong, when there is extreme suffering, it must be a punishment for some great sin. Jesus set them straight. The man was not blind as a result of anyone's special sin, "but this happened so that the work of God might be displayed in his life" (John 9:3).

Job had lost everything. And worse was yet to come. He would lose even his health. In the midst of his suffering, though, all that his friends could think of to comfort him was to tell him that his suffering must be a punishment for some great hidden sin. If he would only repent, everything would be all right again.

The only problem with this advice was that Job had been repentant all along. His faith had been in his Redeemer from the very beginning. He knew it and for that reason rejected his friends' counsel. God knew it too. That's why, in the middle of Job's misfortune, he called Job, "my servant," and "blameless and upright, a man who fears God and shuns evil." Even though Job had lost everything, "he still maintains his integrity." Job's suffering wasn't a punishment. It was an opportunity for this man of faith to hold to his Lord in bad times as well as in good.

When trouble strikes, a job is lost, sickness incapacitates, or a loved one dies, it is good to know that we are still the servants of God through faith in Christ. God himself will say so, just as he praised Job.

As Christians we believe, "there is now no condemnation for those who are in Christ Jesus" (Romans 8:1). There are tests. There are helpful chastisements. But our punishment has already been borne by our Savior, Jesus Christ.

Heroic faith in times of adversity is a faith like Job's. It trusts that God is still with us, still loves us and still calls us his servants.

Lord, give me a strong faith when the dark clouds of adversity threaten, so that I may be comforted by the promise of your everlasting love in Christ Jesus. Amen.

He replied, "I have been very zealous for the LORD God Almighty. The Israelites have rejected your covenant, broken down your altars, and put your prophets to death with the sword. I am the only one left, and now they are trying to kill me too." (1 Kings 19:14)

"IT'S ME AGAINST THE WORLD, GOD"

"It's me against the world, God." Do you recognize this as the almost helpless cry of the beleaguered Christian? It certainly was the cry of the prophet Elijah after his struggle with the prophets of Baal. Just put yourself in his position. He had showed the prophets of Baal on Mt. Carmel who the true God was. .them in the Kishon Valley. What thanks did he get? The king's wife, Jezebel, gave orders for Elijah to be killed.

Elijah, mighty man of God, became the prophet the government sought to silence permanently. Instead of waiting around to be caught and killed, Elijah quickly fled for his life. After running for awhile, he decided it was time to have a talk with God. "I have had enough, Lord. Take my life." In other words, "That's it God. I'm through. Let someone else take the hassle."

What Elijah forgot was that he was not the one who had shown the prophets of Baal who the true God was. He was not the one who made it possible for the prophets of Baal to be put to death. He did not travel for forty days and nights on his own strength. It was the Lord God Almighty who caused these things to happen.

The same Lord God Almighty sends trials into our lives. He does so to strengthen our faith. He does so to remind us that we can and should be absolutely positive that he will take good care of us. He does so to teach us to place his will above ours. He does so that we might listen and obey his word.

In our world which is so dominated by man-centered thought, "It's me against the world, God!" may become a more frequently heard cry among Christians. More and more emphasis is being placed on the indomitable spirit of man rather than on the providence of our gracious God. Many would have us believe that we can control our own destinies. Where will this all end? Let us commit our lives to the good and gracious will of the true God who answers our prayers and rescues us from every evil.

Lord, keep us steadfast in Thy Word;
Curb those who fain by craft and sword
Would wrest the Kingdom from Thy Son
And set at naught all He hath done. Amen.

The LORD is good to those whose hope is in him, to the one who seeks him; it is good to wait quietly for the salvation of the LORD. It is good for a man to bear the yoke while he is young. (Lamentations 3:25-27)

THE LORD DISCIPLINES THOSE HE LOVES

A knife, a saw, an axe—these are instruments designed to cut and to sever. In the wrong hands they can murder or destroy or vandalize, but in the skillful hands of a trained orchardist these same tools can be useful in producing healthy trees which produce bountiful crops. The orchardman uses these tools to cut branches and to prune diseased or excess stock. An untrained observer might be shocked at the appearance of "wanton destruction," but if it were not done, the orchard would quickly deteriorate; because it is done, the orchard flourishes.

Israel's suffering at the hands of its enemies, your suffering a severe financial setback, my grief over the loss of a loved one—these, too, are examples of painful but necessary experiences for those involved. Today's Scripture reading reminds us again that "the Lord disciplines those he loves." A person who doesn't know any better might be led to believe that those who were enduring these or similar afflictions were being punished for some grievous crime of theirs. But a child of God knows that the Lord must also "prune his trees." He must sometimes lay a yoke upon the necks of his people to chasten them because he loves them. "It is good for a man that he bear the yoke."

Our parents, in love, have corrected us; we correct our own children because we are concerned about their spiritual development. Children who are corrected will not turn against their parents, but in later years will bless and thank them every day. The writer to the Hebrews says, "The Lord disciplines those he loves, and he punishes [that is, corrects] everyone he accepts as a son. Endure hardship as discipline; God is treating you as sons. For what son is not disciplined by his father? If you are not disciplined (and everyone undergoes discipline), then you are illegitimate children and not true sons. Moreover, we have all had human fathers who disciplined us and we respected them for it. How much more should we submit to the Father of our spirits and live!" (Hebrews 12:6-9)

Let us be reminded once again that through his discipline our loving Father does whatever needs to be done so that we might be and remain his heirs, here and hereafter.

What God ordains is always good,
His loving thought attends me;
No poison can be in the cup
That my Physician sends me.
My God is true; Each morn anew
I'll trust his grace unending,
My life to Him commending. Amen.

Let him sit alone in silence, for the Lord has laid it on him. Let him bury his face in the dust—there may yet be hope. Let him offer his cheek to one who would strike him, and let him be filled with disgrace. (Lamentations 3:28-30)

WAIT IN HUMBLE SUBMISSION

In these verses we are again reminded of the severe strokes of God's chastening rod which fell upon Israel during the years of the Babylonian Captivity. And yet the believers among the people of this exiled nation were able to endure this misery in patient submission. They humbled themselves under the mighty hand of God. The fact of God's loving concern may not have been evident in the midst of all this misery, but God's people of all ages are gratefully aware that all things work together for the good of those who believe in Christ.

Sometimes, however, we may chafe and squirm under the chastenings of our loving God. We may try in vain to understand how a certain illness or sorrowful experience or tragic loss can possibly be for our well-being. The Lord does not say that we shall always be able to understand immediately and clearly why he is chastening us. It ought to be enough for those whom he loves to know that his ways are not always our ways.

Remember that "thorn in the flesh" which the Apostle Paul speaks about in Second Corinthians? He did not know either, exactly or specifically, just what God's reasons were for permitting him to suffer this affliction. But he endured in humble submission. He writes: "To keep me from becoming conceited because of these surpassingly great revelations, there was given me a thorn in my flesh, a messenger of Satan, to torment me. Three times I pleaded with the Lord to take it away from me. But he said to me, 'My grace is sufficient for you, for my power is made perfect in weakness' " (2 Corinthians 12:7-9).

So here we do have an answer to the questions a Christian may have concerning life in this vale of tears. The Lord's chastisements may have the dual purpose of keeping us from becoming proud and of fortifying our faith so that we might serve him better. With Paul we can "delight in weaknesses. . . . For when I am weak, then I am strong" (2 Corinthians 12:10) in Christ.

The will of God is always best
And shall be done forever
And they who trust in Him are blest;
He will forsake them never.
He helps indeed In time of need,
He chastens with forbearing;
They who depend On God, their Friend,
Shall not be left despairing.
May this, Lord, be our comfort. Amen.

And Ruth the Moabitess said to Naomi, "Let me go to the fields and pick up the leftover grain behind anyone in whose eyes I find favor." Naomi said to her, "Go ahead, my daughter." So she went out and began to glean in the fields behind the harvesters. As it turned out, she found herself working in a field belonging to Boaz, who was from the clan of Elimelech. (Ruth 2:2,3)

THINGS DON'T JUST HAPPEN

How different would your life have been if you had risen an hour later this morning? If you had taken a different route to work last week? If you had moved east instead of west? If you had married someone else instead of your present spouse? On seemingly simple and straightforward occurrences often hang the major events of our lives, and sometimes even the difference between life and death itself.

Take Ruth, for example. She and her mother-in-law, Naomi, had no means of support, so she volunteered to go and pick up cuttings of grain left behind after the reapers went through a field. We are told simply, "it turned out, she found herself working in a field belonging to Boaz." Ruth just "happened" to pick the field of Boaz.

Boaz was a close relative of Ruth's late husband and therefore, according to Levitical law, in line to assume the care of the dead man's property and wife. And thus it turned out that in time Boaz and Ruth were married. Ruth had found herself a kind and loving husband. Boaz had acquired a wife as beautiful of heart as of ap-

pearance. And a child was born to them that would be the ancestor of Jesus the Messiah. All because Ruth "happened" to choose that one particular field to work that day.

Of course, we would be missing the point if we believed these events just "happened." The Lord with his gracious hand was guiding the lives of these people. He was seeing to it that events occurred in such a way to accomplish his good purpose.

In this way he guides also our lives. He allows things to happen which to us may seem indeed to be blessings, or may appear to be punishments, or, most frequently, are unnoticed altogether. Yet, these "happenings" are the workings of our Father, performed in our best interests. He invested the life of his only Son in our eternal welfare. Certainly he is also taking care of us in this life.

Therefore we shall not want to exclude him from anything in our lives. We shall be anxious to consult him before every decision and every undertaking, no matter how insignificant it might seem. And we shall accept his guidance and thank him for it.

I thank you, dear Lord, for your hand in my life. Amen.

Then Joseph said to his brothers, "Come close to me." When they had done so, he said, "I am your brother Joseph, the one you sold into Egypt! And now, do not be distressed and do not be angry with yourselves for selling me here, because it was to save lives that God sent me ahead of you. For two years now there has been famine in the land, and for the next five years there will not be plowing and reaping. But God sent me ahead of you to preserve for you a remnant on earth and to save your lives by a great deliverance. So then, it was not you who sent me here, but God. He made me father to Pharaoh, lord of his entire household and ruler of all Egypt." (Genesis 45:4-8)

ALL THINGS WORK TOGETHER FOR GOOD

"**W**e'll fix him!" With that, Joseph's jealous brothers sold him into slavery in Egypt. Their evil deed removed him from their sight. Not even the unexpected depths of their father's grief could bring them to admit that they had acted rashly and sinfully.

God knew what they were planning, saw what they did and used even this horrible sin against Joseph and their father Jacob to bring about a means to save them ten years later. It is hard for us to understand, how God uses even the evil deeds of evil men to work good for his own. Our question always seems to be, "Why did God permit such a thing to happen?" It is a rather foolish question when we consider that we cannot understand God's ways while we live in a world of sin. The "face to face" seeing (1 Corinthians 13:12) won't be ours until God brings us to heaven.

The best solution for the Christian who is having difficulty understanding what is going on around him is to follow the example of Joseph, who kept his faith focused on his heavenly Father. When he faces his brothers later in Egypt, he realizes the guiding hand of God, which used the evil intended by his brothers for the good of all of them.

Though we may from time to time be able to see, as Joseph did, how God's plan for us unfolds, more often we must simply step forward in faith, knowing God's wisdom and might have the situation well in hand. We can say with David, "My eyes are ever on the LORD" (Psalm 25:15). We read with joy the words which God caused Paul to set forth so clearly, "We know that in all things God works for the good of those who love him" (Romans 8:28). God has clearly told us so!

My God hath all things in His keeping,
He is the ever faithful Friend;
He grants me laughter after weeping,
And all His ways in blessing end.
His love endures eternally;
What pleaseth God, that pleaseth me. Amen.

(Jacob) My father was a wandering Aramean, and he went down to Egypt with a few people and lived there and became a great nation, powerful and numerous. (Deuteronomy 26:5)

A DETOUR FOR A PURPOSE

One of God's precious promises which meant a great deal to the Old Testament Christian was that God would give his people their own land. This would make the event spoken about in our text somewhat surprising. Jacob and his family were living in that promised land, but God uprooted them and sent them down to Egypt. This was only a detour, not a loss of the promised land. And it was a detour for a purpose.

That purpose is hinted at by the words, "He went down into Egypt with a few people . . . and became a great nation, powerful, and numerous." When Jacob and his family went down to Egypt, they numbered seventy. When Israel left Egypt under Moses, they numbered a million, perhaps two million. God took his people to Egypt that they might develop into a large and powerful nation.

But couldn't they have developed into such a nation while living in the promised land? Yes, they could have. But by the time this would have come about, Israel most likely would have been a nation as corrupt as the Canaanites who lived in that same land. Genesis 34 and 38 tell us how easily Jacob's sons were led into moral misconduct by the people living around them.

How was Egypt different? Joseph told his father Jacob that, when he moved with his family to Egypt, they would be put in Goshen because "all shepherds are detestable to the Egyptians." The grain farmers of Egypt would have nothing to do with these shepherds. So the Israelites could live in isolation until they would develop into "a great nation, powerful and numerous."

Detours for a purpose. God also takes us on them in our lives. When we think we are settled into a life which is best for us, unexpectedly God takes us on a detour. Why? For our spiritual good. It was not best for Jacob's family to remain in Palestine. We can be just as sure, if God takes our life on a detour, he is doing it according to his plan of what is best for us. We are his people whom he bought for himself by Jesus' blood. He is leading us on the way to our eternal promised land in heaven. Every detour on which our loving Maker and Savior takes us is intended to bring us safely to that goal.

Lord, lead us to accept the detours in our life as part of the map you have laid out to bring us to yourself in heaven. Amen.

But God remembered Noah and all the wild animals and the livestock that were with him in the ark. (Genesis 8:1)

WAITING FOR DELIVERANCE

We sit in our snug homes and after two or three days of cloudy, rainy weather sadly ask, "Is this rain ever going to quit?" Think of Noah and his family. They had to endure 40 days and nights of a torrential downpour from the heavens and a gushing upheaval out of the earth.

Then followed month after month of waiting within the ark while the waters still covered the earth. How often they must have been tempted to doubt for their safety, asking first if the ark would be able to stand the heavy downpour, then if it would float, and then if it could keep from foundering or capsizing as the waters carried it here and there.

As the days gave way to weeks, and the weeks to months, the hardest trial of all must have been to keep their patience. They must often have asked, "Has God forgotten us? Is there no end to the flood? Shall we never leave this ark?"

Scripture says, "And God remembered Noah." Did he ever forget him? Of course not. Could he ever have forgotten him? Of course not. The only thing that God can and does forget regarding his people is their sin. "For I will forgive their wickedness and will remember their sins no more" (Jeremiah 31:34). But his people he cannot forget. "Can a mother forget the baby at her breast and have no compassion on the child she has borne? Though she may forget, I will not forget you!" (Isaiah 49:15)

"God remembered Noah" means that God, mindful of his promise, mercifully delivered Noah at the right time and in the right way. God so ordered things. The waters went down. The day finally came when Noah and his family could step out on dry ground once more.

Waiting for deliverance is often hard for a Christian. When the days and nights are long, it is easy for the Christian to think that God has forgotten. We should learn from Noah to send such thoughts right back where they come from, namely, the devil who tempts us to sin.

"God remembered Noah." And he also remembers us in his goodness and mercy. Therefore he must and will deliver us, though for the moment he may appear to have hidden his face from us.

Blessed Savior, strengthen us by your Spirit, that in our trials we may never despair of your gracious mercy, help and deliverance. Amen.

I have set the LORD always before me. Because he is at my right hand, I will not be shaken. (Psalm 16:8)

REMEMBER AND APPLY GOD'S WORD

We know that God is our trusted advisor, who provides us with guidance for every day of our lives. But no matter how good an advisor is, he cannot help anyone who does not remember his advice or put it into practice. The guidance we receive from God's Word will benefit us only if we remember it and apply it.

In our text David says, "I have set the LORD always before me." When David went to face Goliath, he took the Lord with him. When he was driven from his home and from the Lord's tabernacle, first by Saul, then by his son Absalom, he took the Lord with him. He could do this because he kept God's Word in his heart. He remembered the things he had learned from his childhood. In some of the darkest hours of his life he wrote some of his most beautiful psalms.

David not only remembered God's Word, he also applied it at the critical times when his faith was tested. When David had the opportunity to kill Saul, he did not do it. He trusted the Lord to deliver him in his own good time. In some of the most terrible trials David kept the Lord always before him. This was not a foolish dream or wishful thinking on David's part. The Lord was not present only in David's mind. He really was at David's right hand, saving him from death time after time. Even when David forgot God and fell into sin, the Lord returned to him and called him to repentance through the prophet Nathan. Even through their best calculated efforts Saul and Absalom could not destroy David. Even with his most diabolical temptations Satan could not tear David away from the Lord. Because the Lord is strong and unshakable, David could not be shaken. David felt secure because he remembered God, but David was secure, in fact, because God remembered him. God remembered his promises to David, and he fulfilled them, not only when David was faithful, but even when David stumbled and fell.

We have promises as sure as those given to David. God has promised us forgiveness of sins. He has promised us eternal life. He has promised to keep us safe from every evil. Because God is unshakable, because his promises are sure, we will not be shaken. Nothing can separate us from the love of God.

Faithful Lord God, we know that we cannot find safety or peace of mind through our own efforts, but since you are at our right hand, we are confident that we will never be shaken. Amen.

The Lord said, ". . . So I have come down to rescue them from the hand of the Egyptians." (Exodus 3:8)

WORDS OF RESCUE

Remember this experience as a child. You climbed up a stepladder. Near the top you looked around and down. You saw the concrete floor was a long distance away. You tried to step down but were afraid of missing a step and falling. The icy fist of fear hit the pit of your stomach. You cried out for help. Dad heard and saw your precarious predicament. "I'll be right there to help you down," he said. What a relief those words brought. They were spoken to assure you of rescue.

Being caught on a high stepladder is a minor danger. What about being stranded on a sinking ship? Or being left in a blazing building? Or being trapped in a gas-filled mine? Should the announcement come, "We will be right there to rescue you," those words would produce a feeling of great relief.

The Lord announced to Moses, "I have come down to rescue them [the Israelites] from the hand of the Egyptians." The toil of working without rest, the whippings of the cruel master, the brutal killing of the infant sons of Israel will end. The eternal Lord was telling Moses that he could count on the rescue taking place as if it already had occurred. What relief the people of Israel must have felt when Moses repeated this divine promise to them. The danger of their own death and their nations' annihilation had been lifted.

A danger stares us in the face today. It is a danger far more serious than death through a catastrophe or extermination by a cruel government. Forever in hell is the peril. Our sin is the cause. "The wages of sin is death."

The eternal Lord spoke and announced our rescue. He proclaimed, "Christ Jesus, . . . has destroyed death." How did he accomplish this feat? "The blood of Jesus, his Son, purifies us from all sin." When did this rescue become our own? "For God so loved the world that he gave his one and only Son, that WHOEVER BELIEVES IN HIM shall not perish but have eternal life."

What a relief to hear these words! They surpass any other rescue announcement we have heard or could hear.

Eternal Lord, thank you for rescuing me from the dangerous result of sin and for announcing the good news to me through the written Word. Make me believe in this deliverance always. Amen.

Taste and see that the LORD is good; blessed is the man who takes refuge in him. (Psalm 34:8)

NOURISHED BY THE WORD

In the familiar parable of the Prodigal Son, we are told that after his "binge" of sinful self-indulgence, "there was a severe famine in that whole country, and he began to be in need." A bit later, after he had gained a lowly, filthy job feeding swine, the prodigal son lamented: "I am starving to death!" Actually that young man had unknowingly been suffering from spiritual want and hunger from the time he left his father's house. Even as he was wasting his inheritance with riotous living, stuffing himself with food and drink, and immersing himself in all sorts of sensual pleasures, that young man was a famine victim. For he failed to feed on the spiritual nourishment offered in God's Word.

So today, in the midst of a prosperous country where churches and Bibles abound, where freedom of religion is casually taken for granted, many people are hungry and in want, spiritually speaking, and worst of all, they generally do not recognize their pitiful condition. In a society that is becoming increasingly secularized and worldly-minded, all of us must be on our guard. We must beware of becoming prodigal sons, straying from our Father's house and despising his Holy Word. Every Saturday we should be eagerly anticipating the opportunity offered us the next day to go into the house of the Lord to gain more comfort, spiritual strength and guidance from God's Word. Indeed, every day we should gladly heed the psalmist David's invitation: "Taste and see that the LORD is good." If we truly trust in the Lord and are faithful children of our heavenly Father, we will never tire of tasting the rich, nourishing food we Christians find in God's Word, for the boundless grace of God in Jesus Christ is exactly the kind of bread we need to sustain our hungry souls.

Remember then, the Father's house here on earth is always open as usual, stocked to the ceiling with a rich supply of the true Bread, Jesus Christ. Don't ignore the Father's loving invitation. Come! Taste! See the goodness and free salvation of the Lord! Don't make the mistake of the prodigal son; don't choose the way of spiritual famine, for there's no denying that the famine of the Word is the worst judgment possible.

On Christ, the true Bread, let us feed,
Let Him to us be drink indeed,
And let us taste with joyfulness
The Holy Spirit's plenteousness. Amen.

Then the woman said to Elijah, "Now I know that you are a man of God and that the word of the LORD from your mouth is the truth." (1 Kings 17:24)

HIS WORD IS TRUTH

God promises mercy, not punishment. He promises that he will not deal with us according to our sins, but for Jesus' sake he will pardon and bless. He promises us unspeakable joy.

But will God keep those promises? Can we count on them? Or should we only take them figuratively? Do his words perhaps only mean that this is what he wishes for us, rather than this is what he will bring about for us?

How much do God's promises count when all we see is failure, and all we feel is despair? It may be easy to sing his praises in church on a bright Sunday morning. Can we do the same, will we do the same when our life seems so dark and depressing that we don't even care if the sun is shining or not?

We might say, "We will, if we have faith!" And that is correct. The writer of the Epistle to the Hebrews reminds us, "Now faith is being sure of what we hope for and certain of what we do not see." But thank God, what we Christians hope for and what we are certain of is not the product of our imagination or our efforts.

We have faith, but it is not blind faith. With St. Paul we can say, "I know whom I have believed." Our faith lays hold of the living God with whom all things are possible.

God has proven himself sufficiently in the past. Jesus came as the fulfillment of his promises. In him we already have all good things. The life, death and resurrection of Jesus are proof beyond all doubt that the promises of God are true. He is not just a God who talks. He is the Lord who acts.

The former heathen widow had come to learn that for herself. She had seen the proof with her own eyes. Now she knew for certain that Elijah was a man of God. But more importantly she knew that the word of the Lord that came from his prophet was the truth.

May we be reminded of this truth by her example. Believing when we cannot see and trusting when we cannot comprehend, may we cling to God's gracious promises. He even promises to give us the strength to do so. We need nothing more.

Eternal God, grant unto your servants the light from on high, so that our hearts and lives may reflect your glory. Amen.

But his delight is in the law of the LORD, and on his law he meditates day and night. (Psalm 1:2)

GOD'S WORD—THE SOURCE OF OUR JOY

The Bible reveals two great doctrines. One is the Law; the other is the Gospel. The Law is always Law and the Gospel is always Gospel. The two may never be mixed. They may never be confused. However, we must be aware that the Bible uses the expression, "the law of the Lord," not only to denote the doctrine of the Law, but in a broader sense, to point to both doctrines—the entire Word of God. That is what the expression, "law of the Lord" refers to in our psalm. That is the single source of true joy in this world. It is experienced when men find their delight in the Word of God.

Why is it that in this vale of tears so little joy and happiness is still sought in that Word of the Lord? Why, for instance, did the prodigal son rather seek his joy in spending his inheritance in a far country where he might live unnoticed, away from the influence of that Word? Why did he seek his joy in riotous living amid harlots, so that he finally ended his quest for happiness in being a guest of swine?

On the other hand, why is it that even among Christians the Bible, "the law of the Lord," is more and more becoming a closed book? Why are many restricting their reading to secular novels and magazines? They may be good ones, but these people let days and months pass without once opening the Law of the Lord.

One cause underlies this all. Bible reading does not come about naturally. By nature the imagination of man's heart is evil, and his mind is enmity against God. It reacts the same way against God's Word and finds no delight in it. Thus sin would cut us off from this source of joy.

Tenderly God coaxes us to turn to his Word as the source of our joy. He reminds us that his Word can make us wise to salvation. It brings us the righteousness of Christ to cover our sin and cheer our heart. It gives us a wondrous knowledge that makes us happier than gold ever could. It is sweeter than honey to our hearts. God would say, "Sinner, come regularly and take this treasure. Break off from this honeycomb and eat. Let your soul delight itself in my Word. It will bring you joy for time and for eternity."

Heavenly Father, teach me to love your sacred Word and view my Savior here. "Oh, may these heavenly pages be my ever dear delight; and still new beauties may I see and still increasing light!" Amen.

O LORD, you will keep us safe and protect us from such people forever. (Psalm 12:7)

HOLD FAST TO THE WORD

Defend Thy truth, O God, and stay
This evil generation;
And from the error of its way
Keep Thine own congregation.
The wicked everywhere abound
And would Thy little flock confound;
But Thou art our Salvation.

(TLH 260:6)

This stanza of Luther's hymn is an earnest prayer that God would keep his congregation safe from the errors of this evil generation of arrogant false prophets. How timely this prayer is for this day and age in which we live! The wicked truly abound everywhere. False doctrine and practice surround us on every side. The little flock of those who hold fast to the full truth of God's Word seems hopelessly outnumbered.

Yet we need not despair. For the Lord is our Salvation. He will fight for us and keep us safe and secure, if we only hold fast to his Word. Think of Gideon and his 300 whom God sent to fight against the Midianite army of 135,000 (cf. Judges 7). They were certainly a little flock, an outwardly small and seemingly insignificant army with an impossible task. But God was with them and gave them the victory. Think of the three men in the fiery furnace (Daniel 3). Their situation also looked hopeless from a human point of view, and yet they, too, were delivered from the hand of the enemy by the Lord to whom they clung in humble faith. Or think of St. Paul. He stood almost as one man against the world in his missionary activity for Christ. Trusting in the Lord, his Strength and Salvation, he conquered the heathen world for the Savior.

And so also shall we, by God's grace, overcome and obtain the victory. For, though taking a firm stand for the truth and against all that is not in full agreement with that truth will mean standing in the minority, yet we shall not be standing alone. For then we shall have the Lord on our side and have nothing to fear, for as St. Paul assures us: "If God is for us, who can be against us?" (Romans 8:31)

May we, then, in these last days of sore distress, hold fast to the Lord our Salvation and to his Word of truth, confident that he will bless us and keep us and bring us safely to our eternal home above!

Oh, grant that in Thy holy Word
We here may live and die, dear Lord;
And when our journey endeth here,
Receive us into glory there. Amen.

Now what I am commanding you today is not too difficult for you or beyond your reach. (Deuteronomy 30:11)

THE WORD IN NEED

Needs and wants are not always distinguished. We may want things we do not need such as possessions, wealth and success. We may also need things we do not want such as punishment, correction or trials. During our lifetime we can count on times of varying needs. We never know what each day will bring, but we live in the constant assurance that the Lord will supply our every need. He does this according to his superior wisdom. He also does this according to his gracious promises. He is never far from us in his word, never beyond our reach.

What are our needs? Has health suddenly deteriorated to a point where our accustomed lifestyle has been severely limited? Psalm 73:26 is near to remind us, "My flesh and my heart may fail, but God is the strength of my heart and my portion forever."

Are the problems piled so high that joy seems to be gone from life? James 1:12 states, "Blessed is the man who perseveres under trial, because when he has stood the test, he will receive the crown of life that God promised to those who love him."

Is our need perhaps a correction because we have brought on our own misery? In the words of Proverbs 28:13 God reminds us, "He who conceals his sins does not prosper, but whoever confesses and renounces them finds mercy."

Are we worried about the future? Have we forgotten the message of Romans 8:32, "He who did not spare his own Son, but gave him up for us all—how will he not also, along with him, graciously give us all things?" Yes, truly, in his Word "the Lord is near to all who call on him in truth."

It is not fitting for a child of God to bemoan his lot in life or to despair of help. We have a heavenly Father who knows us by name. We are members of his family of believers through Jesus Christ. He watches over us and supplies what we need. He does not give us everything we want as a wise father knows is best. But he also does not leave us without help in time of need.

We are not alone and adrift on a stormy sea. We are on the way to the bright shores of heaven where there is no pain, sorrow or need. Our path here is lighted by God's sure Word. Turn to it and see the way through each and every trial, test and temptation.

**Grant, Lord, that from your Word we learn
The wisdom it imparts
And to its heavenly teaching turn
With simple, childlike hearts. Amen.**

The grass withers and the flowers fall, but the word of our God stands forever." (Isaiah 40:8)

THE ETERNAL WORD

If human wisdom and strength were all we had on which to build our lives and hopes, we would be miserable creatures indeed. We would spend our lives in a frantic rush to get as much as we could of what the world has to offer. We would regard every setback as a tragedy. We would have a dreadful fear of death and a sense of complete hopelessness about any future life. We would have no lasting comfort, peace or joy. In tones as solemn as the tolling of the funeral bell Isaiah repeats the unfailing truth that summarizes all of human life, "All men are like grass . . . the grass withers and the flowers fall." How true are the hymnwriter's words, "Change and decay in all around I see."

What a glorious comfort to be reassured by the Lord himself that there is something more important and lasting than the powers and possessions of the world. What a comfort to hear that in a world of death and decay, there is something which lives and abides forever. That something is the Word of God in the Holy Scripture. By the Word of the Lord the world was made. By his Word of power all things are upheld. And by the Living Word hearts are turned from sin to forgiveness and life in Jesus Christ. This Word of God does not change. And it will abide forever.

Those who anchor their faith and hope in the Word will not be put to shame. Trusting in the Word and its promises, believers face the future unafraid. Life's tragedies and reverses do not disturb them. Daily the Word assures them of forgiveness of sins, peace with God and eternal joy. To Israel, God's promises provided the comfort of forgiveness and deliverance. Today that same Word still speaks comfort and peace personally to each of us.

Ask any pastor, and he will tell you that the greatest joy of his ministry is the privilege of bringing the unchanging Word of God, the one thing that really matters, to people in every condition. The eternal Word brings forgiveness to troubled sinners young and old, peace to those searching for the meaning of life, comfort to the sick and hope to the dying. Nor is sharing the Word the privilege of pastors only. Christ has given his Word to all believers, a precious trust to have and to share until his return. May we all ever cling to, abide in and gladly share the eternal Word of Truth!

Preserve among us, O Lord, the treasure of your abiding Word. Amen.

Then the woman said to Elijah, "Now I know that you are a man of God and that the word of the LORD from your mouth is the truth." (1 Kings 17:24)

THE WORD OF THE PROPHETS IS THE WORD OF THE LORD

After Elijah appeared before Ahab and proclaimed a judgment upon Israel by famine and drought, God had him hide by the brook Cherith where ravens brought him food. God then sent him to a widow of Zarephath in Sidon. When he arrived, she was gathering firewood. He asked her for a drink. As she went to get some water, he said, "And bring me, please, a piece of bread."

"As surely as the LORD your God lives," she replied, "I don't have any bread—only a handful of flour in a jar and a little oil in a jug. I am gathering a few sticks to take home and make a meal for myself and my son, that we may eat it—and die."

Elijah said to her, "Don't be afraid. Go home and do as you have said. But first make a small cake of bread for me from what you have and bring it to me, and then make something for yourself and your son. For this is what the LORD, the God of Israel, says: 'The jar of flour will not be used up and the jug of oil will not run dry until the day the LORD gives rain on the land.' " The woman did so, and Elijah stayed with them throughout the famine without the flour or oil failing.

Everything seemed secure and happy when suddenly the widow's son became ill and died. The widow, blinded by grief, said to Elijah, "What do you have against me, man of God?"

Elijah said, "Give me your son." He carried him upstairs to his bedroom, laid him on his bed, and prayed, "O LORD my God, have you brought tragedy also upon this widow I am staying with, by causing her son to die?" Then he stretched himself out on the boy three times and cried to the LORD, "O LORD my God, let this boy's life return to him!"

God heard the prayer of Elijah and restored the child to life. Elijah took him to his mother and said, "Look, your son is alive!" With heartfelt joy she said, "Now I know that you are a man of God and that the word of the LORD from your mouth is the truth."

For both Elijah and the widow this experience became one of great comfort and blessing. It assured them of God's love and abiding presence. It thus prepared them for the future. Our crosses and trials will do likewise if in them we turn to God in faith for help. Through them God wants to help us make him the center of our life and to hope in his love and mercy. Our faith will be helped through them to enable us to say with the widow, "Now I know . . . that the Word of the Lord . . . is truth. I know that all of Scripture, all of its promises are true. They are mine, and nobody can take them from me."

May we, by God's grace, come to live in this certainty of faith through our crosses or trials! In this confidence of faith we will then ever be ready for tomorrow and tomorrow and tomorrow until we finally rest in the "golden tomorrow." God grant us this for Jesus' sake.

Lord, let me know your Word as the truth, both now and forever. Amen.

In you, O LORD, I have taken refuge; let me never be put to shame; deliver me in your righteousness. (Psalm 31:1)

FAITH GROUNDED IN THE WORD

In Thee, Lord, have I put my trust;
Leave me not helpless in the dust,
Let me not be confounded.
Let in Thy Word My faith, O Lord,
Be always firmly grounded.

(TLH 524:1)

The Bible has a message for every condition and circumstance of human life. There are always such among us as have been called to walk in the vale of suffering and sorrow, troubles and tears. For them the Thirty-First Psalm brings a word of comfort, cheer and strength

It is also a word for you who have thus far been spared the cup of suffering, a word that will bring strong consolation and uphold you when trouble does come. If you are a true child of God, you will be beaten and battered by enmity, hatred and ridicule from without, and by fear and trembling from within. But here is divine counsel as to how a Christian is to deport himself in the time of trouble: not murmur, or complain or find fault with God, but trust and pray.

Christianity does not guarantee immunity. A Christian is not exempt from things that hit and hurt. For the Christian, too, life can be extremely frustrating and frightening.

Why do troubles come to the children of God? Sometimes there is a superficial answer given to this question by the unregenerate smart-aleck critic who pounces upon the Christian and says: "This trouble is no doubt the result of some sin on your part." But the Word of God is not that cruel. Christ says: "As many as I love, I rebuke and chasten." It is part of the plan, program and purpose of your life to suffer trials and troubles. "We must go through many hardships to enter the kingdom of God."

Troubles are designed to test us and teach us to trust. Trust in the Word of God is the lesson of the first verse of our psalm: In him we find refuge and rest, safety and security; we shall never be confounded or put to shame and thereby bring shame and disgrace upon him in whom we trust. God is righteous and faithful. He will keep the promises of the covenant he made with David and with us.

Then follow the admonition given by the Christian poet:

Leave all to His direction;
In wisdom He doth reign,
And in a way most wondrous
His course He will maintain.
Soon He, His promise keeping,
With wonder-working skill
Sho'! put away the sorrows
That now thy spirit fill.

(TLH 520:8)

Hear our prayer, O Lord; in your faithfulness answer us, and in your righteousness deliver us. Amen.

He makes springs pour water into the ravines; it flows between the mountains. They give water to all the beasts of the field; the wild donkeys quench their thirst. The birds of the air nest by the waters; they sing among the branches. He waters the mountains from his upper chambers; the earth is satisfied by the fruit of his work. He makes grass grow for the cattle, and plants for man to cultivate—bringing forth food from the earth: wine that gladdens the heart of man, oil to make his face shine, and bread that sustains his heart. (Psalm 104:10-15)

OUR FATHER PROVIDES FOR ALL

The psalmist paints a peaceful and beautiful word-picture for us, a pastoral scene which would be worth reading even if it were not the inspired Word of God saying something special to the family of God. It is a picture of wild and domestic animals, wild grasses and cereal crops, the birds of the air and man the earth-dweller. There is water and air, hill and valley, green and blue. There are the three main products of the Mediterranean world: grapes, olives, and wheat—a delicious picture. All of it is saying: God is a thoughtful and generous Provider. He gives basic nourishment and he adds all the good things of life to it.

He is the Provider of what we all "natural resources." The minerals used for the girders of skyscrapers and the gears of farm machinery and the gauges of delicate instruments — these were placed in the earth for man's use by God's bounty. The wealth of the forest, and the ability to use wood products in an endless variety of ways—these have come from the generosity of the heavenly Provider. The barely investigated wealth of the sea, where each drop of water is a busy world all by itself—the Creator has made it.

In the beginning God spoke and it was so, and it is still so. He speaks and things happen, and they keep on happening. The rich variety of life in the world, the abundant food supplies which do not fail (though man fails in the use of them), the cycle of life and death and regeneration in the creature world—these are evidences that God's creating Word is still effective.

He provides for the least of his creatures in order to preserve his highest creature — man. In the words of Luther, he is "richly and daily providing clothing and shoes, meat and drink, house and home, wife and children, land, cattle, and all my goods, and all that I need to keep my body and life."

Heavenly Father, for all your benefits and bounty, it is our duty to thank and praise and to serve and obey you. As your Son has freed us from sin to serve you, let this duty be our highest joy. Amen.

These all look to you to give them their food at the proper time. When you give it to them, they gather it up; when you open your hand, they are satisfied with good things. When you hide your face, they are terrified; when you take away their breath, they die and return to the dust. When you send your Spirit, they are created, and you renew the face of the earth. (Psalm 104:27-30)

ALL DEPENDS ON OUR FATHER

Some people take the attitude: "God is too great, too busy, too remote, to be interested in me personally." That might be a complaint. It might be false humility. It might be wishful thinking on the part of someone who has a bad conscience and hopes that God is not interested in what he does. But we should not measure God by our standards nor judge him by our limitations. He is God, and so his eye can be on the sparrow and his mind can number the very hairs of our heads. He does not lose sight of our best interests or neglect our needs. He is vitally interested in what we do with the gift of life.

The continued existence of all things depends on the Father-Creator. The seeds which the sparrow eats, the food of the fish in the sea, the crops which men harvest and the food we gather into baskets at the supermarket come from his generous hand. The food itself, the strength to gather it, the ability of our bodies to turn that food into energy and strength are all gifts of his goodness. He is not too great to care about these things. At the wedding of Cana, Jesus did not refuse to provide wine on the basis that he had more important things to do—like redeeming the world. So the Father does not refuse to give any further attention to the creature world on the ground that he is busy gathering the Church from the great mass of sinners. If he should close his hand or turn his face, there would be no life on this earth. Even those who deny his preserving care could not draw another breath without his power and care. Those who refuse to look to him or acknowledge their dependence on him could not live another moment if he were not such a dependable God. The same Spirit who moved over the face of the waters and changed chaos to cosmos is still lending the breath of life to all things, including mankind. Each spring, each renewing of the earth, is evidence of his life-giving ways. It is the same Spirit who teaches us that this is our Father's world and enables us to appreciate that we can also depend on him for eternal life in Jesus Christ, who has taught us to call the Creator and Preserver "Father."

Almighty Father, send your Spirit upon us in rich measure, that we may appreciate and receive with thanksgiving our daily bread. Amen.

You covered it with the deep as with a garment; the waters stood above the mountains. But at your rebuke the waters fled, at the sound of your thunder they took to flight; they flowed over the mountains, they went down into the valleys, to the place you assigned for them.You set a boundary they cannot cross; never again will they cover the earth. (Psalm 104:6-9).

OUR FATHER GOVERNS THE WORLD

We are missing very much in life if we are not interested in the wonders of nature which surround us. Curiosity about the "laws" of nature is part of our humanity, and when we have been made whole in Christ that curiosity is part of our sanctified lives. So we study and respect the balance of nature, the ways in which the multitude of plants and animals depend on one another. We consider the glory of a field of flowers or the mystery of a single flower. We observe the ants and bees with their wonderful organized activity. We read about and watch the marvelous, ordered and predictable ways of the stars and planets. We know about the uniqueness and beauty of each snowflake, the leaf systems of the trees. We confess as the psalmist did: "In wisdom you have made them all."

What keeps it all in order? Not our clever minds! "You set a boundary," says the psalmist. God has established the place and the function of everything in his world. When the earth was "formless and empty. . . . God said, 'Let the water under the sky be gathered to one place, and let dry ground appear: and it was so.' " It was so and it is so. The man who wrote the psalm had the story of Creation in mind. What God had established in the beginning still held true when he wrote. It still holds true today. We observe nature and say, "That's the way things are; that's the way they have to be." But the reason they are that way and can be depended upon to remain that way is that in the beginning "God said."

And you are more important to him than all other creatures. To which of his other creatures has he said: "Have dominion over my creation"? With which of his other creatures does he converse as he converses with us by addressing us in his Word and hearing our prayers? To which of his creatures does he come with the invitation to be his children and heirs of his glory? "The earth is the Lord's, and the fulness thereof," but you are doubly his, for he has also redeemed you at tremendous cost to himself. In Christ Jesus he has restored order to your life by imputing the righteousness of the Holy One to you.

Almighty God, continue to protect, guide and govern your creation. Amen.

As a father has compassion on his children, so the LORD has compassion on those who fear him; for he knows how we are formed, he remembers that we are dust. (Psalm 103:13,14)

OUR FATHER'S HEART

Within two months, death claimed a son and daughter of Daniel Webster. Edward, said that father, was "my heart's delight," and Julia was Edward's "angel sister." The sorrowing father planted two elm trees in his yard in their memory.

Charles Dickens saw his youngest son, just 16, off for Australia. The author-father wrote to a friend, "It was a hard parting . . . he seemed to become once more my youngest and favorite little child . . . I did not think I could have been so shaken."

Abraham loved his son Isaac. With a father's grieving heart he dutifully bound the boy and, at God's command, prepared to sacrifice him.

David's son Absalom tried to steal his father's throne. For it, he was put to death. When David heard it, he went up into a little room over the city gate and, with many tears, wished he had died in his son's place.

Our text uses this example of a father's love to teach us an important truth about God. Our Lord has a great affection for "those who fear him." God is full of pity toward all men, especially toward those who believe in his Son. The reason? "He knows how we are formed; he remembers that we are dust."

Who should know our "frame" better than God! Whether we eat, sleep, work or play, you and I are animated dust. One psalm says that God "planted the ear" and "formed the eye," and the writer of another says to God, "Your hands made me and fashioned me." We are dust-people. We live in dust-bodies. At death the richest and poorest among us again turn to dust.

God knows how weak and frail we really are. Because he pities us, he sent his Son to take on a dust body and, in that body, to pay for the sins of our lost, helpless world. Our Father pities us in our guilt and pronounces us clean in Christ Jesus. He pities us in our troubles and promises to hear our prayers. Because our Father remembers that we are dust, with mortal hearts pulsing in our breasts, he sends his Spirit to strengthen, guide and cheer us.

Why this tenderness, this sympathy? Look inside God's heart! Our Father "has compassion on his children."

Gracious God, continue to pour out upon us the sympathy that fills your fatherly heart. Do it for Jesus' sake. Amen.

The Lord is compassionate and gracious, slow to anger, abounding in love. He will not always accuse, nor will he harbor his anger forever; he does not treat us as our sins deserve or repay us according to our iniquities. For as high as the heavens are above the earth, so great is his love for those who fear him; as far as the east is from the west, so far has he removed our transgressions from us. (Psalm 103:8-12)

OUR FATHER'S MERCY

A German submarine sank a British freighter off Africa in 1941. The sub surfaced amid wreckage, lifeboats and wounded men. When the British were ordered to board the sub, they thought they would be killed or captured. Instead the German captain had his doctor treat their wounds. His crewmen repaired their lifeboats. He gave them food, water, wine and tobacco, then set them on a course for the nearest land.

After the war, one of the British survivors sought out the kind-hearted German captain and invited him to be his guest in England. He was grateful for that wartime act of mercy.

David exults in these verses over God's great mercy to sinners. By the inspiration of the Spirit, he lets us look into God's heart-of-hearts where we see nothing but love, grace and mercy.

You and I should not be permitted to read words like these! We have waged open warfare against God. The grave should swallow us, and we should sink into a sea of torment forever. Jeremiah included us when he wrote, "We lie down in our shame . . . we have sinned against the Lord our God."

Has today been spoiled for you by some new, fresh sin? Does the spectacle of all your life's sin look to you like hell on parade? Does your conscience shout at you until you want to hold your ears? Then go stand by David while he blesses the Lord! Listen while he proclaims the sweetest truth we will ever hear!

God has not dealt with us after our sins. He put our sins on Christ and *dealt with Christ*. He rewarded Christ according to our iniquities. Jesus' *reward* was the bitterness of our hell, a cup of suffering and the cross. But when his awful work was done, Jesus had removed our transgressions as far out of God's sight as east is from west! In God's eyes, we have no sin! The warfare is over. God, plenteous in mercy, has bound our wounds. He has provisioned us with Christ's own holiness. By his Spirit he has set us on a course for heaven.

I thank Thee, O God, for your mercy toward me, a sinner. Amen.

The LORD make his face shine upon you and be gracious to you. (Numbers 6:25)

OUR FATHER'S FACE

Sunshine. Most everybody loves it. In winter months northerners like to travel south to get away from the cold and take in some sunshine. The bright sunshine symbolizes warmth, life and happiness. No wonder people love it. But the sun isn't the only thing that makes us happy when it shines. People do too. When someone is very excited or glad, we say that his face lights up. We love to see it happen. It's contagious. Before we know it, we're smiling along with that person. If it's good when other people smile at us, think of how fantastic it is when God's face lights up and he smiles at us.

By every right we shouldn't expect him to be happy with us. We've done much more to make God frown than smile. Sometimes the Bible talks about God's expression toward sin. The picture then is not of a shining face. Scripture declares, "The face of the Lord is against those who do evil." Certainly we are among "those who do evil." Yet God would much rather smile on us. And he does smile on us every day as he blesses us with schools, churches, homes, family, friends, food, clothing and ten thousand other gifts. He smiles as he blesses us with his Word and sacraments, with forgiveness, life and salvation.

Why does God's face shine toward us? Because of Jesus, "the Sun of righteousness." When he was on the cross, Jesus took our sins up there with him and suffered God's anger in our place. Now God sees us, not as filthy sinners who deserve nothing but punishment, but as his precious children. It was because he looked forward to the joy of saving sinners like us that Jesus the Son of God endured the cross.

This shining love of God is contagious. It lights up our faces and makes us want to smile at others. God loves us. Though at times his bright face may be hidden behind the clouds, we know it hasn't changed. His love remains the same —yesterday, today and forever.

The sun may shine brightly in the sky, but not nearly so brightly as the face of God. Doesn't that make us smile, even if we can't go south for the winter?

God of mercy, God of grace,
Show the brightness of Thy face;
Shine upon us, Savior shine;
Fill Thy church with light divine,
And Thy saving health extend
Unto earth's remotest end. Amen.

The Lord said to Satan, "Very well, then, everything he has is in your hands, but on the man himself do not lay a finger." (Job 1:12)

OUR FATHER IS IN CONTROL

How can there be a just God, with so much misery and suffering in this world? The Scriptures assure us that the Lord reigns. They tell us that Satan is conquered. Yet he seems to have so much power.

Satan is the prince of this world, Satan does go about as a roaring lion seeking whom he may devour. He still does inflict misery and suffering upon his hapless victims whenever and however he can. But he is not without limits.

"But on the man himself do not lay a finger." Here God did set a limit. Satan could do so much and no more. This scene in heaven was hidden from faithful Job. When suffering struck him on earth, he could only ask why and what next. Satan attacked Job with all the forces at his command. But still the Lord overruled the purposes of Satan, so that Job would not be tempted above what he was able to bear.

This hidden transaction in heaven is like the beginning of a drama. Behind the curtain the scenery and props are all in place. The actors take their positions. All the lighting is adjusted just right. And the audience can see none of this until the curtain is finally lifted.

For us God lifts the curtain before we read of the suffering of Job and gives us a glimpse of his heavenly plan. He shows us that he will not allow Satan to pass the limits which he himself sets. He shows us that his only purpose in allowing all this agony is to strengthen and purify Job, and to make the glory of his faith shine with even greater brilliance as he bears his adversity in patience.

Job couldn't see all this. He had to walk by faith, not by sight. And so must we all. If Job had to look around and could not see any end to his suffering, and could look only to the coming Redeemer who would liberate him, we too must confess that the plans of God are dark for us and that faith in Christ is our only light.

God in heaven still limits Satan, so that no matter how hard he tries he cannot do us permanent harm. The whole Book of Revelation shows us the Church suffering and persecuted here on earth, but with a glorious future assured her in heaven.

Job suffered. He didn't always know why. We suffer too. And we can't always see why. But we can be sure of this, that as we suffer with Christ, we shall also be glorified with him. God is still in charge, and he is still the loving Savior.

Lord, lead us to trust that your love still controls our ways. Amen.

Who has measured the waters in the hollow of his hand, or with the breadth of his hand marked off the heavens? Who has held the dust of the earth in a basket, or weighed the mountains on the scales and the hills in a balance? (Isaiah 40:12)

OUR FATHER'S POWER

How much water can you hold in the palm of your hand? How much of the dust of the earth could you take up with a scoop? How would you weigh a mountain? Our limitations, however, are not God's. God measured the waters with his palm. He laid out the universe. He formed the earth and established the size of its mountains.

He is Creator, Preserver—the Almighty God.

At the time Isaiah wrote these words the return of the people of Israel to their homeland seemed impossible. Because human reason said that such a thing was impossible, many concluded that this was also something that God could not accomplish. With the words of this text, God through Isaiah reminded his people that in their thinking they ought not limit God to that which is humanly possible.

Just because we cannot make something out of nothing does not indicate that God cannot do so. Just because it is hard for us to conceive of a flood so great that it covered all the earth does not mean that God could not bring about such a deluge. How wonderful that God's power is vastly superior to ours! Thus he can solve our problems, heal our illnesses, provide for our needs and even make evil work for our good. Because of God's omnipotence we need not fear. "Therefore we will not fear, though the earth give way and the mountains fall into the heart of the sea, though its waters roar and foam and the mountains quake with their surging" (Psalm 46:2,3).

St. Paul wrote, "I am not ashamed of the gospel, because it is the power of God for the salvation of everyone who believes"(Rom. 1:16). The Gospel of Christ, the Good News that he is our Savior, is the power of God that turned us from unbelief to saving faith. For this power, which also sustains our faith, we ought daily to thank God.

Scripture tells us that it was Abraham who "Against all hope . . . in hope believed . . . being fully persuaded that God had power to do what he had promised" (Romans 4:18,21). Abraham believed God's promises because he knew that God could do vastly more than that which is possible for man to accomplish. Abraham believed that "The Lord God OMNIPOTENT reigneth."

Lord, I believe. Help mine unbelief. Amen.

Lord, I have heard of your fame; I stand in awe of your deeds, O Lord. Renew them in our day in our time make them known. (Habakkuk 3:2)

OUR FATHER'S FAME ENDURES

A few decades ago one of the popular songs regularly heard on the radio was the Ballad of Davy Crockett. The song related the legendary exploits and heroic deeds of the early American frontiersman. Davy Crockett was larger than life to the youngsters who delighted to hear about his amazing strength and fantastic accomplishments. But feats of Davy Crockett or of any other hero, real or legendary, are nothing in comparison with the real deeds of the Lord God Almighty.

Habakkuk, the prophet, had learned about the Lord's deeds, and he stood in awe of them. Habakkuk had heard how the Lord created the earth and the universe and everything in them in six days. He had heard how the Lord sent a great flood to destroy the world and all the people in it except Noah and his family. Habakkuk had heard how the Lord delivered the people of Israel from the Egyptians by parting the waters of the Red Sea and drowning the soldiers of Egypt in the sea. Habakkuk stood in awe of what the Lord had done, and he prayed that the Lord would lead his contemporaries to understand and to appreciate his mighty deeds too.

How awe-struck are you by what the Lord has done? It's so easy to forget or to fail fully to appreciate the Lord's great deeds. Often we find ourselves more impressed by man's feeble accomplishments. We need seriously to reflect on the awesome deeds of the Lord in the past. We also need to stand in awe of God's deeds performed all around us every day. We should remember who makes the sun to shine, the rain to fall, the crops to grow; who placed the power in the atom; who sustains and preserves the lives of all his creatures. It is God who guides and governs men and nations. It is God the Holy Ghost who works the miracle of faith in every believer's heart.

The most awesome of all God's deeds was when he sent his one and only Son into this world to assume our human nature. He lived a perfect life on behalf of all mankind. He took upon himself the sins of all people of all time and endured God's wrath in our stead so that we might be saved eternally. This is the deed we pray he would continue to make known through us to all the people in the world.

We stand in awe of your deeds, O Lord. Cause the good news of your love and salvation in Jesus to fill my heart and the hearts of people everywhere with awe and praise for you, in Jesus' name. Amen.

"Lift up your eyes and look about you: All assemble and come to you; your sons come from afar, and your daughters are carried on the arm." (Isaiah 60:4)

OUR FATHER'S GLORY

What has God been doing about conditions in the world today? This is a question scoffers ask so often of faithful Christians. Indeed, sometimes the problems of this world in which we live seem to overwhelm us; sometimes God seems to be so far away. We live in an age of economic and political unrest, to be sure. But let us not permit either this or the muttering of the prophets of doom to cause us to go about our daily lives with eyes downcast in despair.

Just what is God doing? Let us heed the words of the prophet Isaiah, "Lift up your eyes and look about you." All right, let us look up from our troubles. What shall we see? Wars and political crises? Crime? An impending energy crisis? No! The prophet is not directing us to look upon the mess that sinful mankind has made of this world. We find no comfort there.

Let us today look where the prophet would have us direct our eyes, to the family of God. Let us see the people who are coming to the Light of the world in faith. These are precious souls redeemed by the saving work of Jesus.

God's family is called the Church. Each Sunday we confess in the words of the Apostles' Creed: "I believe in the holy Christian Church, the communion of saints." Let us believe in our hearts what we confess with our mouths.

Jesus has come, and by God's grace you believe in him as your only Savior. You are God's sons and daughters. Yes, children of God, lift up your eyes! See the blessings that are yours both now in this life and for all eternity. But you are not alone.

What is God doing? While the world trembles in the throes of sin and with the fear of destruction, God is quietly carrying out his plan of salvation through the still, small voice of his gospel. Daily the family to which we belong, the communion of saints, is growing. And what a wonderful family it is! It knows no cultural, racial or national barriers or boundaries. Membership in this family is based solely upon faith in Jesus Christ as one's personal Savior.

Let us look up and see what God is doing. People the world over are hearing and by God's grace are believing the gospel. God has not forgotten us. His kingdom is being enlarged daily through the power of his Holy Spirit.

Lord, we thank you for the grace you have shown us and all your children. Amen.

Do you not know? Have you not heard? The Lord is the everlasting God, the Creator of the ends of the earth. He will not grow tired or weary, and his understanding no one can fathom. (Isaiah 40:28)

HE WATCHES OVER US DAY AND NIGHT

To know God in the truest sense of the word is to believe him and trust in him under all circumstances, no matter how trying. Israel in its misery had forgotten God and failed to remember what he could do. Thus, in their despair, the people of Israel feared they were out of reach of God's help.

There are many daily difficulties that we face that tend to discourage and depress us. The boring routine of work has father wishing the weekend were already here. Mother can't make the budget stretch to feed and clothe the family, and company is coming. The children are rowdy, and they must be reminded again and again to do even the simplest of their chores. But is this all so strange? Is not this exactly what God told Adam and Eve that life would be like when they had fallen into sin? (See Genesis 3:16-19)

Our troubles are not because God does not know what is going on, or because he is tired and sleeping while we suffer. The very opposite is true. He does know, and he carefully watches over us day and night. Our problem is our own sinful nature.

And part of our sinful nature is forgetfulness.

Today's Scripture verse is a call for us to remember who God is. He is everlasting, that is, he has always been and will always continue to exist. Also, he is the Creator. Don't ever let any evolutionistic idea rob you of that truth. For to lose sight of God as Creator is to forget that he is Lord, that is, in full command of heaven and earth.

Remember also the past. To be sure, there have been problems and hard times. But our God has always sustained us. If that were not true, not one of us would be alive today.

Finally, look to the future. God has a great salvation prepared for us. Through a plan so simple, yet so far beyond our understanding, God placed our sin on his Son. He permitted his Son, Jesus Christ, to die the death of the cross so that by faith (trust) in him we might have life eternal as a free gift. To keep us in this faith, God graciously watches over us every moment of every day and night. Let no one say that God is asleep or that he doesn't care.

Lord, my Shepherd, I shall not want. I will fear no evil for you are with me. Surely goodness and mercy shall be mine forever. Amen.

Therefore the law is paralyzed, and justice never prevails. The wicked hem in the righteous, so that justice is perverted. (Habakkuk 1:4)

GOD IS IN CONTROL

"The way things are going in this life it appears that God has lost control. It appears that Satan is ruling. There doesn't seem to be any hope for anything." These are the thoughts and words of some depressed Christians.

This world does seem out of control. It appears that criminals are well off and honest people are losing their shirts. It appears that the unscrupulous are immorally using legalities to free the guilty and oppress the innocent. The laws seem paralyzed and unable to help the downtrodden. It seems that wicked people are in control and justice is perverted. The days we are living in and the times of Habakkuk appear to have many similarities.

In these days of frustration we ought to remember that "our God is in heaven: he does whatever pleases him." God allows people to reject his love and bring destruction upon themselves and others. He does not force people to believe in him and serve him. Yet history is "his story." God is in control. He is with his believers and will deliver them from evil.

God causes good to come to the Christians in the days of trouble. Evil days move us to look more frequently to God for help. Oppression and affliction force us to exercise our faith. In the dark days of injustice we have opportunity to let the light of Christ shine brightly in our daily life.

Our God will never test our faith beyond our ability to endure afflictions. He will give us the strength to bear every burden. He will allow evil to go only so far and then will deliver his people. Human laws are often paralyzed, and human justice is often perverted. Our God's law is not paralyzed or his justice perverted. He is almighty to save, and his ways are more than just.

Satan and evil people may be allowed to take our earthly treasures. But they cannot take away the forgiveness and eternal life Jesus earned for us. Nothing but our own unbelief can rob us of the love and salvation of God. Our God is in control and will make all things work together for the good of those who trust in him.

Our Father, deliver us from evil, for the kingdom and the power and the glory are yours forever and ever. Amen.

Praise be to the name of God for ever and ever; wisdom and power are his. He changes times and seasons; he sets up kings and deposes them. He gives wisdom to the wise and knowledge to the discerning. (Daniel 2:20,21)

IN GOD'S HANDS

God is always in control. He may allow killing frosts to come to Florida two years in a row. He may allow floods to rampage along the Ohio River valley. He may turn much of Africa into a desert. It may seem that nature is going out of control, but God is always in control. He still changes the seasons and provides the earth with "seedtime and harvest."

God is also in control of the people of this earth, even the great kings and leaders. They are like puppets on a string. They may rage and fume, but they can go no farther than God allows. Nebuchadnezzar, the King of Babylon, thought that he was high and mighty. But in the same day that he boasted of his greatness, Nebuchadnezzar was deprived of his sanity. God reduced his mental powers to those of a wild beast. Later God restored Nebuchadnezzar's sanity, and the king confessed that this humiliation was necessary so that he might know God and honor him.

Belshazzar, his successor to the throne, did not learn his lesson. He dared to defile the sacred vessels that had been confiscated from the temple in Jerusalem. He and his wives and concubines used them to toast the false gods of Babylon. Belshazzar saw the original "handwriting on the wall." It prophesied Belshazzar's death and the destruction of Babylon. It happened that very night, because Belshazzar dared to despise the true God.

Believers can say confidently with another king, King David, "My times are in your hands." The only reason David became king of Israel was because God chose him and set him on his throne. As he looked back, David acknowledged the special goodness God had shown him.

God controls our lives in the same way as he did King David's. He has shown us his goodness and mercy. He has shown himself worthy of our trust. We do not have to look to men for guidance. We do not have to fear what evil men may do to us. We have the sure Word of God—God's unfailing wisdom and love are revealed in the Bible. There God reveals himself to us in Christ and leads us to eternal glory. We are in very good hands—God's hands.

**Thou art the Life; the rending tomb
Proclaims Thy conqu'ring arm;
And those who put their trust in Thee
Nor death nor hell shall harm. Amen.**

Nathan replied, "The Lord has taken away your sin. You are not going to die."(2 Samuel 12:13)

WHAT COMFORT—SIN FORGIVEN!

The Bible is a very truthful book. It presents God's people to us just as they are. It shows us the children of God in their triumphs and victories. It shows us the children of God in their failures and sins. It is a sad thing for us to watch David, this great king, this man after God's own heart, brought down into the dust to cry out, "I have sinned against the Lord." Yet it is all there for a reason. The Bible says that these things were written in order that we might learn from them.

David's double sin of adultery and murder was great indeed. It is hard to imagine two more terrible sins against God and man than these. However, we learn from our text that David was forgiven for what he had done. No sooner had David confessed with all his heart and soul, "I have sinned against the Lord," than the prophet replied, "The Lord has taken away your sin. You are not going to die."

How can this be? If God is just and righteous and if God is serious about his commandments, how can God forgive David's sin and not punish him for it? The answer is found in the death of our Lord Jesus Christ on the cross. Jesus took David's sins upon himself and paid the penalty David deserved. Jesus suffered the punishment that David so justly merited. For the sake of Jesus Christ, Nathan could say to David, "The Lord has taken away your sin."

But how can this be? Jesus had not even been born when David sinned. No matter. With God there is no past or future. He sees all things as present. He saw David's sins and at the same time the all-atoning sacrifice of Jesus for the sins of the whole world. David not only confessed his sins, but he also had faith in the precious promise of God to send a Savior into the world. David's faith in that Savior assured him that his sins were truly forgiven.

What a blessed comfort this is to us! We too have sinned against God and have deserved nothing from him but his wrath and punishment. For Jesus' sake God forgives. He forgave David his sins of adultery and murder. He forgave Paul his sins of persecution against the church of Christ. He forgave Peter his threefold denial of the Lord. Best of all, God forgives us.

Jesus, redeem, restore, forgive us through your precious blood. As heirs of our home in heaven we praise our pardoning God. Amen.

I am with you and will watch over you wherever you go, and I will bring you back to this land. I will not leave you until I have done what I have promised you." (Genesis 28:15)

ALWAYS AT OUR SIDE

People on the move. That is pretty much the story of our society today. But it's also the story of many a biblical character. Think how God called Abraham to make a move that would change his whole life. God called Abraham from Ur of the Chaldees to a land he had never seen before. Later, Israel moved from Egypt to the Promised Land. Later yet Israel made the journey to Babylon as captives and returned home safely. Jesus moved from place to place in Palestine preaching the Gospel. St. Paul and the rest of the apostles were no strangers to far travels, either.

We Christians live in a very mobile world. About one out of every five people move to a different location every year. People move looking for new jobs. Companies transfer their workers. People move to get a new outlook on life or to escape the past. Some move for reasons of health. Others for reasons of ease, retirement or careers.

Jacob decided to move to avoid the anger of his brother Esau. Remember, Jacob tricked his father to give him the best inheritance. This made Esau angry enough to kill Jacob. But Jacob left home, probably with a guilt-laden conscience, to seek his security and livelihood at his uncle Laban's, far away from home.

It wasn't an easy move for Jacob. As a boy, he loved his home. He was favored by his mother. Packing his belongings meant leaving his homeland. He was leaving the land which God promised to him and his descendants. Maybe he thought to himself, "Am I doing the right thing?"

How wonderful was the promise that came to him from heaven on the first night of his journey! The Lord said to Jacob, "I am with you. I will protect you wherever you go. I will bring you back to this land someday, and I will not leave you until I have done all that I promised." What a comfort to Jacob!

What a comfort for every believer! We cannot run away from God's presence. He is always in control, even though we attempt to fashion our own destiny. Who knows where we might move to in our lifetime? Remember, wherever we are, the Lord is at our side to lighten the load, to guide the way and to secure the future. Depend on him in faith!

Lord, grant me serenity knowing that you are with me always. Amen.

The Sovereign LORD is my strength; he makes my feet like the feet of a deer, he enables me to go on the heights. (Habakkuk 3:19)

A NEVER-FAILING SOURCE OF STRENGTH

Two men once visited a factory. The tour guide showed them the huge rooms where the machines were running and making a great deal of noise. Then the guide led them to a much smaller room where it was very quiet. One of the men said, "There isn't much going on in here, is there?" The guide smiled and replied, "This is the most important room of all. This is where the power comes from to run the great machines." With that the visitors looked in wonder at the huge, almost noiseless dynamos.

Our lives are often like a factory with its noise and activity. But perhaps we sometimes forget where the power source is and that if the power were not on we couldn't produce a thing. The Lord is our power source. The same power he used to create the world he uses today to keep all things in existence. "In him all things hold together," the Bible says (Colossians 1:17). God is not resting somewhere in the heavens, but he is constantly and actively present with us keeping and sustaining us, directing and governing us. "In him we live and move and have our being," Paul reminded the philosophers in Athens (Acts 17:28).

Habakkuk realized that. Habakkuk knew that if left on his own he would only tremble and falter. His heart would pound. His lips would quiver. Decay would creep into his bones, and his legs would tremble. But with the Lord as his strength he says he can run like a deer and bound up steep slopes. The Apostle Paul in his letter to the Philippians says the same thing in slightly different words. "I can do everything through him who gives me strength" (Philippians 4:13).

Dynamos can break down. Batteries can die. But the Lord is a never-failing source of strength.

The greatest thing of all is that by his strength the Lord redeemed us. It took more than a mere man to crush Satan's head and to defeat sin and death. It took the almighty Son of God, the God-man. By his own power Jesus rose victorious from the grave. By the gospel the Holy Spirit works powerfully in our hearts to bring us to faith in Jesus our Savior. By that same power he keeps our faith alive. By the Lord's strength we live our lives for him. By his strength and power the Lord will raise us from the dead and take us to eternal life in heaven. The Lord is our never-failing source of strength.

Lord God, keep us mindful that without you we can do nothing. Keep our faith alive and well, and give us strength to serve you faithfully. Amen.

"Is anything too hard for the Lord? I will return to you at the appointed time next year and Sarah will have a son." (Genesis 18:14)

WITH GOD NOTHING IS IMPOSSIBLE

Broken promises! How many times has not a promise been made to us that was never kept? Why so many broken promises? There are of course people who will just lie to us and never intend to make good on their promises. But there are also many sincere people who make promises but do not carry them out. One of the major reasons that there are so many broken promises is because the person, although he has good intentions, oftentimes finds that he is just unable to do what he has promised.

Let us be thankful that God and his promises are different. He never lacks the power or ability to carry them out. Solomon recognized this when he wrote in 1 Kings 8:56, "Praise be to the Lord. . . . Not one word has failed of all the good promises he gave."

We have already seen that God's promise to Abraham and Sarah was one such promise. God's great power and wisdom had no problem in rearranging the laws of nature, so that the child could be conceived and born. The miraculous birth of Isaac reminds us of the great miracle of the birth of Jesus, our Savior. Contrary to the laws of nature, Isaac was born.

He was born because God had promised it. Contrary to the laws of nature, Jesus was born. Again it was because God had made a promise: "Behold a virgin shall conceive and bear a son" (Isaiah 7:14).

God's power was at work to make sure what he had promised would come to pass. By God's power faith was worked in Sarah's heart. God also put his power to work in her body, to make sure that his precious promise would come to pass. In Hebrews 11:11 we read, "Through faith Sarah herself received renewed strength (power) to conceive seed, and was delivered of a child when she was past age." God's power fulfilled his precious promise.

"With God nothing shall be impossible." When we hear God's promises to us in our times of trouble, guilt and fear, we are to find the same comfort and assurance that Abraham and Sarah found. God will surely bring to pass by his power what he has promised.

The promise stands: "With God nothing shall be impossible," not the creation of the world, not the adorning of the heavens with millions of stars, and God be praised, not even the salvation of mankind!

Lord, move us always to trust each of your promises as sure and certain, because you have the almighty power to bring them to pass. Amen.

As a mother comforts her child, so will I comfort you; and you will be comforted over Jerusalem. (Isaiah 66:13)

COMFORT LIKE ONLY A MOTHER CAN

A toothless smile grins into the TV and mouths the words, "Hi, Mom!" The burly football player has just recovered a fumble in the big game. The isolation camera picks him out on the sideline and in the midst of his jubilation, the first person he thinks of is his mother—the woman who brought him into the world, the person to whom he owes so much.

Perhaps it is a natural instinct to recall those early childhood experiences, lost deep in the recesses of our subconscious. Then our two biggest worries, a full stomach and a dry diaper, were just taken care of automatically. Consequently the thought of mother remains a comforting fixture in our minds throughout our life.

So the Lord uses this expression to indicate his loving concern for the faithful remnant of Israel. Just as a mother consoles her child, God promises to take pity on his people. He will rescue them out of the Babylonian captivity which awaited the inhabitants of Judah not many years after Isaiah wrote. They will be restored to their native Jerusalem. It will be rebuilt and resettled seventy years after the destruction of the temple. Thus they will be comforted.

This is ancient history, of course. Because we know it happened just as the Lord said it would, we can be assured of his comforting love as well. We find ourselves in need of it quite frequently, in fact. When we have sinned and gone astray, each one to our own way, it is good to know that the Lord will come looking for us like a mother searches for a lost child. When we have fallen and hurt ourselves, because we stumbled carelessly over temptation, it is a warm feeling to be picked up and brushed off by the forgiving hands of the Lord. When we wake up frightened in the night of danger, it is reassuring to be able to call out to God for help and know that he is right there.

Earlier in Isaiah's book the Lord illustrates his love for us by comparing it to the bond that exists between a mother and child regardless of what intervenes over the years. "Can a mother forget the baby at her breast and have no compassion on the child she has borne? Though she may forget, I will not forget you" (Isaiah 49:15). Here we have a guarantee of comfort from our God to keep us ever content.

Loving God, we thank you for the comfort you have given to us in all circumstances of life. Amen.

The LORD said, ". . . I am concerned about their suffering." (Exodus 3:7)

GOD'S CONCERN FOR OUR SUFFERING

Have you ever been the object of concern? Showered with get-well cards and mobbed by visitors when ill? Overwhelmed with food, clothing and helping hands after a misfortune? Swamped with mail and telephone calls in grief? It's a heartwarming experience. It feels good to know others care and want to help. It brings hope during those dark hours.

Imagine what Moses must have felt when the living God from the burning bush said, "I am concerned about their suffering." The eternal Lord was aware of Israel's affliction. He cared and wanted to help them in their distress. The Lord's words raised hope in Moses. His people would receive help in their dark hours.

The Lord's words stirred up hope in the hearts of the suffering Israelites. Moses relayed the Lord's message to them. "And when they [the Israelites] heard that the Lord was concerned about them and had seen their misery, they bowed down and worshiped" (Exodus 4:31). The Lord's words offered them comfort and hope. The Israelites praised and worshiped the Lord.

Acquaintances are not always aware of our sufferings. Marriage faltering. Loneliness. Lack of self-confidence. Disobedient children. Bills overdue. More than likely we hear no expression of concern from others. We are not aware that others care and want to help. That makes suffering doubly painful.

There is One, however, who is concerned about our suffering. It is the One who cared for and wanted to help suffering Israel—the eternal Lord. Through his Word he says, "Never will I leave you; never will I forsake you," and "Call upon me in the day of trouble; I will deliver you." With these promises the eternal Lord is saying, "I am aware. I care. I want to help. I will help."

Do sufferings afflict us? Set aside for handy reference the eternal Lord's promises cited in the previous paragraph. Read them again when you need to know that someone is concerned. God's promises give comfort and raise hope during our dark hours.

Eternal Lord, during my sufferings may your promises remind me of your concern and your willingness to help. Amen.

So the L<small>ORD</small> brought us out of Egypt with a mighty hand . . . and with miraculous signs and wonders. (Deuteronomy 26:8)

GOD DELIVERS HIS PEOPLE FROM HARM

The same mighty miracles with which God judged the Egyptians were also the means by which God delivered his people. When the first nine plagues fell on Egypt, God spared his people from harm. In the last plague, the angel of death passed over every home which had the blood of a lamb on the doorposts. God spared the firstborn sons in Israel from death.

At the Red Sea God parted the waters, so that his people could get safely to the other side and away from the pursuing Egyptian army. In joy the people sang, "The Lord is my strength and my song; he has become my salvation." In the desert when Israel had needs, God provided water and manna and quail. The people of Israel found joy in constantly calling to mind these mighty acts by which God delivered them from Egypt and rescued them from harm while on their way to the promised land.

Does God deliver us from harm in exactly the same way? Yes and no. Yes, sometimes we experience a miraculous deliverance from an accident or illness. But no, God does not always use miraculous means to deliver us from harm. He may use those whom he has placed over us, our parents or the government. No matter how he does it, he keeps his promise, "No harm will befall you."

This promise does not mean our lives will be free of trouble. It does mean that God will control and direct any trouble in our lives for our good. And in the midst of such trouble our Good Shepherd will give us the strength we need and will comfort us with his rod and his staff.

We know that God will deliver us completely from all harm when he takes us home to heaven. With Paul we can say, "The Lord will rescue me from every evil attack and will bring me safely to his heavenly kingdom." There we will sing Israel's song of deliverance one more time as we stand safely on the heavenly shore, "The Lord is my strength and my song; he has become my salvation."

Oh, magnify the Lord with me,
With me exalt His name!
When in distress to Him I cried,
He to my rescue came.
The hosts of God encamp around
The dwellings of the just;
Deliv'rance He affords to all
Who on His succor trust. Amen.

The LORD . . . be gracious to you. (Numbers 6:25)

GETTING WHAT WE DESERVE

Someone put it this way: Justice is getting what you deserve; mercy is not getting what you deserve; and grace is getting what you don't deserve.

That sums up the Christian faith pretty well. We are all sinners who continually have displeased and angered our Creator by breaking his commandments in our thoughts and words and deeds. Justice demands that we forever be banished from God's presence. But God is merciful and doesn't punish us with an eternity in hell. And then he takes it a step farther. Although none of us deserve God's love and blessing, that's exactly what he gives us— eternally. That's grace!

The Scriptures declare that the earth is filled with God's unfailing love or grace. We see this in the works of nature. The Lord God Almighty has created the heavens and the earth. In his grace he continues to care for his creation, even though it has fallen into sin. He sends the sunshine and rain to make the crops grow, so we have food to eat. He gives us our bodies, souls, minds and abilities. Our health, our wealth, our families, our friends— whatever we have is from our gracious God.

God's grace is most evident in our salvation. "We are justified freely by his grace," writes the Apostle Paul. Through the life, death and resurrection of Jesus Christ we enjoy God's grace.

As a young man John Newton was an unbeliever and a slave trader. By God's grace he came to faith in Christ. Newton was moved to write the beautiful hymn: "Amazing grace! how sweet the sound, that saved a wretch like me." Perhaps we have known God's grace so long that we take it for granted. We shouldn't. God's grace is equally amazing in each of our lives.

This whole notion runs counter to the spirit of our day which tells us just the opposite: "You deserve the best. . . . You're number one." Though the Bible starts by telling us how unworthy we are, it ends by giving us a dignity the world could never even conceive of. We can hold our heads up high. We know we are worthwhile. We own the best gifts God himself can offer. We are part of God's family and will live with him forever.

When you think about it, that's mind-boggling, isn't it? The Lord is gracious to us. We are getting what we don't deserve.

**From all pain and imperfection,
Gracious Lord, deliver me,
Heaven's glory let me see.
Keep me under Thy direction
That the grace Thou gavest me
I may praise eternally. Amen.**

VOLUME TWO
Comfort
From

Meditations

For
Such a
Time as This

GOSPELS

NORTHWESTERN PUBLISHING HOUSE
Milwaukee, Wisconsin

CONTENTS

Comfort through Prayer

Comfort for Troubled Hearts

Our Good Shepherd

Living in Peace and Joy

What a Friend We Have in Jesus

The Summons to Glory

On the Road from Grace to Glory

Expectant Christians

EDITOR'S PREFACE

For Such a Time as This. The title of this three volume set of devotions comes from a thought that Mordecai brought to Queen Esther's attention during days of trial and tribulation for the Old Testament people of God. "For such a time as this," Mordecai suggested, God had placed Esther in a position of honor and influence so she could bring God's promised help to God's people (Esther 4:14).

For Such a Time as This. Days of trial and tribulation are no strangers to God's people today. Trials and troubles challenge us, spiritual enemies beset us, fiery trials scorch our faith, our own frailty and mortality frightens us, tragic losses mount, guilt plagues our consciences, personal problems put us on the verge of despair, and sometimes even daily life seems difficult and discouraging.

For Such a Time as This. In times such as these Christians of all ages have turned to God in prayer seeking his help, his promised deliverance, his comfort. They have turned to his Word to find what he has to say to them, and for the past thirty-three years *Meditations* has helped to lead Christians to that comfort of God's Word. Comfort in the fact that God knows who we are, where we are, what we are. Comfort in that God knows the story of our lives and has seen to it through Jesus Christ that it has a happy ending. Comfort in that Jesus has promised to guide us through every trouble, even through the valley of the shadow of death, until we safely stand with him at God's right hand.

For Such a Time as This. Now 300 of those messages of comfort have been selected for inclusion in these three volumes. Each volume contains 100 devotions based on texts chosen from the Gospels, the Epistles, and the Old Testament. Pastor Henry Paustian of Watertown, Wisconsin read through some 12,045 devotions and selected the best of these comfort meditations. Minor changes have been made in some of the original devotions to bring them into line with current procedures. All Scripture quotations and citations are from the NIV; capitalization and punctuation principles reflect current style; titles now are solely the themes of individual devotions instead of a weekly series.

For Such a time as This. Note that on the cover the letters "h-i-s" in the word **this** are printed in another color. That was done to remind all of us that no matter in what situation we may find ourselves, this is still **his,** God's time, that our lives and the events in our lives happen not by chance but under the providential direction of our Father in heaven. As the cover illustration further indicates, we are always safe in his hands.

May the reader find God's comfort in these devotions.

Lyle Albrecht

Who of you by worrying can add a single hour to his life? . . . Therefore do not worry about tomorrow, for tomorrow will worry about itself. Each day has enough trouble of its own. (Matthew 6:27,34)

A LESSON FOR THE WORRIER

You can't change the past, but you can ruin a perfectly good present by worrying about tomorrow. And how many of us haven't let worry ruin a perfectly good day?

Worry brings about results. It brings about ulcers, nervousness, headaches, temper flare-ups and sleepless nights, to name a few. It makes us miserable and unhappy. It creates problems rather than solves them.

Christ teaches us that no one has ever added years to his life by worrying about it. And no one ever will. How foolish, then, to worry! How useless to be anxious!

But how we forget! In our sinfulness we find all kinds of things to worry about. Worry is a sin, and it reveals a lack of trust in God and his providence. A worrying Christian on the one hand acknowledges God's almighty power, but on the other is saying, "I am not so sure you have everything under control, Lord."

We must never forget that God is constant. He doesn't vary. He isn't fickle. He doesn't forget about us, or shortchange us on his blessings. He takes complete care of our lives, every detail and every moment. Worry won't remove sickness, put food on the table, pay bills or solve problems. But God will. He graciously invites us to come to him in prayer and give him all our cares, worries, anxieties, troubles.

Give them to God. Let him take care of them. There is no need to lose sleep at night. There is no need to get ulcers, or lead a miserable existence of fretting and anxiety. God is in control!

Our lives can get pretty hectic and complex, and we may feel we are at the end of our rope. How wonderful to be able to pour out our hearts to God with complete trust in him to take charge and do what's best! Worrying is a sin. Let us give our concerns to God, in prayer.

What a Friend we have in Jesus,
All our sins and griefs to bear!
What a privilege to carry
Everything to God in prayer!
Oh, what peace we often forfeit,
Oh, what needless pain we bear,
All because we do not carry
Everything to God in prayer! Amen.

Now when he saw the crowds, he went up on a mountainside and sat down. His disciples came to him, and he began to teach them, saying: "Blessed are the poor in spirit, for theirs is the kingdom of heaven." (Matthew 5:1-3)

BLESSED ARE THE POOR IN SPIRIT!

When you think of God, do you think of him first as a God who wants to take something from you? Do you think of him first as a God who makes demands?

Jesus teaches us to think of God first as a God who gives, a God who is eager to give us his richest blessings. Jesus came to the people of Galilee, and he comes to us with promises of wonderful blessings. May we gladly receive the blessings our Savior brings!

In his first "beatitude," or word of blessing, Jesus promises God's blessing for all who are poor in spirit.

We can understand what it means to be poor in spirit by thinking about what it means to be poor in body, or physically poor. Many poor people do not have enough food. Many do not have sufficient clothing. Many don't even have a house to live in. They are in need, and they depend on others to give them food, clothing and shelter.

Likewise, people who are poor in spirit are people who are in need. Our souls need to be fed by the Word of God, because man "does not live on bread alone, but on every word that comes from the mouth of God." We are sinners who need to be clothed by God, because "all our righteous acts are like filthy rags." And God in love does clothe us, in the gleaming garments of Christ's righteousness. We need to be sheltered by God because on this earth we have no permanent home. But Jesus gives us a heavenly and eternal home.

Let us be people who are poor in spirit and admit our spiritual needs. Let us turn to Jesus our Savior, who promises to bless us in every spiritual need. He promises to feed us with his Word! He will forgive our sins day by day! He will shelter us in his everlasting arms! Let us also be poor in spirit, because then we will be eternally rich. "Blessed are the poor in spirit," says our Lord, "for theirs is the kingdom of heaven!"

Lord Jesus, thank you for coming to us with promises of wonderful blessings. Help us to know that we are poor and needy in spirit, and help us to turn to you as the only One who can meet our needs. Give us joy in the certainty that ours is the kingdom of heaven. Amen.

Blessed are those who mourn, for they will be comforted. (Matthew 5:4)

BLESSED ARE THOSE WHO MOURN!

It is sad to see people in mourning who will not be comforted. A woman whose child has died wails in utter and unconsolable grief. A man whose body is wasted by dread disease bemoans the loss of health, job and happiness; he curses God and refuses to be comforted. It is sad to see people thus, because Jesus offers the great blessing of divine comfort for all who mourn.

As children of God we mourn because of our sins. We know the grief they cause our heavenly Father. We know the pain and sorrow they caused our Savior as he suffered and died on the cross. We know the grief they cause our loved ones and ourselves. We mourn because we do not have the strength or ability to overcome our sins, to put them behind us once and for all.

Yes, we mourn because of our sins—but Jesus comforts us in our mourning. He assures us that he loves us in spite of our sins. In fact, he came to this earth for the very purpose of saving just such sinners as we are. He tells us that he has forgiven us—he has washed our sins away in his own blood. He gives us the Holy Spirit, who strengthens us and enables us to bring forth fruits of repentance, and who enables us to live a new and holier life today. Yes, we mourn because of our sins —but in Jesus our Savior we have the forgiveness of sins and eternal salvation!

As children of God we also mourn because of the trials and troubles of life. We are not exempt from these sorrows just because we are Christians. We are not strangers to sickness, death, tragic accidents or personal failure. Jesus said, "In this world you will have trouble," and times of trouble bring grief and mourning. But our eyes need not be blinded by the tears of our mourning. Let us look through the tears and see Jesus at our side! Let us look beyond the sorrows of here and now to the joys of eternity! One day soon our Savior will deliver us from this world of sin. He will wipe all tears from our eyes, and we will be comforted! Surely we mourn because of our sins, and surely we mourn because of the troubles of life, but in all our mourning the Savior's promise holds true: "Blessed are those who mourn, for they will be comforted!"

Lord Jesus, thank you for the comforting message of the gospel. Comfort us in all our griefs, and help us bring the comfort of your love to others. Amen.

"Who of you by worrying can add a single cubit to his height?"
(Matthew 6:27)

NO PROFIT IN WORRY

A mother worries about her son who is out with his friends on a Friday night. She knows that he is a good, responsible boy, but she worries nevertheless. So many things could happen to him.

Her husband worries about his job. Will the problems at the shop continue to increase until he is forced to look for other work? Where will he find something that pays enough to meet all the family expenses .

The son, a junior in high school, worries about his grades. Suppose he doesn't pass the last chemistry test! Will he fail the course? If he fails, will he be able to go on to college?

His older sister is off at the university now and finds the classes quite easy. But she worries about not finding someone suitable to marry. She is already 20 years old and has no steady boy friend.

This family is far more typical than it ought to be. They represent many sleepless hours, countless helpings of good food pushed back on the table, and hours upon hours of irritableness.

But what are father, mother, son and daughter accomplishing by their worry? About as much as they would accomplish if each of them by their powers of concentration were trying to grow an inch. Worry does not solve problems. It only adds to our woes.

Enough of such foolishness. Let us commit our way to the Lord and trust in him. He will bring matters to a successful conclusion for us. He will watch over Junior while he is out with his friends and will guide him into the right career, whether it be through a college education or not. He will find Sis a good husband, if in his wisdom he chooses to join her to a man in holy matrimony. Unless the Lord knows that it is best to lay a heavy cross on the whole family, father will continue to be able to support his wife, his children and himself.

In every case, whether things work out exactly as we hope or some other way, our heavenly Father is sending us those things only which he knows to be in our best interest. He knows our needs, and he knows best how to meet them so that we may remain his children.

Let us step back and give our dear Father room to work. Our brains were made for solving the problems that are within our reach, not those beyond our control. Our hearts were made for faith and love, not for anxiety. Let the Lord add the cubits to our stature. He knows how tall we should be.

Dear Lord, deliver us from sinful, painful worry. Amen.

Therefore I tell you, do not worry about your life, what you will eat or drink, or about your body, what you will wear. Is not life more important than food, and the body more important than clothes? Look at the birds of the air; they do not sow or reap or store away in barns, and yet your heavenly Father feeds them. Are you not much more valuable than they? (Matthew 6:25,26)

A LESSON FROM LITTLE BIRDS

If you ever need some cheering up, and you want to hear someone with an optimistic viewpoint, just watch and listen to some birds. Birds by their very nature are carefree, lightspirited, happy creatures. Martin Luther pictured little birds as "live saints" who sing praises to God without the least worry and are fed by him day by day.

God expects us to work for a living, using wisely his gifts for our good. Birds aren't expected to work. For them there is no seedtime or harvest. They have no barns or granaries in which they store food. But their tables are always set. Sometimes they have the choicest food, sometimes just enough to sustain life. But they eat, because God takes care of them!

How foolish we would be not to learn from them! We have the same almighty God, only our relationship is a deeper one, because he is our heavenly Father and we are his dear children. He loves us and will give us everything we need. After all, he gave us our body. How could he fail to take care of its nourishment?

But as sinful creatures we many times put our noses to the grindstone and forget to look up to our Provider. We may worry about what we will eat, how long we will keep our job, whether or not we can afford our house payment. Such anxiety over our physical necessities shows a lack of trust in the Giver of all things. Worrying indicates that we are trying to make it alone, forgetting that all things come from God. In our sinfulness, Christ comes to us with the example of the little birds, and tells us to cast our cares upon him and he will care for us. May we trust in him without hesitation, resting on his providence.

What is the world to me!
My Jesus is my Treasure,
My Life, my Health, my Wealth,
My Friend, my Love, my Pleasure,
My Joy, my Crown, my All,
My Bliss eternally.
Once more, then, I declare:
What is the world to me! Amen.

"Therefore I tell you, do not worry about your life, what you will eat or drink; or about your body, what you will wear. Is not life more important than food, and the body more important than clothes? Look at the birds of the air; they do not sow or reap or store away in barns, and yet your heavenly Father feeds them. Are you not much more valuable than they?" (Matthew 6:25,26)

GOD PROVIDES

Many times we feel we don't have everything we need. We need a new car and the money just isn't there. That living-room chair is ready to fall apart. The room addition we had planned —well, there's no need of even thinking of it now. And we could go on. We never have enough.

But is this true? Are we really lacking the things we need? What is meant by "need"? It varies from one person to another. If we examine the situation, we will probably find that the things we don't have are things we really don't need. The old car really could be repaired. We don't absolutely need the room addition. And we do have other chairs in the living room. The things we really need, the basic necessities of life we still have. God has never failed to give us these.

God has actually given us more than the basic things in life. We have television sets, boats and "convenience foods." Many of our families have two cars. We take pleasant vacations. If we are honest, we must admit that God has given us many luxuries.

Our text, however, is not mainly concerned with luxuries. It speaks of basic necessities. Jesus says, "Don't be concerned about even the basic things. The Father will give them to you." He assures us of this promise when he says, "Is not life more important than food, and the body more important than clothes?" In other words, if God has given us the greater gift, life, won't he also give us the lesser gift, our food? If he has given us the greater gift, our body, won't he also give us the lesser gift, clothing for our body? He also refers to birds. Martin Luther pictures birds as "live saints who sing their praise to God without the least worry and are fed by him day after day." They cannot do what we can do, namely, sow seed, harvest the fruit and store it for the future. Yet God takes care of them. Certainly, we are much higher in his eyes than the birds. He'll care for us.

Dear heavenly Father, you care for us so much that you provide us with everything we need. Help us to remember that, and not be too much concerned about our physical welfare. Amen.

And why do you worry about clothes? See how the lilies of the field grow. They do not labor or spin. Yet I tell you that not even Solomon in all his splendor was dressed like one of these. If that is how God clothes the grass of the field, which is here today and tomorrow is thrown into the fire, will he not much more clothe you, O you of little faith? So do not worry, saying "What shall we eat?" or "What shall we drink?" or "What shall we wear?" For the pagans run after all these things, and your heavenly Father knows that you need them. (Matthew 6:28-32)

A LESSON FROM THE LILIES

What a beautiful lesson our Savior teaches us! What a simple lesson from the flowers of the field! Christ directs us to one of the flowers commonly seen in Palestine—a pretty lily that thrived without cultivation.

Its beauty was such that even Solomon, in the splendor of his attire, could not be compared with it.

While the natives of Palestine burned these little flowers for fuel and held them in low esteem, God esteemed them enough to clothe them in splendid colors, more gorgeous than the apparel of Israel's richest king. Even these little flowers were in his almighty care.

Are we also not cared for? Yet, are we not often anxious about the clothing we need, and the other necessities of life? We worry about being without, even though God has seen fit to put us into a land of plenty, in the midst of abundance. Such worrying is a sure indicator that our faith needs a boost.

Christ teaches us to find comfort in the fact that our heavenly Father knows what we need. He takes care of everything. The ungodly worship the god of materialism. The child of God is to know better, and not be identified with such a spirit.

There is nothing wrong with seeking after food, clothing and a place to live. God wants us to work faithfully and provide for ourselves and others. But Christ cautions us not to give our hearts to these things and make them our dearest treasures in life. Much more important is raiment for our soul, the robe of Christ's righteousness, with which God covers our rags of sin. Seek after this clothing for your soul, revealed in the gospel of God's love in Jesus, and you have the clothing that lasts for eternity.

I am trusting Thee to guide me;
Thou alone shalt lead,
Ev'ry day and hour supplying
All my need. Amen.

Are not two sparrows sold for a penny? Yet not one of them will fall to the ground apart from the will of your Father. And even the very hairs of your head are all numbered. So don't be afraid; you are worth more than many sparrows. (Matthew 10:29-31)

DARE TO TRUST!

The daring discipleship to which Jesus calls each Christian is full of challenges. Meeting them often means suffering. The faithful disciple cannot help but be opposed by the forces of Satan in many forms.

As we accept the challenges of our Christian faith, we need God's care. If physical persecution is absent, we still have to deal with being called unloving, antagonistic, divisive and prejudiced by the unbelieving world. All this and more afflicts the daring disciple.

We have to add to that inner challenges. No Christian is completely free from feelings of doubt. Sin rears its ugly head and attempts to kill each disciple's hope. Even our failures to live up to Christ's challenges to daring discipleship gnaw at our hearts.

In this desperate situation we have an all-powerful Lord who cares. We can see how he provides for and watches over the creatures of this world. Not even sparrows, which seem so valueless at times, are outside of his concern. "Not one of them will fall to the ground apart from the will of your Father."

From that we can be sure that God also cares for our physical well-being. All the hairs of our heads are numbered. Not one of them is lost apart from our heavenly Father's will either.

Just think, if God cares so much about our bodies, how much more must he care about our eternal souls! In this truth, Jesus challenges, actually invites, us to trust in God for everything.

He sits at the Father's right hand to watch over our every physical and spiritual need. He knows firsthand the challenges we face. He was tempted. He was afflicted. He was despised.

And Jesus will provide. He cared enough to die for us on the cross. He loved us enough to shed his blood to pay for our sins.

He gives strength for every moment of weakness. He sends joy for every sorrow. He grants peace for every trouble.

This challenge to be daring disciples is really no challenge at all. God graciously supplies the strength, the faith to accept his gracious promises. Let us simply put our trust in him.

I am trusting Thee, Lord Jesus;
Never let me fall.
I am trusting Thee forever
And for all. Amen.

"And do not set your heart on what you will eat or drink; do not worry about it. For the pagan world runs after all such things, and your Father knows that you need them. But seek his kingdom, and these things will be given to you as well. "(Luke 12:29-31)

THE ONLY VALID PRIORITY

The world is full of such who do not believe. But that's not all. Christians also live in this world. And like the unbelievers, Christians have a great need for "things." Things like a job to provide income, food for nourishment, clothing for warmth, homes for shelter and families for happiness. And as long as Christians are in this world, these needs will daily continue to confront them.

The difference is that the unbeliever thinks that these things are all that count in life. The Christian, on the other hand, knows that he needs something else even more. As important as it is to provide an education for our children, to establish a good and enjoyable family life and to obtain all the luxuries that somehow have become necessities, the Christian has an even deeper yearning for that which Jesus Christ alone can give. That is the assurance of God's love, the joy of forgiveness and the hope of everlasting salvation. Only Jesus can offer this, because Jesus is the only Savior whom God sent to make it all possible. It happened on the cross.

Ever since the day he came, Jesus has tried to impress on his followers that if we put him first on our list of needs, everything else will be taken care of by God. And we will never have to worry for one minute about our bodily needs. That's an overwhelming promise. But it's reliable, because it comes from Jesus—from Jesus who was sent by the Father in heaven and came to take our place.

Come next Christmas, many of us will be looking for a bonus from our boss. A bonus is "something extra." And that's what Jesus offers us here: a bonus, something extra. "Seek ye the kingdom of God and all these things shall be added unto you." It is as though Jesus said, "Hold on to me and cling to me as your Savior. Trust me when I tell you that my blood covers all your sins. Make heaven the first goal of your life. Give priority to the needs of your soul, for they are your greatest needs. And I promise—on God's honor—that you will always have everything that you will ever need for your body." What a promise! What a blessed freedom from worry if we only believe it!

Dear Savior, help me keep you first in my life, to make the concerns of your kingdom my priority. Amen.

Then Jesus said to his disciples: "Therefore I tell you, do not worry about your life, what you will eat; or about your body, what you will wear. Life is more than food, and the body more than clothes. . . . And do not set your heart on what you will eat or drink; do not worry about it. For the pagan world runs after all such things, and your Father knows that you need them. But seek his kingdom, and these things will be given to you as well." (Luke 12:22,23,29-31)

CAST CARE ASIDE!

There are feelings and attitudes which do not conflict with our Christianity. One attitude, however, is under all circumstances completely at odds with our creed and conviction. It is worry. That is why our Lord exhorts us, "Do not worry about your life." That is why the Lord's Apostle Paul encourages us, "Do not be anxious about anything" (Philippians 4:6).

This world of sin is a vast breeding ground for all sorts of cares. People worry about their daily bread and daily job, about their debts or investments, about sickness and the health of their bodies, about sin and the state of their souls. They worry about their parents or children, about husband or wife, about their country and community, about their church and congregation. Such cares seek to invade and to infest every home and heart. All of them are included in the warning word, "Do not worry about it!"

When all is said and done, all these cares come from a single source and acquire weight through the same burden. This common source and burden is sin. Christ came to take away our sin. Our faith in him makes us free from care and worry. He is our burden-bearer. God our Father took the whole ugly burden of our guilt and cast it upon his Son, our Savior. For the sake of that Son and Savior our Father invites us to cast the whole heavy burden of our care upon him.

Between his first and second comings, Christ's believers need never anxiously ask, "What shall we eat or drink or wear?" They can trust that the faithful Lord, who sent them the Savior, will also with that Savior freely give them all things. They can cast care away. They can cast it, with the strong arm of faith and with hands folded for prayer, on the eternal, almighty, omniscient, merciful, loving Lord who cares for them.

"So be it," then I say
With all my heart each day,
We, too, dear Lord, adore thee,
We sing for joy before thee.
Guide us while here we wander
Until we praise thee yonder. Amen.

"So he got up and went to his father. But while he was still a long way off, his father saw him and was filled with compassion for him; he ran to his son, threw his arms around him and kissed him. The son said to him, 'Father, I have sinned against heaven and against you. I am no longer worthy to be called your son.' But the father said to his servants, 'Quick! Bring the best robe and put it on him. Put a ring on his finger and sandals on his feet. Bring the fattened calf and kill it. Let's have a feast and celebrate. For this son of mine was dead and is alive again; he was lost and is found.' So they began to celebrate." (Luke 15:20-24)

THIS IS HOW GOD IS

Everyone has favorite people. My favorite people are a supermarket stocker, a mailman, a Sunday school teacher and a man and woman who sit across the aisle from each other on Sunday mornings. Each has a smile on his face and a twinkle in his eye. A person feels good because they are glad to see you, to talk to you, to be with you. The son in our Scripture reading discovered that he had a father like that.

Earlier in Jesus' parable, the boy had decided he could manage his life without the help of Father, Mother or God. He had left home with his share of his father's wealth and made a disaster of his life. When all was gone, he came to his senses and decided to return home. He would confess all and plead, even beg, for a chance to be a menial servant in the house. But he didn't know his father well. The father ran out to meet him, forgave him everything and celebrated his return with a joyous feast.

Jesus told this parable so that we would know that the smile on the father's face, his open arms and his joy are pictures of God as he receives a sinner who repents.

A person might get the idea from watching certain Christians that we are supposed to be sad, longfaced people. It is good to be serious about worship, but Jesus wants us to know that God meets us like that father in the parable. God has open arms for us when we admit our sins and come to him for help. God provides us with a beautiful robe, the robe of Jesus' righteousness. He invites us to a splendid feast, the feast of his Word and his Sacrament. What love!

When we, on our part, know that God loves us like this, we, too, will reflect his love in a big smile on our face as we meet, work and play with people. Happy Christians ought to be everybody's favorite people because through Christians other people learn that God forgives and loves them, too.

Heavenly Father, let us never lose sight of your open arms. Draw us back to you if we stray. Let the inner joy we feel light our faces and draw others to the warmth of your love. Amen.

"For God so loved the world that he gave his one and only Son, that whoever believes in him shall not perish but have eternal life." (John 3:16)

REJOICE IN THE GOSPEL OF GOD'S LOVE

There is beauty in simplicity. Some of the most beautiful and precious truths of our Christian faith are expressed in language so simple that even a child can understand them. The familiar and beloved verse before us today is a classic example.

It tells us that God, the holy and righteous Lord of all, loved the world—notice, "loved" not "liked," for how could God like a sinful, foul, stinking world? But he could and did love it, love all the poor, miserable sinners in it, love it so much that he gave his one and only Son. He gave him to be born, to live, to suffer and die and rise again for the world's redemption. He gave him to pay in full for all the sins of all the sinners, so that whoever believes in him—and here everyone of us is invited to write in his or her own name—shall not perish but have eternal life. That's the simple, beautiful, great good news that Jesus brought to Nicodemus and that he brings to us.

To be sure, this good news of the gospel is foolishness to natural man. To human reason it seems all wrong that God should sacrifice his Son to save sinners of every kind, that

publicans and harlots who repent and believe in him shall not perish, while respectable people who try to do what is right are condemned if they do not believe. But this is the offense of the gospel, the fact that salvation is entirely by God's grace and not by man's goodness.

But in this offense of the gospel lies also its greatest glory, for the gospel doesn't demand, it gives. It doesn't require that we meet God halfway, but assures us that he went all the way for us. It offers eternal life to infants who cannot yet do any good works and to old sinners who have broken God's law again and again. It takes hold of publicans like Matthew and harlots like Rahab, and by the power of the Holy Spirit operating through it makes them repentant and believing saints. It gives the thief on the cross the sure hope of heaven, and it gives you and me, as vile as he, that same hope and fills us with all joy and peace in believing.

That's the gospel, the simple but surpassingly beautiful good news that is at the very heart of Christianity. May we never grow tired of hearing it but rejoice in it daily and share it eagerly.

Lord, you have revealed your saving grace in beautiful simplicity. Help us to rejoice in it with a simple, childlike faith. Amen.

"For God so loved. . . . Just as Moses lifted up the snake in the desert, so the Son of Man must be lifted up." (John 3:16,14)

GOD WROTE THE BOOK ON LOVE

How do you show love for God? We can't see him. We know he's there, but we don't have that face-to-face relationship with him that would allow us to exhibit our love for him in the ways we can for family or friends.

It helps first to identify just what kind of love we're talking about. If we want to know what love is and how to show it, we should ask God, because "God is love," the Bible says. He is the author of love. He wrote the book on love.

And not being content with merely lecturing the world on the subject of love, he put his love into action. He sent us love in the form of his own Son, Jesus Christ. Jesus loves us with more than just a friendship kind of love, although he certainly is our friend. To help us understand his love for us, Scripture calls him the bridegroom and the church his bride.

Jesus' love is more than a feeling or emotion. His is the "doing" kind of love. Jesus loved us and died for us before we ever learned the first lesson on love. We became Christians, not because we loved God, but because God first loved us. His love prompted him to take steps toward our salvation before we even knew we needed saving.

Already in Moses' day God revealed his plans for our salvation in some striking ways. When, for example, the Israelites were dying in the desert after being bitten by poisonous snakes, Moses, at God's bidding, lifted up a bronze serpent for them to look at and be cured. Their looking didn't save them. It was the power of God's promise associated with their looking.

This Old Testament episode was a preview of how God in love would one day let his Son be lifted up on a cross and how that Son's death would be the remedy for all sin. We must look to Calvary for eternal life. Just as the Israelite was saved with a look, so the sinner is saved by looking to Jesus.

We call that the great exchange, when God substituted his Son's life for us worthless sinners. Isaiah 53 tells the whole story: "Surely he took up our infirmities and carried our sorrows . . . the Lord has laid on him the iniquity of us all." God had one perfect Son. He was willing to give that one and only Son, that he might one day have a whole kingdom of sons and daughters.

Through faith in Christ you are one of God's children, and God finds many ways to show his love for you. You are dear to him. When you are feeling worthless and blue, remember that God loved you so much that he sacrificed his only begotten Son to redeem you.

Father, how can you love us so much? Teach us your kind of love, that we may be more like you. Amen.

"For God so loved the world that he gave his one and only Son, that whoever believes in him shall not perish but have eternal life." (John 3:16)

GOD LOVES THE WORLD—GREAT NEWS!

If you circle the first letter of the 2d word, the 11th, the 14th, the 22d, the 25th and the 26th words in the Bible verse above, they spell gospel. John 3:16 is often called "the gospel in a nutshell" since it tells you the good—no, make that the greatest—news you could ever hope to hear: GOD LOVES THE WORLD!

Since you are part of the world, God loves you! In spite of your sins, he does not disqualify you from his kingdom. Instead he gave his Son to be your Savior. Isn't that good news? God doesn't want anyone to suffer eternal punishment in hell. He wants you to spend your forever life with him and his Son in heaven.

Once you have read John 3:16, you need never again doubt God's feelings toward you. Whoever believes will not perish but will live forever.

The word whoever appears in God's Book 179 times. Whenever the term applies to salvation, it means "anyone without exception."

Contrary to God's wishes, there will be some, come judgment day, who will be condemned, but it will be their will, not God's. If God had his way, everyone would respond to the good news, repent and be saved.

If you still have your doubts, read John 3:16 again. This time insert your own name where it says "the world" and "whoever." "For God so loved . . . that he gave his one and only Son that . . . believes in him [and] shall not perish but have eternal life." Thanks to Jesus and his cross your name is also written in "the Lamb's book of life." That's good news!

The "good news" for others is that there still is room. God once lifted up his Son, whose death is God's remedy for sin. It is now our mission to "lift up" the Messiah that the world might see and believe. God loves the cosmos.

This coming week tell that good news to someone you meet who may not yet know his or her Savior. Pray that God will give you opportunities to tell and supply the words you need to share the good news. Jesus once said, "I have other sheep that are not of this sheep pen. I must bring them also." God so loved them too; they just don't know about it yet.

Dear God, when doubts about my salvation appear in my mind and heart, send me back to your good news. Send me back to John 3:16, which says it all, for me and for everyone. Amen.

"For God so loved the world that he gave. . . ." (John 3:16)

THE WORLD'S GREATEST ACT OF LOVE

A runner in a marathon race crosses the line and finishes fourth. "He gave it his all," his coach says. A little girl's eyes widen as she sees her dad open his wallet and take out all the cash—four $20s—and drop it into the offering plate in church. "He gave all his money," she thinks to herself. But in these examples it isn't really "all." It may be a lot, but for the runner there's always a little more strength and energy to draw upon; otherwise he would drop over dead. The dad isn't really broke or bankrupt; there's money in savings he could use and there's another paycheck coming soon.

But when God gave, he did "give his all." He gave with no reservations; there were no back-up Sons to send later. He has only one Son, and yet he willingly gave him up to be the world's Savior from sin. God gave the most lavish gift the world has ever seen. He gave this gift to you and me. Because his gift was perfect for you, solving all your basic spiritual needs—forgiveness of sins, life, salvation, freedom from guilt and then some—you surely want to give God a gift in return. You can do that! St. Paul tells you to live your whole life as a gift to God by dedicating everything you do to his glory. But remember! You're not doing this to earn your way into God's good graces. You are merely saying, "Thank you, God. You really did give your all so that I could be yours."

Everything about God's gift was unique. No one else compares with God's Son. Nothing else compares with his act of salvation. Never before and never since Jesus has a baby been born of a virgin. Ever since Adam no man except Jesus lived an absolutely sin-free life. No one else has been able to do the miracles he did. If other individuals died for the sake of another, their sacrifice, no matter how noble, did nothing about sin. Not one person who has died has ever come back from death on his own.

And, finally, Jesus' resurrection was the absolute proof that in him and in what he did God accomplished for us what we could never hope to do on our own—overcome sin and death and make us fit for heaven.

God "gave his all" because he loves you. When a woman told her pastor that she did not think she was saved because she did not love God enough, the pastor simply replied, "That doesn't matter. He loves you." Engrave these words in your memory. Hang them on the wall on your heart. God loves you. The cross is all the proof you need.

Dear Father, when I worry about being saved, remove all anxiety and care from my heart. Help me remember each day that in Jesus you love me. That will never change and nothing else really matters. Motivate me to return your love in all I think, say and do. Amen.

The soldiers led Jesus away into the palace (that is, the Praetorium) and called together the whole company of soldiers. They put a purple robe on him. (Mark 15:16,17)

HIS ROBE

"The royal purple" people called it in days gone by. In olden days kings and queens wore robes of purple, for only they could afford the costly dye required in making such robes. The purple robe then became a symbol of the magnificent palaces, gilded chariots and rich splendor which surrounded royalty.

That Good Friday in Pilate's palace another king wore the royal purple. But what a king he was and what a robe he wore! Some soldier had found it in some corner of the barracks and draped it over Jesus' naked shoulders. And if the color was somewhat faded, that didn't matter. It would soon be darkened again by the blood from his torn back. A king he was supposed to be, so with coarse taunts the soldiers outfitted him like one, in a purple robe stained by his own blood.

They placed the robe on his back in mockery that day, but a moment's worth of deeper reflection will show how fitting it was. If anyone could wear "the royal purple," Jesus could. Let earthly kings have their halls of marble and homes of splendor, Jesus had the Father's house above. Let earthly kings fill their closets with fashion's latest, he had the heavenly brightness which dazzled his disciples on the Mount of Transfiguration. Let earthly kings struggle to win and hold their paltry kingdoms, he made and rules over all.

And yet he must wear a cheap, cast-off cloak. This King of kings has chosen to leave behind heaven's splendor for a life on earth as a humble servant. He who owns all has to borrow a place to lay his head, a boat to cross a lake, a cape to cloak his body, a tomb to hold his corpse. Willingly he chooses to endure poverty and pain, self-denial and death. Never has the world seen royalty like this!

That bloodstained robe reminds us of his royalty. It reminds us also of something else. How he must love us! All this he endured to pay for our sins, rescue us from hell, equip us for heaven. All this he endured to weave another robe, the robe of his righteousness which he drapes over our shoulders. Because of that robe we can stand before our God in heaven and even rule with him, our King, forever.

"King," they said in mockery that day. "King, indeed!" we respond as he puts the robe of righteousness on us, "King of kings and Lord of lords!"

**Jesus, thy blood and righteousness
My beauty are, my glorious dress;
Midst flaming worlds, in these arrayed,
With joy shall I lift up my head. Amen.**

16

They . . . twisted together a crown of thorns and set it on him. (Mark 15:17)

HIS CROWN

Earthly kings wear crowns, some of them simple circles of gold, others elaborate rings studded with gems. From Egypt's ancient dynasties to Europe's modern monarchs, the sovereign wears a crown.

King Jesus must also have a crown, so the mocking soldiers thought. A prickly branch was found, twined together, and placed on his royal head. But it lacked the sparkle of precious stones. No problem; that could easily be supplied. A few blows on that circle of thorns brought drops of his blood to glisten like rubies.

They placed that crown of thorns on his brow in mockery that day, but a moment's worth of deeper reflection will show how fitting it was. Let others wear golden crowns with cold and lifeless gems, Jesus wears a crown adorned with his own blood, blood more precious than all earth's treasures, blood able to win that which nothing else could buy. That crown, touched with his blood, speaks of victory, victory over sin, death and the devil.

Only victors wear crowns, and Jesus hardly looked like a victor that day. Yet Easter Sunday brought news of victory complete. And now in heaven the Victor rules. In heaven the angels who have ever been there and the saints who have gone before us join in the chorus, "Worthy is the Lamb, who was slain, to receive power and wealth and wisdom and strength and honor and glory and praise!"

Shall we not join them? Can we be silent while angels sing the great Redeemer's praise? Is it not rather, "Oh, that with yonder sacred throng we at his feet may fall. We'll join the everlasting song and crown him Lord of all"? Why wait for heaven to crown our eternal King? The time to start is now! Let's give him the throne room in our hearts. Let's daily retake that oath of allegiance to him that we first spoke on our confirmation day. Let's sing with the heroes of old to that King of Creation, "Truly I'd love thee, truly I'd serve thee, Light of my soul, my Joy, my Crown."

May that Savior, whose sacred head was scornfully surrounded with thorns as his only crown, forgive our frequent lack of loyalty and faint-hearted service to him. May he move us to surrender our hearts and lives in willing homage to him.

"King," they said in mockery that day. "King, indeed!" we respond as he offers us the crown of glory, "King of kings and Lord of lords!"

Dear Jesus, give us hearts of faith to hold you and lives of love to serve you all our days. Amen.

And they began to call out to him, "Hail, king of the Jews!" Again and again they struck him on the head with a staff and spit on him. Falling on their knees, they paid homage to him. (Mark 15:18,19)

HIS HOMAGE

The crowds cheered and the flags waved as we stood on the main avenue in Mexico City on November 20, the anniversary of their revolution, and watched as the president of Mexico went by. Rulers are used to receiving homage from their people.

King Jesus also must have homage, so the cruel soldiers thought. "Hail, king of the Jews!" they mocked, bowing low before him. Then they spit on him. Disgusting, dirty spittle for his face, such was the homage considered worthy for this king. Others amused themselves snatching the reed from his hand and rapping him over the head with it. Such was the respect they had for this king.

They bowed before him in mockery that day, but how fitting homage is for this king. Before them stood one who was more than just Jesus, the Son of Mary. He was Jesus, the sinless, almighty Son of God, co-ruler of heaven and earth. One word from his lips and angels could have flocked to his defense. One sentence and rough soldiers would have sprawled on the pavement. One glance and Pilate would have been rendered powerless.

They were manhandling the King of kings. Finally they would even put him on the cross, not because he couldn't stop them, but because he didn't want to. His love wouldn't let him stop them. In love he was "laying down his life for the sheep," just as he said he would. Here's the true glory of our King! Willingly he lays down his life for the sins of the world that we might inherit an eternal kingdom.

So where are our cheers and flags? Certainly we want to be on our knees before him, sending prayers and praises to him. But that's the easy part. Far more difficult is it to keep on waving those flags and shouting those praises in the daily routine we call life. Let our fellow church members see by the way we worship him each Sunday; let our family members see by the way we lead them daily to this throne; let our fellow workers see by the way we dedicate workday matters to him that we know who our King is, what he has done for us and how worthy he is to receive our homage.

"King," they said in mockery that day. "King indeed!" we respond as we serve him in his kingdom, "King of kings and Lord of lords!"

Dear Jesus, remind us of the kingdom which is ours through your innocent suffering and death, that we may serve you willingly. Amen.

18

And when they had mocked him, they took off the purple robe and put his own clothes on him. Then they led him out to crucify him. (Mark 15:20)

HIS THRONE

Kings must have their thrones as seats of honor and proof of power. In the royal palace in Madrid, Spain, stands such a throne, overlaid with the richest gold and upholstered with the finest velvet.

King Jesus also had his throne, a most unlikely one at that. It was a seat reserved for the worst criminal, the lowest slave, and God's Son! Today we bronze it and position it on our altars. We gild it and put it on chains. We polish it and place it on our steeples. But in Jesus' day it meant the worst disgrace and the deepest pain.

Who can describe the pain of rough nails tearing through flesh as nerve endings screamed out? Who can lay out in words what it meant to hang on that rough wood and wait for life to ebb slowly, all too slowly, from a pain-wracked body? Still worse, who can plumb the depths of what it meant for Jesus to have hell's punishment wash over him, one crashing wave after the other, as payment for every sin in the world was demanded? Who can detail what it meant for him to drink that cup of suffering to its bitter end on the cross where he was enthroned?

Even more—who can fully describe the love behind it all? Love is never easy to define, the love of parent for child, lover for spouse, friend for another. But love that would bring God down from his glorious throne on high where he was surrounded by angels to be enthroned on a cross and encircled by thieves, where do we find the words? In John 15:13 the King told his disciples, "Greater love has no one than this, that one lay down his life for his friends." Later, one of those disciples, after having stood beneath the King's cross, wrote, "This is how we know what love is: Jesus Christ laid down his life for us." And that love becomes even more indescribable when we realize Christ died not for friends, but for enemies.

Earthly monarchs can have their thrones of gold and velvet. The cross of our King is infinitely more beautiful and far more valuable. For the believer that cross spells God's love and the sinner's salvation in shining letters. For the believer that cross is his Savior's glorious throne.

"King," they said in mockery that day as they lifted him up on the cross. "King indeed!" we respond as we kneel in humble thanks before our Savior on his throne of love, "King of kings and Lord of lords!"

Dear Jesus, draw us to your cross in life and death. Amen.

While they were eating, Jesus took bread, gave thanks and broke it and gave it to his disciples, saying, "Take it; this is my body." Then he took the cup, gave thanks and offered it to them, and they all drank from it. "This is my blood of the covenant, which is poured out for many," he said to them. (Mark 14:22-24)

HIS LEGACY

Kings work mightily to extend the borders of their realms and enlarge their riches. They want more for themselves and more to leave as legacies for their children. But so often earth's riches are ripped from their grasp or squandered by their descendants.

King Jesus also has a legacy for us. And he worked hard to get it. It took him to the cross to give up his life in payment for the world's sins. Forgiveness was the rich treasure he would win and leave for all people.

This forgiveness our King offers in a very special way. As he ate the Passover with his disciples on the night before he went to Calvary, he left his forgiveness in a unique form. Taking the unleavened bread and the cup of wine on the table, he gave them to his disciples and said, "Take it; this is my body. . . . This is my blood of the covenant." Miraculously, but really, he gave them his body and blood along with that bread and wine to assure them of the forgiveness of all their sins.

What a legacy! Jesus knew how often his followers would be weak and wobbly, how often their faith would flicker and fade, how often they would need to be assured of forgiveness. So he gave them the miracle of his Holy Supper. In that Supper along with the bread and the wine he gives us the very body and blood he used to prepare forgiveness. Who can doubt that sins are gone and heaven opened as he receives the very body and blood of his Savior?

What do you do with a legacy? Lock it away in a bank vault or stash it on a closet shelf? Far better when new sins alarm us and old guilt won't let go, far better when faith needs feeding and Christian muscles cry out for strengthening, to stand at his table and to hear him tell us again, "Here, this is my body; I gave it for YOU. Here, this is my blood; I shed it for YOU. YOUR sins are forgiven. YOU depart in peace."

Our King has left us a wondrous legacy. As we use it regularly, we can't help but exclaim, "He's a King indeed! He's King of kings and Lord of lords!"

Dear Jesus, let your Holy Supper refresh us today and often. Amen.

With that, he bowed his head and gave up his spirit. (John 19:30)

HIS DEATH

Television programs are interrupted for special bulletins. Reporters come from afar when one of earth's royalty dies and is buried.

That Good Friday another King died. His soul left its home in his body. His head dropped down; his cheeks turned pale; his eyes lost their luster. Those who watched realized he was dead just like so many kings before and after him.

Yet his death was different. Death is always something solemn. When we stand at a deathbed, we feel God's nearness and realize he's speaking to us. If true with the death of an ordinary mortal, how much more so when the God-man closes his eyes? If we can feel the deep mystery in human dying, how much more so when the everlasting Christ hangs dead on the cross? With the hymnwriter we have to marvel, "O sorrow dread, God's Son is dead."

The King who died was different; so was the way he died. We know why we die. It's because we have to. We may want to live longer, but our strength gives out, our heart stops, and we die. Nothing on earth can add one second to our life. With Jesus it was far different. He was not dying because he was powerless to stop the process. He was dying because he loved us and wanted to die for us. He even set the time of his death, for we are told, "He gave up his spirit." Death did not capture Jesus, but he went forward to meet it. He who once said, "I lay down my life—only to take it up again. No one takes it from me, but I lay it down of my own accord," now proved this fact as he committed his soul into the hands of his heavenly Father.

And we? Yes, we must die. Yes, there is nothing we can do about it. But because of Jesus' death, for us death is no longer the king of terrors and the unbeatable foe. When God's children must give up their souls, they hand them over to no stranger or enemy, but into the loving hands of an eternal Father. He will take us home safely to those mansions prepared by his Son on Calvary's cross.

Our King died that day. No television shows were interrupted and no reporters came. But his death has meant life for thousands like us and ever will.

Must we not say it, "A King indeed! Yes, King of kings and Lord of lords!"

Dear Savior, let your triumphant death be my comfort now and in the hour of my death. Amen.

When he had received the drink, Jesus said, "It is finished." (John 19:30)

HIS VICTORY

It was early morning, May 7, 1945. Some of us can remember the day. Five years, eight months and seven days after war had been declared with Germany, it was over. Victory was ours!

It was close to 3:00 on a Friday afternoon about A.D. 30. All of us need to remember that day. The war was over, one raging ever since sin had closed Eden's door. And the victory was ours!

Out on Calvary scarcely had the sponge soaked with sour wine moistened our King's lips when he spoke. "It is finished," he said. One word of four syllables in Greek, and yet it was the most important word the world would ever hear. The Greeks wrote this word on tax bills to show that they were paid in full. Now our Savior shouted it from his cross. What did it mean? What was over?

Jesus did not speak in the whisper of dying men which you must lean low to hear. No, he spoke, as the Gospel writer tells us, with "a loud voice" so that all might hear. He shouted, "I have won! My work of salvation is done. I have kept the law perfectly for all people. I have paid for all sins, not one remains. I have suffered the agonies of hell which were reserved for sinners. I have endured the full punishment and righteous anger of my Father over sin. I have shed my precious blood to redeem all mankind. And now it, my work of salvation, is completely finished." Our precious Savior from his position on the cross could turn his gaze from the first sinner to the last and see no one for whom he had not paid.

Talk about victory! Does our conscience tell us, "You are a great sinner and deserve eternal punishment"? "Not any longer," the voice of our King from Calvary answers. "It is finished. My blood cleanses you from all sin."

Talk about victory! Does an inner voice whisper to us, "You are a child of death, a sure victim of that king of terrors"? "Not any longer," the voice of our King from Calvary answers. "It is finished. I have abolished death and brought life and immortality."

Talk about victory! Does Satan still try to handcuff us to him in sin's slavery? "Not any longer," the voice of our King from Calvary answers. "It is finished. One little word can fell him."

But to talk about victory means to talk about the King. He did it! He is a King indeed! He is King of kings and Lord of lords!

Dear Savior, remind us ever of your Good Friday victory. Amen.

Now on his way to Jerusalem, Jesus traveled along the border between Samaria and Galilee. As he was going into a village, ten men who had leprosy met him. They stood at a distance and called out in a loud voice, "Jesus, Master, have pity on us!" (Luke 17:11-13)

ASK JESUS!

When trouble strikes, the natural reaction of man is to cry out for help. Men cry out to whatever they think will help them, be it someone in their family, or a doctor, or the government, or a god—someone stronger and wiser than themselves, someone to help in a need they cannot handle themselves.

But much of the time men cry out to what is unable to help them, to false gods, who do not exist, or to doctors and friends, who are limited in their wisdom and power. Much of the time, men cry out in vain.

We do not know how many times these ten lepers had cried out for help during the many years of their affliction with leprosy. Nor do we know whom they asked for help. We do know that no one did help them, for their leprosy continued and troubled them more with each passing year.

No one helped them—until they came to Jesus and asked Jesus to have mercy upon them. The measure of help is determined by the strength and ability of the helper. When all is said and done, there is only One who is powerful and able to help in every need. That is Jesus. He is the Son of God. He is true God from eternity to eternity. He has all wisdom and power in heaven and on earth.

As we hear of these lepers turning to Jesus for help, we remember that Jesus has invited all of us to bring our needs to him. And he has assured us that he will help us: "Call upon me in the day of trouble; I will deliver you, and you will honor me" (Psalm 50:15).

Days of trouble will come our way during our lives. Indeed, each day has enough sorrows of its own. In our need we cry out for help. And our help is in the name of the Lord. He made us, redeemed us, and will preserve us and all who call upon him unto his heavenly kingdom.

All that for my soul is needful
He with loving care provides,
Nor of that is He unheedful
Which my body needs besides.
In my need He doth not fail me.
All things else have but their day,
God's great love abides for aye. Amen.

As he was going into a village, ten men who had leprosy met him. They stood at a distance and called out in a loud voice, "Jesus, Master, have pity on us!" (Luke 17:12,13)

ASK JESUS IN ALL THE NEEDS OF LIFE

Leprosy was the common cancer in the days of the New Testament. Like cancer, leprosy was dreaded and feared. Like cancer, leprosy struck with no distinction of sex or age or previous health. Today cancer (and leprosy) can sometimes be treated, but 2,000 years ago there was no cure for leprosy. When a leper was detected, he was considered ceremonially unclean and sent away from his home and family; he was forbidden contact with society; he could not work but had to beg for his food and clothing; he could only suffer until his leprosy brought its own relief in death. Because lepers were so separated from other people, it is understandable that these ten lepers had banded together to aid and comfort one another in their hopeless situation.

Standing afar off, because they could not come close to those who did not have leprosy, the ten called out loudly to Jesus, that he might hear them and help them. They cried out to Jesus, for their need was great.

As those who know and trust Jesus, we also cry out to him in our needs. We needn't wait until we have a great need, for Jesus wants us to come to him in all the needs of life. He is not a helper only when things get to be "too much for us to handle." He is a helper for us in matters great and small, in every concern of life. No matter that we bring to Jesus is too small—or too great—for him.

He especially invites us to come to him to be cleansed of our leprosy—the leprosy of sin. Our sins have made us unclean and have separated us from God's fellowship. Our sins will bring us eternal death—unless they are cured. And we have a perfect cure in Christ, who shed his blood on the cross for us.

The invitation to come to Jesus is well expressed in one of our hymns:

Come in poverty and meanness,
Come defiled, without, within;
From infection and uncleanness,
From the leprosy of sin,
Wash your robes and make them white;
Ye shall walk with God in light.

(TLH 149:2)

Whatever our need, be it a need of the body or of the soul, Jesus always can help. And he always will help, for he is our Savior. He is our God.

Lord Jesus, have mercy upon us. Amen.

When he saw them, he said, "Go, show yourselves to the priests." (Luke 17:14)

ASK IN FAITH

Jesus' answer to the ten lepers sounds strange to us. They had asked for healing, but Jesus said only, "Go, show yourselves to the priests." Though this answer puzzles us, the lepers understood it very well. The Old Testament regulations (in Leviticus 13 and 14) had a provision that priests were to serve as inspectors. They had the responsibility to certify that a person had leprosy and to certify it if a person were healed of leprosy. Jesus told these men to go to the priest so that he could pronounce them clean and welcome them back, as it were, into the "land of the living." In telling them to go to the priest, Jesus was promising them that they would be healed of their leprosy. This answer of Jesus to the ten lepers invited them to trust him. They had as of yet no physical indication of healing. They had only the promise of Jesus that they would be healed. By giving this kind of answer, Jesus sought to give the lepers a lesson in faith. He taught them to trust him as the Son of God and their Savior. They were to learn to trust him, not only for the healing of their bodies, but also, and especially, for the healing of their souls. They were to learn that in all their needs they could count on the help of Jesus.

We too have been given promises by Jesus. Like the lepers who heard this promise, we do not yet see the fulfillment of many of Jesus' promises to us. He has said that we are cleansed and purified from the leprosy of sin, but we still see sin in our lives. He has said that we have been delivered from death, but we still see the grave ahead of us. He has said that he is with us always, but none of us has ever seen Jesus face to face. He has said that we will see heaven, but all we see now is the pain and misery of this world.

In making such promises to us, Jesus is calling upon us to put our faith in him. As Jesus said, "Blessed are those who have not seen and yet have believed" (John 20:29). Blessed are we, who trust the promises Jesus has made to us. Blessed are we, who believe that he has cleansed our bodies of the leprosy of sin, that he has freed us from death, and that in him we have newness of life and immortality. Blessed are we, who believe the gospel of salvation. Blessed indeed! For all who believe it possess what it offers.

Our Father in heaven, we thank you for having brought us to faith in Jesus, your Son. Preserve our faith unto the end, for his sake. Amen.

Once more he visited Cana in Galilee, where he had turned the water into wine. And there was a certain royal official whose son lay sick at Capernaum. When this man heard that Jesus had arrived in Galilee from Judea, he went to him and begged him to come and heal his son, who was close to death. "Unless you people see miraculous signs and wonders," Jesus told him, "you will never believe." The royal official said, "Sir, come down before my child dies." Jesus replied, "You may go. Your son will live." The man took Jesus at his word and departed. (John 4:46-50)

LESS THAN WHAT HE ASKED FOR—AND MORE

A boy was sick. Help was badly needed. His father remembered Jesus. Faith sought the Lord. It made its plea. It asked Christ to come. And Jesus said no!

Or did he? It's true, Jesus didn't answer the father's prayer in the manner in which the father wanted him to answer it. And it was a good thing he didn't, for the father would have shorted himself. Jesus gave him less than what he asked for—and more!

The Lord gave the man less in that he did not accompany him to his house as he desired. In a manner of speaking, his request wasn't answered at all. Instead, the Lord gave the father a word of promise. He indicated that the lad would be healed, that if the father would simply return home he would find his petition granted. And this was the much greater gift, since it required faith on the part of the man to accept and believe the word of Jesus. He had faith in his heart already, or else he would not have sought out the Lord in the first place. Jesus' word of promise caused that faith to grow and become stronger. Don't you see that the Lord gave him much more than he asked for? When the man arrived home, not only was his son well, but he himself had been strengthened in his faith in the Savior.

There's a lesson in that for us. Whenever we go to the Lord in prayer, when we seek his assistance and help, let's never tie his almighty hands as this father almost did. We must learn to allow the Lord to answer our needs in the manner he thinks best. We would often shortchange ourselves. And when he answers our prayers in a way that is a bit different than we had anticipated, let's learn to look a bit more deeply, and we shall see that Jesus has granted us not less, but more, much more than we asked for. He knows much better than we do what we really need.

The father's strengthened faith is a fine example for our faith. Let us ever look for the word of promise our Savior gives us in Scripture, believe it, and trust in it. His promises give us all we need—and more!

Lord Jesus, grant me a faith that never doubts, but ever believes. As you answer my prayers, strengthen my faith to cling firmly to the promises of forgiveness and life eternal found in your glorious gospel. Amen.

A Canaanite woman from that vicinity came to him, crying out, "Lord, Son of David, have mercy on me! My daughter is suffering terribly from demon-possession." (Matthew 15:22)

LORD, I MUST TALK TO YOU!

The land of Syrophenicia began about 35 miles northwest of the Sea of Galilee. In Old Testament times the heathen Canaanite people fled to this valuable seacoast region to escape the children of Israel. This region was never subdued by God's chosen people. Tyre and Sidon—two famous commercial cities of the ancient world—were once located here. But long before the coming of Christ they had fallen under the wrath of God for their wicked, idolatrous ways and were completely destroyed.

But some of these heathen people had been exposed to the Jewish religion. They had heard of the Messiah who was to come to the Israelites. Nor were they ignorant of Jesus, whom many in neighboring Galilee believed to be this Messiah or Savior sent from God. When the Canaanite woman in our text heard of the miracles that Jesus was doing in Galilee and heard of his message concerning the kingdom of heaven, she was convinced that he was of God and could help her.

Tragedy and sadness had entered her home. The devil had taken possession of her daughter and made her life ugly and uncontrollable. Up to this point, life had seemed hopeless. Not that the woman hadn't sought help from her heathen religion. She had, but to no avail. Her gods were no gods. But in Jesus Christ lay hope. He not only claimed to be the Son of God who had come to save the people from their sins, but even did the works of God to prove it, including the casting out of devils. She had to talk to Jesus and ask his help!

But it wasn't only the POWER of Jesus that attracted her. It was also the COMPASSION. Jesus was easily touched with the feeling of sinful man's infirmities. Her former gods showed no compassion, but Jesus loved and pitied and helped people. She was convinced that her words of prayer would speak heart to heart and the Lord would help. She must talk to Jesus! Saving faith looks always to Jesus.

Jesus is our compassionate Lord and Savior. When our life is weary and sad; when we feel tempted by devil, world and flesh; when sickness strikes our body, or sin smites our conscience—whatever the need —let our heart cry, "Lord, I must talk to you!" Sinner, heart answers heart whenever we speak to Jesus. Only believe! Ever pray!

Lord, in all times of trial and need teach us to talk to you. Amen.

Jesus did not answer a word. (Matthew 15:23)

PATIENTLY WAIT FOR GOD'S ANSWER

" **J**esus did not answer a word." How strange the words sound! He did not say yes to her as we would expect. He did not say no. He just remained silent. Why? One reason was that Jesus was not sent to the Gentiles but to the Jewish people. But there is also another purpose for his silence. That was to teach her patience. The time was not exactly right for him to respond to her plea. He had heard it. He would answer. But he would do it when he knew it was best.

Does Jesus answer our prayers? This is a question which often faces the Christian. I know of old people who are suffering the pains of old age and long to die. They pray that the Lord will take them. Yet he remains silent. I know of people who pray for a healing, but it seems that the Lord is not hearing them; instead their disease continues to grow worse. I know of people who pray for a job where they can earn a decent living, but the days go by and there is no work or the pay is not enough. I know of students who pray for good grades and in spite of their diligent work continue to do poorly. I know of people who pray for their children who have fallen away from

the church, but the pleas seem to go unanswered. Is Jesus hearing our prayers? Yes, Jesus is hearing our prayers. The problem is that we are not hearing the answer.

First of all, whenever we pray for spiritual blessings from Jesus, we can be sure that he gives us the answer in his Word. When we pray for the forgiveness of sins, he answers in his Word, "Your sins are forgiven." He has paid for all of them. When you pray for a strong faith, he answers that prayer through his Word and the Lord's Supper. He begins strengthening our faith immediately.

Secondly, whenever we pray for earthly or temporal blessings, he answers those prayers, but at his own time in the way that is best for us. Many times the things for which we pray would be harmful for us. We must learn that he knows what is best for our life so that we reach eternal life. Many times he delays the answer to our prayers to teach us patience. We are products of modern America, and as such we want instant satisfaction in everything. As Christians we must learn to be patient. May the Lord grant us patience as we wait for the answer we know the Lord will give.

Lord Jesus, teach us to pray with the certainty that our prayers are heard and answered. Give us the patience to wait for the answer that is best for our welfare now and forever. Amen.

The woman came and knelt before him. "Lord, help me!" she said. (Matthew 15:25)

JESUS INSTRUCTS US ABOUT PERSEVERANCE

"I quit. I give up." Very often this is our response when we try something for a while and it does not work out. But this is not to be our response when prayers seem to go unanswered.

Even though Jesus had told his disciples, "I was sent only to the lost sheep of Israel," the Canaanite woman did not give up in her efforts to have Jesus deliver her child from demon-possession. In fact it seems that this pause when Jesus spoke to his disciples gave the woman time to catch up with them. "She came and knelt before him." With all humility she bowed before her Lord. Her plea was, "Lord, help me." She still recognized Jesus as her Lord and only source of help for her daughter. She would not give up.

It would be interesting to know just what this woman had heard about Jesus. She must have heard of the way he healed all that were brought to him. Had she also heard of the teaching of Jesus, "All that the father gives me will come to me, and whoever comes to me I will never drive away" (John 6:37)? Had she heard the invitation of Jesus, "Come to me, all you who are weary and burdened, and I will give you rest" (Matthew 11:28)? We have no way of knowing the answers to these questions. What is important is that we learn from this woman to persevere in our faith in Jesus Christ.

We have a wealth of Scripture passages which show us that Jesus is able to do whatever we ask him. All of the miracles have been recorded for that purpose. We also know of the promises which he gave to his disciples. We know of his great invitation to come to him for rest. We have the examples of people in the Old Testament who were strong in their faith. We know how Abraham trusted that God would give him a child even though it seemed impossible. He persevered. We know how Jacob struggled with the Lord until the Lord blessed him. We know how the Lord listened to the pleading of Moses and spared the children of Israel.

Above all we know the love of the Lord Jesus for us. He was willing to come to earth, suffer and die for us. He was willing to take our place so that we might have eternal life. Because we know of his love toward us and that he also invites us to pray, we persevere in our faith in him.

Lord Jesus, when we hear your word, send your Holy Spirit into our hearts and work a faith which will persevere through all the trials of this life. Amen.

Then one of the synagogue rulers, named Jairus, came there. Seeing Jesus, he fell at his feet and pleaded earnestly with him, "My little daughter is dying. Please come and put your hands on her so that she will be healed and live." So Jesus went with him. (Mark 5:23,24)

TROUBLE UNDERNEATH—POWER UP ABOVE

When the sun shines and the breezes blow gently, the Sea of Galilee seems so peaceful. From the heights overlooking Tiberias one can observe sparkling waters and green hillsides sloping up from the lake. Appearances deceive. It is not always so calm. Some days there are strong winds, waves and danger.

Even so, many will still insist that Galilee is a delightful place to visit. An ideal place to vacation. So peaceful!

Jesus chose to live in a village in this area. The people of Galilee became his friends. He called some to be his witnesses. They would travel far and go to busy places. Could they ever forget this calm place?

But every peaceful scene may be the opposite underneath. Sin, trouble, sickness, despair and death emerge. All destroy peace. Wherever these are present—and this is everywhere—the quantity and quality of peace is limited.

Everything may have looked outwardly peaceful one day when Jesus discussed fasting with John's disciples. But several people had troubles that day. It took Jesus to restore peace. One home in Capernaum was far from peaceful. A little girl lay near death, the only daughter of the ruler of the synagogue. Peace disturbed by critical illness!

The death angel seemed close when the father, Jairus, went to Jesus with a simple request. When trouble finally disturbed his house, he felt that his neighbor, Jesus, had the power to help, as he had helped others.

The Savior's response? "Jesus went with him." So did the disciples. All went to where trouble underneath threatened to destroy Jairus's life.

No one lives in continual peace. Nothing grants immunity from occasional heartache. Where is help?

When trouble underneath disturbs our lives, Christians remember where the best help is—Jesus, through prayer. The centuries have not diminished his power to help. He can still rise from the right hand of power and come to our house when asked.

Dear Jesus, when there is trouble underneath, always be our power up above. Amen.

While Jesus was still speaking, someone came from the house of Jairus, the synagogue ruler. "Your daughter is dead," he said. "Don't bother the teacher any more." (Luke 8:49)

DONT BE AFRAID; JUST BELIEVE

The villagers of Capernaum had seen Jesus perform many miracles. A nobleman's son, a demoniac, Peter's mother-in-law, a palsied man and numerous invalids and cripples had felt the healing touch of the Great Physician. Fishermen had reported that the Sea of Galilee had calmed one night at Jesus' command. Yes, Jesus' neighbors experienced his power to heal and to control the elements.

But overcome death? That might be different. Who had done that since Elijah and Elisha? Did the friend who met Jairus returning home with Jesus think this?

Probably. The news he bears is bad. "Your daughter is dead; don't bother the teacher any more." A crushing message!

"Why did I wait so long before going to Jesus?" he may have thought. Or asked, "Why didn't Jesus come sooner?" Yes, no sense bothering Jesus now. A dear treasure, his one and only daughter is gone!

But the bruised reed, shocked and confused like most bereaved humans, is not broken off. Jesus' eye is on the broken father. He encourages, "Don't be afraid; just believe, and she will be healed."

How? The daughter was not sick anymore. She was dead! What could Jesus do about that?

Much, actually. Jesus can do much more about anything than even his children believe he can do. Shortsighted individuals forget that with God all things are possible. God's power is not limited. Jairus would have to trust that also.

How many hearts in trouble find it hard to hope like that? Many hesitant or qualified prayers seem to admit, "Jesus can do one thing but not another. I dare to ask for little but not for big things." So while they ask boldly for some things, they will not trouble the Master whenever the request seems like an impossible one.

Jesus does not scold Jairus's friends. Jairus is his concern. "Don't be afraid; just believe." That has to be enough for now. Jairus accepts. And waits. They continue on their way.

Tuck those words away in your hearts, believers! On our way through life remember that Jesus urges us also, "Don't be afraid; just believe." Even when the outlook seems completely hopeless and insurmountable, do not fear to trouble him further.

I know, Jesus, when my faith trusts you, you will honor my request for help. Amen.

He told her, "Go, call your husband and come back." "I have no husband," she replied. Jesus said to her, "You are right when you say you have no husband. The fact is, you have had five husbands, and the man you now have is not your husband. What you have just said is quite true." "Sir," the woman said, "I can see that you are a prophet." (John 4:16-19)

KNOWING ALL THEIR NEED

We are afraid to tell people what we need; sometimes even our friends. We are afraid they will laugh at us or hurt us. Or even worse that they will ignore us. Though this woman had some real problems, she had no one to talk to. Jesus showed her that he knew what she needed and that she could talk to him.

At first she did not say much; it was too painful. Her past had left deep scars on her heart. She had nothing to be proud of. She did not want to be reminded, though she needed to tell someone. Jesus understood. He showed her that he knew all about her. Nothing about any of us escapes his eye. He knows us just as we are. Because he loves us, he accepts us and forgives us.

He wants us to be open and honest with him. He invites us to pray to him, to lay all needs on him. As he says through Peter, "Cast all your anxiety on him because he cares for you." We may bring our big needs and our little ones, everything that is important to us. Jesus will not laugh at us or hurt us. He will do whatever is best for us. He will give us whatever is best for us.

He knows us better than we know ourselves. Because he is our good friend, he will help us with needs we are not even aware of. We are never left alone to struggle with our needs. Jesus sticks with us. He assures us, "I will never leave you nor forsake you." Everything will turn out for our good—that is his promise.

He can make such promises because he is the Lord of all creation. He makes everything we see, and he keeps it all running. He has the power to do what he promises; he earned it. He did everything his Father asked. With such willingness and love, he met our biggest need, our need to be forgiven. We have no reason to fear. Rather, "Let us then approach the throne of grace with confidence, so that we may receive mercy and find grace to help us in our time of need."

Dear Jesus, we hurt more than we can say. We have more needs than we know. But we are not afraid anymore, because we can tell you what we need. We know that you can help us in every need. We trust that you will help us and do what is best for us, because you have already loved us so much. Amen.

When they could not find a way to do this because of the crowd, they went up on the roof and lowered him on his mat through the tiles into the middle of the crowd, right in front of Jesus. (Luke 5:19)

BE PERSISTENT

How easily good intentions can evaporate when faced with a little resistance. We know how that works. A pastor intends to call on that member. But after several phone calls with no answer, and then no one home when he stops by, he lets that call wait until "later." A member intends to talk with his pastor. But when he finally gets up the courage to do so, there are too many people around, and he decides it wasn't that important. Think of how many sales have been lost, gardens not hoed, church services missed, because we let a little resistance stand in the way and don't persist.

God wants us to persevere in our faith, and in all that we ask for in faith. This is true, also, when we come to him for healing like these men did in our text. Did they say, "It's too crowded; no one will let us through with this stretcher; we'd better not bother Jesus when he's so busy; let's go home." No! They persisted. Faith finds a way. In this case, they moved back the movable tiles and went through the roof. They didn't give up until they had presented their case right in front of Jesus to let him decide what to do.

Jesus himself sets the best example of persistence for us. His human nature did not relish the thought of going any further in Gethsemane. Nevertheless he persisted in doing his Father's will and went all the way to Golgotha. And look at the blessings that resulted! Forgiveness for all our sins. Peace for our souls. Life with God forever in heaven. Jesus has given us spiritual healing and eternal good health because he persisted.

When it comes to seeking out Jesus also for earthly blessings—including healing—God wants us to be persistent. Remember the Syrophoenician woman and her crumbs? God hasn't promised always to heal us in the way we want it or according to our timetable. Sometimes he says, "My grace is sufficient for you." But he also says, "You do not have, because you do not ask God." He says we "should always pray and not give up." Be persistent. It may not seem like you can find a way at first. But persevere in faith to bring all your needs right in front of Jesus. And let him decide.

Dear Jesus, sometimes I get discouraged in my faith. Help me to be persistent in bringing all my needs to you until you meet them in your way. Amen.

Jesus said, "Have the people sit down." There was plenty of grass in that place, and the men sat down, about five thousand of them. Jesus then took the loaves, gave thanks, and distributed to those who were seated as much as they wanted. He did the same with the fish. (John 6:10,11)

PRAYER—BAROMETER OF FAITH

A barometer is an instrument which measures air pressure. When the pressure is high and steady, then the sky is clear, the sun shines, and the weather is enjoyable. When the barometer drops, it indicates that there is going to be a change in the weather. When the weather is unstable, the sky is probably cloudy, and there is a threat of severe storms.

Our prayer-life serves as a barometer of our Christian faith. Prayer does not create faith any more than a barometer causes the weather. But prayer is an accurate gauge and measure of the strength of our faith. If it reads high, if we are praying a lot, it is an indication that our faith is strong and that our hearts are unclouded. If the barometer is low, if we pray little or not at all, we may well take that as a sign that our faith is growing weak and expect storm clouds to appear on the horizon.

Before Jesus had his disciples distribute the bread and fish to the hungry people who had followed him, he prayed. Jesus' prayer is an example to every believing heart. By his prayer Jesus showed that the blessing of food which was to follow was a gift from God. His prayer of thanks was his way of professing that God deserves the credit for providing our food, drink, clothing, shelter, family, friends, good weather, good health and all that we need for our body and life.

When we give thanks to God for our daily bread it is an evidence of faith. For our prayer of gratitude acknowledges the Creator's love and ability to preserve our life. It flows from our knowledge of our Redeemer's sacrificial love. And it is a product of the Comforter's work of having brought us to faith in Jesus. According to that faith, let us daily join the psalmist, who experienced God's gracious providence, and foresaw and believed his promises in Christ. He prayed: "Give thanks to the Lord, for he is good; his love endures forever."

Oh, may we ne'er with thankless heart
Forget from whom our blessings flow!
Still, Lord, Thy heav'nly grace impart;
Still teach us what to Thee we owe.
Lord, may our lives with fruit divine
Return Thy care and prove us Thine. Amen.

Deliver us from evil. (Luke 11:4)

THE LORD TURNS EVIL INTO GOOD

Only the very inexperienced are surprised when something breaks, fails to function, or goes wrong. The older you get the more you realize that sooner or later everything in the world wears out, clogs up, rusts, becomes diseased, withers, rots, dies or becomes useless. This is the disastrous result of sin. Sin covers creation like dew. Nothing escapes. Everything is affected. Everything is doomed.

When you think about the world covered with the curse of sin, you almost want to yell out, "Get me out of here!" God will, in due time, get us out of this vale of tears. But in the mean time we should cherish our life as priceless. Our life is God's gift. Eternal life is his greater gift. True, we are still in an evil world, but we will overcome. "He who overcomes will inherit all this, and I will be his God and he will be my son" (Revelation 21:17).

While we trudge through this sin-cursed world we pray, "Lord, deliver us from evil." We don't expect to be engulfed in a pink cloud and be spared all the agonies, disappoint-ments and heartaches of life. Evil is part of life.

When we pray "Deliver us from evil," we pray that God in his good pleasure might turn some of that evil into good as he turned the hatred of Joseph's eleven brothers into the good of raising Joseph to the position of leadership in Egypt, or as the Lord strengthened Job through affliction.

My favorite comfort passage at the bedside of a down-hearted Christian is Romans 8:28, "And we know that in all things God works for the good of those who love him, who have been called according to his purpose."

God can and does turn the evil of life into great blessings for his children. The other evening my wife and I were together with three Christian couples. Two couples had already buried one of their children; the other couple is raising a handicapped daughter. But these are devout and contented people because they are in Christ and they have learned to glory even in their tribulation.

We pray in this petition, as the sum of all, that our Father in heaven would deliver us from every evil of body and soul, of property and honor, and finally, when our last hour shall come, grant us a blessed end, and graciously take us from this vale of tears to himself In heaven. Amen.

Jesus, knowing that they intended to come and make him king by force, withdrew again to a mountain by himself. (John 6:15)

GOD GIVES US WHAT WE REALLY NEED

Would you like to be able to command God to do just what you want him to do in your life? Would you like him to give you a blank check on which you could fill in any desired amount? Jesus knew what these people wanted from him—even before they asked. And he refused their request for their own good.

When the crowd realized that Jesus was able to perform miracles, they wanted to make the most of his presence in their midst. They wanted him to be their king and free them from the oppression of the Roman authorities. They wanted Jesus to provide for all their needs with no effort on their part. They wanted him to be their bread king.

Jesus had something much better in mind for them. He would let them continue to live with the responsibilities that God had given them in this life. But he would gain eternal life for them, so that they might have permanent happiness and freedom from cares in the life to come. Those were much greater blessings than any earthly king could provide for them.

When Jesus satisfied the demands of God's justice on the cross, he was not suffering judgment for his own sins. He was dying for the sins of all the people. He took God's anger over our sins upon himself, that we might bask in God's favor and love for all of time and eternity. He died that we might live forevermore.

Beyond that, he rose that we might rise to life eternal at the last day, as well as have life in him now. In all these ways he showed that he really cares for us. He would not let this eager crowd turn him from his love-wrought purpose. He withdrew from them, because he wanted to do what was really good for them. He went to give his life in their place.

We can be happy that when we pray to God, he does not always give us exactly what we want. We may pray for all good things that we desire, but we often do not understand what would really be good for us. But God knows all things. He knows what is best for us, and that is what he gives us. "We do not know what we ought to pray, but the Spirit himself intercedes for us with groans that words cannot express." In this way God gives us what is really good for us.

Dear Jesus, I thank you that you care for me. Thank you for giving me the best gift of all, the everlasting salvation purchased with your precious blood and your innocent suffering and death. In your name I pray. Amen.

"Take my yoke upon you and learn from me, for I am gentle and humble in heart, and you will find rest for your souls. For my yoke is easy and my burden is light." (Matthew 11:29-30)

"COME UNTO ME YE WEARY"

"Come unto Me, ye weary, and I will give you rest" is one of those hymns that strikes the chords of joyous melody in our hearts, and well it might. For it comes to those whose hearts are oppressed and promises them "pardon, grace and peace—of joy that hath no ending, of love which cannot cease." To the wanderers, to those whose hearts are filled with sadness, it promises "gladness and songs at break of day." To those who are "fainting" it promises life; to those engaged in a fierce struggle against Satan it promises strength to win the victory.

Christ continually invites us to leave our heavy burden of sin and shame on his shoulders and in return to accept a light burden from him. Those who leave their heavy burden of sin with Christ, are not going to be without a burden altogether. Christ will give them another in its place, a light burden though, one that is actually a privilege. It is the yoke of the cross, which Christians must be prepared to bear in this world as disciples of him who first bore the cross for us. Though the heavy burden of sin has been lifted, there will still be trials and tribulations, for the disciple is not above his master. This burden will prove irksome to our flesh.

And yet, compared with the heavy burden of sin which has been lifted from us, the yoke of Christ is easy and his burden is light. The Christian knows that these crosses do not come upon him by chance or accident. They are sent into his life by a loving God and are intended for his good. The Christian also knows that God will never let the cross become heavier than he is able to bear. With each trial of faith God will also provide the ability to endure. God will supply the necessary strength for each new day. Hence, the burden of Christ, far from separating us from the love of God, will only draw us much closer to him. The affliction of the body will be turned to the eternal good of our soul.

Whenever we are crushed by the heavy burden of sin, or when we become anxious and troubled by the problems that we face in a world of sin, let us immediately go to the right place, to him who graciously tells us:

And whosoever cometh,
I will not cast him out.
O patient love of Jesus,
Which drives away our doubt,
Which, tho' we be unworthy
Of love so great and free,
Invites us very sinners
To come dear Lord to Thee. Amen.

Then Jesus went up on the hillside and sat down with his disciples. The Jewish Passover Feast was near. When Jesus looked up and saw a great crowd coming toward him, he said to Philip, "Where shall we buy bread for these people to eat?" He asked this only to test him, for he already had in mind what he was going to do. (John 6:3-6)

TESTS FOR DISCIPLES

Giving a test still seems to be one of the best ways for a teacher to gauge the progress of his pupils. Throughout our lives we are required to pass various kinds of tests to determine our level of achievement. We must pass a driver's license examination in order to use the highways. Various types of psychological and aptitude testing are done by companies in connection with the employment and advancement of their workers.

When a multitude of people followed Jesus around the Sea of Galilee, Jesus gave a test to his student, his disciple Philip. He asked him, "How can we buy enough bread to feed all those people?" The test which Jesus gave, however, was not like those which an ordinary teacher might give to his pupils. Because Jesus was the Son of God, he already knew everything there was to know about Philip. He knew how strong Philip's faith was. He knew what Philip was thinking when he saw a multitude of people coming to Jesus. Jesus' test of Philip was not to determine Philip's aptitude or ability. Jesus was testing or trying Philip's faith so that it might become stronger.

God tests all Christians in this same way. He tests our faith to make it stronger. He exercises our faith by allowing questions and problems to enter into our daily lives. His purpose is not to hurt us, but to strengthen us. "God is faithful; he will not let you be tempted beyond what you can bear. But when you are tempted, he will also provide a way out so that you can stand up under it."

This is a comforting thought for us, who are tempted by Satan to doubt God's love and to question his purposes in the midst of suffering. God promises that, for Jesus' sake, he will allow his people to suffer only for their good. It is true that "no discipline seems pleasant at the time, but painful. Later on, however, it produces a harvest of righteousness and peace for those who have been trained by it."

From dark temptation's power,
From Satan's wiles, defend.
Deliver in the evil hour
And guide us to the end. Amen.

When Jesus looked up and saw a great crowd coming toward him, he said to Philip, "Where shall we buy bread for these people to eat?" He asked this only to test him, for he already had in mind what he was going to do. Philip answered him, "Eight months' wages would not buy enough bread for each one to have a bite!" Another of his disciples, Andrew, Simon Peter's brother, spoke up, "Here is a boy with five small barley loaves and two small fish, but how far will they go among so many?" (John 6:5-9)

HE GENTLY BRINGS OUT FAITH

There are times when we feel there is nowhere to turn. We feel trapped. Philip could see no way out of the predicament the people were in. It was impossible for Philip to buy food for them because there was not enough money available.

There are times when we don't have enough money to take care of all our expenses. We may get desperate. Perhaps we look for a second income, or we go deeper into debt. Sooner or later we have to tighten our belts and lower our standard of living until we earn our way out. But in the meantime we may frantically enter every sweepstakes or contest that comes in the mail, or we may waste our meager resources on lottery tickets. We may even rely on such things rather than trusting in God to provide.

Philip did not know where to get food for all the people. So Jesus asked a question to test him. He wanted Philip to be aware of his own inadequacies, and then he wanted Philip to look to his Savior for the solution for this pressing problem.

Jesus is right beside us all the time, too. We need to place our cares and our worries into his hands. "Cast all your anxiety on him because he cares for you." He is strong enough and wise enough to make everything turn out right.

It is difficult for us to trust God to take care of all our problems. Perhaps we feel he takes care of our spiritual problems, our sins, but we are responsible for our physical needs. He invites us to cast all our cares upon him, for he cares for us, and "we know that in all things God works for the good of those who love him, who have been called according to his purpose."

Lord Jesus, help me to realize every time a problem comes into my life that you care for me and you will provide the right solution in the proper time. I place my life into your hands. Amen.

When they had all had enough to eat, he said to his disciples, "Gather the pieces that are left over. Let nothing be wasted." So they gathered them and filled twelve baskets with pieces of the five barley loaves left over by those who had eaten. (John 6:12,13)

GOD KNOWS OUR NEEDS

Worry is a sin against the First Commandment. The First Commandment requires an absolute trust in God and his promises to provide for us. Worry and consternation are the very opposite of trust and confidence in God. Worry suggests that God is unconcerned about his people, unwilling to help them or perhaps even unable to do so. Among Jesus' disciples there had been much concern, if not worry, about the five thousand men who were without food on the eastern shores of the Sea of Galilee. Philip pointed out that there was not enough money to buy food. Andrew looked at the loaves that were available and said, "But how far will they go among so many?"

Have we ever been guilty of sinful worrying, as though God were incapable of handling our situation? In his "Sermon on the Mount" Jesus told us not to worry. He said, "So do not worry, saying, 'What shall we eat?' or 'What shall we drink?' or 'What shall we wear?' For the pagans run after all these things, and your heavenly Father knows that you need them."

When he fed the five thousand, Jesus demonstrated the heavenly Father's attention to our daily needs. Not only did God provide, but he provided so much and so well that they needed twelve baskets to gather the food that remained. So we are daily led to an appreciation of God's great love when we see how he provides for us in spite of our worry and far beyond that which we even have time to request.

But this should come as no surprise. For God showed his love a long time ago in a way much more generous than anyone ever could have imagined. How can we worry when we know by faith what great love he first demonstrated by sending Jesus to be our Savior! "For God so loved the world that he gave his one and only Son, that whoever believes in him shall not perish but have eternal life." In Christ, God has taken care of the greatest and most vital needs of our souls. How then can we think for a moment that he cannot see or provide the lesser, namely, what we need for our daily, bodily life!

Yes, God gives daily bread indeed without our asking, even to all the wicked; but we pray that he would lead us to receive ours with thankful appreciation.

Our Father in heaven, give us this day our daily bread, and lead us to receive it every day with gratitude in Jesus' name. Amen.

He looked up to heaven and with a deep sigh said to him, "Ephphatha!" (which means, "Be opened!"). (Mark 7:34)

THE LORD'S CONCERN FOR THE INDIVIDUAL

People communicate very effectively with sounds other than words. For example, a parents' gasp says that their daredevil two-year-old has struck again. An executive's deep sigh signifies a hard day at the office. The cheers of the crowd give approval to the home team. Sounds that people make are significant, even if many of them are not real words.

Our Lord Jesus was a master communicator. He could express himself not only with words but also with other sounds. We notice one sound, a sympathetic sigh, in the Scripture verse above.

As Jesus looked at the man standing in front of him, unable to speak and unable to hear, he could not but pity him. Here was a human being, whose ancestor, Adam, had been created perfectly in God's own image and yet upon whom human sinfulness had taken its physical and spiritual toll. Jesus sighed because in this man he saw the pitiful condition typical of all people, for all are heirs of Adam's sinful nature and are guilty of many sinful deeds of their own.

Jesus healed many people day after day, but none of his healings were just impersonal demonstrations of his power. Our Lord took a personal interest in every person who came or was brought to him for healing. His sigh shows his concern for this individual.

Take Jesus' sigh as a sign to you that he is also concerned about you and all your troubles. He has experienced everything that you can imagine. Are you hurting because you have lost a loved one? Jesus knows what that is like. Are you fighting against a repeated temptation which seems more difficult to resist each time? Jesus can sympathize with you. Are you tired of carrying your own problems as well as those of others? Jesus sighs with you. You are not alone. Anything you experience Jesus has gone through too, but without sin.

The sympathetic sigh of your Savior also tells you that Jesus had an earnest desire to help, and help he did. What greater burden could you bring to God than the burden of your sins and their sentence of death? Yet Jesus was so sympathetic toward you that he carried your sins and the burden of your debt on his own shoulders. He sympathized with you to the point of giving his life to pay off what you could not pay—the debt of all your sins.

You are never alone. Jesus is always present with you. He sympathizes with you in all your problems and temptations. He provides the only solution to the disaster of sin. Lean on and trust in him. He is your sympathetic Savior.

Lord, thank you for the comfort of your sympathy. Amen.

He looked up to heaven and with a deep sigh said to him, "Ephphatha!" (which means, "Be opened!"). At this, the man's ears were opened, his tongue was loosened and he began to speak plainly. (Mark 7:34,35)

THE WONDERFUL WORD OF POWER

T.G.I.F. Some weeks are so hectic and tiresome that people have coined the phrase, "Thank God It's Friday!" After a week of work and other activities we may welcome the weekend as a time to regain some lost energy. Where will you look this weekend to recharge yourself? Where will you look for help today?

Jesus used something very powerful to heal this man. It was not a special potion. It was not a prescription drug. The power to heal lay in Jesus' almighty word. He simply said, "Be opened!" and the man's ears and tongue were healed. When we think of words of power, we are reminded of the creation account in Genesis 1. The psalmist writes, "By the word of the LORD were the heavens made." For the man who was deaf and mute, Jesus' word was also filled with God's power.

Jesus' word is still powerful to heal. St. Paul calls the Word of God and especially the good news of Jesus "the power of God for the salvation of everyone who believes." Without the Word we would not come to know of Jesus. Without the Word we could not believe in Jesus. Without the Word we could not be forgiven. With the Word all this and much, much more is accomplished. Jesus' word is the power of God which brings us to faith and salvation in Jesus Christ.

We can consult God's Word for other reasons also. Do you need guidance for your life? Do you need to have your energy level recharged? Get in touch with the gospel of Jesus in his Word, in baptism and in the Lord's Supper. Familiarize yourself with all God's promises to you for now and for eternity, and be filled with enthusiasm and energy from God.

When you feel drained of your energy, the only thing that helps is rest. Jesus promises that, if we come to him wearied and burdened, he will give us the ultimate in rest— rest for our souls. Get into the habit of enjoying such rest daily through his wonderful word of power, and thank God for opportunities to serve him with gladness every day of the week.

Almighty God, by your Word give us strength and energy for each new day. Amen.

When he had finished speaking, he said to Simon, "Put out into deep water, and let down the nets for a catch." Simon answered, "Master, we've worked hard all night and haven't caught anything. But because you say so, I will let down the nets." When they had done so, they caught such a large number of fish that their nets began to break. (Luke 5:4-6)

FAITH IS ALWAYS HONORED

Are you kidding, Lord? Fish aren't caught in deep water. Besides, we have been trying all night. I don't think we had better do this. We'll make fools of ourselves and everyone will laugh at us. Are you absolutely sure that this is what you want us to do?

Yes, Peter could have made such statements in answer to the Lord's command. Might not we have answered in much the same way? But Peter didn't. He believed Jesus' words. And faith was honored!

If this were a principle that is new, a principle not found elsewhere in the Scriptures, we might not give it a great deal of attention. But it happens to be a principle that is repeated in nearly every chapter of the Bible. Faith which believes the Word is always honored. Never, let me repeat, never, has our God failed to make good on a promise which he has asked us to accept in faith. Now, that's a claim no one else can make for himself. Our best friends, the most trusted members of our family circle, our most dependable acquaintances cannot say that they have never failed us, that they have never gone back on their word. Neither can we. But God can!

That's why it is so imperative that we believe the Word of our God. All his promises concerning our physical well-being here on earth are promises he will keep. And far more important, all his promises concerning our spiritual well-being, both now and for eternity, will come to pass. Because of what his Son did for us on Calvary's cross, our God can say to us, "You are mine." And we can trust that the relationship which is ours through the forgiveness purchased by our Savior is a relationship which has everlasting implications. It is not a relationship which will dim with time, as so many earthly friendships do. Rather, it is something that has substance.

The writer to the Hebrews says of faith, "Now faith is the substance of things hoped for, the evidence of things not seen." God keeps his promises. They are for real. By faith we know that God will keep them, just as surely as Peter found the fish in his net.

O Holy Spirit, overcome my doubts and allow faith to take over in my heart. May I believe your Word, and through such believing enter the mansions above! Amen.

Some men came carrying a paralytic on a mat and tried to take him into the house to lay him before Jesus. (Luke 5:18)

BASE YOUR HOPE ON JESUS

Good health is one of God's best earthly blessings. When we don't have it, we really miss it. When we do have it, we should appreciate it and remember to praise God for it.

Unfortunately, good health is not automatic in this world of sin. The healthy young athlete may take for granted his ability to race down the sideline under a pass, or circle the bases on a long line drive. But when he's confined to a wheelchair following a car accident, then what wouldn't he give not to be paralyzed? Is there any hope he'll walk again?

The answer to that question lies in the hands of the same person to whom some men carried a paralytic in our text. They came to the house where Jesus was and sought to lay their friend before him. They based their hope for help on Jesus.

What about you? Maybe you are one who is reading this devotion on your back in a hospital bed. Maybe it is your loved one awaiting lab tests on a tumor. What are your hopes for recovery? Do what these men did. Base your hopes on Jesus and lay your needs before him. Yes, go to that cardiologist if your doctor feels it would be helpful to call in a heart specialist. Yes, make that appointment at the Mayo Clinic if your medical needs require it. Doctors and hospitals are among the natural means that God has given to help provide for our earthly lives.

But, above all else, look to Jesus. Like the tearful child who brings the broken bike to his father and lays it before him for fixing; like the fearful mother who brings her feverish infant to the doctor and lays it before him for healing, so, first and foremost, we should bring all our needs to the Lord and lay them before him. "Cast all your anxiety on him because he cares for you."

Jesus does care for you. He cared enough to suffer for your sins. He cared enough to endure hell for you on the cross, to die, in order to fix your broken life and heal your sinsick soul. If he cared that much for you, do you not think he will care about your earthly needs also, whether they are emotional, or medical, or financial or anything?

Trust him. We do not know whether he has healing in store for our earthly lives. But we do know he loves us. We know he hears our prayers and will bring to pass what he knows is best for us. And we can't ask for anything better than that. Base your hopes on him.

Lord, help me to look to you for healing, and for everything. Amen.

Jesus knew what they were thinking and asked, "Why are you thinking these things in your hearts? Which is easier: to say, 'Your sins are forgiven,' or to say, 'Get up and walk'? But that you may know that the Son of Man has authority on earth to forgive sins. . . ." He said to the paralyzed man, "I tell you, get up, take your mat and go home." (Luke 5:22-24)

GOOD REASON TO HOPE

Hopeless! Sometimes that's the way we feel about things. My doctor says there is nothing more he can do for me, and I don't have any hope for getting better. My feelings tell me I have sinned too greatly for God to forgive me, and I feel my situation is hopeless.

But that's our human nature speaking. Let faith prevail! Listen to the words that Jesus speaks and let them assure you that our situation is never hopeless. With Jesus as our God we have good reason to hope.

Look at the assurance in our text. Some skeptical religious scholars privately doubted that Jesus had the authority to forgive sins. That was an amazing contradiction in itself. They apparently were willing to concede that Jesus could perform miracles of healing. The evidence of that was all over Galilee. But they didn't think Jesus was God and could forgive sins. Sometimes we reverse their doubts. We are willing to concede that Jesus is God and forgives our sins, and then we begin to doubt that Jesus cares about us enough, or has the ability, to heal our bodies.

To this Jesus says, "I know what you are thinking. Why do you doubt me? Which is easier to do, forgive sins or heal diseases?" Only God can do either one. Only God can forgive sins, though he may use ministers and other spokesmen in the church to pronounce that forgiveness. And only God can heal bodies, though he may use medicines and doctors to accomplish that end. To prove his authority, as God, to forgive sins, Jesus said to the paralyzed man, "Get up and walk."

Here is our reason for hope. With God nothing is impossible. Who can take a shriveled limb and, without surgery or therapy, make it whole? No miracle drug, only God himself. Who can take terminally ill souls and with the balm of his grace heal us of our sins and give us eternal life? No mere man, only the God-man.

God has not promised that he will always heal our bodies the way we desire. But he has promised to care for our earthly lives as a loving Father and give us what is best for our faith—without exception. He has promised that where his church is, he, too, is present with the forgiveness of sins and all his blessings. And what God says, he does. We have every reason to hope.

Dear Lord Jesus, help me always to place my hope in you. Amen.

Immediately he stood up in front of them, took what he had been lying on and went home praising God. (Luke 5:25)

HOPE IS REWARDED

The paralyzed man is healed! His faith, and that of his friends, was rewarded. Their prayers were granted. The skeptics were silenced. What telling testimony to the truth that those who place their hope in God are not disappointed.

There are two kinds of healing that people require. There is healing of the body, which we all need at times. For it is a rare person who at age eighty can say that he has never been to the doctor's office or spent a day in bed with the flu. And there is healing of the soul, which we all need at all times. For there is no one born who is without sin. For both kinds of healing we can turn to our Lord in hope and trust that he will help us.

The paralyzed man in our text had his hope rewarded. His concerns over sin were dispelled when Jesus forgave him his sins. And his desire for bodily health was granted when Jesus told him to get up. And he did. No assistance was needed to steady him. No weak muscles needed to be strengthened. There was no lengthy period of rehabilitation. "Immediately" he stood up and was able to carry home the stretcher that had carried him there.

God will not disappoint our hopes in him either. He may not give us immediate recovery from illness or accident. In fact, in most cases the healing process he gives us involves things like walkers and I-Vs. But whether we "miraculously" recover as one on whom the doctors had given up hope, or chronically continue on, we "know that in all things God works for the good of those who love him." Our faith and hope in God will not be disappointed.

With the healing of our souls, on the other hand, our recovery is always immediate and complete. No delays. No partial forgiveness. When we turn in repentance and faith to our God for help, we rejoice in the fact that he has already healed us. "If we confess our sins, he is faithful and just and will forgive us our sins and purify us from all unrighteousness." We will not have to suffer or die for our sins, because Christ already suffered and died for us— 2,000 years ago. Our hope in him will never be disappointed.

One more thing. Do not forget what the formerly paralyzed man did on his way home. He "went home praising God." Hopes that are realized lead to happiness and thankfulness. In your homes, in your hymns and in your hearts remember always to praise the God of your salvation.

I praise you with my whole heart, O God, for all your goodness to me. Amen.

Say in a word, and my servant shall be healed. (Luke 7:7)

CONFIDENT FAITH

What is a man's word worth today? Nothing gripes this writer more than empty promises made by repairmen, contractors, salesmen, or, for that matter, friends.

"It will be done tomorrow," he says.

You take him at his word. You drive the distance to his shop only to hear, "It's not ready yet." And you come to the bitter conclusion that you were only being strung along.

You and I do not like being strung along by anyone for any length of time. And we have been "taken" so often by the business world and by friends (I use that word "friends" quite loosely). Therefore we might fault God for stringing us along with something that is very important with us, such as: Will our sick dear one get better? Will I grow in faith? Will I carry out my desire to be a better Christian?

We make our request known in prayer to our Lord on Sunday morning and expect an answer by Sunday afternoon. And when it takes a while for us to see God's answer to our prayers in our life, we might accuse him of stringing us along.

So I will rephrase the initial question. What is God's Word worth today? Can it be taken to mean something? Will God's promise mean action in my life?

Jesus simply had to speak the word, and the centurion's servant would be healed. That is what the centurion believed, and it was enough for him. And if Jesus chose to carry out his request in miracle form in that way, that is the way it would be done.

When we take our broken hearts, lives and souls to the Repairman from Nazareth, results are guaranteed. They will be long lasting because Jesus is God. He has earned our salvation by his death on Calvary's cross. He is also our Good Shepherd.

We won't be put off with our problems when we go to Jesus for a solution. We won't be put down because our names do not carry any weight. Jesus knows us by name. Nor will we be put to the bottom of the list. Jesus plays no favorites.

Jesus' word means action in our life. Action now . . . for now and eternity.

O Lord, I wait patiently for your answer. I am confident that it is already on the way for Jesus' sake. Amen.

When Jesus had again crossed over by boat to the other side of the lake, a large crowd gathered around him while he was by the lake. Then one of the synagogue rulers, named Jairus, came there. Seeing Jesus, he fell at his feet and pleaded earnestly with him, "My little daughter is dying. Please come and put your hands on her so that she will be healed and live." (Mark 5:21-23)

DESPERATION

St. Mark will tell us later that Jairus's daughter was twelve years old. St. Luke adds that she was "his only daughter." We aren't told what disease she had. But it doesn't really matter, does it? The one thing that mattered most of all to Jairus was that his little girl's life was slowly slipping away. And there didn't seem to be much of anything he could do about it. Helplessness gradually gave way to desperation. He had to do something.

It was hard to walk out of the house. For all he knew, by the time he could get back to her, his little girl would be dead. And if she had to die, he certainly wanted to be there as she drew her last breath. But as hard as it was to leave, it would have been even harder to stay and wait for the inevitable without doing anything to try to help her.

Jairus had to do something, but he didn't know if he would be able to find Jesus. Perhaps Jesus was not even in Capernaum at the moment. He had recently crossed over to the other side of the Sea of Galilee to visit the region of the Gadarenes.

Jairus had no way of knowing when Jesus would return. But how could he ever forgive himself if he were to let his daughter die without even trying to locate Jesus?

With a sense of desperation, Jairus left his wife with his dying daughter and headed down toward the water, and once again we see God performing one of his almost invisible miracles of timing. It was more than a coincidence that Jesus' boat had just landed and "a large crowd gathered around him while he was by the lake." He was easy to find.

Everyone wanted to get close to Jesus, but maybe they recognized Jairus as "one of the synagogue rulers" and let him through out of respect for his office. And no doubt they could see the desperation on his face and in his movements as he made his way through the crowd and fell at Jesus' feet to beg for help.

Desperate people don't always think clearly, but in Jairus we see an example worthy of imitation. When you are feeling desperate, go and find Jesus and fall at his feet. He will not disappoint you.

Lord, please lay your hands on me so that I may live. Amen.

"Every branch that does bear fruit he prunes so that it will be even more fruitful." (John 15:2)

PRUNED BRANCHES

"God doesn't love me anymore!" Sometimes we feel this way when we are experiencing suffering and adversity. We make this mistake because we tend to equate love exclusively with blessing and happiness. We must learn not to pity ourselves when we are experiencing God's chastening. Remember, you and I are branches of God's vine. He is trimming us to make us useful. He must either prune us or sever us.

This is not to say that pruning is not painful. It is only to say that pruning is better than being "cut off." Anything is better than to have God abandon us in this life to the wiles of the devil and in the hereafter to the horrors of hell. Trust God to remove from your life what he knows would hurt you.

A man visiting a chrysanthemum show stood amazed at the beautiful blossoms. He noted the wide variety of colors and forms, but was impressed most of all by their size. "How do you produce such marvelous blooms?" he asked one of the gardeners. "We concentrate the strength of the plant on just one or two blossoms," the gardener replied. "If we allowed the plant to bear all the flowers it would like to, none of them would be worth showing. If we are to have a prize-winning plant, we must be content with one or two blossoms instead of a dozen."

This gardener described the way God works. In order to help us grow more like him, he cuts away the useless shoots of pride, greed or lust, so that we have singleness of purpose. He also uses his pruning knife to teach us that we cannot sin with impunity. Though we are not punished for our sins as unbelievers are, yet the consequences of our sins are often visited upon us, and thus we come to understand the heinousness of sin in God's sight. As we allow God to prune away the things harmful to our spiritual lives, our faith is strengthened until we become "more fruitful" branches fit for the gardens of eternity.

Remember, pruning is not punishment. Thanks be to God, Jesus has borne that. If sometimes we suffer under God's knife, let's try to imagine how we would agonize under his wrath, and then let's thank our Savior anew for enduring that wrath for us. God's pruning is never done in wrath. "The Lord disciplines those he loves."

O loving heavenly Father, when you send chastisements, help us to bear them and benefit from them and be comforted in your love. We pray in our Savior's name. Amen.

When the Counselor comes, whom I will send to you from the Father, . . . he will tesify about me. (John 15:26)

SOMEONE TO COMFORT YOU

In India, along the winding roads, especially in the hill countries, there are little resting places for travelers. They are similar to our waysides in appearance, and they are called "samatanga." Here a person may rest his weary feet, lay down his burden, and pause to talk with other travelers like himself. Then, rested, refreshed and encouraged, he may resume his journey.

How well we could use such places of rest as we travel the road called life! Along the way we encounter and must shoulder many sorrows which weigh us down. We grieve over the loved ones who have passed into the Lord's presence, leaving an empty place in our lives which no one else can fill. We wrestle with discouraging and painful personal and family problems which seem to gnaw away at our hearts night and day, robbing us of peace and joy in life. We fall to our knees under the crosses which our Lord in his wisdom allows us to bear from time to time. We grow weary under the burden of our guilt and sins. How we long for a spiritual "samatanga," a place where we can find a moment's peace, breathe a sigh of relief, find at least some refreshment for our souls.

Our Lord has provided us with just such a place. You know where it is— at the foot of the cross of Jesus. There we find the assurance that all is well between God and us, no matter how rough the road of life might become. And in case we have trouble finding this place when we need it and, blinded by grief and sorrow, should lose our way, Jesus has sent his Comforter, the Holy Ghost, to be our guide. It is this Comforter who takes us by the hand and leads us back to Calvary. There we are reminded that God is no longer angry with us, that he poured out on his Son the wrath we deserved. There he gave us righteousness, and hope, and life. And no man or devil can take it away from us!

So if the cares and worries of life are threatening to overwhelm you; if you feel yourself sinking under a tremendous load, then go back to the promises of God in Christ. For in them you will find not only a passing "samatanga," but eternal rest and comfort for your souls.

Come, Holy Ghost, in love
Shed on us from above
Thine own bright ray.
Divinely good Thou art.
Thy sacred gifts impart
To gladden each sad heart.
Oh, come today! Amen.

So he came to a town in Samaria called Sychar, near the plot of ground Jacob had given to his son Joseph. Jacob's well was there, and Jesus, tired as he was from the journey, sat down by the well. It was about the sixth hour. (John 4:5,6)

THE MIRACLE OF GOD'S LOVE

After a bitter argument between friends, a husband and wife, or brothers and sisters, someone has to make the move, the first move to bring them back together. It works best if the one who did the hurting or began the trouble, makes that first move. How hard it is! But how necessary, if things are to be healed. Only love enables us to rise above our hurt and pride to forgive and to ask forgiveness.

Here is the miracle of God's love. Though he has been offended, and ignored, and denied, he makes the first move. We can only run away and hide. We sin against him and him alone more than we can ever know. His anger against our sin is greater than we dare to admit. We know not how or when or where to come to him. Here is the miracle. He grabbed hold of us before the world began. He saved us, for "while we were still sinners, Christ died for us." Again and again he makes the first move, coming to us.

In our reading the miracle unfolds. Jesus comes in more than promise; he comes himself. He comes not as judge and destroyer, as well he could, but he comes in the flesh as one of us.

"Tired as he was from the journey," our text reads. How encouraging those words are. He knows and understands, for he "was tempted in every way, just as we are—yet was without sin." He gives us what we could never give ourselves. He gives us freedom from death, because he entered death and broke its power. He gives us peace, because he brings us back together with God. He offers us help for our every need. And he is there when we need him.

It was no accident that Jesus sat by this well, alone. He was waiting for someone to come; someone who needed him desperately. And he would be there. He is always there. He has come to each of us in our baptism and taken us for himself. He enters and stays in our lives. He remains always close to us. For he is not far from any one of us. We have his Word. We have him as we receive his very body and blood in the sacrament. By these means, he embraces us and remains with us always.

Dear Lord Jesus, left to ourselves, we would never find you. We thank you that you have found us and that you have forgiven our sins. We rejoice that you take us as we are and that you make us over again. We know that you remain with us in Word and sacrament. Continue to be with us and ever hold us fast until we are with you forever. Amen.

When Jesus landed and saw a large crowd, he had compassion on them and healed their sick. (Matthew 14:14)

MEETING OUR REAL NEEDS

Compassion leads to action. Jesus not only felt, he acted.

Matthew gives us a summary statement here: "and Jesus healed them." The other three gospel writers fill in the details. Mark writes, "So he began teaching them many things." Luke comments, "He welcomed them and spoke to them about the kingdom of God, and healed those who needed healing."

Jesus, as true God, saw the real needs of these people—both spiritual and physical. He saw how desperate and forlorn they were, like sheep without a shepherd. As the great Physician, he would treat not only the symptoms, but also the cause. The physical ailments and needs these people had were only the symptoms of a much greater disease: the sickness of sin. If Jesus were to address only the physical, it would have been like treating a brain tumor with aspirin.

Jesus' first priority was their spiritual depravity. He instructed them from the Word of God about the kingdom of God. This kingdom, which God had promised to David and his descendants, was to be established by David's Son, Jesus of Nazareth, who stood before them. This would not be a physical or worldly kingdom, but a spiritual kingdom—established within them through faith in him, the Christ of God.

Having cared for their souls, our healing Lord now attended to their bodies. Those who had physical ills he healed immediately and completely. His power to heal physical ills reinforced the truth of his power to heal their spiritual ills.

The compassion of our Lord is not restricted to our spiritual ills. He is also concerned with our physical health. He has created our bodies with tremendous recuperative powers. He has given physicians and surgeons the skills and technology needed to treat severe physical ills. He wants us to appreciate and use them as gifts and blessings from him.

We have a healing Lord. Let us not forget this. Go to him for healing —spiritual and physical.

Be thou our Joy and Brightness,
Our Cheer in pain and loss,
Our Sun in darkest terror,
The Glory round our cross,
A Star for sinking spirits,
A Beacon in distress,
Physician, Friend, in sickness,
In death our Happiness.

O Lord, our great Physician, you know our needs, both physical and spiritual. Send us your healing power. Amen.

Jesus said again, "I tell you the truth, I am the gate for the sheep." (John 10:7)

OUR GOOD SHEPHERD OFFERS PROTECTION

If a shepherd could use only one word in describing the sheep under his care, the word he would probably choose is "helpless." Why "helpless"? Because sheep truly are helpless animals. They cannot defend themselves from predators. They easily lose their way and become lost. Sometimes they cannot even find food that is as close as thirty feet away!

A good shepherd knows this. To care for them he knows he must provide constant, abiding protection.

Our Lord Jesus knows that we also need constant, abiding protection. This is one of the reasons he calls himself "the gate" in today's reading. Shepherds in Bible times often would spend the night in the gateway of the sheep pen. By doing this, predators could not get in nor could sheep wander away without their shepherds knowing it.

The moment the Holy Spirit creates faith in our heart we come under the ever-watchful eye of our Good Shepherd. While a human shepherd may doze and sleep, God's Word assures us, "He who watches over you will not slumber; indeed, he who watches over Israel will neither slumber nor sleep. . . . The Lord will keep you from all harm—he will watch over your life; the Lord will watch over your coming and going both now and forevermore."

Death and destruction, heartache and hurt are all around us. They are caused by sin. And like predators they threaten to overwhelm us. If we were on our own, we would surely fall. But our Shepherd is there. He stands between us and our enemies and promises, "Fear not, for I have redeemed you; I have called you by name; you are mine. When you pass through the waters I will be with you; and when you pass through the rivers, they will not sweep over you."

Our sinful hearts may tempt us to wander along dangerous ways. But once again, our Shepherd is there to protect us. Like a gate he stands in our way and turns us back to safety.

He is by our side constantly, around the clock. He is ready to help in every time of need. How blessed are we!

Yea, tho' I walk in death's dark vale,
Yet will I fear no ill;
For Thou art with me, and Thy rod
And staff me comfort still. Amen.

The thief comes only to steal and kill and destroy; I have come that they may have life and have it to the full. (John 10:10)

HE IS THE LIFESAVER OF HIS FLOCK

Sometimes the shepherd's life is a dangerous one. David tells us of two such instances in 1 Samuel 17:34,35: "When a lion or a bear came and carried off a sheep from the flock, I went after it, struck it and rescued the sheep from its mouth. When it turned on me, I seized it by its hair, struck it and killed it. Your servant has killed both the lion and the bear."

David risked his own life for the sake of his sheep. He did it willingly. He did it out of love. He did it because he was a good shepherd.

The Bible tells us that Jesus not only risked his life, he gave his life as "the atoning sacrifice for our sins, and not only for ours but also for the sins of the whole world." Jesus is the Good Shepherd. He saw us hopelessly caught in the grasp of sin and trapped in the jaws of death. We could not escape. Because he is both true God and true man, only Jesus Christ could help us; and he did not hesitate to come to our rescue.

Christ did not fail. He saved his sheep by laying down his life for them. God's law had demanded death as punishment for sin, and Jesus took upon himself the punishment we deserved. He died in our place. We surely did not merit such sacrifice and love. As the hymnwriter says:

> What punishment so strange
> is suffered yonder!
> The Shepherd dies for sheep
> that loved to wander.

What love our Good Shepherd has for us! What pain he suffered for us! He truly is our Savior, our lifesaver! Because of his resurrection we know we have life in his name. And in addition to such a gracious gift, our Lord promises us much more! "He who did not spare his own Son, but gave him up for us all—how will he not also, along with him, graciously give us all things?" How can we ever thank God for giving us such a Good Shepherd? May we daily ask the Holy Spirit to fill us with love and gratitude, that our whole life will be one hearty "thank you" to our Good Shepherd, our lifesaver.

**Perverse and foolish, oft I strayed,
But yet in love He sought me
And on His shoulder gently laid
And home, rejoicing, brought me. Amen.**

And there shall be one fold and one Shepherd. (John 10:16)

THE RULING SHEPHERD

Jesus concludes the picture of himself as the Good Shepherd by describing his flock. Jesus' sheep are his believers. He gathers them from every age and nation by the power of his gospel. They are young and old, male and female, Jew and Gentile, rich and poor. Yet together they constitute one flock under the one Shepherd.

Jesus is speaking here of his church. The church is one, not in the sense of being one outward, visible organization, but one in the blessed fellowship of faith which binds together all who follow Jesus as their Good Shepherd. Its members are all who, by the Spirit's work in their hearts, believe that Jesus took their sins away through his death on the cross. They listen to his voice and follow him. Through the gospel they know him and look forward to eternal life with him. This spiritual flock makes no racial or social distinctions. It breaks down every barrier and brings all who believe in Jesus as their Savior together into his one fold.

The Good Shepherd leads and rules his flock. He knows his sheep, and he guides them. He speaks to them in his Word, providing them with all they need to remain in the fold. He governs the events of history to serve the welfare of his flock. And on the last day he will make his one fold, now invisible, visible in heaven.

Like every other aspect of Jesus' picture of himself as the Good Shepherd, his assurance that he is the One Shepherd ruling over his one flock is rich in comfort. Though to the world we appear to be in the most miserable, scattered and unattended condition, in reality the very opposite is true. For we are all members of the undivided Body of Christ. We all have been baptized with one and the same baptism. We worship one Lord, who is above all and through all and who dwells by faith in the hearts of all who worship him. Though plagued and tempted and persecuted, we look for strength to the same heavenly Father and follow the voice of the same Good Shepherd. And in heaven we shall rejoice together forever in the sunshine of his love.

Few pictures in Scripture are as rich in comfort, joy and peace as is the picture of Jesus as our Good Shepherd. May he bless us with his Word and preserve us as his sheep, here and in eternity!

Come, faithful Shepherd, feed Thy sheep;
In Thine own arms the lambs enfold.
Give help to climb the heavenward steep
Till Thy full glory we behold. Amen.

"I am the good shepherd. The good shepherd lays down his life for the sheep. . . . No one takes it from me, but I lay it down of my own accord. I have authority to lay it down and authority to take it up again." (John 10:11,18)

THE GOOD SHEPHERD LAYS DOWN HIS LIFE

Was he a victim of circumstances? In no way. On the contrary, he was the author of the circumstances! He was in control, doing exactly what had to be done. To lay down his life was the purpose for which he had come. No one could keep him from it. Long ago this had been planned and authorized by his heavenly Father.

The good shepherd's plan to lay down his life for his sheep is the central theme of the Bible. The death of the Messiah was announced after the fall into sin. It was repeatedly announced throughout the time of the Old Testament. It is the focus of the New Testament.

But in all of Scripture there is no passage that portrays this theme more clearly than Isaiah's prophecy in chapter 53. "Surely he took up our infirmities and carried our sorrows, yet we considered him stricken by God, smitten by him, and afflicted. But he was pierced for our transgressions, he was crushed for our iniquities; the punishment that brought us peace was upon him, and by his wounds we are healed. We all, like sheep, have gone astray, each of us has turned to his own way; and the LORD has laid on him the iniquity of us all." Here we see, with a clarity unsurpassed in the Bible, a picture of the good shepherd laying down his life for the sheep.

It is your shepherd who speaks these words. He speaks them to you to comfort you with the forgiveness of sins. It cost his life, but he considered your salvation worth the cost.

Why did he do it? To gather a people who would live for him and serve him. The Apostle Peter (himself a wayward sheep at times) summed it up like this: "He himself bore our sins in his body on the tree, so that we might die to sins and live for righteousness; by his wounds you have been healed. For you were like sheep going astray, but now you have returned to the Shepherd and Overseer of your souls."

Dear Savior and Good Shepherd, what tremendous love I see in your death on the cross. It was for wayward sheep like me that you died. The punishment that you suffered brought me peace with God. Help me to see that message as the focal point of your Word. To thank you, I will serve you with my entire life. Amen.

"I have other sheep that are not of this sheep pen. I must bring them also. They too will listen to my voice, and there shall be one flock and one shepherd." (John 10:16)

CHRIST, THE GOOD SHEPHERD FOR ALL

Of all the titles which Jesus claims for himself, no doubt "The Good Shepherd" is one of the most revealing and comforting to the Christian. A real shepherd will always be concerned about his sheep. He will not only look after the entire flock, leading it to green pasture and good water and protecting it from vicious animals that would destroy the sheep, but as a good shepherd will be interested and concerned about the well-being of each individual sheep in his flock. He calls each one by name, gives it special care and attention when it is sick or injured, searches for it when it has strayed from the flock.

A sheep is among the most helpless of all creatures when left to itself. When straying, it will wander away until it is completely lost, for it does not have a sense of direction to guide it home. It is unable to find good pasture by itself. It cannot scent and find good water to drink. It is not equipped to defend itself from it's natural enemies. Left to itself, it would soon perish of hunger and thirst in a wilderness or fall an easy victim to vicious animals. But this is also a picture of man as he is by nature. The prophet Isaiah describes man's condition by saying: "All we like sheep have gone astray; we have turned everyone to his own way."

But Jesus, the Good Shepherd, has come "to seek and to save that which was lost." He was sent by the Father "unto the lost sheep of the house of Israel." He was born of the Jews, lived and worked and carried out his public ministry and completed God's plan of salvation in Israel. But that did not mean that salvation was intended only for them. In our text Jesus says: "Other sheep I have, which are not of this fold; them also I must bring." The Good Shepherd has in mind the multitudes of Gentiles who are lost without a shepherd's care. Them also he has come to seek and to save. God "will have all men to be saved, and to come unto the knowledge of the truth." Jesus is the Good Shepherd for all.

It matters not who we are, where we live, what we have done; Jesus had us in mind, too. Though we may have been wandering far from our Good Shepherd, lost and in danger of perishing eternally, Jesus has come to seek us and to bring us safely into his fold.

Lord, help us to heed the voice of our Good Shepherd so that we may follow him in faith as he leads us into his eternal fold. Amen.

"Peace I leave with you; my peace I give you. I do not give to you as the world gives. Do not let your hearts be troubled and do not be afraid. You heard me say, 'I am going away and I am coming back to you.' If you loved me, you would be glad that I am going to the Father, for the Father is greater than I. I have told you now before it happens, so that when it does happen you will believe." (John 14:27-29)

JESUS GIVES US HIS PEACE

Martin Luther found a great deal of comfort in these words of Holy Scripture. Luther knew that he had not deserved eternal life from a holy God. Therefore when the Savior announced, "Peace I leave with you," these words filled his heart with joy.

Many people today, unfortunately, do not share Luther's attitude toward sin. As far as the world is concerned, sin is only a "sickness" or a "weakness" in the human soul. Because the world does not view sin as a real problem, the world does not appreciate the Savior's announcement of real peace. Unless we first of all learn to confess, "Lord, I am by nature sinful and unclean; I also have sinned against you in thought, word and deed," the Savior's words will mean nothing to us.

But after God's law has shown us how poor and wretched and needy we really are, then the Savior's words of comfort bring great joy to our hearts. "Peace I leave with you; my peace I give you. . . . Do not let your hearts be troubled and do not be afraid." His peace is not another kind of temporary peace such as the world has to offer. It is a peace between God and us. It is a permanent peace, the peace of knowing that God will give us every blessing, for Jesus' sake. It is the peace which settled over the disciples once they realized that Jesus had risen from the grave. It is the peace which the Holy Spirit, the Comforter, brought to them and still brings to us through the gospel.

This peace, which is ours in Christ, is the cause for endless joy. Jesus has now returned to the throne of his Father's majesty on high. Jesus did humble himself—even to the extent of dying a shameful death on the cross. And he did it all for us. But now Jesus, having completed his work here on earth, sits in glory at the right hand of the Father. From his exalted position in heaven Jesus continues to assure us, "My peace I give you!" And he offers it to us again and again through his Word and Sacraments.

The peace of this world may be very attractive, but it is also very temporary. The peace which Jesus offers, on the other hand, though it appears much less attractive, even irrelevant, to the eyes of men, is real and eternal.

Grant us your peace, O Lord! Amen.

On the evening of the first day of the week, when the disciples were together, with the doors locked for fear of the Jews, Jesus came and stood among them and said, "Peace be with you!" (John 20:19)

THE GIFT OF PEACE

The disciples had deserted Jesus, denied him and ignored his promises. In his suffering and death Jesus had been left to stand alone. But now he was standing among them. He had not forsaken his disciples as they had forsaken him. In fact, he did not even come to them with harsh words of rebuke and scorn. He came to them with peace.

The Lord has not left us alone either. He has promised to be with us always, even to the end of the world. And on Pentecost, Christ sent his Holy Spirit to comfort and direct his church on earth, until that day when we can stand with our Lord in the rooms of his Father's heavenly home.

In this world people have attempted to find peace through treaties, wars to end wars, nuclear arms, drugs and the like. But sin, hatred, anger, bloodshed, violence and wars continue to fill the headlines of life. And yet, no matter how much trouble we see in this life, we Christians still possess the gift of peace, which Jesus gave to his disciples that evening.

We cannot explain this peace to an unbeliever, because it surpasses all human understanding. But we know what it means for us. It is peace with our conscience, when we know that our sins are forgiven in Christ. It is peace with God, when we look to the cross of Christ as full payment for all our sins. It is peace of mind, when we cast all our cares upon the Lord, who cares for us. It is the hope of eternal peace, as we look forward to the coming of our Lord on Judgment Day. It is a peaceful night's rest, as we leave behind the tensions of the day in prayer.

We don't deserve this gift of peace any more than the disciples did in that locked room. And we certainly cannot make this peace for ourselves. It is another daily evidence of the miraculous grace of God, with which he continues to love us, in spite of our own sin and unfaithfulness. There is nothing else in the world like it. As Jesus assures us, "Peace I leave with you; my peace I give you. I do not give to you as the world gives. Do not let your hearts be troubled and do not be afraid."

O Lord, we give you thanks for the gift of peace, which you have so graciously bestowed upon us. May the power and comfort of your Spirit calm our troubled hearts, until the day of your coming. Amen.

Jesus . . . said, "Peace be with you!" After he said this, he showed them his hands and side. (John 20:19,20)

THE PRICE OF PEACE

Almost thirty million fatalities and more than one trillion dollars! That, history tells us, was the staggering cost of World War II. Of course, such bare statistics do not tell the whole story. Only those who lived through the war can do that. Only they can tell of loved ones who went away to war never to be seen again, of people displaced from their homes and never allowed to return, of the terrible economic sacrifice and the lingering emotional and psychological trauma suffered by so many of the war's victims.

As great as the cost of World War II was, what if the outcome of the war had been different and our freedom had been lost? Then the cost would have been even greater! We may be sad that all that money and all those lives were spent, but we rejoice that they were not spent in vain. We rejoice that the cost of the war became the price of peace. Peace did come. It was peace with honor and freedom.

In the same way we find both tragedy and joy in the sufferings, death and crucifixion of our Savior. It was tragic that the very Son of God had to die because of the sins of men. It was tragic that the most precious blood in the world had to be shed. It was tragic that the most loving Father there ever was had to turn his back on the most loving and perfect Son there ever was, if only for a short time. In fact, we can think of no greater tragedy in all the world than this.

Yet this was the price of our peace, peace with God, a glorious peace, a lasting peace, a peace that gives us joy and freedom as God's dear children. Our hearts are filled with sadness when we see what a great price was paid for our peace, but at the same time we are most happy and grateful that that price was paid. Our Lord's pierced hands and wounded side bring tears to our eyes, but they are also reason for joy. They tell us that our sins are gone.

How, then, can any of us continue to live in sin as if nothing has happened? As those who suffered through World War II surely said, "Never again!" and increased their vigilance against tyranny, so we who have escaped an even greater, eternal disaster ought to cleanse our hearts and lives to act like the children of God he wants us to be. We have ample reason to shun sin and all its shame. All we need to do is to consider his love and the price of our peace.

Thank you, Lord, for paying the great price that was necessary for our peace. Amen.

Jesus came and stood among them and said, "Peace be with you!" After he said this, he showed them his hands and side. The disciples were overjoyed when they saw the Lord. (John 20:19,20)

NO ORDINARY PEACE

On the evening of that first Easter day the disciples were full of fears, disappointments and doubts. Their Lord Jesus was dead. Now that he had allowed himself to be crucified, how could he be the earthly king some of them were looking for? And how could he be their Savior from sin? A dead Savior cannot save.

Furthermore, it might only be a matter of time before the authorities came knocking on the door and took them away. And even if the reports of the women, of Simon and of the two from Emmaus were true, even if Jesus were alive, why would he want anything to do with them? Hadn't they all forsaken him and fled? They had betrayed him. They had given up their faith. Surely, they would never see him again.

No wonder the disciples were overjoyed when Jesus suddenly appeared among them. Not only was he alive, not only had the enemy not defeated him, but Jesus was not at all angry with them. In one short statement he immediately assured them that he had forgiven them everything. "Peace be with you!" he said.

Who can measure what those words mean to us today? There are times when we, like the disciples, are in the depths of despair. It may be that a loved one has left us, some fond hope has been dashed to pieces, or sin has taken such a toll that we wonder whether the Lord will ever have anything to do with us again. But then Jesus says to us, "Peace be with you!" And immediately the darkness and gloom disappear. We are forgiven. We are still God's and he is still ours. He is at peace with us.

This is no ordinary peace, but the peace of knowing that our eternal future is secure. This is no temporary armistice between warring nations or quarreling neighbors, this is an eternal peace with God established for all people for all time.

Stories are told of news reporters near the end of World War II hoping to be the first to tell the world that peace had finally arrived. Oh, the happy person who would be the first to break the news! But if the news of that armistice was worthy to be passed on, so is the news of the peace we have with God through the shedding of Jesus' blood. Surely that, more than any other, is no ordinary peace, and the news of it should be spread to the four corners of the earth.

Lord, lead us to treasure your peace more than any other. Amen.

The disciples were overjoyed when they saw the Lord. (John 20:20)

HAPPINESS IS . . .

"**H**appiness is a warm slice of banana bread right out of the oven, smothered with butter." Or "happiness is a warm puppy." We make such statements, but do we really believe that's what happiness is? Banana bread soon gets cold and stale. Puppies soon grow up. God's creation is so wonderful that we find a little bit of happiness in a lot of things, but lasting happiness is hard to find.

For most people happiness is something that's just around the corner. They almost have it, but not yet. Ask a child, and he may tell you that happiness is finally being old enough to go to school. Ask the person who's in school, and he may tell you that happiness is getting out of school, getting his first job, and being on his own. Ask the family man, and he may tell you that happiness will come when the children are grown, when he's retired and finally has the time to do all the things he's always wanted to do. Ask the retired person, and he may tell you that he hasn't quite found happiness either. Like a mirage in the desert, happiness seems to move away just when we get close.

What was it that made the disciples happy that first Easter evening? They saw Jesus! "The disciples were overjoyed when they saw the Lord." Jesus, their Savior, was alive! He had risen from the dead! And he was the same loving friend to them he had always been!

Someday we too will see Jesus, face to face, his arms outstretched, welcoming us home to heaven. Never again will we hunger. Never again will we thirst. There will be no more death or crying or pain, for the old order of things will have passed away. No more will happiness move away just when we get close, but it will cover us like a blanket on the outside, and permeate our whole inner being.

But if happiness is seeing Jesus, let's remember that we don't have to wait until eternity to see him. We can see him today in his Word. In his Word we can already see Jesus loving us, helping us along life's road, forgiving all our sins, interceding for us before our heavenly Father's throne. We can see Jesus being the same friend to us that he was to the disciples. Seeing Jesus in this way not only makes us happy. Like the disciples, we are overjoyed.

Lord, how anxiously we await the joys you have in store for us in heaven. But how happy you have made us already, now that we have seen you in your Word. Amen.

Again Jesus said, "Peace be with you!" (John 20:21)

A WORD OF PEACE—A WORD OF POWER

Have you noticed that whenever a person blesses or curses something by his own authority, nothing really happens? Many a neighbor's dog or errant hammer has been cursed with no apparent result. No lightning came down from heaven to punish the person or thing that was cursed. The accursed thing did not wither away or suddenly disappear. Man's curse is only an empty wish on his part. He huffs and puffs, but accomplishes nothing. And so it is when man blesses by his own authority. He wishes and hopes, but he has no power to make it come to pass. Many a "Bless you!" has been spoken with little result.

But when God blesses or curses, things happen. When God utters a curse, the ground opens up and swallows hundreds of people at once, fire and brimstone come down from heaven and destroy whole cities, and entire armies lose their will to fight. Likewise, when God speaks a blessing. When Jesus told the paralytic that his sins were forgiven and that he should get up and walk, the forgiveness and the healing were contained in his words. It was already done.

God's word is a word of power. When God speaks, things happen. In creation God said, "Let there be!" and there it was. He spoke, and it was done. When God announced that Adam and Eve were banished from the Garden, it was accomplished immediately, perhaps even in mid-sentence and before our first parents could hear all that God said.

So it was also when Jesus stood before his disciples that first Easter evening and said, "Peace be with you!" This was no mere empty wish of a common mortal hoping that his friends would have a nice day. This was a word of power which contained within itself the ability to effect what it expressed. He said, "Peace be with you!" and it was so. The words not only gave comfort, they produced saving faith. They established peace as the disciples believed them.

As the Prince of Peace, Jesus brought about the peace that now exists between God and man. And now he offers that peace to us. He says to each of us, "Peace be with you!" May those words of Jesus be to us, as they were to the disciples, words of power which awaken and strengthen faith. Remember, these are not the words of mortal man. They are words of power which grant the peace of which they speak. Peace is ours. The life, the death and the words of Jesus make it so.

Lord, bless your word of peace that it may be a word of power establishing in our hearts that precious peace which we so earnestly desire. Amen.

After he said this, he showed them his hands and side. The disciples were overjoyed when they saw the Lord. (John 20:20)

THE GIFT OF JOY

I ask you, "How could anyone be overjoyed while looking at someone who has been mortally wounded?" Jesus had been wounded in the hands, feet and side. He was showing these wounds to his disciples, but what was their reaction? Sorrow or sympathy? No. They were overjoyed at seeing their wounded Lord; not because he was wounded, rather because he had risen from the grave.

The wounds of our risen Savior are the marks of victory. They are visible proof that Jesus Christ is true God and true Man, David's Son and David's Lord. When we look upon the wounds of Jesus, we see the wonderful message of our salvation. Eternal God became mortal man, in order to humble himself under his own law. After a life of perfect righteousness, the Lord of all creation gave his life in death, to satisfy the curse of the law upon the sins of all mankind. Because he made full payment for all our sins, the Lord is able to give us forgiveness and salvation.

If we were looking upon the wounds of a dead man lying in a grave, we would have reason to sorrow. But this is Jesus himself showing us his wounds—Jesus, who once was dead but now lives. We have reason to be overjoyed. Every victory celebration is meant to be a joyous occasion. And the gift of joy, which the Lord gave to his disciples, lives on for all eternity. The message of Christ's death and resurrection brought joy to thousands of repentant hearts on the first Pentecost. And it continues to bring joy to countless thousands of sinners all over the world, who have come to know Jesus as their Savior.

The gift of joy in Christ is a wonderful blessing from the Lord. In our daily lives, when frustrations and afflictions bring frowns to our faces, there can still be joy in our hearts. For our Lord is faithful and powerful and promises to deliver us from all evil. And when we Christians face death (be it our own, or that of a loved one), in the midst of sorrow we can know the joy of a personal victory in Christ. For as the Lord rose and lives again, so also in death we live and will rise again.

Only with such joy in his heart could the Apostle Paul have written, "Yes, and I will continue to rejoice. . . . For to me, to live is Christ and to die is gain."

O Lord, fill our hearts with joy in Christ, now and forevermore. Amen.

After he said this, he showed them his hands and side. The disciples were overjoyed when they saw the Lord. (John 20:20)

THE SECRET OF LASTING PEACE AND JOY

A casual reading of the New Testament might lead some to assume that events after our Lord's glorious resurrection were rather scrambled. We know that he appeared to Mary, to the other women and to the disciples on the road to Emmaus. Since Jesus had predicted his return from the grave, we might expect his followers to be waiting with calm hope and living joy. Instead, they brooded in grief. His return from the grave was utterly unexpected.

Luke, chapter 24, informs us that the disciples even doubted the testimony of their own eyes when Jesus appeared to them on Easter Sunday evening. Initially, they thought that he was a ghost. Their fears and doubts must have been frustrating for Jesus.

But Jesus was patient with them. He gently invited them to look at the puncture marks in his hands and feet. He encouraged them to touch him. Even though in his glorified state he no longer needed food, Jesus ate before their eyes, providing their senses ample opportunity to verify that it really was he. Jesus really had risen. He was not a ghost.

What a change came over the disciples' hearts that Easter night! His words and wounds drove despair from their minds and hearts. We can well imagine that they were surprised to see him. Their hearts must have skipped a beat when he suddenly appeared. They forgot their fear of the Jews. Their apprehension vanished. They were certain that Jesus was alive. Hope was revived; confidence was restored. "The disciples were overjoyed when they saw the Lord."

Their joy in the presence of our risen Lord teaches us that the secret of lasting peace and joy lies in looking to the living Lord Jesus. True peace cannot be bought or manufactured. Lasting joy cannot be achieved through money, learning or feverish activity. They are a gift from Jesus. "Therefore, there is now no condemnation for those who are in Christ Jesus" (Romans 8:1). Our God has stopped at nothing to remove the threat of sin, death and hell. Will he not assist us with our lesser fears and anxieties! Let us not shame our Savior by living as if he were still dead!

I am content! Lord, draw me unto Thee
And wake me from the dead
That I may rise forevermore to be
With Thee, my living Head. Amen.

Now Thomas (called Didymus), one of the Twelve, was not with the disciples when Jesus came. So the other disciples told him, "We have seen the Lord!" (John 20:24,25)

IN NEED OF PEACE OF MIND

Three men were talking one day about the frailties of people. Said one man, "The trouble with most people is that they eat too much." The second man objected, and said, "It isn't how much you eat, but what you eat that counts." The third man, a doctor, said, "It's neither what you eat nor how much. It's what's eating you that is important." The doctor hit the nail on the head.

The trouble most people have today is that gnawing inside of them. There are so many things to do. There are so many doubts. There are so many problems to be solved. Each of these eats away at a person's peace of mind. They haunt his waking hours and disturb his sleep.

Thomas had the same problem. Thomas was a faithful follower of the Lord. He loved Jesus with all his heart. In fact, Thomas was one of the first to realize that Jesus would have to die. When Jesus went to Bethany to see his friend Lazarus, it was Thomas who said, "Let us also go that we may die with him." And yet Thomas's heart was filled with uncertainty. When Jesus spoke of the many mansions in his Father's house and of how he would go and prepare a way to those mansions, it was Thomas who said, "Lord, we don't know where you are going, so how can we know the way?" Thomas loved his Lord but wasn't sure what his mission was.

What was true of Thomas was also true of the rest of the disciples. But on the day of our text, the doubts, the questions and the uncertainties were gone for them. They said, "We have seen the Lord. We have seen Jesus. He is alive. He lives." The disciples saw in Christ's resurrection the answer to all the problems in their lives. They wanted Thomas to have that same peace of mind.

Is there someone in your family who needs that peace of mind? Take them to Calvary and from Calvary to the empty tomb. Tell them, "We have seen the Lord." We have found in him the answer to all our problems. He has shown us the way to live and to love, to sing and to shout his glory. No problem, no doubt, no situation is too hopeless, for we have seen the Lord.

Dearest Lord Jesus, we have seen you through the eyes of faith. We know that you are alive and will ever live. Come live in each of our lives with your love. Help us to share you with each other and with those around us. In your name we pray. Amen.

"I am coming to you now, but I say these things while I am still in the world, so that they may have the full measure of my joy within them." (John 17:13)

KEEPING HAPPY

"**I**s everybody HAPPY?" Thus Al Jolson would begin his comedy routine. He asked the question because he felt a responsibility to make and to keep his audience happy.

The departing Lord Jesus also wanted the disciples he was leaving behind to be happy. He knew that this world does not, as a rule, tend to make its inhabitants happy. He also knew that at this time his disciples were anything but happy. They had begun to realize that he would soon be taken from them in death. Jesus therefore prayed to the Father that they might have the full measure of his joy in them.

The words "his joy" tell us that Jesus himself was happy. Yes, even in the face of betrayal by a disciple; in the face of crucifixion by his own people, Jesus was full of joy. It was not the "keep them rolling in the aisles with jokes" kind of happiness. It was the kind of joy that is quietly confident of victory against impossible odds.

The Lord wanted his disciples to have this kind of joy, then and in the difficult days to come. That is why he was going to the cross to die for them. That is why he would rise again and proclaim his victory over sin and death. That was why he prayed for them as he did—so that they might have the full measure of his joy in them.

Jesus' prayer was answered by the Father. Through his word and the Holy Spirit the disciples were able to rejoice later on, even in the face of persecution. They were happy in their ascended Lord.

How about you and me? Jesus was praying for us in his high priestly prayer as well as for those in the upper room. Are we happy? With life in this world being what it is we can't always expect to be as ecstatic as the disciples were on Easter Sunday. But do we have that quiet joy that comes from knowing that he who died for us is alive again? Do we have the happiness of which the Lord said earlier that night, "No one will take away our joy"? This is the joy that comes from the sure hope of eternal life, the joy that will stay with us even through our darkest days. May the full measure of our Savior's joy find a place in our hearts.

Heavenly Father, there are so many things that make us sad. Give us the full measure of the joy that can be ours only through faith in our risen Lord. Amen.

Now a man named Lazarus was sick. He was from Bethany, the village of Mary and her sister Martha. . . . So the sisters sent word to Jesus, "Lord, the one you love is sick." (John 11:1,3)

A FRIEND IN THE DAY OF TROUBLE

With what body of water mentioned in the Scriptures are we modern-day friends of Jesus most familiar? Most will answer, the Sea of Galilee. On the northwest shore of the Sea of Galilee stood the city of Capernaum. Capernaum served as Jesus' headquarters during the early years of his ministry. Four of his twelve disciples —Peter, James, John and Andrew— had made their living from the Sea of Galilee as commercial fishermen prior to their acceptance of Jesus' call. Several more of Jesus' disciples called Capernaum or one of its suburbs "home."

Occasionally the usually calm Sea of Galilee was lashed by fierce storms. Cyclonic winds would suddenly come swooping down from the high hills that ringed this body of water. Within minutes the Sea of Galilee could become extremely dangerous to anyone caught on its waters. We remember a time when Jesus and his disciples were caught in such a storm.

Most of the time our lives are like the Sea of Galilee on a calm day. Our hearts are light. God seems to be smiling upon us. He daily provides us with all that we need to stay alive and healthy. He brings joy to our hearts with his gospel.

Things apparently had been going well for Mary and Martha and Lazarus. We do not hear that they had any financial worries. They seemed to be enjoying good health. Best of all Jesus was their friend.

But suddenly and unexpectedly Lazarus became seriously ill. One can imagine how concerned Mary and Martha became as Lazarus's condition steadily worsened. Jesus had permitted trouble to come into the lives of his Bethany friends.

But has Jesus ever promised those who believe in him trouble-free earthly lives? No, he has not. Sickness, disease and other evils do occur. Since the fall of man into sin evils of every kind are found in this world. These evils may strike not only the unbelievers, but also those who are Jesus' friends. Sin has made this world a vale of tears. And because of the sin that still clings to us who are Jesus' friends, daily woes and heartaches are all that we deserve.

The Lord Jesus in his infinite wisdom may not immediately subdue every trouble that comes into our lives. May he grant us the grace to accept all things with patience and with confidence in his mercy, as did his three friends in Bethany.

Jesus, Savior, pilot me
Over life's tempestuous sea. Amen.

When he heard this, Jesus said, "This sickness will not end in death. No, it is for God's glory so that God's Son may be glorified through it." (John 11:4)

JESUS PROMISES TO HELP HIS FRIENDS

Sorry, we can't help you! In our society it is becoming more and more difficult to get help in an emergency. Years ago when a doctor received a call for help, he felt duty bound to respond immediately. Today this is not always the case. Some doctors have become quite independent. The mechanical answering device replies: "Sorry, Dr. Jones is not in. Will you please leave a message." Sometimes even a call to the hospital doesn't bring the results we want. Our best decision is to rush the seriously ill person or accident victim to the hospital emergency room and hope the physician on duty is available.

Jesus' friends are never put off, or given the run-around, when they call upon him for help. With Jesus we never have to make an appointment in advance or sign our name to some hospital or insurance forms. To be sure, proper procedure in human affairs dictates that we make such appointments and fill out forms. But how comforting to know that when we call upon Jesus for help, we can count on gaining his attention immediately. Later Mary and Martha found that out.

When their message, "Lord, the one you love is sick," reached Jesus, Jesus at once considered and diagnosed the case, "This sickness will not end in death. No, it is for God's glory so that God's Son may be glorified through it." And we can assume that Jesus asked the messenger who informed him of Lazarus's illness to deliver the response to Mary and Martha.

That response constituted a promise on the part of Jesus, a promise that all would be well with Lazarus— also a promise that God would be glorified. What comforting promises we, too, have, when we turn to Jesus for help: "Call upon me in the day of trouble; I will deliver you, and you will honor me."

The Lord Jesus assures us that he is both willing and able to resolve all of our problems. True, his response to our call for help may not always be what we would like it to be. But Scripture assures us that "all things work together for good to them that love God"!

What God ordains is always good.
He never will deceive me;
He leads me in His own right way,
And never will He leave me. Amen.

When he heard this, Jesus said, "This sickness will not end in death. No, it is for God's glory so that God's Son may be glorified through it." Yet when he heard that Lazarus was sick, he stayed where he was two more days. . . . After he had said this, he went on to tell them, "Our friend Lazarus has fallen asleep; but I am going there to wake him up." . . . So then he told them plainly, "Lazarus is dead." (John 11:4,6,11,14)

JESUS KNOWS WHEN TO HELP HIS FRIENDS

We friends of Jesus may sometimes wish that we were omniscient. Jesus is omniscient, that is, he knows all things. We may wish that we were omniscient so that we could be of greater service to our fellow human beings. Every now and then we learn that someone whom we know and care about is in trouble. We may feel that if only we had known sooner, we might have been able to do something to help.

Jesus, our all-loving Savior, knew exactly when to respond to the illness of this friend, Lazarus, who lived in Bethany. It may surprise us to learn that Jesus deliberately delayed journeying to Bethany for two days. Though Lazarus was seriously ill, Jesus made no immediate move to help. Mary and Martha may have wondered why it took so long for Jesus to arrive. Had he perhaps decided not to come?

But Jesus knew what he was doing. He waited until he could say to his disciples, "Our friend Lazarus is asleep." Lazarus had died. Now it was time to go to Bethany. The disciples, with perhaps the exception of John, did not understand what Jesus meant. "Then said Jesus unto them plainly, 'Lazarus is dead.' "

Why did Jesus wait until Lazarus was dead? Jesus had already answered that question. He had said, "This sickness will not end in death. No, it is for God's glory so that God's Son may be glorified through it." How would Jesus be glorified by a man's death? Or by waiting until Lazarus's body had lain in the tomb for four days? Yes, Jesus waited—he waited until many relatives and friends of the family had arrived in Bethany to offer their condolences to Mary and Martha. But then, when he arrived, Jesus called Lazarus back to life.

As believers, that is, friends of Jesus, we have the comfort that he knows when to help us. He knows that much better than we do. If he was willing to suffer the shame and disgrace of the cross for us, will he not also deliver us in every other need and trouble!

Lord Jesus, grant that we might always be willing to await your answer to our prayers. Amen.

When he heard this, Jesus said, "This sickness will not end in death. No, it is for God's glory so that God's Son may be glorified through it." . . . After he had said this, he went on to tell them, "Our friend Lazarus has fallen asleep; but I am going there to wake him up." (John 11:4,11)

JESUS KNOWS HOW TO HELP HIS FRIENDS

When a loved one suddenly becomes seriously ill, we may be at a loss what to do. Even the doctor may be stymied. If the doctor is unable to diagnose the illness, how can he know what to do? But the Lord Jesus is never at a loss. He always knows how to help. He certainly knew how to help in the case of his friends at Bethany.

How? First of all, by not immediately hastening to Bethany when the message arrived that Lazarus was ill. We are told that Jesus deliberately waited to start out for Bethany until after Lazarus's death. Jesus had no intention of healing Lazarus of his illness. Why not? Because Jesus had something better in mind.

After Lazarus had died, Jesus said to his disciples: "Our friend Lazarus has fallen asleep; but I am going there to wake him up." Jesus here announced that he would be raising Lazarus from death. The disciples did not question what Jesus said. Had they not with their own eyes seen Jesus raise the young man of Nain and the daughter of Jairus from the dead?

But Jesus here was not thinking only of the effect that his raising of Lazarus would have on his disciples. He also was thinking of the salutary effect it was to have upon Mary and Martha and also upon their many relatives and friends—yes, of the effect it would have on all of Jerusalem and Judea.

So Jesus made it a point not to arrive at Bethany until after Lazarus's body had been in the tomb for four days. This meant that the process of decay was already well under way. Recall that Jesus had raised the young man of Nain and the daughter of Jairus shortly after they had died. Unbelieving Jews may have suggested that in those cases the dead person had not really been dead, but only unconscious. In Lazarus's case there was plenty of proof that he was dead. Thus, as Jesus had said, the raising of Lazarus would glorify God.

It did. We are told that the raising of Lazarus made such an impression on people that many came to faith in Jesus (John 11:45).

Lord Jesus, you always know much better than we do how to help us in the troubles that come upon us. Deliver us from every evil. Amen.

On his arrival, Jesus found that Lazarus had already been in the tomb for four days. . . . When Martha heard that Jesus was coming, she went out to meet him, but Mary stayed at home. "Lord," Martha said to Jesus, "if you had been here, my brother would not have died. But I know that even now God will give you whatever you ask." (John 11:17-22)

A FRIEND TO RELY ON

It is said of sports that timing is everything. A mistake in timing can turn a touchdown into a loss of yardage, a home run into a pop-up.

Suspense in the theater is all a matter of timing. "Will the hero arrive in time to save the lady in distress?" Timing can affect our real lives quite dramatically, too. Much of what the world calls success depends on being "in the right place at the right time."

Martha considered timing to be critical in the case of her brother's death. If Jesus had been there, she lamented, Lazarus would not have died. It wasn't that Jesus carried some wonder drug with him to cure diseases. Martha had seen Jesus regularly heal the sick by his divine power, by speaking the word. She knew (such was her faith) that Jesus would have healed Lazarus if he had arrived sooner.

But now it was too late. The touchdown pass was blocked. The ball game was over. Lazarus had died. Or was it too late? Martha undoubtedly remembered the message Jesus sent back when he heard of Lazarus's illness. "This sickness will not end in death," he had said. Jesus had never lied about anything or deceived anyone. Could that mean that he would still work a miracle? Would he raise Lazarus from the dead? He had raised the dead before this on two occasions. The body of Lazarus, however, lay decaying in the grave.

Martha was torn between grief and hope, but her faith told her to rely on Jesus. She could not understand it, but she confessed, "I know that even now God will give you whatever you ask." "Even now!" she said. Her brother lay dead; still she trusted in the Lord.

Jesus always stands ready to help those who believe. He does not abandon us. Let us not abandon him. He gave himself into death to redeem us from sin and death. He opened the way to eternal life for us by rising victorious from the dead. No matter how hopeless we might consider matters to be at times, we still have reason to rely on Christ. By his works and his words, we know he will answer our prayers and give us all that we need.

Blessed Lord Jesus, teach us to trust in you for all things. Amen.

But some of them said, "Could not he who opened the eyes of the blind man have kept this man from dying?" (John 11:37)

A FRIEND WITH OUR BEST INTERESTS AT HEART

Why did this tragedy happen? Why to him? Why to her? Why to them? Why to me? Why now? Why?

How often this question troubles us—"Why?" When the ways of life do not fall into the pattern which we have in our minds, the question, "Why?" rises to the surface. It was no different for the people who knew Jesus, who knew Lazarus and his sisters, Mary and Martha. They all wondered why it had to happen that Lazarus died.

Mary and Martha reasoned this way: Had not Jesus performed many miracles? He gave sight to the blind; he restored hearing to the deaf; he gave speech to the dumb; he made the paralytic walk again. Jesus could have healed Lazarus from his sickness. He had done so many other miracles. Surely he could have helped his dear friend, Lazarus.

Such a question troubles all of us at one time or another. We also wonder why things could not be different; why they could not be the way we would like them to be.

However, when we give serious thought to the matter of why the Lord does what he does, we must again grow thankful that we do not have to decide matters.

We sometimes ask questions touching very basic teachings of the Bible. Why did God make man the way he did? Why did God permit man to fall into sin? Why did God devise the plan of saving man the way he did? Why did God give us his revelation concerning this plan of salvation? Such questions and many more could come to mind if we permitted our reason to run rampant.

All these questions are simply answered—because it is God's will and way! God has his own purpose; his ways are higher than our ways. He knows what is best for us. He has our best interests, that is, the best interests of his believers, at heart at all times. We might ask the question, "Why?" But let us answer it just as quickly —"It is God's will." Let the whys give place to the certain promises of God that we have in our Savior, Jesus Christ. And let us confidently pray with the hymnwriter:

Tho' dark my path and sad my lot,
Let me be still and murmur not
Or breathe the prayer divinely taught,
"Thy will be done." Amen.

Jesus was sleeping. The disciples went and woke him, saying, "Lord, save us! We're going to drown!" (Matthew 8:24,25)

A FRIEND IN TIME OF DANGER

It had been a very busy day for Jesus and his disciples. The hours had passed in teaching and healing the crowds that had gathered around. At sunset Jesus and his disciples stepped into the boat to cross the lake and find time for meditation and communion with the heavenly Father. Jesus lay down in the stern of the ship and was soon asleep.

The storm that raged that night was one of no ordinary violence. The men in the boat had been accustomed to the lake from childhood, as many of them plied the trade of commercial fishing, and they were accustomed to all its moods and dangers. But here was a storm which struck fear to their hearts, and even these experienced men saw themselves heading for a watery grave. It has been said that there are few situations where a man realizes how helpless he is as when he is engulfed in such a devastating storm at sea.

From the midst of this storm comes a cry in the night, "Lord, save us! We're going to drown!" Suddenly they knew that all their skill, their cunning as sailors was of no avail. There was only one who could save them. In their distress they went to the Lord as master of wind and wave, as guardian of their bodies and souls. Facing death, they knew him to be their only help and salvation. And Jesus answered their prayers.

The account of the storm on the lake is an historical incident in the life of our Lord and his disciples. But as we think about it a little further, it also becomes a parable of man's existence. We are the occupants of that boat, crossing the stormy seas of life.

While people have their health, and they seem to be able to control things, there often seems to be only a lukewarm acceptance of Jesus. But when trouble and sickness comes, when the leprosy of their sins begins to eat into their souls, when a serious or terminal illness strikes and storms seem to buffet them on every side, then they want to know that Christ is there at their side, that he is the One who is able to save. Then sounds forth the cry of distress, "Lord, save us."

And that is the right word, "save." For when we have that, we have all. Jesus came "to seek and to save that which was lost." Jesus does help us in all our undertakings. But the greatest prayer we can bring to Christ is this, "Lord, save me."

Gracious Lord, save us from all dangers, but above all save us for eternity through your precious blood and merit. Amen.

When Jesus had entered Capernaum, a centurion came to him, asking for help. (Matthew 8:5)

JESUS WOULD BE HIS FRIEND

"**D**oris, I have been transferred, again," said her husband. "We have to move to Los Angeles in six weeks."

A soldier of Rome received the same type of orders 2,000 years ago. "Caesar wants you!" The centurion answered his emperor's call to military service and was stationed more than 1,500 miles from Rome in Capernaum of Galilee. It was not the worst place to be on duty in the Roman Empire. Still, it was not home either.

The centurion could sulk—after all he was far removed from loved ones and friends, or he could resolve to make the best of it. There would be new things to see . . . a new culture to learn . . . and new friends to make.

Plus, he had promised to serve the emperor by being the best possible representative of his country. There would be plenty to do to keep busy, soldiering and otherwise.

While in Capernaum, this officer heard of and committed his allegiance to the Lord of lords and King of kings—Jesus Christ. We don't know exactly when or how it happened; that is not important. It is important that it did happen.

Jesus, his Savior, would conquer his sin and remove the fear of death even in a far-off land. Jesus would be his friend—someone this soldier could go to when he was lonely. Now, there would always be available strength and limitless comfort no matter where he would be stationed. Capernaum was a comfortable place to be after all!

A change of address can often be traumatic. Moving because of work, age or serving our country in the armed services can be cause for some worry, even some fears. What will it be like there? Whom will I meet? Who will replace my former friends and neighbors?

On the other hand, some things never change. Even though a move means change, Jesus Christ, our Savior and Friend who is the same yesterday, today and tomorrow, will be waiting for us when we move to our new city and into our new home. It is comforting for every Christian to know this.

Oh, spread Thy covering wings around
Till all our wanderings cease
And at our Father's loved abode
Our souls arrive in peace. Amen.

In that day you will no longer ask me anything. I tell you the truth, my Father will give you whatever you ask in my name. Until now you have not asked for anything in my name. Ask and you will receive, and your joy will be complete. Though I have been speaking figuratively, a time is coming when I will no longer use this kind of language but will tell you plainly about my Father. In that day you will ask in my name. I am not saying that I will ask the Father on your behalf. No, the Father himself loves you because you have loved me and have believed that I came from God. (John 16:23-27)

WHAT A FRIEND WE HAVE IN JESUS

To the Philippians (4:6) Paul wrote, "In everything, by prayer and petition, with thanksgiving, present your requests to God." These words are preceded by the saying, "Do not be anxious about anything." They present the Bible's own remedy for worry, the sure cure for care. That cure for care is prayer in all cases.

People try to cope with their cares in many different ways but somehow always seem to neglect the sure and effective way. Some drag their worries around with themselves all day long. They get up with their problem in the morning and take it to bed with them at night. That is folly, useless folly. Others with sublime and supreme indifference shrug off their problems or assume they can drink or dance them away. That's folly, too.

We are not to hoard our worries, as the miser hoards his money. We are not to toss them blithely into the blue, as the gambler casts a pair of dice. We are not to entrust them primarily and exclusively to our fellow men, who often are unable or unwilling to help us. No matter what the case or the care may be, we are to let our requests be made known to God by prayer and supplication with thanksgiving.

This is the God who sent his Son into the world as the Savior from sin. The love he manifested then still reaches out to gather in our requests. The believer who trusts in God and embraces the merits of his Son will be able to send his supplications and thanksgiving up to the throne of grace. He will be able to pray as a dear child to his dear Father in heaven.

The time will come when prayers are no longer needed, but that will not be before the final judgment. Until then we can drive away all cares and worries by requesting the aid of our all-powerful, all-wise, all-merciful Father in heaven. He will help us and bless us.

Lord, I come to Thee for rest,
Take possession of my breast;
There Thy blood-bought right maintain
And without a rival reign. Amen.

Jesus answered her, "If you knew the gift of God and who it is that asks you for a drink, you would have asked him and he would have given you living water." "Sir," the woman said, "you have nothing to draw with and the well is deep. Where can you get this living water? Are you greater than our father Jacob, who gave us the well and drank from it himself, as did also his sons and his flocks and herds?" (John 4:10-12)

JESUS, FRIEND OF SINNERS

Nothing about his appearance gave any hint. He looked like just another ordinary traveler. Yet he made great promises, offering more than the ancient patriarch himself. She wondered to herself, "What can he give me?"

We remember the beggar who sat on the temple steps. He was lame from the time of his birth. As he saw the apostles Peter and John approaching, he too wondered, "What will they give me?" "Can they give me anything?" What a surprise he received. No silver or gold, but the greatest of gifts—he walked for the first time. He came to faith in the Savior of all men. He was given salvation.

We may have wondered, "What can he give us?" The answer is plain. He gives us God's own righteousness. Because he suffered and died in our place, he gives us the forgiveness of sins. What we do not deserve, what we could not earn, is ours as a gift. He wipes away our sin. He covers us with the robe of his righteousness. He washes away every stain and spot.

Through that forgiveness he makes us members of his family. He teaches us that God is our Father. How important! We finally know who we are. Our search is over; we have found our roots. We have an identity. With his help, we begin to live differently. We aim for those things which are good and pleasing in his sight. We live more for him than for ourselves.

We look to the future with confidence. Our life still remains a mystery to us. There is much that we do not understand. But we know that whatever happens will turn out for the best. Above all we know what the end will be. He has promised to return. He has promised to take us with him to be members of his family forever. He has promised us eternal life. And we know that he gives what he promises.

Dear Jesus, we could never come to life without you. Open our eyes to see the greatness of the treasures you offer us. Continue to forgive us. Enable us to live as members of your family. Help us not to lose our way or to become discouraged. Keep our hearts fixed on the promise of your return and eternal life. Amen.

Soon afterward, Jesus went to a town called Nain, and his disciples and a large crowd went along with him. As he approached the town gate, a dead person was being carried out—the only son of his mother, and she was a widow. And a large crowd from the town was with her. (Luke 7:11,12)

DEATH—WHERE LIFE BEGINS

Nain means "pleasantness" or "beauty." But there was nothing pleasant or beautiful the day Jesus came to a town called Nain. There were only tears and death.

Our Lord had just come from the town of Capernaum, where he healed a centurion's servant. As a result of this miracle, a large crowd followed Jesus as he walked a day's journey southwest of Capernaum to the slopes of Little Hermon, where Nain was located. When Jesus came near the gate of the town, he saw a dead man being carried out. It was a gloomy event, at least for many of the people. Death, humanly speaking, is the loss of everything. But Jesus knew otherwise. There was hope which he alone could bring. He alone could offer and present hope because he alone is the Prince of Hope and the Prince of Life.

As visitors and travelers on this earth, we observe death everywhere. We open the newspaper and read the obituary column; we drive downtown and pass a funeral home; we tour the countryside and see a cemetery. Death is all around us, and the words of St. Paul in Romans 6:23 pierce our ears and hearts: "For the wages of sin is death!" No one looks forward to death. However, if we look at the perfect redeeming work of the Visitor who came to Nain, we see that he has power over sin and death.

Because of Jesus we don't have to fear death any more than our bed. Thankfully, St. Paul's Romans 6:23 passage does not stop at a dead end, but rather tells us, that for all who believe in Christ, that is where life begins—eternal life! Listen closely to Paul's entire passage: "For the wages of sin is death, but the gift of God is eternal life in Christ Jesus our Lord."

He gives us hope and peace and life. With his promises in view, each new sunrise reminds us that a glorious eternal day will dawn for us. And the evening shadows teach us to say with childlike confidence:

Now I lay me down to sleep;
I pray the Lord my soul to keep.
If I should die before I wake,
I pray the Lord my soul to take. Amen.

When the Lord saw her, his heart went out to her and he said, "Don't cry." (Luke 7:13)

DON'T CRY!

On November 11, 1975, the Edmund Fitzgerald, a 721-foot ore ship, was on a run from Superior, Wisconsin, to Whitefish Bay, Ontario. It never reached its destination. The high winds and 30-foot waves of Lake Superior made this journey its last one. Twenty-nine men died. The relatives of these sailors were all too familiar with tragedies of this kind. And pain filled their hearts as they heard the church bell ring 29 times. Other mariners and friends were filled with compassion for the surviving families, but nothing could be done. Only words of sympathy could be offered.

The same feelings of compassion filled the heart of Jesus as he approached the gate of Nain and the widow, the corpse, the mournful procession. He came up to her and said, "Don't cry!" Jesus was not implying that it is wrong to cry at a funeral. We know that Jesus wept at the grave of his friend, Lazarus, and we know the Bible says, "Mourn with those who mourn" (Romans 12:15). Tears have a way of releasing the buildup of our sorrow. The message Jesus wanted to communicate to the widow of Nain was this: "Dry your eyes, for you have hope."

Jesus wants to communicate that same message to us today. He wants us to know that we have hope—eternal hope. The Apostle Paul spelled out that hope to the Thessalonian Christians: "Brothers, we do not want you to be ignorant about those who fall asleep, or to grieve like the rest of men, who have no hope. We believe that Jesus died and rose again and so we believe that God will bring with Jesus those who have fallen asleep in him" (1 Thessalonians 4:13,14).

"Stop crying" sounds like an unbelievable request, especially when we see a loved one lowered into the grave. But the message of the forgiveness of sins and the good news of Jesus' love and mercy enables us in due time to dry our tears. They impart the certain hope that we and all who believe in Christ will meet again, nevermore to die.

For the same Christ who said, "Arise!" to the widow's son and, "Come forth!" to Lazarus, will say the same to his people on the last day. And we shall arise and come forth.

Why do we mourn departing friends
Or shake at death's alarms?
'Tis but the voice that Jesus sends
To call them to his arms. Amen.

Then he went up and touched the coffin, and those carrying it stood still. He said, "Young man, I say to you, get up!" (Luke 7:14)

A SUMMONS FROM THE SAVIOR

Imagine yourself following the pallbearers to the graveside. Suddenly a stranger approaches, stops the procession, raises the lid on the coffin, and commands the corpse to sit up. Would there be a few eyebrows raised? Most likely everyone would wonder if the person was in his right mind. Yet, if we simply read the words of our text, it's quite clear that this is exactly what Jesus did. He walked up to the bier, that is, the bed on which the dead man lay, and said, "Get up!" He did not use any theatrical devices. There was no puff of smoke, no spotlight, no drum roll. Jesus just spoke the word. It was by his own power that Jesus ordered this young dead man to arise. And to the amazement of all, he arose.

We might recall that it was this same power that the disciples were given when they first went out to spread the gospel. It was the word of the Lord which allowed the lame to walk and the deaf to hear. And Psalm 33:6 makes it easy for us to believe that it is so. There the psalmist reminds us, "By the word of the LORD were the heavens made, their starry host by the breath of his mouth." If God could do the greater, namely, create the universe and all that is in it, out of nothing, simply by speaking the word—so he can certainly do the lesser, that is, knit a soul and body, which has already been created, back together again.

God's Word, the Bible, is still effective today. The Holy Spirit comes to us in that Word, convinces us of our complete sinfulness and guilt before God, and convinces us that in Christ God has put away our sin and guilt. And we believe and confess that that same word of God will search out every corner of the globe on judgment day and call forth all the dead. Then the unbelievers will be assigned to eternal punishment and the believers to eternal joy.

Some may raise their eyebrows at this teaching. Others will ridicule it. But when the day arrives, and Christ says, "Get up"—all will get up, like it or not. For God's Word is powerful and true. And all who believe it look forward to the last day and that final summons from our Savior: "Come, you who are blessed by my Father; take your inheritance, the kingdom prepared for you since the creation of the world" (Matthew 25:34).

**"Forever with the Lord!"
Amen! so let it be.
Life from the dead is in that word,
'Tis immortality. Amen.**

The dead man sat up and began to talk, and Jesus gave him back to his mother. (Luke 7:15)

A DEAD MAN SPEAKS

The motion picture industry can produce amazing happenings. It can put us on a wagon train and transport us across the Great Plains. It can strap us in a fantastic spaceship bound for Mars and bring us safely back. A good camera and a good imagination can produce illusions in endless variety.

But on this otherwise ordinary day in the Galilean village of Nain there were no movie cameras and no special effects—just historical facts. A young man who was dead sat up and spoke. The miracle was clear. Everyone who witnessed it knew it for what it was. Only crass unbelief tries to write it off as a hoax or dismiss it as an illusion.

The Bible is filled with many similar events that are out of the ordinary, but true, like the feeding of the 5,000 with only five barley loaves and two small fish, Jesus' walking on the water and the healing of the blind man. As believers in Christ, we accept these miracles as true. Our confession is that of the Apostle Paul, who said, "We live by faith, not by sight" (2 Corinthians 5:7).

Yet we know that the devil, the world and our sinful flesh try to destroy that faith which the Holy Spirit has put into our hearts through baptism, the Lord's Supper and the message of the Bible. Oh, how we continually need the Holy Spirit's help to flee every temptation! We daily need to pray: "I do believe; help me overcome my unbelief!" (Mark 9:24).

Today's Bible reading is one of the weapons by which we are able to overcome the enemy. It clearly tells us that this dead man from Nain sat up and spoke and that Jesus presented him to his mother. We do not know what the young man said, but we do know that he did speak and that he went back home again with his mother. It was not an illusion. It was a fact. And this fact and all the other Bible facts still remain true today. It is true that the Son of God came to this earth as a baby; he lived a perfect life and died for our sins; he physically rose from the dead, ascended into heaven and will return again. These are facts. And as we read about them, study them and take them to heart, the Holy Spirit convinces us that they are true.

To thine almighty Spirit be
Immortal glory giv'n,
Whose teachings bring us near to Thee
And train us up for heav'n. Amen.

They were all filled with awe and praised God. "A great prophet has appeared among us," they said. "God has come to help his people." (Luke 7:16)

GOD IS IN OUR TOWN

The people of Nain said, "God has come to help his people." Their statement was more accurate than some of them may have intended it to be. It was true that God visited his people by bringing a young man back to life. But this miracle was not performed by an ordinary representative of God; this miracle was performed personally by God himself—by the God-man, Jesus Christ. The Apostle Paul once wrote to the Colossian Christians, "For in Christ all the fullness of the Deity lives in bodily form" (Colossians 2:9). The people of Nain had not only seen the miracle in which a dead man came back to life, but they actually saw God himself perform it!

All of this is a mystery to us. The doctrine of the Trinity and of Jesus' incarnation are beyond our comprehension. How can God be in heaven as a spirit (who has no flesh and bones), and at the same time be on earth as a man? We cannot understand this any better now than we did when we were small children. Yet, as when we were children, we believe that it is true.

Although the teaching that God is everywhere is a mystery to our intellect, it is a comfort to our heart. It is comforting to know that wherever we are living, God the Father who made us still continues to preserve us. It is comforting to know that Jesus Christ who redeemed us from sin, still walks next to us in this life. It is comforting to know that God the Holy Spirit who has brought us to faith in Christ, continues to keep us in that faith.

From a spectacular miracle we know that the Triune God was active in the town of Nain about 2,000 years ago. But his Word informs us that he still is active today in our town and among us. It does not matter where we live. For Jesus' sake, our God is with us; he will help us; he will forgive us; he will guide us.

If our doubts ever arise concerning God's presence, all we have to do is turn to Isaiah 41:10 and read God's own words and promises: "Do not fear, for I am with you; do not be dismayed, for I am your God. I will strengthen you and help you; I will uphold you with my righteous right hand." God is with us, that we might reign with him.

**Our God, our Help in ages past,
Our Hope for years to come,
Be Thou our Guard while troubles last
And our eternal Home! Amen.**

When the Lord saw her, his heart went out to her and he said, "Don't cry." Then he went up and touched the coffin, and those carrying it stood still. He said, "Young man, I say to you, get up!" The dead man sat up and began to talk, and Jesus gave him back to his mother. (Luke 7:13-15)

DEATH CANNOT HOLD US

Who is Jesus Christ? "He's our God and our Savior." That's the answer we Christians give, but that isn't the answer the average man on the street gives. "Jesus was a frustrated political reformer." "Jesus was a great teacher who set an excellent example for us to follow in our associations with others." That's what others say.

How can we be sure who's right? Pro-football fans all over the country feel that their team is the best when the season begins, but at the end the contest narrows down to two teams. It's the best of the NFC against the best of the AFC. The winner is undisputed champion because he has beaten the best.

That's what Jesus did. The powers of darkness put their best up against him—death. Mere man would have wilted facing that power. He would have been bombed out of the stadium. But Jesus was no mere man, and when he came face to face with death, death met its conqueror.

The story is a very sad one. A woman who lived at Nain had already lost her husband. Now her son, the last joy and comfort of her life, was dead too. Everyone was very sympathetic. They wanted to help her, but what can anyone do in the face of death? Once a person is dead, all hope is gone. Or is it?

When Jesus and his disciples came along and realized what had happened, we're told that "his heart went out to her." He felt genuinely sorry for her and quickly took an action that turned her sorrow into joy. He stopped the funeral procession, walked up to the dead man, and said, "Young man, get up!"

What a joke it would be for a mere man to try something like that! But Jesus is no mere man. He is our God and our Savior, and even the dead have to obey him. The young man arose! The great enemy, death, could not hold him.

Death could not hold Christ either. It tried! The church and the state of that day crucified Christ. He died. He was buried. But on the third day the grave had to give up its victim again. Death could not hold the Lord Jesus.

Neither will it be able to hold us. The day is coming when all of us will fall asleep in death, but we need not be afraid. There's no reason for us to be afraid, for we have a Savior who met death and conquered it for us!

Jesus, thank you for taking away our fear of death. Amen.

So he replied to the messengers, "Go back and report to John what you have seen and heard: The blind receive sight, the lame walk, those who have leprosy are cured, the deaf hear, the dead are raised, and the good news is preached to the poor. Blessed is the man who does not fall away on account of me." (Luke 7:22,23)

PEACE—EVEN IN THE HOUR OF DEATH

"**D**id you hear what he said?" said one of John's followers to the others. "Why, he took credit for those healings. He claimed that he is the preacher of good tidings. And what's more, he maintained that it was he himself who raised those people from the dead. You know, I'm beginning to understand how our master, John, can face death so unafraid." Trusting in the Living Word, one need have no fear even when facing death.

Now we're down to brass tacks, down to the nitty gritty, aren't we? When we can maintain that believing the Word can bring power and peace, even when facing death, then we are talking about something both mighty and useful. It seems that everyone is afraid of death, or at least doesn't relish the thought of death too much. But the believer can banish all such fear and anxiety. He knows where he's going. He sees death for what it really is, that through the efforts of Jesus his Savior, death is the door to life eternal in heaven. The consolation which such knowledge brings is enough to give a man peace, even and especially, in the hour of death.

Look at John the Baptist. Imprisoned, certain death awaiting him, he nevertheless is calm. He sends his followers to hear from the Lord's own lips that it is he who is the long awaited Messiah. The Living Word has convinced him, and he knows that Christ's words will also be able to convince them. In the power of Christ's promise, John was ready to die in peace. Our Lord said of him, "Then what did you go out to see? A prophet? Yes, I tell you, and more than a prophet." When death came, John did not despair. He had Jesus' word. He could die in peace, for he believed his words.

That very same certainty that Christ has forgiven us our sins and that he will raise us from the dead will enable us to meet the hour of our own death without fear and trembling. Trusting in the one who will never fail us, we know that our departure here will be a glorious arrival there, where "He will wipe every tear from their eyes. There will be no more death or mourning or crying or pain, for the old order of things has passed away."

Let your Word comfort me in death and lead me to life. Amen.

When he had said this, Jesus called in a loud voice, "Lazarus, come out!" The dead man came out, his hands and feet wrapped with strips of linen, and a cloth around his face. Jesus said to them, "Take off the grave clothes and let him go." Therefore many of the Jews who had come to visit Mary, and had seen what Jesus did, put their faith in him. (John 11:43-45)

WHEN THE LORD CALLS US FROM THE GRAVE

"If Jesus had not called Lazarus by name," an elderly gentleman is quoted as saying, "the whole graveyard at Bethany would have emptied its tombs." Such is the power of a word from Jesus. He speaks, and the grip of death is broken. At the last day, say the Scriptures, "all who are in their graves will hear his voice, and come out."

Think of the scene at Bethany when, at the command of the Lord Jesus, Lazarus came walking out of a tomb that had held his dead, decaying body for four days. It's an astounding picture—Lazarus, the corpse, wrapped in grave clothes, stepping out of his tomb. Then transfer the picture to the day of judgment and imagine, if you can, the billions of graves in the world opening at one time and all the bodies coming out alive. From the small cemetery next to your church to the depths of the ocean, the dead will rise and will come before Jesus for the judgment, summoned by his voice.

There is at least one important difference between our rising on the last day and the raising of Lazarus. Lazarus was raised from the dead to continue this life until the natural processes of death took over again. We shall be raised in a glorified body that cannot die again. We see something of that difference indicated by the references to the grave clothes in the resurrections of Lazarus and of Jesus. Lazarus, still in his earthly body, came out of the tomb struggling with the clothes still wrapped around him. Jesus, in his glorified body, rose free from the grave clothes, which remained in place where his body had been lying. The glorified body will not be hindered by earthly things as our earthly bodies would be. We will have glorified bodies eternally free of decay and disease.

We will be like the Lord who will call us from the grave. We will "see him as he is." We will be caught up to meet him in the clouds of heaven and will live with him forever. Joy and thanksgiving will fill our hearts. For us and all who believe in Christ it will be a wonderful day when the Lord commands all the dead to come forth.

Come quickly, Lord Jesus. Amen.

Then Jesus told him, "Because you have seen me, you have believed; blessed are those who have not seen and yet have believed." (John 20:29)

FAITH WITHOUT SIGHT

Thomas believed because he saw. In our case, "Faith comes from hearing the message, and the message is heard through the word of Christ" (Romans 10:17). The bliss and happiness of saving faith does not rest upon the evidence of the senses, upon our feelings or even our reason, but alone on the word of the gospel. The Word of God brings Christ to us; the Word of God brings us to Christ.

Jesus approved the firm confession of Thomas with a word that shines like a beacon down through the centuries: "Because you have seen me, you have believed; blessed are those who have not seen and yet have believed." The words were spoken for our benefit. Jesus is not making a comparison between the faith of Thomas, who was privileged to see, and the faith of those who have not seen. As it is with us, Thomas was saved by faith in Christ as the promised Messiah, the Son of God. Yet, the words of our text bestow a special blessing on those who do not enjoy the same opportunity of the first disciples.

Our Savior undoubtedly granted them visible proof of his resurrection because he wished them to have an impressive demonstration of his successful redemptive work. His personal appearance would sustain their courage in this early era of the New Testament Church.

The resurrection is a reality. We believe this. We need not see Jesus visibly or personally. The disciples saw him and reported it to us in God's own inspired Word. Our faith is not some vague dream or wishful thinking. Our confidence rests on the powerful testimony of God the Holy Ghost. Behind these words stand all the power, the love, the wisdom and the truth of our Creator and Savior. Can we ask for better assurance or stronger evidence of the reality of our salvation!

Peter was a witness to this whole episode involving Thomas. His comforting words to us have a familiar echo: "Though you have not seen [Jesus], you love him; and even though you do not see him now, you believe in him and are filled with an inexpressible and glorious joy, for you are receiving the goal of your faith, the salvation of your souls" (1 Peter 1:8,9).

Gracious Savior, nourish our faith with your Word until we share in the fullness of your glory in heaven. Amen.

So the women hurried away from the tomb, afraid yet filled with joy, and ran to tell his disciples. (Matthew 28:8)

BRIGHT WITH JOY

A funeral director once commented, "I can tell when a grieving family comes into my establishment whether they are Christian or not. Christians have an altogether different way of handling their grief. There's a certain peace, almost an inner joy, even when they mourn."

The women who had met the angel at the tomb exemplify what that funeral director had observed. As they left the tomb, they were afraid. Perhaps their fear was the result of seeing a holy angel. Maybe the fear was that they would never be believed, or that what the angel had said was too good to be true. We are told that they felt that normal human emotion we call fear.

But that fear did not prevent them from being "filled with joy." Joy overcame their fears. Joy gave swiftness to their feet. It was the resurrection of Jesus that provided that fear-conquering joy. The grave was empty. Jesus had left it, using the power that he has over death. Gradually the meaning of the event must have occurred to them. Jesus lives! Death couldn't hold him. Then death has lost its hold on us, too!

The resurrection of Christ is the source of Christian joy. To be sure, Christians can and do often weep over the death of loved ones. But the tears shed by Christians over one who is now "asleep in Jesus" do not change the joy that is in their heart; in fact, it is that joy that comforts the Christian even as he mourns. It is joy over the fact of Christ's resurrection that keeps tears of sorrow from becoming tears of bitterness or despair, as must be the case with the nonbeliever.

The resurrection joy is a joy that fills the Christian's life. It doesn't come and go. In fact, it can't be shattered, even when tragedy strikes. It is a lasting joy, because it enables us to look past all the present sorrows and see our resurrected Lord, the Lord who promised, "Now is your time of grief, but I will see you again and you will rejoice, and no one will take away your joy."

Lord Jesus, your victory over death has filled us with joy. Lead us by the brightness of the resurrection to the eternal joy that you have prepared for us in heaven. Amen.

Jesus replied, "Go back and report to John what you hear and see: The blind receive sight, the lame walk, those who have leprosy are cured, the deaf hear, the dead are raised, and the good news is preached to the poor." (Matthew 11:4,5)

WHAT'S REALLY IMPORTANT

"**M**essiah!" "Son of God!" "Savior!" The works of Jesus shouted out: "Here is the one you were waiting for!" Were the individual miracles important? Ask the once blind Bartimaeus as he reads the *Jerusalem Times* over a cup of coffee! Ask the Samaritan leper hugging his wife after a hard day at the office. There hadn't been much hugging in the leper colony! Go to the parents, sisters, brothers and friends of the healed and the risen. Do you hear them singing? Can you see the lame man dancing? Each wonder touched tens and hundreds; each wonder was important in itself.

But, and we must hastily add this, the miracles were even more important as signs of who Jesus was. Jesus wanted, yes, he still wants, to be accepted not as a miracle-worker, but even more as the Savior from eternal death. Jesus used words to present himself to the world as the Savior, but he used works to prove that he was the Messiah the Old Testament predicted, and, therefore, our Savior.

To those who had trouble believing the words he would say, "At least believe me on account of the works."

The substance of Jesus, that is, the real, important stuff, was not and is not salvation from physical lameness, blindness or even death. The lame who walked, the blind who saw and the dead who rose remained sinners—sinners who would die and were headed for an unbearable eternity. No, the substance is the good news preached to poor and rich alike. It is news of a much more important salvation. It is the guarantee of a resurrection to eternal life, because the one who proclaimed the news also established it by turning away God's punishment from man back upon himself.

Let's keep our spiritual glasses on! To be healed is wonderful; to seek Jesus' help in physical distress is God's will for us. To be raised for a time is cause to jump and shout. But to live forever in God's presence is the true substance of the good news. And it is ours for the believing!

Lord Jesus, David's Son and Lord, keep our eyes turned heavenward. Deliver us from evils of body; but, most of all deliver us from hell's eternal evils. We praise your great salvation. Amen.

"The Counselor, the Holy Spirit, whom the Father will send in my name, will teach you all things and will remind you of everything I have said to you." (John 14:26)

LISTEN AS GOD SPEAKS

"Sure! You Christians quote from the Bible. But the Bible was written by men. And men can make mistakes."

That is what the unbeliever says. With that kind of reasoning the unbeliever tries to shake the Christian's faith and tries to make the Bible look like an unreliable book. But in today's Scripture verse Jesus himself contradicts that mistaken human opinion.

We all know how quickly people can forget what happened. We all know how quickly people can get the facts and the details mixed up. If the apostles had been left to themselves, they also would have misrepresented many of the things that Jesus said and did. If the disciples had been left on their own, they would have gotten the facts and the details mixed up. Their writings and their teachings would have been filled with all sorts of contradictions.

But God did not permit this to happen. Jesus did not let them wander off on their own. But it happened to them as he said in our Scripture lesson, "The Holy Spirit will remind you of everything I have said to you." The Holy Spirit caused the New Testament writers to remember exactly what Jesus had spoken and exactly what Jesus had done. The words which they spoke and wrote were given by inspiration of God the Holy Spirit. Therefore we have the assurance that the Bible is an accurate record of the Savior's words and deeds. It is the truth.

Therefore let us not idly sit back and hope that God will somehow appear to us or directly inform us of his will. If we want to hear God speak and be assured that it is truly God, and not the devil, speaking, we must go to his Word, the Bible. For that is where Jesus comes to us and makes himself known to us. We can hear and read the Bible with the confidence that Jesus himself is standing before us and instructing us. When the Bible reveals our sinfulness and our need for a Savior, Jesus is speaking. When the Bible tells us that "God so loved the world that he gave his only-begotten Son," Jesus himself is offering us his comfort. Let us then be eager to hear and to read the words of that sacred Book. And let us believe them.

Dear Savior, thank you for coming to us in your Word. Give us hearts that are eager to hear and to learn and to believe it. Amen.

Jesus answered, "I tell you the truth, no one can enter the kingdom of God unless he is born of water and the Spirit. Flesh gives birth to flesh, but the Spirit gives birth to spirit." (John 3:5,6)

BORN-AGAIN CHRISTIANS

What does it mean to be "born again"? Nicodemus had a problem understanding that, and there are people today who have a similar problem. There are those who claim to be "born-again Christians." We are happy to hear anyone confess allegiance to Christ, but we wonder a bit about the use of the term "born again." The implication seems to be that there are two kinds of Christians, those who are born again and those who are not. Some say that to be a real Christian one must be able to point to an extraordinary emotional experience at some specific time and place; without such a "Damascus road decision for Christ" a person is not a Christian in the full sense of the word.

But in its true scriptural sense to be born again simply means to become a believer in Christ. Everyone who has been brought to faith in the Savior is thus a born-again Christian. To this spiritual rebirth we contribute as little as we did to our natural birth into this world. The Holy Spirit, and he alone, is the Lord and Giver of life. He regenerates spiritually dead sinners who cannot by their own reason or strength believe in Jesus Christ, their Lord, or come to him. It is not our decision for Christ but the Spirit's gracious and powerful working in our hearts that gives us a new birth.

How does the Holy Spirit accomplish this miracle of regeneration? Through the means of grace, the gospel in word and sacraments. For most of us our spiritual rebirth took place when we were baptized as babies. There we were born again of water and Spirit, called into the kingdom of grace, made children of God and heirs of heaven. We need not look for some other unique or spectacular experience. All of the wonderful promises of the triune God apply to us whom the Spirit has called to faith by the gospel, God's power for our salvation.

May we appreciate the Spirit's work, and may we continue to use the Spirit's means so that our faith may be nourished and sustained. The Spirit does indeed work where and when he pleases, but always and only through the means of grace. That means is readily available to us. It is as close as our Bible, as close as the church pew, the baptismal font and the communion rail. God's grace is there for us to enjoy in the gospel. May we come and get it.

O Holy Spirit, enter in and in our hearts thy work begin. Amen.

"Go, tell his disciples and Peter, 'He is going ahead of you into Galilee. There you will see him, just as he told you.' " (Mark 16:7)

BENEFITING FROM GOD'S PROMISES

It is incredible how all the people who deny the physical resurrection of Jesus disregard the many undeniable proofs of it. From the testimony of eyewitnesses to the silence of his enemies, evidence abounds to support the fact that Jesus returned to life.

Just as incredible is the way that Jesus' followers were shocked and surprised by his resurrection. Jesus had told them, right from the start, that he was going to rise again. They had the promise of Easter. Mary Magdalene had the promise—and assumed Jesus' body was stolen. The disciples had the promise—and locked their doors in fear. Thomas had the promise—and demanded to see and touch.

The promise was there for them, but they did not benefit from it because they did not accept it by faith. Even when the empty tomb demonstrated that the promise had been fulfilled, they were slow to believe. That's a mistake that should be easy for us to avoid. We can start with Easter. We know that God has fulfilled that promise for us already. We rejoice that Jesus has risen.

But let's not stop there. God promises to hear and answer the prayers of his people, and he never fails to keep that promise. So we are encouraged to come before the throne of grace often with our petitions and thanksgivings.

God promises to forgive all our sins. He has told us the death of Christ was full payment for all sins. He guaranteed this in Jesus' resurrection. Cast your guilt at Jesus' feet and draw on the grace of God for daily comfort.

God promises to look after us in this world. His angels watch over us. He sustains us in every suffering and makes all things work together for our good. Rely on him and his love no matter how dark the road or painful the trial.

All these promises have been fulfilled for us. But one remains, the promise of heaven. Don't wait for Jesus to return before you believe. Put your faith in him now for your promised eternal salvation. Enjoy the blessings of knowing that paradise waits for us before the promise is changed to fulfillment. Then you will daily know and experience the great changes that the empty tomb of Jesus has brought about.

As we believe your promises, O Lord, give us comfort, peace, and joy that will be perfected when you take us to yourself in heaven. Amen.

The kingdom of heaven is like a landowner who went out early in the morning to hire men to work in his vineyard. . . . About the third hour he went out and saw others standing in the marketplace doing nothing. . . . He went out again about the sixth hour and the ninth hour and did the same thing. About the eleventh hour he went out and found still others standing around. (Matthew 20:1,3,5,6)

CALLED AT DIFFERENT TIMES

Some years ago I sat at the bedside of an elderly man in the hospital. He had asked me to pray for him. I was very glad and thankful for his request. I was also amazed. A few weeks ago when I came into this same room to visit a fellow Christian, this man shook his head and said, "I don't want any part of that religious nonsense!" My visits continued, and thankfully the condition of our Christian friend in the bed next to this aged man improved. Although he didn't want to admit it, this often crotchety man listened to our devotions.

It was on the day that our friend was moved to another room that this man asked me to pray for him. The power of the Word had had its desired effect. Over the next weeks I had the privilege of sharing the rich blessings of God's Word and the great treasure of forgiveness with a now willing listener. On one bright afternoon the man confided, "I'm glad the Lord didn't give up on me. I'm so happy he called me even at this late date." Jesus had indeed been patiently knocking at the door of his heart and finally entered by the Spirit's power.

God calls his people into the kingdom at different times. For some of us it is early in our lives at the time of our baptism. For others it is during the young searching years of life. For still others, it comes at a time when all others have given up on the person, all others except God, that is. Think of the Apostle Paul. God called him to preach the gospel to the Gentiles. This calling amazed a lot of people, for Paul had been a zealous persecutor of the Lord's church.

Remember that God has set us aside for himself before the world began. He who numbers our days knows those who are his. Even though human reason cannot see hope for someone, God knows that hope will live in the hearts of those he calls—no matter how late in life. Thank God for his persistent grace! Keep sharing the message of that grace—even with those who at first say, "No."

Merciful Lord, let us never underestimate the power of your grace upon our lives. Let us never tire of sharing the message of your love through Jesus, even when we wonder if if does any good. Amen.

Then they worshiped him and returned to Jerusalem with great joy. (Luke 24:52)

JOY!

Like a golden stream, the theme of joy runs from one end of the Bible to the other. "You [O Lord] will fill me with joy in your presence," says the Psalmist David. "With joy you will draw water from the wells of salvation," writes the Prophet Isaiah. "You will rejoice," says Jesus, "and no one will take away your joy." "I am full of joy," declares the Apostle Paul.

We are also told that immediately following Jesus' ascension into heaven, the disciples "returned to Jerusalem with great joy." It would seem that they had little reason for joy, especially not for "great joy." Their Savior had just vanished from their sight. They would never see him again this side of eternity. They also knew that ahead of them lay persecution and even death. Jesus had told them to expect this. They knew that many would reject their message. On top of all that, they were returning to Jerusalem, the hotbed of opposition to Jesus and everything he stood for.

Yet they returned "with great joy." Why? There were many reasons. Although they no longer saw Jesus, they knew he was still with them. His returning to heaven was another instance of his keeping his word; he had said he would go there to prepare a place for them. And, in spite of all the problems they would face, Jesus had promised them their work would be successful. He had given them the astounding promise, "I tell you the truth, anyone who has faith in me will do what I have been doing. He will do even greater things than these, because I am going to the Father. And I will do whatever you ask in my name."

In this life we can be sure we will have our share of troubles. At the same time we can rejoice with the disciples—and for the same reasons. Jesus is with us, though we don't see him. He is preparing a place for us, and will bring us to himself someday. God's Word assures us that our work for him is never in vain.

The psalmist aptly described the joy of Christ's ascension, when he wrote long before the event: "God has ascended amid shouts of joy!" Long after the event we have every reason to live joyful lives. Our Savior, who has won our salvation, is now ruling over all things and using them for our eternal good. Let us do all within our power to share that joy with others!

Jesus, our ascended Lord, amid life's troubles keep us from losing sight of the lasting joy we have in you. Amen.

While he was blessing them, he left them and was taken up into heaven. (Luke 24:51)

"HE LEFT THEM"

"**H**e left them." These three little words sum up one of the most momentous moments in the history of our planet.

For thirty-three years Immanuel—"God with us"—had lived among us. Clothed in human flesh, the almighty, eternal God became our brother. The Apostle John describes how he and the other disciples "have heard, . . . have seen with our eyes . . . and our hands have touched" God incarnate, God in-the-flesh. Not only did he take on our flesh and blood, but Jesus Christ also took on our sorrows and our griefs. He became like us in all things, except that he was without sin. He, the innocent one, laid down his life for us the sinners.

Now we read that "he left them." Now the bringer of joy and life no longer walks among us. No longer can the sick feel the physical touch of his healing hand. No longer can his disciples hear his reassuring voice or see the forgiving look of love in his eyes.

"He left them." But notice that Luke does not say, "He deserted them." Far from it. It was not Christ's purpose merely to tease the world with a brief moment of heavenly light and love. He is visibly gone but has not left us alone. He has promised to send us the Holy Spirit, the Comforter. And Jesus has also promised his own unseen presence with the words, "Surely I am with you always."

"He left them." Some people have a sense of confidence from the fact that they do not see God. They think it means that God doesn't see them either, and so they can ignore God's commandments. This is wicked and foolish thinking. For even though Jesus has left the earth, he still sees everything that goes on here, including the very thoughts and desires of our hearts. Someday he will return to judge the world.

In the book of Acts Luke records how angels told the disciples, "This same Jesus, who has been taken from you into heaven, will come back in the same way you have seen him go."

"He left them." There's one more important truth here. When he left this world, Jesus did not leave his humanity behind. The almighty God is still our brother. He is preparing a place for us in heaven, that someday we may be with him. And he will never leave us.

O Savior, precious Savior, whom yet unseen we love, comfort us with the assurance that you are with us always. Hasten the day of your return, so that we may see you face to face. Amen.

And they stayed continually at the temple praising God. (Luke 24:53)

PRAISE GOD!

In the second chapter of his Gospel, St. Luke writes that when Jesus was born "a great company of the heavenly host appeared with the angel, praising God and saying, 'Glory to God in the highest. . . .' "

Today's Scripture passage is the closing verse of Luke's Gospel. A lot had happened in the thirty-three years since the angels praised God at the Savior's birth. Jesus had lived out his life on earth. He had completed his mission. He had suffered, died, risen again and ascended into heaven. And now, Luke tells us, it is the disciples of Jesus who are praising God. The angels knew the wonderful work that Jesus came to do; now the disciples knew it as an accomplished fact.

It is interesting that we find them praising God "at the temple." Jesus had told them to wait in Jerusalem until the Holy Spirit came to them. After he came, they were to go everywhere proclaiming the gospel. But for now they continually remained in the temple. This was where Jesus had taught when in Jerusalem, where he had chased out the merchants and the money-changers. Here he had been confronted by his enemies the Sadducees and Pharisees.

It must have felt strange for the disciples to return to the temple. As they watched the many sacrificial animals being offered there, they had to think of the supreme sacrifice for sin: Jesus' death on the cross. As they heard the Old Testament scriptures read, they could not but think of the fulfiller of all the prophecies. He had come and gone. As they thought about these things, the disciples could not but praise God.

According to one dictionary, to praise means "to commend the worth of." We can never say enough about the worth of Jesus and what he has done for us. He has done what all the world's gold and silver could not do—redeemed us from sin. He has done what all the world's wisdom and power cannot do—won for us eternal life.

May we follow the disciples' example. Let us live our lives for our ascended Lord and continually praise his name. At the right hand of God—that is, with almighty power—he rules over all creation. "Praise him for his acts of power," exalts the psalmist, "praise him for his surpassing greatness." Yes, yes, praise the Lord!

Oh, grant, dear Lord, this grace to me,
Recalling Thine ascension,
That I may ever walk with Thee,
Adorning Thy redemption.
And then, when all my days shall cease,
Let me depart in joy and peace,
In answer to my pleading. Amen.

At that time the king dom of heaven will be like ten virgins who took their lamps and went ou to meet the bridegroom. (Matthew 25:1)

EXPECTANT CHRISTIANS

Ten bridesmaids are waiting for a wedding reception to begin. Can you imagine a more carefree, excited group of people? The heavy responsibilities of preparing for the wedding went to someone else. All they had to do was stand there and look pretty. Now the serious part of the ceremony is over and the fun part is about to begin: to laugh and play and eat and drink, perhaps till the wee hours of the morning. These bridesmaids have everything to look forward to, whether the wedding takes place at the time of Christ, or in the twentieth century.

Jesus compares these excited bridesmaids to his disciples, the members of the holy Christian church on earth. They are looking forward to something far better than a wedding reception. They are looking forward to the glories of heaven.

Jesus has promised that he will return. "I am going there to prepare a place for you. And if I go and prepare a place for you, I will come back and take you to be with me that you also may be where I am." The Revelation of St. John describes heaven as a beautiful city with streets of gold so pure that it shines like glass, filled with light that proceeds from God himself, where saints and angels sing joyful praises to the Lamb who poured out his blood for their salvation.

That's what Christians are looking forward to. That's what you and I are looking forward to. And when we think about it like that, the prospect of our Lord's return is far more exciting than a wedding reception. For this is one celebration that's going to last forever!

At the same time Christians are not only looking forward. They're also looking backward, at the grief and misery that surrounds them in this world. Not only the unemployment and poverty and disease and death, but also man's inhumanity to man, the baby-killing, the child abuse, the broken marriages and broken minds and spirits that come from broken homes. And on top of all this an immorality that scorns the Christian sense of right and wrong, a value system that makes mockery of the treasures of salvation that God has given us. And the sorrow of seeing fellow Christians swept away by the mounting ungodliness, until we say, "If God does not shorten these days how shall even God's elect be saved?"

The bridesmaids waiting to get into the wedding reception are not nearly as eager to get in as Christians who are waiting for the return of their heavenly Bridegroom.

Come quickly, Lord Jesus, come quickly. Amen.

"Do not let your hearts be troubled. Trust in God; trust also in me." (John 14:1)

FACING THE FUTURE WITH FAITH

I t was going to be a night of doubt and despair for the Twelve. It was the night of Jesus' betrayal and trial and sentence of death. Before twenty-four hours had passed he would be crucified, dead and buried. They would wonder if they could still think of him as Savior, whether God was still their loving Father. They had been so secure in his company while he taught the multitudes and healed the sick and raised the dead. But before morning they would see him arrested and degraded.

To prepare them for that terrible experience which would tempt them to despair, Jesus said: "Trust in God; trust also in me." My Father can be trusted. He has always proved himself to be trustworthy. I can be trusted. Place your confidence in me and don't let panic rob your hearts of faith.

There are things in our future which we cannot foresee. But we know from the Word of God and from human experience that our lives can change so quickly. Today prosperous and secure, tomorrow unemployed. Today cheerful and content, tomorrow broken and weak. Today confident in the loving concern of our Savior, tomorrow wondering whether he still cares.

It is just that last condition that he wants to prevent by speaking these words of our text to his disciples and leaving them for us in the pages of Holy Scripture. "Do not let your hearts be troubled."

Don't leap to any false conclusions about me and my concern for you. I cared enough to join the human race when I could have just continued in my majesty forever. I suffered for the human race, suffered more than you will ever suffer. I did my Father's will and finished my Father's work. I carried out his plan for your salvation as your Representative before his bar of justice. He raised me again to demonstrate that his justice is satisfied and you are forgiven. See my hands and my side, my empty tomb. Can you doubt my good will?

"You trust in God; trust also in me." The important thing to concentrate on here is that he is strong and loving. We quickly find out how weak our faith is. But our God is strong. It is not that we are so good at trusting, but that he is trustworthy. Where shall we find confidence for the future? In his cross, his empty grave.

Who shall help us in the strife
Lest the Foe confound us?
Thou only, Lord, Thou only. Amen.

"In my Father's house are many rooms; if it were not so, I would have told you. I am going there to prepare a place for you." (John 14:2)

THERE IS A PLACE FOR YOU!

Have you ever felt "out of place"—perhaps at a party, in a new school or in a strange neighborhood? The feeling that you just don't belong is not a pleasant one, is it? But you don't feel "out of place" in your own home, do you? You know you belong there. And you don't feel out of place at your church, do you? You know you belong there, too. And today Jesus assures us that in heaven we will also feel right at home, for heaven is our Father's house, and there is a nice, cozy place for each of us there.

Heaven is our Father's house. Our loving Creator dwells there. Our loving Savior is also there. And the Spirit who sanctifies us is there. The holy angels who watch over us are there, and all of our loved ones who have fallen asleep in Christ are there.

Heaven is a large house. It has many rooms, Jesus says. He does not say exactly how many rooms our heavenly mansion has, but it must be very many. In the Revelation to St. John Jesus reveals that heaven is like a vast, holy city. He describes its dimensions as over 1,400 miles wide, by 1,400 miles long, by 1,400 miles high. That would mean that one side of this heavenly cube is equal to half the distance from New York to Los Angeles. If we estimate that each story of the city is fifteen feet high, the city would have 528 stories. Thus, the total square footage of heaven would be 1,188,000,000,000 square miles. If we would divide that by the total estimated population of the world since the beginning of time (about 30,000,000,000), that would leave 198 square miles for every family! Now, of course, this picture of the heavenly city is a symbolic picture not to be taken literally, but it does symbolize a heaven with plenty of room for everyone.

You may still think that you will feel out of place in heaven since it is a holy place occupied by the holy God, holy angels and holy saints. And you know very well that you are totally sinful. Won't you be out of place there? Not at all! Jesus went to Calvary to prepare a place in heaven for you. He paid for all your sin. Don't be afraid of moving in to your new heavenly home! God has declared you holy because of Jesus' perfect life, death and resurrection. Heaven is your home. There is a place for you there.

Precious Savior, thank you for preparing a room in heaven for me. Amen.

"Do not let your hearts be troubled. Trust in God ; trust also in me. In my Father's house are many rooms; if it were not so, I would have told you. I am going there to prepare a place for you. And if I go and prepare a place for you, I will come back and take you to be with me that you also may be where I am. (John 14:1-3)

CHRIST WILL COME AGAIN TO TAKE US HOME

The parable of the ten virgins points out that there was only distress and everlasting misery in store for the five who foolishly failed to have oil in their lamps. The bridegroom's sudden arrival caught them unprepared. Any last moment attempt to correct the past came too late. The door was shut. That was final. "Then they will go away to eternal punishment" (Matthew 25:46).

"The door was shut." That is a hard sentence. Does it apply to us? How dreadful if that were the case! The selfsame Bridegroom who shut the door to the foolish also said, "Come, you who are blessed by my Father; take your inheritance, the kingdom prepared for you since the creation of the world" (Matthew 25:34).

When we view our life in the light of God's holy commandments, we have reason to stand in dread of "the Great Day of the Lord." We have sinned and come short of the glory of God (Romans 3:27). We would despair if God's Word did not tell us, "Blessed is he whose transgressions are forgiven, whose sins are covered" (Psalm 32:1).

This is our comfort and joy. The Bridegroom, our Savior Jesus Christ, has completely covered our sins. Clothed in the garment of his righteousness we have nothing to fear. His promise goes far beyond our fondest hopes and dreams. Not only are we assured that God no longer sees our guilt, but our Savior also promises us a place in heaven with him! More than that. He tells us that he himself has prepared this place for us. And when our last hour shall come, when we walk through the valley of the shadow of death, we know that he will be at our side. His promise is: "I go and prepare a place for you; I will come back and take you to be with me that you also may be where I am." There is no greater promise than that!

Whatever tribulations the Christian may have to endure as a faithful witness of Christ here on earth, the promise of God removes all weeping and sighing, for "the Lamb at the center of the throne will be their shepherd; he will lead them to springs of living water. And God will wipe away every tear from their eyes" (Revelation 7:17).

Be Thou at my right hand,
Then can I never fail.
Uphold Thou me, and I shall stand;
Fight Thou, and I'll prevail. Amen.

Do not let your hearts be troubled. Trust in God; trust also in me. (John 14:1)

TRUST ME!

"**J**ust trust me! I know what I'm doing!" Tom's wife was afraid that his decision to change careers would only result in financial hardship and more unhappiness for the family. But Tom insisted that he knew what he was doing. If his family would just trust him!

We have often heard the same words from a family member when making a financial investment, choosing a travel route or making an important decision. Experience has shown that people may not always know what they are doing, but there is one who can always be trusted.

"Just trust me," is what Jesus said to his disciples in the Upper Room on the night before his crucifixion. Their hearts were deeply troubled that night. They were confused by Jesus' solemn announcement that he would suffer, die and rise again. They were frightened and disturbed by Jesus' declaration that he would soon go away and leave them. They were shaken by Jesus' disclosure that one of them would betray him. The future looked bleak. On what strange course was the Lord leading them? Was he doing the right thing? Would it only end in disaster for him—and them?

We can understand how they felt that night. There have been, there may be now, or someday there will be moments when we wonder: "Is he leading me in the right direction? Does he know what he is doing?" In those moments our Savior still speaks to our troubled hearts: "Just trust me!"

In contrast to the troubled disciples, Jesus was remarkably calm that evening. He was fully aware of the anguish and agony which would soon come upon him as he sacrificed his holy life in payment for all sin, but he was not thinking of himself. Loving them to the end, he told his anxious and worried disciples: "Continue trusting in God . . . and continue to trust in me." Even in the shadows of suffering and death there was no need to fear. He knew what he was doing. He was still in control. "Just trust," he said, "everything will turn out well."

This is still true. He is always in control. Our Lord knows what he is doing. Don't be afraid—just trust him!

I am trusting Thee, Lord Jesus;
Never let me fall.
I am trusting Thee forever
And for all. Amen.

VOLUME THREE

Comfort From

Meditations

For Such a Time as This

EPISTLES

NORTHWESTERN PUBLISHING HOUSE
Milwaukee, Wisconsin

CONTENTS

Through Suffering to Glory

The Wonderful Ways of God

A Matter of Death and Life

Children in God's Family

A Call to Prayer

The Disciple Looks to the Future

Divine Counsel for Troubled Christians

God's Grace in Our Lives

Living in Hope

Living in Confidence

EDITOR'S PREFACE

For Such a Time as This. The title of this three volume set of devotions comes from a thought that Mordecai brought to Queen Esther's attention during days of trial and tribulation for the Old Testament people of God. "For such a time as this," Mordecai suggested, God had placed Esther in a position of honor and influence so she could bring God's promised help to God's people (Esther 4:14).

For Such a Time as This. Days of trial and tribulation are no strangers to God's people today. Trials and troubles challenge us, spiritual enemies beset us, fiery trials scorch our faith, our own frailty and mortality frightens us, tragic losses mount, guilt plagues our consciences, personal problems put us on the verge of despair, and sometimes even daily life seems difficult and discouraging.

For Such a Time as This. In times such as these Christians of all ages have turned to God in prayer seeking his help, his promised deliverance, his comfort. They have turned to his Word to find what he has to say to them, and for the past thirty-three years *Meditations* has helped to lead Christians to that comfort of God's Word. Comfort in the fact that God knows who we are, where we are, what we are. Comfort in that God knows the story of our lives and has seen to it through Jesus Christ that it has a happy ending. Comfort in that Jesus has promised to guide us through every trouble, even through the valley of the shadow of death, until we safely stand with him at God's right hand.

For Such a Time as This. Now 300 of those messages of comfort have been selected for inclusion in these three volumes. Each volume contains 100 devotions based on texts chosen from the Gospels, the Epistles, and the Old Testament. Pastor Henry Paustian of Watertown, Wisconsin read through some 12,045 devotions and selected the best of these comfort meditations. Minor changes have been made in some of the original devotions to bring them into line with current procedures. All Scripture quotations and citations are from the NIV; capitalization and punctuation principles reflect current style; titles now are solely the themes of individual devotions instead of a weekly series.

For Such a time as This. Note that on the cover the letters "h-i-s" in the word **this** are printed in another color. That was done to remind all of us that no matter in what situation we may find ourselves, this is still **his,** God's time, that our lives and the events in our lives happen not by chance but under the providential direction of our Father in heaven. As the cover illustration further indicates, we are always safe in his hands.

May the reader find God's comfort in these devotions.

Lyle Albrecht

In this you greatly rejoice, though now for a little while you may have had to suffer grief in all kinds of trials. These have come so that your faith—of greater worth than gold, which perishes even though refined by fire—may be proved genuine and may result in praise, glory and honor when Jesus Christ is revealed. (1 Peter 1:6,7)

THANK GOD YOU'RE TESTED

A test involves pressure. Whether an engine, a structural beam or a person is being tested, the method is the same. Pressure or stress of some kind is applied to the object of the test. Without stress, the test wouldn't really be a test. Giving a second-grade math test to high school seniors wouldn't be a true test.

The purpose of all testing is the same, too. A test is meant to discover any weakness so that it can be corrected, so that the product (whatever it is) can be improved. If the object passes the test, of course, it has been proven to be genuine, the real thing. It is fit for its purpose.

Now we see why the Apostle Peter speaks so highly of trials in the Christian's life. They are all important tests of our faith, and they have wonderful results, because God's own purpose is behind them.

Even while we rejoice in our eternal inheritance, Peter says, we may be suffering grief in all kinds of trials. Sometimes the cross—suffering because of our confession of Christ. Sometimes the loss—of people or things dear to us. Some-times physical pain and weakness, or disappointment or another kind of trouble.

Difficult, yes! Distressing, yes! But thank God when you're tested! For it is your gracious God himself who tests your faith. He himself is in the test. He applies pressure to reveal and to correct any weakness. And if he brings you through the fire of affliction, it is not to harm you, but only to refine, to purify, to temper and to strengthen your faith.

"One Christian who has been tried," wrote Luther, "is worth a hundred who have not been tried, for the blessing of God grows in trials. . . . When faith is thus tried, all that is dross and false must pass off and drop away. Then will result a glorious reward, praise and commendation when Christ will be revealed."

It's great to be alive, even when you're being tested in the fire, for your loving God is purifying and proving your faith. He is refining and strengthening it for your eternal benefit. You can indeed thank God when you're tested and continue to "rejoice."

Lord Jesus, help me to rejoice even in my trials, and to come through every test with a stronger and better faith. Amen.

I consider that our present sufferings are not worth comparing with the glory that will be revealed in us. (Romans 8:18)

A WORD ABOUT SUFFERING

Suffering is a fact of life. It strikes young and old, rich and poor. Its root cause is sin. We all suffer from sicknesses and diseases because we live in a sinful world. Who could describe all the forms of physical, mental and spiritual suffering as they exist in our world today?

Thank God that in his suffering Servant he has given us an answer to suffering. Our Substitute suffered it all. He suffered trial, temptation, poverty, pain, sorrow, rejection and death. He was indeed a man who was familiar with suffering. Jesus suffered so that we would not have to suffer the eternal torments of hell.

That accomplished fact directly affects our view, as God's people, on suffering. By faith in Christ we know that God is our loving Father. In our Father's hand suffering is a tool by which he would draw us closer to himself, train us or give us an opportunity to witness to his undeserved love.

Many of us have experienced passing through a period of suffering. We learned from that experience that man's life truly does not consist in the amount of things he possesses. God's promises became even more valuable, and in that way he drew us closer to himself

We all experience the suffering which our Father sends into our lives as discipline. Scripture says, "God disciplines us for our good, that we may share in his holiness. No discipline seems pleasant at the time, but painful. Later on, however, it produces a harvest of righteousness and peace for those who have been trained by it."

Sometimes God permits suffering to come upon us so that by faithful patience and endurance we might witness to others. Seldom do we think of suffering as an opportunity, but often that's what it is.

In the middle of suffering we can at times lose perspective. Our word about life for today puts all suffering into perspective. When all is said and done, it isn't worth comparing with the heavenly glory and joy that awaits us. We have God's Word for that.

Should Thy mercy send me
Sorrow, toil and woe,
Or should pain attend me
On my path below,
Grant that I may never
Fail Thy hand to see;
Grant that I may ever
Cast my care on Thee. Amen.

To keep me from becoming conceited because of these surpassingly great revelations, there was given me a thorn in my flesh, a messenger of Satan, to torment me. (2 Corinthians 12:7)

A THORN IN THE FLESH

It's very difficult to look upon troubles and afflictions, sufferings and hardships—those unpleasant aspects of our lives—as being connected at all with God's grace. "Why is God doing this to me?" is the first question that comes to mind. "What am I being punished for? What wrong have I done?"

In the throes of suffering we are tempted to question the grace and mercy of God, even his fairness and justice. "How can this come from the hand of a loving Lord?"

Job searched for an answer to his sufferings. He could only come up with the same questions, until God revealed the truth.

That the Lord never withdraws his loving hand from his children and that we are always the objects of his gracious care are assurances of which we need to be reminded constantly. We draw such assurance from God's Word. "For the Lord will not reject his people; he will never forsake his inheritance." It is his promise, "Never will I leave you; never will I forsake you."

The Apostle Paul was given a thorn in his flesh—a particular kind of affliction. We don't know the exact nature of it, but it was something that troubled him considerably. He said it kept him from being conceited because of the great revelations he had received. He also described it as a messenger of Satan to torment him.

Can a messenger of Satan given to torment someone be consistent with God's loving care? Can it be a manifestation of his grace? Paul saw it as that, not because it was a reasonable way to look at it, but because his faith had grown to trust his Lord's concern for him in everything that happened to him. He knew God had a purpose, a good purpose for allowing him to suffer this affliction.

In that faith Paul could assert so positively, "We know that in all things God works for the good of those who love him, who have been called according to his purpose."

God deals with his children today no differently than he did with Paul. He has not made us immune to sufferings, to afflictions or trials, but we can be certain that those difficult times in our lives are not for our harm but come with the Lord's knowledge and will serve the good purpose he has in mind for us.

Gracious Lord, we trust your love in the good things you give us. Help us to see your love in adversity, too. Amen.

I consider that our present sufferings are not worth comparing with the glory that will be revealed in us. (Romans 8:18)

NO COMPARISON

Cancer! Heart-attack! Bankruptcy! What do these three seemingly unrelated items have in common? They all identify sufferings of one kind or another. We see these sufferings all around us. Friends, relatives and even we ourselves may have experienced them in our lives.

The Apostle Paul was well acquainted with sufferings. He tells us, "Five times I received from the Jews forty lashes minus one. Three times I was beaten with rods, once I was stoned, three times I was shipwrecked, I spent a night and a day in the open sea." Yet in spite of all these problems, Paul was not discouraged or fed up with life. He looked beyond his present situation to the glories which would be his in heaven. For Paul there was no comparison between his present suffering and his future glory. All the pain, grief and heartaches of this life were quickly replaced as Paul thought of sharing in Christ's glory in heaven.

Is our life much different from Paul's? We may suffer under different circumstances than Paul did. Nevertheless, suffering and grief in varying degrees have affected all of us. We cannot escape it in this life. The cause of all suffering, sin, is as much a part of our world today as it was of Paul's world. Ever since the fall of man into sin, suffering has been an ever present part of man's life. At times though it receives too much attention. We rob ourselves of the joy which is ours by faith in Christ.

While sin has brought suffering into this world, Christ has made us heirs of a glorious inheritance in heaven. Through faith we have become the children of God. Just preceding our verse St. Paul reminds us that "we are heirs—heirs of God and coheirs with Christ, if indeed we share in his sufferings in order that we may also share in his glory." To share in Christ's glory is beyond description. Everything that we consider beautiful and glorious today, is still infected with sin. How much more beautiful and glorious eternity is, we shall simply have to wait and see.

St. John described some of the beauty of that eternal glory when he wrote, "Never again will they hunger; never again will they thirst. The sun will not beat upon them, nor any scorching heat. . . . And God will wipe away every tear from their eyes." There's no comparison! As we endure the sufferings of this life, let us look forward to future glory in Christ.

O Lord, be with me in all the sufferings of this life that I may share in eternal glories with you. Amen.

In this you greatly rejoice, though now for a little while you may have had to suffer grief in all kinds of trials. These have come so that your faith . . . may be proved genuine and result in praise, glory and honor when Jesus Christ is revealed. (1 Peter 1:6,7)

STRENGTH IN TRIALS

When things are not going quite right, a bit of advice frequently handed out is to keep a stiff upper lip. The advice suggests that there are certain difficulties you can expect in life, and the only way to cope with them is to grit your teeth and make the best of it.

The Christian has a different view of life's difficulties. First of all, he understands their origin. They result from sin. All problems, all suffering, all sorrows, all difficulties, all misery, all frustrations have a common origin. They result from sin. Sin has contaminated the whole human race, and the believer also suffers from that contamination.

In addition, the Christian has another view of the difficulties he encounters in life. He knows that they are under God's control and that they are intended for his good. Granted, there are times when this is extremely hard to understand and accept. Yet the Bible stresses this again and again. God sends corrective measures into our lives, just as parents do with their children. Peter wrote to his readers that the trials which they were encountering had come "so that your faith . . . may be proved genuine and result in praise, glory and honor when Jesus Christ is revealed."

God's love for us is so great that he wants nothing to lure us from living and abiding in his saving grace. It is our trials in life, our problems, our tribulations which keep us from becoming too wrapped up in worldly affairs. If everything went along smoothly in life, if every day brought nothing but joy and pleasure, if every week and every month were nothing but one big pleasure trip, we would face the grave danger of becoming very attached to this world.

But we are strangers on this earth. Heaven is our home. The trials of life remind us of this. With the strength God provides, we can endure these trials. The resurrection of Jesus Christ from the dead is God's assurance that he will give us that strength. This is a very important part of our living Easter hope. How rich we are that God strengthens us in all the trials of life!

O Lord, grant us strength as we encounter the trials and difficulties of life. Help us realize that they serve our good and will continue only for a short season until we live with you in heaven. Amen.

For you were like sheep going astray, but now you have returned to the Shepherd and Overseer of your souls. (1 Peter 2:25)

WANDERERS AT HOME

The picture Peter portrays for us here is not as vivid for us as it must have been for his first readers. Most of us do not live in a farming community as many of our grandparents did. And even fewer of us have ever raised sheep.

Sheep have a terrible tendency to wander. It's not that they're so curious to find out what the rest of the world looks like. It's just that they tend to become so preoccupied with what they're doing that they don't pay any attention to where they are. If a sheep is grazing, he simply keeps his head down and goes from one good clump of grass to another. If he's not carefully watched, he will just keep walking and eating until he becomes hopelessly lost. Alone and helpless he is then choice prey for any wild animal.

That's exactly the way it is also for those who are not under the watchful eye and protecting staff of the Good Shepherd, Jesus. They simply wander around, go from one earthly pleasure to another and are unaware of any danger. They too are choice prey for the devil, who "prowls around like a roaring lion looking for someone to devour" (1 Peter 5:8).

We too were once in that situation, lost and helpless and in danger. But we are no longer. Through the life and death of Jesus Christ we have been brought back into the shelter of his protecting arms. Once again we have a Shepherd and Overseer for our souls. Gently he leads us toward our eternal home, always aware of our helpless condition.

In times of suffering how comforting it is to know that we're not alone. Jesus is still there to care for us and to guide everything so that it serves our welfare. Every day he leads us back from wandering and another step closer to our eternal home in heaven. With a shepherd such as this we are of all people truly blessed—even in sufferings.

Jesus, the Good Shepherd, lead me in the paths of righteousness and keep me in your protecting arms. Comfort me with your word and finally deliver me from all evil by taking me to be with you in heaven. Amen.

The creation waits in eager expectation for the sons of God to be revealed. But if we hope for what we do not yet have, we wait for it patiently. (Romans 8:19,25)

PATIENCE ON THE ROAD TO GLORY

In an age of "instant gratification" people find it hard to wait. But "wait patiently" is what Christians are told to do when they are burdened by trials and sufferings of all kinds.

God's whole creation has been crippled by the effects of sin. And Christians are not immune to these troubles. Even though we have become children of God through faith in Jesus, the redemption of our bodies is still unfulfilled. That means they continue to fall into sin. And they still experience disease and handicaps of all kinds. Sin and its consequences are evident in the life of every Christian.

But the promise of God is that a day is coming when also the physical world will be set free from the effects of sin. All creation "will be liberated from its bondage to decay and brought into the glorious freedom of the children of God." Our own bodies cry out for that day of redemption. So for now we must wait for these things. We wait in the knowledge that

God will most certainly keep the promises he has made.

Being patient in time of trouble will not take away the trouble. But as we wait in faith and hope, our attitude toward our trouble can change. We see the trouble as part of God's righteous judgment on a world of sin. We see it as temporary. We see it as something that will end when God completes the work of redemption that has already freed us from the guilt of our sins.

How patient are we while we wait? Patience is certainly not easy. Days and years of suffering go by very slowly. Sometimes the loss is so overwhelming we can hardly think about anything else. Who can be patient in such circumstances?

God's Word encourages us by comparing present sufferings with future glory. The more we concentrate on the glory, the more we will be able to endure the sufferings.

Be patient and await his leisure
In cheerful hope, with heart content
To take whate'er thy Father's pleasure
And his discerning love hath sent.

Dear Father, grant me patience while I wait for the glorious day when all my troubles will come to an end. Amen.

And the God of all grace, who called you to his eternal glory in Christ, after you have suffered a little while, will himself restore you and make you strong, firm and steadfast. (1 Peter 5:10)

THE WHOLESOME EFFECT OF SUFFERING

There is no end to what the ungodly will suffer in hell. And what they suffer here on earth is but a preview of their damnation. To us, who look to Christ for our salvation, however, the misery of this life is a preview of what we shall escape. For us it is a wholesome sorrow, by which God refines our faith and preserves our hope.

No matter what may befall us here, our God is still "the God of all grace, who called you to his eternal glory in Christ." He is still with us. He still feeds, shelters and protects us. He still forgives our sins and assures us of our eternal inheritance.

Knowing that we have a Father in heaven, what do we have to fear on earth? Since God is for us, who can oppose us? Even if the thorns of Satan tear at our flesh and inflict the worst physical pain and mental anguish, we know that they cannot touch our soul. Nothing can sever us from the love and promises of Christ.

Even if it were our lot to writhe on a bed of pain for a thousand years, we still would be able to shout victoriously with Paul, "Who shall separate us from the love of Christ? Shall trouble or hardship or persecution or famine or nakedness or danger or sword? As it is written: 'For your sake we face death all day long; we are considered as sheep to be slaughtered. No, in all these things we are more than conquerors through him who loved us. For I am convinced that neither death nor life, neither angels nor demons, neither the present nor the future, nor any powers, neither height nor depth, nor anything else in all creation, will be able to separate us from the love of God that is in Christ Jesus our Lord.' " (Romans 8:35-39).

God is merciful and kind. He will not let us suffer beyond our ability. But he does let suffering come when it is for our good. Like a loving, faithful father,he chastises us in order to rid us of our foolishness and to save us from disaster. In a marvelous way, he uses those same sorrows (which give the ungodly a foretaste of hell) in order to perfect, establish, strengthen and settle us on our way to eternal glory.

Dear Lord Jesus, do not let us despair when suffering comes, but cause it to perfect our faith and to strengthen our hope in you. Amen.

Don't be deceived, my dear brothers. Every good and perfect gift is from above, coming down from the Father of the heavenly lights, who does not change like shifting shadows. (James 1:16,17)

LOOK TO THE SOURCE OF YOUR BLESSINGS!

James wrote his letter to the church at a time when persecution was her close companion. So his words are immediately fresh and powerful and apply to every Christian of every time in every place. For when has Satan ever gone to sleep or ceased to voice his hatred for the Body of Christ and its members? Or when has the world, which is in bondage to Satan, ever stopped opposing the church and the gospel? Our enemies may change their tactics from generation to generation, but not their purpose.

As a man who knew the meaning of persecution and temptation, James was equipped to rally our courage and to cheer us. "Consider it pure joy," he said, "whenever you face trials of many kinds, because you know that the testing of your faith develops perseverance. Perseverance must finish its work so that you may be mature and complete, not lacking anything"; and "blessed is the man who perseveres under trial, because when he has stood the test, he will receive the victor's crown of life that God has promised to those who love him" (James 1:2-4,12).

So in his opening chapter James not only lifts our thoughts up and away from our present suffering, but he also bids them to dwell on the crown of glory awaiting us in heaven and on the one who has prepared it for us. In one short statement he recalls both the love and the great power of the God we worship. He is the "Father of lights"—the source of every good and perfect gift. He is our Creator, who separated the light from the darkness and has promised that, as surely as the sun will rise on schedule, he will continue to provide for our earthly needs. He is our Redeemer, Jesus Christ, who came as the very Light of the World to free us from death, hell and the "prince of darkness." He is the Holy Spirit, who has illuminated our hearts with the light of the gospel and has given us the sure hope of eternal life.

So let the trials come! Let the devil roar. Let him open his jaws and gape at us. Let the whole world disapprove of us and vent their displeasure. These are things which James and all of the apostles teach us we can expect here as members of the Body of Christ. But these are things which even add to our joy; for they are evidence that we are not the children of this world, but the children of a heavenly Father and the heirs of every good and perfect gift.

Dear Father in heaven, continue to bless us, for Jesus' sake. Amen.

Now if we are children, then we are heirs—heirs of God and co-heirs with Christ, if indeed we share in his sufferings in order that we may also share in his glory. (Romans 8:17)

THROUGH SUFFERING TO GLORY

With one bold stroke of his pen, the inspired Apostle Paul summarizes our new relationship with God in Christ. Eloquently he leads us through an understanding of our present status and carries us to the very gates of heaven.

The Holy Spirit has graciously called us to believe the Gospel of Christ. Through that saving Word he enlightens us, purifies us and preserves our faith in him. Therefore, according to that same Word, we are rightly called the "children" of God. But who can fathom all that this implies! Even the wise and aged John had to pause in amazement at the thought and declared "How great is the love the Father has lavished on us, that we should be called children of God (1 John 3:1).

"And if we are children, then we are heirs," Paul continues, "heirs of God and co-heirs with Christ." We, who were at one time no people at all, now have the unspeakable honor of being called the people of God. By our sins we deserved to inherit the whirlwind of his wrath. But now we possess the promise of an inheritance which makes the wealthiest man on earth look like a wretched beggar by comparison. For Jesus' sake, we have become heirs of eternal life. All who believe in him will never die.

"If indeed we share in his sufferings in order that we may also share in his glory," Paul concludes. It is impossible to escape suffering in this hostile world. Christ suffered here, and so will we. "A student is not above his teacher, nor a servant above his master" (Matthew 10:24). Paul makes it clear: no suffering, no glory.

But "our present sufferings are not worth comparing with the glory that will be revealed in us" (Romans 8:18). Who of us can imagine the glories of heaven! "However, as it is written: 'No eye has seen, no ear has heard, no mind has conceived what God has prepared for those who love him' " (1 Corinthians 2:9). With our eyes of flesh we look around us and see nothing but temptations, disease, death and decay. With our ears of flesh we hear about wars, earthquakes, fires and floods. But with our eyes and ears of faith we hear of God's mercy and forgiveness in Christ and look forward to the glory which shall be revealed in us.

O Holy Spirit, give us the strength to bear whatever suffering comes our way, and refresh us through the blessed hope of eternal life; for Jesus' sake. Amen.

How unsearchable his judgments, and his paths beyond tracing out!
(Romans 11:33)

WHEN MY FOOLISH HEART ASKS WHY

How many people don't approach life in the same way that Beethoven departed it—shaking his fist at the sky! They complain that life isn't fair. They look for someone to blame and inevitably point at God. They consider the constant threat or presence of war, famine, natural disaster and human injustice; and they conclude that either there is no God or that he is a harsh and unreasonable tyrant. Even we, who are Christians, are often tempted to complain and to ask why: "Why must I, a faithful member of the church, suffer with cancer?" "Why did my husband have to die, while so many immoral men go on living?" "Why was our child born with a handicap?"

The world cannot produce a satisfactory answer. And where the Bible gives us an answer, the children of men refuse to accept it. We all know the temptation to doubt that God's purposes are good, for we are all made of the same flesh. And our natural mind of flesh is opposed to God and his word. Besides this, Satan is continually at our backs and whispering, "Yea, hath God said? Does God really mean it when he says that he loves you? Why, look at all you are suffering! Do you really think God means to bring something good out of this?"

When thoughts like this come to us, let us recognize them as the lies of Satan. God has already given us all the answers we need in his holy Word. So we can turn and say: "Satan, get out of here! My God has never promised me a perfect life of bliss on this earth. And when suffering comes my way, it is only further evidence of his truth and love. He is teaching me not to fall in love with this world and drawing me closer to himself and to his promises in Christ. And even if I am about to die, you cannot touch me. For my Redeemer lives, and he will raise me from the dead again and give me eternal life.

"I cannot say exactly why or how all the events of my life fit into God's overall plan. But that is none of my business. For 'My thoughts are not your thoughts, neither are your ways my ways, declares the Lord' (Isaiah 55:8). 'Our God is in heaven; he does whatever pleases him' (Psalm 115:3). And that is good enough for me. For I know that he was pleased to send me a Savior from sin. And 'He who did not spare his own Son, but gave him up for us all—how will he not also, along with him, graciously give us all things?' " (Romans 8:32)

When my foolish heart asks why, quiet me with your words, "Be still, and know that I am God." Amen.

Who has been his counselor? (Romans 11:34)

SOME GOOD ADVICE

Downcast and dejected, the man stepped into the counselor's office. "What seems to be the trouble?" the counselor asked. "I don't know exactly. All I know is that I'm not happy. Is there anything you can suggest to help me?" The counselor looked at the man for a moment and then he said, "I hear a famous comedian is in town playing to a packed house every evening. They say people come away from his performance holding their sides from laughing so hard. Why don't you go to his performance tonight and forget your troubles?" The man looked down at the floor for a moment, and then he said, "Sir, I am that comedian."

That counselor's advice was as wrong and foolish as the kind of advice people sometimes like to give God. Some would like to advise God that he doesn't really understand human nature and the times in which we live when he forbids marital unfaithfulness, perversion and fornication. They suggest that God's words are impractical and out of date. They would like to tell God that sin isn't as serious as he has said it is, and that the punishment for sin surely shouldn't be something as severe as eternal punishment in hell. God ought to relax his standards today, they insist.

Then, too, they would like to advise God that he has made the way to heaven too restrictive. Anyone who is sincere and honest and tries to do what is right ought to be able to go to heaven, they feel. "Can't we be considered Christians without believing everything the Bible says?" they ask. "How important is belief in the Bible's account of creation or the virgin birth or the resurrection from the dead?" As ridiculous as it sounds, they suppose that they can counsel almighty God!

But that's turning things completely around. It is God who is our Counselor. On the night of his betrayal Jesus promised to send his disciples another Counselor who would be with them forever. That Counselor is the Holy Spirit, who advises and counsels us by means of the Scriptures. He informs us that our sins are many, that they are serious, and that they indeed deserve eternal punishment. But he also assures us that God has declared us righteous for the sake of the innocent sufferings and death of the Savior. He comforts us with the knowledge that God will make everything in life serve a good purpose for us and that he will take us to heaven. That is good counsel—the kind of counsel that the comedian needed too!

Lord, help me always to listen attentively to the counsel of your holy Word. Amen.

Oh, the depth of the riches of the wisdom and knowledge of God! (Romans 11:33)

THE FATHER KNOWS BEST

"**M**y daddy knows everything!" At least that's what I thought at age five. He could fix anything, make everything right. He had answers for all my questions. I don't think Dad grew stupid while I got smart; but at fifteen I was no longer sure that father knew best. At twenty-five, though, I was ready to go back to him for advice.

Likewise the Christian with a childlike faith knows that his heavenly Father knows best. It is the spiritual adolescent who questions God's wisdom and knowledge. But Christians, matured by Scripture and experience, recover that childlike awe, and with St. Paul they marvel, "Oh, the depth of the riches of the wisdom and knowledge of God!"

How far God's wisdom and knowledge are above our own! The current arguments and ideas of men may sound good. They claim to offer quick and easy answers to life's problems, immediate gratification for human desires, simplified explanations for the events and purposes of life. So we look around us in this world. We see something that we like and immediately think that it must be good for us—simply because we like it. God, on the other hand, is able to see far beyond our likes and dislikes. And, like a good father, he permits his children to receive only that which is best for them in the end, whether for the moment they like it or not. Patience discovers the wisdom of God and exposes the folly of men.

Only on the Sixth Day could the perfect wisdom of God be seen in his Creation. Only on Easter could the perfect wisdom of God be seen in his plan of salvation. Only in eternity will we fully see what the wisdom of God has accomplished in the life and world through which he now leads us. Until then we will find comfort and joy only in trusting the answers he has already worked out for our good; and by praising him for his vast and hidden wisdom.

Yes, God knows everything. That means he also knows us. God knows our sins and weaknesses. Long before we were born, he foresaw our predicament and determined in love to send us a Savior from sin. And that Savior is Jesus Christ, the good Shepherd, who laid down his life for the sheep, and who said of us before we were born, "My sheep listen to my voice; I know them, and they follow me. I give them eternal life" (John 10:27,28).

Dear Lord and Savior, teach us to trust in you alone and to depend on your wisdom and judgment. Amen.

Humble yourselves, therefore, under God's mighty hand, that he may lift you up in due time. (1 Peter 5:6)

GOD'S TIME IS THE BEST TIME

We all have days, even weeks and months, when everything in life seems to be going our way. But then suddenly, altogether unexpectedly, everything shifts into reverse. One day the sun is shining brightly; the next day all is dark and overcast. One week we are actively carrying out our responsibilities; the next week we are lying helpless on a hospital bed. Every day the world turns over on someone who has just been sitting on top of it.

Where is there a Christian who has not had this kind of an experience? Where is there a Christian who has never asked: "If God can let suffering and sorrow come that quickly into my life, why won't he remove it just as quickly?"

Often people deeply resent it when suffering or sorrow disrupt their blissful plans. They grow bitter and cynical and consider the temptation to curse God and die. But God has given us a powerful weapon against these temptations in the Scriptures. In our devotional text the Apostle Peter gives a special word of encouragement.

God is the Lord. He rules his creation with a "mighty hand." So doesn't he know what he is doing when he lets suffering come? And doesn't he also know when it is best to remove it? "Humble yourselves, therefore, under God's mighty hand," Peter writes, "that he may lift you up in due time."

When we pray to God in our time of need, we may do so with confidence, knowing that the God who sent his Son to die for us certainly will also hear and answer our prayers. Sometimes the answer may be yes; sometimes it may be no. Most often, experience has taught us, the answer is "Wait!"

God's ways certainly are not our ways. Nor is his time our time. And how long his "due time" usually seems to linger! But our comfort lies in the fact that it is his time—a time not established by our nearsighted emotions, but by his far-reaching wisdom.

Someone once said there are two ways to open a flower bud. You can force the petals apart (and, in doing so, destroy the flower), or you can leave it alone until God slowly, but surely, unfolds it. By ranting and complaining we can hinder our own blessings. But by patiently depending on Christ and his mercy, we will never be disappointed. "Humble yourselves, therefore, under God's mighty hand, that he may lift you up in due time."

Help us, O Lord, patiently to bear all things; for Jesus sake. Amen.

They passed the first and second guards and came to the iron gate leading to the city. It opened for them by itself, and they went through it. When they had walked the length of one street, suddenly the angel left him. Then Peter came to himself and said, "Now I know without a doubt that the Lord sent his angel and rescued me from Herod's clutches and from everything the Jewish people were anticipating." (Acts 12:10,11)

GOD'S MASTER PLAN

When we look ahead, life is a blur. Even as we experience it, life is usually out of focus. But when we look back, we often see life with 20-20 vision.

This is what Peter discovered when the angel left him. Sitting in prison, Peter had placed his life in the Lord's hands without really knowing what would happen. Even while he was participating in the escape, he was only dimly conscious of what was going on. But once outside the prison, after the angel had left him, he could see one thing clearly in all that happened: the Lord's hand.

Peter's observation also holds true for the rest of the early church. When Jesus ascended to heaven, the disciples knew that Jesus had commissioned them to bring the gospel to all lands. But they had no idea how it would happen. Now Peter could look back and see a pattern in all that happened. Pentecost, the preaching of the gospel to the Gentiles, even persecution itself—all was directed by the Lord as part of his master plan.

Christians may look back on all of history and clearly see the guiding hand of the Lord. In his first recorded sermon, the Apostle Paul emphasized that God directed the affairs of Israel to make possible the coming of the Savior. We also observe that it was no accident that the mighty Caesar Augustus issued the taxation decree. As a result, prophecy was fulfilled, and the Savior was born in Bethlehem. It was no accident that the persecutions sent the Christians from the city of Jerusalem. As a result they carried the saving gospel with them to people far away.

All Christians can look back on life and see the Lord's guiding hand. God has arranged lives to bring Christians to faith and to strengthen them in it. The chance acquaintance and the passing event may have seemed of no importance at the time. Years later the Christian sees how the Lord arranged them for the believer's eternal welfare. Only heaven itself will reveal how carefully the Lord has guided us along the way.

Help me in life and death, O God,
Help me through Jesus' dying blood;
Help me as thou hast helped me. Amen.

For the eyes of the Lord are on the righteous and his ears are attentive to their prayer, but the face of the Lord is against those who do evil. (1 Peter 3:1,2)

HE WATCHES OVER US

The heathen do not expend any effort to bring up their children in God's ways. They have no reservations about flying in the face of God's Commandments. And they not only "get by" with it but even earn the respect of many people. There almost appears to be a rule that the wicked will prosper and the righteous suffer.

Are not these thoughts similar to what must have gone through Job's mind? Within a short time, everything went wrong for him. He lost his holdings to bands of thieves. His children died in a storm. His wife blamed and rejected him. False friends increased his misery by suggesting that God was punishing him for some evil deed.

Why do the righteous suffer? God tells us that it is according to his will, and that he will not abandon us in our suffering. He did not merely plan some distant salvation for us and then leave us to grope our way through life alone. He has also promised to protect and to care for us in spite of our suffering, even while we are in the midst of it. And that is good enough for us!

We cannot see God. He is a spirit. His being and his ways are beyond our comprehension. When Job began to wonder why God lets the righteous suffer, God taught him a valuable lesson. He said, "Can you really understand my ways, Job? Where were you when I laid the foundation of the world ? Where were you when I made the ox and measured out the first crocodile?" and Job answered, "I know that you can do all things" (Job 42:2). Job conceded to the will and wisdom of God.

The Lord, our God, can do all things. In loving kindness he keeps watch over us night and day. He hears and sees everything that our enemies try to do against us. If anyone harms us, his ear is quick to catch our faintest sigh. "For the eyes of the Lord are over the righteous, and his ears are open to their prayers."

Should we then be concerned when we see that the wicked prosper here on earth? Let God himself give the answer on the day of judgment. In the long run, evil will receive its reward. Our God is still in heaven, and his "face . . . is against those who do evil." But we can live in cheerful confidence. For we have learned to know him as our gracious God and Redeemer, who watches over us and answers our prayers. Let us follow him.

Lord God, remind us of your watchful presence and refresh us on our way through this valley of tears till we reach our home at last. Amen.

Who has known the mind of the Lord? Or who has been his counselor? (Romans 11:34)

RELY ON GOD'S PERFECT WISDOM

"**G**od doesn't know what he's doing." When things do not happen the way we think they should, we are tempted to question God's ways. "Why, God?" We angrily demand that he explain himself and show us the justice of his actions. "Why do you permit so much evil and violence? How can you let so many babies be murdered before birth? Why did you let my parent become an alcoholic? Why did you let my sister get hooked on drugs? Why did you give me an unfaithful spouse? Why am I sick? God, you messed up again!"

Shall we blame God? Blame him for what? Incompetence, impotence or a lack of love and compassion? Perhaps God needs us to tell him how to run this universe. Our advice would soon straighten out this mess! If only we were in charge.

Oh, really? But what kind of counselors would we be? We are so selfish, so vengeful, so merciless and unforgiving.

For example, our Lord does not desire the "death of the wicked, but rather that they turn from their ways and live." Yet how often do we who have experienced this love still "damn" something or somebody? That curse slips out so easily, so thoughtlessly. What if God would take our advice when we damn our trick knee or when we damn our neighbor for whom Christ died, too?

Thank God he doesn't rely on our confused and self-centered counsel! How dare we challenge the all-knowing, all-wise and almighty Lord God? How dare we make him accountable to us?

We can trust the wisdom of the One who devised and executed salvation. He is our ever-faithful Savior-God, who assures us that nothing happens to us by chance. Our Lord also promises us that it is his unfailing love that controls all things in order to bless us. His perfect wisdom can even overrule sin and Satan, so that they must serve God's purposes. Even our cry, "Why, God?" will become a blessing for us if it drives us to his Word.

And if God chooses to veil the specific "why" of his actions, then let us humbly bow before his perfect wisdom, steadfastly relying on his eternal love. For how can we doubt our merciful Savior who gave his life to redeem us?

Precious Lord, who can understand why you would die to save us wretched sinners? Strengthen our faith greatly, so we trust your wisdom, not only for salvation but for all things. Amen.

Not many of you were wise by human standards; not many were influential; not many were of noble birth. (1 Corinthians 1:26)

WHO'S WHO—BEFORE GOD

"**W**hy, Lord, why?" That was the question the lady on the phone asked. She had just received news that her sister-in-law and two children had died. A train/car accident took their lives at an unmarked crossing.

The ever-recurring question is, "Why?" Just ask any parent. But other people ask it too. A Christian might ask, "Why me, Lord?" when considering the Lord's call to follow him in humble faith.

In the daily course of life, people are chosen for special favors because of who they are or what they have made of themselves or whom they know. One wouldn't expect to see the president of the United States standing at the end of a long line at the bank or supermarket. Authority, power and birth mean something before men.

Human reason might presume that God calls people to be members of his family of believers for the same reasons. But Paul reminded the Corinthian Christians that God's way of doing things is not comparable to man's. Few among them could lay claim to great wisdom, superior posi-tions of authority or favored birth in noble families. Yet they were members of the family of believers.

Everything depends on God's grace. "It is by grace you have been saved, through faith—and this not from yourselves, it is the gift of God —not by works, so that no one can boast" (Ephesians 2:8,9).

God's undeserved love presented Jesus as Savior to a world lost in sin. God's undeserved love brought Jesus from the dead on that third day. God's undeserved love called us through his word to be members of his family through faith in Jesus Christ.

God's undeserved love moves him daily to keep us physically and spir-itually as his children. And finally God's undeserved love for us will cause him to take our hand and walk with us through the doorway of death into the glory of our eternal home. Truly, by the grace of God alone, I am what I am—his child, an heir of his eternal heaven.

Forbid it, Lord, that I should boast
Save in the death of Christ, my God;
All the vain things that charm me most,
I sacrifice them to his blood.

Were the whole realm of nature mine
That were a tribute far too small;
Love so amazing, so divine,
Demands my soul, my life, my all. Amen.

And you also were included in Christ when you heard the word of truth, the gospel of your salvation. (Ephesians 1:13)

IF ONLY I HAD A STRONGER FAITH

"**I**f only I had a faith like his!" People are often heard to make such a remark. But in admiring the faith of a fellow Christian, we dare not overlook the fact that we, too, have been greatly blessed by God. We, too, are a part of Christ's church. As Luther reminds us, "Jesus did not die only for Peter and Paul but also for you." And in the inspired words of St. Paul, "You also—as an individual—were included in Christ."

What an honor it is to be numbered along with great men and women of faith, people like Abraham, Paul, Peter, James, John and Mary! Yes, Christ's peace is also for you. You were "included in Christ."

Remember the Lord's life on earth. How often he left the crowds to heal or speak to one single person. On Calvary he not only prayed that the entire throng be forgiven their sinful, ignorant actions, but Jesus also assured an individual sinner, "Today you will be with me in paradise." After his resurrection Jesus appeared to the eleven disciples at once and to over 500 believers at one time. But he also met personally with Mary Magdalene.

At your baptism the triune God entered a covenant with you alone. Jesus was born, suffered, died and rose for you as an individual, just as much as for the entire race of mankind. God's peace was planned and performed for you. God's peace was performed to give you strength in every conflict with sin. God's peace is promised to you through "the word of truth, the gospel of your salvation." God's peace is given to you to comfort you in the midst of the many sorrows in life.

Yes, we may admire other Christians and look up to the Bible's heroes and heroines of faith. But let's not forget we have the same Savior and the same word of truth. May each of us grow in that word.

And may God's peace ever dwell in your heart and cause you to overflow with joy.

Chief of sinners though I be,
Jesus shed his blood for me;
Died that I might live on high,
Lived that I might never die.
As the branch is to the vine,
I am His, and He is mine. Amen.

We know that in all things God works for the good of those who love him, who have been called according to his purpose. (Romans 8:28)

GOD HAS A PLAN

At the beginning of the automobile assembly line an ugly piece of metal is forcefully attached to another piece of equally unattractive steel. A process begins. To a person who has never seen the finished product this scene might be viewed as a disastrous waste of time, material and machinery. But those who have seen the end of the assembly line know the final result, a brand new car. From this vantage point the beginning of the process makes sense.

More than 13,000 parts go into a car. Each has its specific place. If the auto worker attaches the wrong part, or forgets a part, or does a poor job of attaching it, the quality of the car is impaired. Maybe it won't run at all. Therefore each assembly-line worker must carefully follow his instructions to every minute detail.

In his eternal counsels God has prepared a blueprint for each one of us. "Called according to his purpose" means that our lives fit into his master plan. Right now the assembly line of our lives is in progress. The master planner is closely watching that assembly and is making sure that everything fits together perfectly piece by piece and step by step.

The assembly line of our lives does not end until we cross the threshold of heaven. The finished product is a life, totally perfected in every way, of eternal happiness. By faith we know what that finished product will be, even though our eyes have never seen it. As St. Paul says, "We live by faith, not by sight."

What a comfort to know that God has a plan for our lives and that we "have been called according to his purpose." With that understanding it is much easier to accept our troubles and bear with our tears. They are part of God's marvelous plan for us. We can't see the finished product now, but we know that it will be perfect and beautiful.

The remarkable thing is that God accomplishes his plan for us in spite of our sins. We often get in the way with our stubborn will and self-chosen deeds. It's only by grace that we are among those who love him and desire to have his plan fulfilled for our lives.

O Lord, help my faith to accept your plan for my life and not to stand in its way by my sins. I pray in my Redeemer's name. Amen.

And he died for all, that those who live should no longer live for themselves but for him who died for them and was raised again. (2 Corinthians 5:15)

A NEW VIEW OF DEATH

What is death? Most definitions view death as an end, the end of life, the end of biological functions, when it's all over and done.

Christ our Savior died and changed our view of death. He didn't change the scientific or physical nature of death, but the spiritual aspect of death has been radically changed. The original cause of death was removed when Christ died. And because he died for all, death has been conquered for all.

Dying started when sin entered the world, and since sin passes from one generation to the next, so does dying. Christ came and broke this deadly cycle. When he died, he took everyone's place and experienced once and for all that death which is sin's just punishment. He carried the sins of the world and paid for them by dying, not only physically, but by suffering all the wrath of a holy God against sin. That's what has changed everything and has given us a brand new life and a new view of death.

The old and natural view of death is that it is an awful and dreadful experience. Before Jesus conquered death for us, it hung over our heads as a menacing reality. Worst of all, it brought to mind the problem of finding ourselves face to face with God, whom we had offended in so many ways.

Now we have a new view of death. It still is frightening to us even though it has been conquered, but now we know that when we die, we aren't being punished. The death of Christ took care of that kind of death for us. Now we can see death as the way to a new life. Our death, thanks to the death and resurrection of Christ, is nothing more than a sleep from which we will awaken totally refreshed and glorified to live in the eternal mansions which Jesus went to prepare for us.

When Christ died, he rose again and so did we. We died with him as far as sin is concerned; when we were baptized, we were buried with him, and we also rose with him to a new life. Now we don't live to ourselves. Why should I live to myself? What have I ever done or what could I ever do to deserve being the center of my life? But Jesus did far more than we could ever have hoped or imagined. He conquered sin, death and hell for us. Let's live for him!

Jesus, thank you for conquering death for me. I will live for you. Amen.

While they were stoning him, Stephen prayed, "Lord Jesus, receive my spirit." (Acts 7:59)

UNAFRAID OF DEATH

Are we afraid to die? Many people are. We might think that something as important and as certain as death would be thought of and prepared for by everybody. But that is not the case. Many people live their lives trying to forget about death. They put off thinking about death until it stares them in the face.

Stephen wasn't afraid to die. He boldly testified in front of his enemies even though he could see that it was working them up into a murderous rage. Stephen did not carelessly put his life in danger, but he certainly was not going to deny his Savior to save it.

Stephen did not see death as the end of all things but rather as a deliverance, a gateway to heaven and eternal life. On Stephen's lips was also the same confession that the Apostle Paul made, "We are confident, I say, and would prefer to be away from the body and at home with the Lord" (2 Corinthians 5:8). Although death may have caused temporary separation from his fellow Christians on earth, it meant an eternal reunion with his Lord and Savior whom he loved.

This bold disciple was certain of eternal life because he died in the name of the Lord Jesus. Death could not hold Jesus who paid for Stephen's sins, so it would not be able to triumph over him either. The great Apostle Paul mocked the power of death. "Where, O death, is your victory? Where, O death, is your sting? . . . But thanks be to God! He gives us the victory through our Lord Jesus Christ" (1 Corinthians 15:55,57).

Stephen faced death as fearlessly as he faced his enemies. The Lord Jesus had not deserted him in this life. He would not desert him in death either. Meeting his death confident of the Lord's deliverance was the last great triumph of Stephen's faith here on this earth.

We do not have to fear dying any more than Stephen or Paul did. Our Savior has destroyed the fear of death. We are told in the verse following today's text that Stephen fell asleep. That doesn't sound very fearful, does it? Our death also will be a sleep from which our Savior can easily awaken us.

We trust in Jesus as our Savior from sin. Let us also be confident that he will grant us deliverance from death. Believe his promise, "I am the resurrection and the life. He who believes in me will live, even though he dies" (John 11:25).

Lord Jesus, remove all fear of death from me. Help me to see in death a deliverance from this world to be with you forever. Amen.

And if we die, we die to the Lord. (Romans 14:8)

DEATH—THE BEGINNING OF A WHOLE NEW LIFE

Paul's statement, "And if we die, we die to the Lord," like his statement, "If we live, we live to the Lord," expresses an expectation. A Christian is expected to die to the Lord.

But what does that mean, to die to the Lord? It means, first of all, recognizing that the time and place of your dying is not in your hands. That is something which must be left entirely in the hands of the Lord Jesus. The thought, "It's my life, and I can end it if I want," is not the attitude of one seeking to please the Lord.

Dying to the Lord also means willingly accepting the Lord's final summons to leave this world. Dying to the Lord means commending your soul into his care when he calls you from this life. Dying to the Lord means confidently looking forward to being with the Lord forever in the eternal bliss of heaven.

Rather than shrinking away from this expectation stated by Paul, pray God that you are among those of whom it can be said, "They died to the Lord."

Death is the final door through which everyone must pass before entering eternity. For some that door represents the absolute end to everything, beyond which there is nothing. For others, passing through that door is a cause for fear, because it leads to the unknown or because it leads to judgment and condemnation.

Through the example of his resurrection the Lord Jesus demonstrated that death is not the absolute end. Rather it is the beginning of a whole new existence. Through his saving work the Lord Jesus has made it possible for Christians to face the final judgment confident of God's reward rather than his punishment.

Christ Jesus has told his followers that for them the life to come will be a blessed and happy existence. The Lord Jesus has made it possible for believers to face death without fear. To use St. Paul's words, Jesus has made it possible "to die to the Lord."

Blessed are those who die to the Lord! Lord Jesus, strengthen our faith so that we are among them.

With peace and joy I now depart;
God's child I am with all my heart.
I thank thee, death, thou leadest me
To that true life where I would be.
So cleansed by Christ, I fear not death.
Lord Jesus, strengthen Thou my faith. Amen.

While they were stoning him, Stephen prayed, "Lord Jesus, receive my spirit." (Acts 7:59)

FAITHFUL TO THE END

"**W**hy? Why did he have to die? He was such a faithful follower of Jesus. He actively served the Lord and was sorely needed by the early church. Why did the Lord take him so soon?"

The questions are familiar to many of us. I'm sure they were familiar to the earliest Christians. When Stephen was stoned to death, he was a highly respected church member. But why did he have to die in such a way and at what appeared to be the prime of his life? The answer is simply: it was God's will. The death of Stephen has remained one of the finest examples of being faithful to the end, and many a Christian has been strengthened by Stephen's example. When he was being murdered, he did not curse the name of Jesus, nor did he voice the question, "Why must I die now, Lord?" Rather, it is written that with his last ounce of courage and faith Stephen confidently prayed: "Lord Jesus, receive my spirit." There was no doubt in his mind. Jesus was his Savior from sin, death and hell.

What an example Stephen is for us! He was faithful to the end. He accepted God's will as good. Even though in this life the will of God occasionally seems hard to understand, we too can continue to find the peace and hope that Stephen found. It is a peace and hope which moved him and can move us to pray at our last hour: "Lord Jesus, receive my spirit."

If you know of someone who is dying, share with him the story of Stephen, for through it God the Holy Spirit offers peace and courage, strength and conviction—offers that same hope of eternal glory which Stephen had in Christ.

Oh, for a faith that will not shrink
Tho' pressed by many a foe;
That will not tremble on the brink
Of poverty or woe;

A faith that keeps the narrow way
Till life's last spark is fled
And with a pure and heavenly ray
Lights up the dying bed.

Lord, give us such a faith as this;
And then, whate'er may come,
We'll taste e'en now the hallowed bliss
Of an eternal home. Amen.

I thank my God every time I remember you. In all my prayers for all of you, I always pray with joy because of your partnership in the gospel from the first day until now, being confident of this, that he who began a good work in you will carry it on to completion until the day of Christ Jesus. (Philippians 1:3-6)

WILL I BE A CHRISTIAN WHEN I DIE?

This question frequently suggests itself to those who realize the value of their Christian faith. They've read the warnings in the Bible not to fall from faith. They've tasted the sweetness of sure forgiveness, love and hope which faith possesses. They've memorized the passages which remind them that "by grace are ye saved, through faith . . ." and they know that "without faith it is impossible to please him (God)."

How can I know if I will still have my Christian faith when that last test of death comes my way? Parents sometimes ask about their children, "How can I know that our children, rooted in the Word of God, will remain anchored in it when they leave our home?" Can anyone be sure that he will remain a Christian until his dying day?

If we didn't have Paul's reminder to the Philippians and other emphatic statements of the Scriptures, we might answer, "No one can be sure." If we had to depend upon our own self-discipline, determination and strength of character to keep ourselves in the Christian faith, we'd have to answer, "I don't know if I will stay a Christian."

But we have a more sure foundation for our hope than our self-service efforts. Paul points us to our only source of confidence, "He who began a good work in you." God has called Christians to the faith they possess. God created the Gospel fellowship Paul joyfully recalls. God equipped the Philippian Christians for their faithfulness "from the first day until now." Later in this letter Paul reminds the Philippians that it is "God who works in you to will and to act according to his good purpose" (2:13). And what is that good purpose? That we believe his Gospel and have eternal life! God is going to keep us in the Christian faith. How long?

He "will perform it (the good work of faith which he began) until the day of Jesus Christ." God will not fail nor break his promise. "Faith comes from hearing the message, and the message is heard through the word of Christ." Faith is preserved by that same Word through the power of God. We "are shielded by God's power until the coming of the salvation that is ready to be revealed in the last time" (1 Peter 1:5).

O Father, draw me close to Jesus. Keep me close to him in faith, throughout all the storms of life, through death, forever in him. Amen.

For we know, brothers loved by God, that he has chosen you because our gospel came to you not simply with words, but also with power, with the Holy Spirit and with deep conviction. (1 Thessalonians 1:4,5)

HOW CAN YOU BE SO SURE

" **J**erry, you're sure that you're gong to heaven after you die," the young welder said to his friend across the lunch table. "That's neat! But how can you be so sure? I mean, how can anyone be sure that God has chosen them for heaven?" Paul wrote to the congregation in Thessalonica, "We know that he has chosen you." The obvious question they might have asked was, "How can you be sure?" Paul and his co-workers didn't have God's throne room bugged. They didn't receive golden tablets from an angel with the names of these Christians on them. Yet they could speak with authority and say, "We know."

Paul and the other missionaries based their statement, not on a dream or feelings they had about these people, but on facts that were readily observable. The gospel came to these people "not simply with words" but "with power." The Thessalonians didn't treat the gospel like a fable. They received it as "the power of God for the salvation of everyone who believes" and as the "words of eternal life." The gospel of Jesus Christ changed their lives. They were never the same after they heard it.

Along with the gospel came the Holy Ghost with his gifts of love, joy, peace, patience and kindness. These trademarks of the Holy Spirit were evident in these people. The "deep conviction" these Christians displayed in the face of persecution indicated to the missionaries that they were elect of God. Paul knew that where there was Christian faith, love and hope, there were God's chosen ones. Most of all, Paul was confident that the preaching of the gospel would not be without its effect. For God had promised through the Prophet Isaiah, "My word will not return to me empty, but will accomplish what I desire and achieve the purpose for which I sent it."

If we have one of those days when nothing seems to go right, or if our doctor schedules us for our second major surgery in less than six months, we may not feel very chosen. But thank God, being chosen isn't a matter of feeling. God has verified that he has forgiven us and opened heaven through Christ. That's a fact. The powerful effect that message has had upon our hearts and lives is clearly visible. "The Spirit himself testifies with our spirit that we are God's children."

Holy Spirit, teach me to stop searching for the certainty of salvation within me but rather in my crucified Savior. Amen.

We believe that Jesus died and rose again and so we believe that God will bring with Jesus those who have fallen asleep in him. (1 Thessalonians 4:14)

OUR BLESSED HOPE

In a world that is filled with all sorts of doubts about death and what happens to the body after death, it is understandable that hopelessness and insecurity will mark people's attitudes toward the deaths of those dear to them. God's people will not be unaffected by these attitudes of a world lost in sin.

But if "we believe that Jesus died and rose again," then there is no reason to grieve over our deceased loved ones as those without hope. Thus Paul encouraged the Thessalonians that they might conquer their grief born out of the hopeless views of an unbelieving world. It is the same faith that needs to be firmly established in us to help us bear our grief when death strikes.

To experience hope in the midst of grief, believe in the living Jesus. When Jesus' good friend Lazarus died and his sisters were grief-stricken, Jesus turned their attention to himself. "Your brother will rise again. . . . I am the resurrection and the life. He who believes in me will live, even though he dies; and whoever lives and believes in me will never die."

Anticipate the resurrection when the cloud of death hovers overhead. That is something the Thessalonians did not do, and it's something even Jesus' disciples did not do. One would think the disciples would have been waiting at the grave of Jesus on Easter Sunday for him to come out. Instead they went into hiding when they heard the grave was empty. Though Jesus had told them he would spend no more than three days in the grave and though they had visible proof in the resurrection miracles, the disciples were despondent and without hope in the moment of Jesus' death because they did not anticipate the blessed hope of the resurrection.

Next time we stand at the coffin of a loved one or contemplate our own death, let us not forget our blessed hope. We know most assuredly that those who die in Jesus, God will raise from the dead. And he will bring their souls together with their risen bodies to enjoy the happiness of heaven forever. May our sorrowing hearts be uplifted in this blessed hope!

Lord Jesus, my resurrected Savior, teach me to anticipate with the hope of faith the glorious resurrection of all those who live and die in you. Amen.

He had James, the brother of John, put to death with the sword. (Acts 12:2)

A DEATH THAT BEFITS A CHRISTIAN

How do you want to die? In your sleep? Perhaps you've never thought about it.

Few people would choose to die as James did—beheaded by an executioner. It was not that he had done anything wrong. He was not a criminal. King Herod merely wanted to make a show of killing a Christian to please the people. James was arrested and executed. Thus one of Jesus' closest disciples became the first apostle to suffer martyrdom—to die for his faith. He drank his cup of suffering.

Yet we could wish that all people could die as James did, not in the sense of being executed, but in the sense of being faithful to Christ till death. No amount of tears could change the fact that James died a blessed death. For his death merely opened the door to eternal life in heaven. His death boldly proclaimed to the world that Christians have something worth living for and worth dying for. Death has no hold on Christians. Christ has removed death's sting.

We pray that God would also give us a blessed end. That has nothing to do with the type of death, whether natural, or accidental or violent (though it is certainly proper to pray for a peaceful type of death). Rather we want to have a blessed end in the same sense that James did. We want to approach death with a firm faith in Christ as our Savior. We want the assurance that death will be the entrance to heaven. We want to know that no sin can condemn us, for Christ has suffered for all our sins. Because he lives, we shall live forever with him.

We also pray that our end may be blessed in the sense of it being a bold confession of our faith. As James willingly bowed to the executioner's sword rather than deny Christ, so we pray we may bravely accept whatever end God has in store for us. If others would see us going to our grave complaining, that would not speak well of our faith. But if others see us praising God and voicing our confidence in the eternal life awaiting us, they will be witnessing one of the strongest Christian testimonies we could give.

We don't have to die a martyr's death to have a blessed end. Every Christian who dies believing in Christ as his Savior and confessing his faith in whatever ways are available has just as blessed an end as James. May God give us all such a death.

Lord, keep my faith growing, so I may die as befits a Christian. Amen.

For to me, to live is Christ and to die is gain. (Philippians 1:21)

WITH THE LORD IN LIFE AND DEATH

For me to live is Jesus,
To die is gain for me;
Then, whensoe'er he pleases,
I meet death willingly.

Meet death willingly? Yes. The hymnist could do it. St. Paul could do it. So can we. How? Isn't death something to be feared? Not when we know that death has lost its victory and sting. Not when we know that the Lord has paid for our sins with his death on the cross. Death must no longer be feared, for on the other side of death's door lies the gift of eternal life in heaven for every child of God.

What a glorious place heaven will be! Scripture tells us that in heaven we will personally be with our Savior. We will be his people. God himself will be with us. He will wipe every tear from our eyes. There will be no more death or mourning or crying or pain. The old order of things will have passed away. No wonder St. Paul refers to death as a "gain" for himself in today's text. Forever with the Lord—that is the glorious hope every child of God may have.

But St. Paul could also proclaim, "For to me, to live is Christ." Paul is simply stating that all his living activity is centered in Christ and that Christ controls his life on this earth. The will of the Lord directed Paul's thoughts, words and deeds in this life. St. Paul was totally dedicated to his Savior. By the power of the Holy Spirit Paul was with the Lord, and the Lord was with Paul in life and death.

Will we not also want to be with the Savior in life and in death? Absolutely! Think of his love for us. We have broken God's holy law, but Jesus kept it perfectly in our stead. He credits our account with his perfect holiness. The punishment we deserved for breaking God's law— Jesus has suffered that too in our stead. He died on the cross to pay for our sins. We have not deserved it, but out of the love of his heart he has given us the hope of eternal life in heaven. What love we will want to give our Savior in return! We will want him to guide, control and direct our life on this earth and our life with him in heaven. By the power the Holy Spirit alone can give, we with St. Paul proclaim, "For to me, to live is Christ and to die is gain!"

Take my will and make it thine,
It shall be no longer mine;
Take my heart, it is thine own,
It shall be thy royal throne.
Take my love, my Lord, I pour
At thy feet its treasure-store;
Take myself, and I will be
Ever, only, all, for thee. Amen.

As it is written: "For your sake we face death all day long." (Romans 8:36)

LIVE FOR HIM UNTIL HE CALLS US HOME

She was well along in years. No longer was she able to leave her room or her bed without assistance. Often she felt totally useless. "What am I still good for? Why does the Lord want me to live in this helplessness?"

This is a common feeling among the shut-ins and elderly. They prefer to leave this world as soon as possible. Sometimes they feel resentful toward God himself for still letting them live. What good can their lives bring to them or anyone else? They feel they are a burden on others.

In Paul's time it wasn't so much the fear of old age and the nearness of death for which he counseled the Christians in Rome; it was death by persecution. "We face death all day long." Paul's willingness to suffer all, even death, came because there was another who had done the same for him. In fact, Paul knew the truth that the same man who gave his life for him did so for everyone. This made Paul, who knew how undeserving he was, humbly take on the responsibility of becoming a missionary for the cause of this unselfish man.

The man, of course, was Jesus Christ, the Son of God and the Son of man. Paul's sinfulness could not be put aside by anything he did, but Jesus proved by his resurrection from the dead that he had conquered sin, death and the devil. Jesus substituted his righteousness for the unrighteousness of Paul and all sinners.

The joy of receiving this free gift of salvation set Paul to the task of preaching the message of salvation through Jesus Christ. When we realize Paul's willingness to give even his life for the sake of spreading the good news, it brings shame on those of us who grumble and complain about the situation today.

The shut-ins and elderly who don't know for what reason God has kept them alive must count their blessings under God and realize their purpose as his children. They can smile, for God is with them. They can thank God for food and warmth. They can pray every day thanking God for every gift, asking for his mercy upon them and others and interceding for others who have needs. Their kindness, patience and love—all fruits of faith in their Savior-God—can be a good example to many.

Yes, God has a purpose for all of us here on earth, until he wills to bring us home.

Lord, still use us for heaven's sake. Amen.

How great is the love the Father has lavished on us, that we should be called the children of God! And that is what we are! (1 John 3:1)

REMEMBER—YOU ARE GOD'S OWN

Have you ever considered how unusual the love of God for us sinners is? In the original language of the Bible the expression translated "how great" suggests the thought of being foreign. God's love for us sinners is so unusual that we might say it is foreign to our way of thinking and acting.

We would never have thought of, much less carried out, the idea of freeing guilty people by paying the cost of their guilt and then receiving them into our own household. But this is what God has done for us.

The fact that we are sons and daughters in God's family is not something to be taken for granted. It is a gracious gift from God, and it ought to fill our hearts and minds with wonder. Just think of it. God calls us son or daughter! He is calling us his very own.

Of course, it would be one thing to be called a son or a daughter and then have the facts reveal that what we are called and what we actually are happen to be two different things. For example, people may call you a "tightwad" when in reality you are quite generous. On the other hand when God calls us "children," that is exactly what we are. God doesn't give us an empty title. His Word is truth. It always means what it says and says what it means. So when God says we are his "children," he really means it.

The reason this is so hard to believe is because this is not natural to us. We are by nature corrupt and sinful, enemies of God. Only by his grace have we been renewed. God doesn't just talk about this; he takes action! His love moves him to action. He "lavishes" his love on us by making us his people.

What a wonderful way to begin each day! What a wonderful way to close each day! I am God's own. He made me his own and he keeps me as his own.

Dear Lord, we stand in awe of your love for us. It is too wonderful for us to comprehend, but we praise and thank you for it. Strengthen us in the confidence and the comfort of knowing that we are your people. Help us also to act like we are yours. Bless our lives as our effective witness to the power of your love and grace. Amen.

But you received the Spirit of sonship. And by him we cry, "Abba, Father."(Romans 8:15)

CHILDREN IN A LOVING RELATIONSHIP

It starts with the first "ma-ma, da-da." It grows into messages like "Hi, Mom! Hi, Dad!" It is a relationship of love between parents and children. The simple words bring a feeling of joy and warmth to the hearts of mothers and fathers everywhere. By voicing them, children show that they regard their parents as friends, not foes, as partners in the process of living and not adversaries.

It takes work to build up that kind of spirit in a human family. Trust and confidence, acceptance and forgiveness must be mutually exchanged. That is not to say that parents shouldn't be parents. For the benefit of all, there must be order and authority. There must be a head of the family who finalizes decisions. And children know that. They need it and want it.

God's children in his spiritual family of faith recognize that also. They know that God is still God. To us, he is not just a "spiritual pal." He is still in control; his will is still the last word. He is deserving of honor and respect to the utmost degree.

But there is a relationship of love between us and our heavenly Father which pervades our entire being. He is the one who chose to make us his children through his Spirit. He is the one who took action to adopt us into his family. He is the one who sent our Redeemer to give us the robe of righteousness. He is the one who stands at the gate eager to welcome us prodigals back home.

Is it any wonder that we delight in calling him by that familiar, but meaningful term "Father"? In that loving relationship is embodied some marvelous blessings and privileges.

First, there is the privilege of talking with him as a true friend. Every day, in every circumstance, we can place our hand in his through prayer. We can place upon him our perplexity, our problems, our sorrow, our woe and our worry.

Then there is peaceful confidence. It is the trust that our Father will not give us a stone when what we really need is bread. It is the serenity that comes from knowing that he makes all things—yes, all—work for our benefit.

Finally, there is his abiding presence; we are never out of his care or concern. We are never at a loss for someone stronger or wiser. He is our Father.

Keep me, Father, as your dear child, now and forever. Amen.

We share in his sufferings in order that we may also share in his glory. (Romans 8:17)

CHILDREN FOR AN ETERNITY OF GLORY

Children have remarkable impatience. "How much farther, Dad?" "How much longer, Mom?" "Can we do it right away?" All are common childhood questions. It's only as we get older that we realize time goes fast enough as it is. "Don't wish your life away" is the oft-voiced advice from the older generation to the younger.

In a sense, we children of God never really grow up. We also are numbered among those who just can't wait. We live in eager anticipation of what is to come in eternity. Right now our existence is all tied up in the progressive ploddings of everyday life, much as school children bear the Monday to Friday schedule in anticipation of the coming weekend.

It is not so much unhappiness with the present situation that keeps us going as it is the anticipation for the future. In fact, it is the expectation, no, the certainty of a better future which makes the present bearable.

Children of God certainly have happy, joyful and satisfying moments in this earthly life. The enjoyment of God's gracious blessings in family and friends, possessions and activities is pleasing to them. But they don't last. They change, rust and disappear. Even on the brightest day, there is always a gray cloud. The weekend is always followed by Monday morning.

Yet we know the time is coming when things are not only going to get better; they are going to become perfect. And they are going to stay that way. There will be a fullness of joy, without any trouble spot to diminish it. There will be happiness forever, without any passage of time to detract from it. There will be radiant, glorious bodies and souls, without any tears or tribulations to trouble them.

For the child of God, the prospect of an eternity of glory shared with our Savior is the light at the end of the tunnel. Our Spirit-wrought faith has so united us with Christ that we share everything: the blessings of his redemptive work, the cross of suffering in this world—but as the ultimate—the glory which he already enjoys.

Pretty hard to wait for that, isn't it? Pretty difficult to be patient when it seems so long and so far. But it's just that remarkable impatience which marks us as CHILDREN IN GOD'S FAMILY.

Lord, give me patience, both to deal with the sorrows of this life and to wait for the day of sorrowless glory. Amen.

Our citizenship is in heaven. (Philippians 3:20)

CHILDREN OF GOD—CITIZENS OF HEAVEN

"Citizens of heaven" is more than a pious phrase that has a pleasing sound. It is descriptive of the great honor which God is pleased to bestow on us for Jesus' sake. Citizenship in Israel was highly prized in Old Testament times. Roman citizenship was highly prized in New Testament times. American citizenship is highly prized in our day. But how can we ever begin to compare any of these with citizenship in heaven?

The kingdoms of this world come to an end. They are constantly vulnerable. Citizens of this world have to switch allegiance as their rulers and governments change. Earthly citizenship is never sure, and its eventual loss is inevitable. But the citizen of heaven belongs to a kingdom that will never end and never change. It stands firm and sure, for Jesus is defending it and those in it. The citizen of heaven will not have his citizenship taken from him, nor will his citizenship end when he dies. He has an "inheritance that can never perish, spoil or fade—kept in heaven" (1 Peter 1:4).

The heart of the blessing of citizenship in heaven is that its citizens are the redeemed people of God. They are the people to whom God has granted his mercy in Jesus Christ. They are people who have been delivered from the condemnation and destruction which will belong to the enemies of God. Rather than being separated from God as foreigners and strangers, because of Christ we have become fellow citizens with the saints and members of his family.

We ought to prize our citizenship highly. It is not something man can achieve or merit by his own efforts, but it is a citizenship awarded by the grace of God. We are citizens of heaven because Jesus won a place for us there by his atoning death on the cross. He sealed our citizenship in heaven by his resurrection from the dead. And he ascended into heaven to prepare a place for us there.

Through the gospel invitation the Holy Spirit led us to believe these wonderful truths concerning Christ. By the powerful promises of God in the Scriptures, we are assured that we belong to Christ and that heaven belongs to us. Men may steal our earthly life. But no one, no, nothing, can separate us from the love of God in Christ or deprive us of our citizenship in heaven.

We thank you, O Lord, that you have called us into your kingdom of grace and mercy. We rejoice that you have forgiven our sins and written our names in the Book of Life. Amen.

Our citizenship is in heaven. (Philippians 3:20)

CHILDREN OF GOD—LOOK FORWARD

During his lifetime Abraham lived in tents and led his herds across Canaan. He had no permanent home, nor did he own any land except for the family burial plot. He was a stranger, a foreigner, in the land in which he lived. Nevertheless, God promised him that one day his descendants would call the whole land of Canaan their possession and their home.

Citizens of heaven are also strangers and outsiders in this world. Here we have no lasting home. Indeed, we are warned not to make too much of the things of this world nor to set our hearts upon them. For we have been promised an inheritance far richer and better than anything in this world. As believers in Christ and citizens of heaven, we will have a new heaven and a new earth for our home. We walk now on streets of earth or of stone, but then we shall walk on streets of gold through gates of pearl in the Paradise of God.

We look forward to our homecoming. Each day here brings us one day closer to it. Still we have to be on our guard. For each day also threatens to overwhelm us with its cares and temptations. But we are not alone. Our Lord Jesus is present with us in his word and sacraments. He assures and reassures us that our sins have been forgiven, that we are the children of God, and that our names have been written in the Book of Life. Each day we can turn to his word for strength and encouragement. Each day through that word he leads our thoughts heavenward and shows us how we are to live as citizens of heaven.

Without the word of God we would soon become discouraged and lose our way. But with its message in our hearts, we are encouraged to look forward and to sing:

My walk is heavenward all the way;
Await, my soul, the morrow,
When thou shalt find release for aye
From all thy sin and sorrow.
All worldly pomp, begone!
To heaven I now press on.
For all the world I would not stay;
My walk is heavenward all the way.

Bless the days of our lives, O Lord, that each day may indeed bring us closer to heaven. Forgive us our sins, and guide us on our way. Help us to appreciate the fact of our heavenly citizenship and to rejoice in your salvation. Amen.

Brothers, think of what you were when you were called. (1 Corinthians 1:26)

CHILDREN OF GOD—REJOICE!

The past can bring to mind sorrows or joys. The painful memories of immorality, materialism and idolatry brought sorrow to the minds of Christians in Corinth as they remembered the way they were. They realized how far they were from what God wants his people to be. Like sheep that had gone astray, they were once helplessly and hopelessly lost in the depths of sin. What a sorrowful state to be in!

Their reminiscing was to be also the source of rejoicing. For Paul reminded them that they were "called." That brings to mind the amazing grace of God, who calls people to be his own. That call is even more wondrous when one realizes that God has called people who aren't worthy of his call. God "has saved us and called us to a holy life—not because of anything we have done but because of his own purpose and grace [which] was given us in Christ Jesus" (2 Timothy 1:9).

Our membership in God's family depends on his action for us and in us as the Holy Spirit touches our hearts through the word. God alone stands at center stage with the spotlight shining on his grace revealed brilliantly at the cross of Christ. Remembering what we are in the light of what we were brings joy in Christ to the hearts of God's people. With rejoicing God's people confess that "Jesus Christ . . . has redeemed me, a lost and condemned creature, purchased and won me from all sins, from death and from the power of the devil, not with gold or silver, but with his holy, precious blood and with his innocent suffering and death."

We were "made alive with Christ even when we were dead in transgressions" (Ephesians 2:5). Indeed, we are special people by the grace of God, who loves us with an everlasting love.

All that I was, my sin, my guilt,
My death was all mine own;
All that I am I owe to thee,
My gracious God, alone.
Thy Word first made me feel my sin,
It taught me to believe;
Then, in believing, peace I found,
And now I live, I live!

All that I am, e'en here on earth,
All that I hope to be,
When Jesus comes and glory dawns,
I owe it, Lord, to Thee. Amen.

How great is the love the Father has lavished on us, that we should be called children of God! (1 John 3:1)

CHILDREN OF GOD—LOVED BY THE FATHER

A teacher once asked her pupils what was most amazing about God. A child responded, "He knows all about me, and yet he still loves me." Indeed, God's love for us is amazing. He does know all about us. He knows about our defying his commandments, our failing to carry out his will, our unloving thoughts and unkind words. He knows we deserve nothing but his wrath. Yet, he still loves us. He loves us so much that he was willing to send his Son to die for our sins.

In our text, John tells us that the Father has lavished his love on us. God loves us very dearly. In fact, we could say that his love for us is so vast that we cannot even begin to measure it.

The fact that we are God's children tells us that God has lavished his love on us. We do not deserve to be God's children. We forfeited this privilege because of our sins. Yet God in his love for us satisfied his justice. He made us acceptable to himself. He brought us to faith in Jesus. Through faith we possess Christ's righteousness. We stand before God acceptable to him through his Son. We are God's sons and daughters. We will inherit the heavenly kingdom our Father has prepared for us.

What a comfort it is to know God loves us. There are times when our conscience condemns us. We recognize our sinfulness and wonder how God can let us into heaven. When problems arise, we may feel God doesn't care about us anymore. At times such as these we need to look beyond our feelings and reason. By faith we lay hold of the words and promises of God. It is not how we feel about God that gives us comfort. The fact that God loves us gives us hope.

"How great is the love the Father has lavished on us, that we should be called children of God!" What a joy it is to bask in the radiance of these words. We are sinners, it is true. We deserve nothing but God's wrath. Yet, God loves us. Christ paid for our sins. We are God's children. Heaven is ours. This is a fact. Thank God for that!

Was it for crimes that I had done
He groaned upon the tree?
Amazing pity, grace unknown,
And love beyond degree!

God made him who had no sin to be sin for us, so that in him we might become the righteousness of God. (2 Corinthians 5:21)

CHILDREN OF GOD—SAINTS

Jesus had no sin. He was born without sin and he lived without sin. When he was put on trial, he was declared innocent of all charges by Pontius Pilate. God the Father also had declared him to be innocent when he said from heaven: "This is my Son whom I love, whom I have chosen; with him I am well pleased."

For us, God made him to be sin. He charged the sins of all mankind against Jesus. He suffered the curse of sin and endured its just punishment. This is one part of the great exchange. God took the guilt of all the world and laid it on his own sinless Son.

The other part of this great exchange is that the perfect holiness of Jesus is ours by faith. In Christ we have a new and perfect righteousness. It is a holiness just as genuine as the sinless life of Christ. It is a holiness which God himself accepts as perfect; after all, it comes from him. We are saints. That's what God has made us, and that's how God treats us because of what Jesus has done.

The righteousness that is ours by faith in Christ is complete. It doesn't need additives or any final touches. It's not like instant coffee or soup where you need to add water. It's compared in the Bible to a garment that's already sewn and ready to wear. By faith we put it on and we appear before God looking beautifully and impeccably dressed.

Let's remember this when we feel depressed. This perfect righteousness takes away our guilt and our fears. It takes away our tendencies to look at ourselves as mere faces lost in the crowd, run-of-the-mill human beings. We're saints. God made us holy; God treats us as though we had never sinned. That makes our life a brand new life in Christ.

The more we can see ourselves as God sees us, the more we will grow in our own personal holiness as well. I'm a child of God, a saint. I'm not going to follow any and everyone who invites me or encourages me to play in the garbage of sin. My brand new, sparkling white robe of righteousness in Christ makes me want to stay far away from the dirt.

Jesus, thy blood and righteousness
My beauty are, my glorious dress;
Midst flaming worlds, in these arrayed,
With joy shall I lift up my head. Amen.

The Spirit himself testifies with our spirit that we are God's children. (Romans 8:16)

CHILDREN WITH PERFECT SECURITY

Have you ever been in a group where you felt you really didn't belong? Not just because you shouldn't have been there, but because you just didn't feel part of the group? Because everyone else knew one another and you were the stranger? Because you had nothing in common with the rest of the crowd? Uncomfortable, uneasy, uncertain, unsure?

Sometimes we are also more than a bit uncertain about our relationship within the family of God. The devil uses our doubts and our worries, our sins and our weaknesses, to lead us to ask, "Do I really belong? Am I really one of God's children? Is he really my loving, caring heavenly Father? Or am I just deluding myself into thinking that all is well?"

So much of what we do and say in our everyday lives is tied up in those emotions we call our "feelings." And in normal conditions, our feelings can well be a barometer of what's going on inside of us. We may accurately read the signs of the party crowd around us, and then say, "I feel I'm not really wanted; I don't really belong."

It would be easy to make the mistake of carrying over this emphasis on feelings into our spiritual lives. We could get the impression that you must "feel saved" in order to be saved. Oh, yes, at the high points of our Christian lives, maybe Christmas or Easter, we feel pretty faith-filled. But all too often our faith is weak, questions are unanswered, doubts prevail, not-so-notable sins plague the conscience, and our spirit fades and fails. We feel, "Am I really wanted? Do I really belong to God's family?"

God's children, however, have a vital and eternally true assurance. It comes not from within us, but from outside of us. It is not based on how we feel, but on how God feels; his Spirit speaks to us in a thousand places in the written Word. Over and over again he says: "You may feel unlovable, but I love you. You may feel you are an outcast, but I have adopted you to be my child."

It is just when we have those weak and failing feelings that we are invited to come back to him through his Word. To perk up your spirit, let his Spirit speak. You'll be blessed with the perfect security of knowing, "I really belong."

O Lord, give me your Spirit so that by your Word of promise I may trust that I am truly one of your children. Amen.

And you also are among those who are called to belong to Jesus Christ. (Romans 1:6)

CHILDREN OF GOD—WANTED BY THE FATHER

Some of you may remember those words jumping out at you during World War II from a poster. Our government, caricatured in the figure of Uncle Sam, pointed a demanding finger in our direction and implied that we were needed and had an obligation to fulfill. "I want you," said the poster.

One of the greatest of human needs is just that, the need to feel wanted. We need to be assured someone cares for us, and we are important to that person. Yet there are many dark times in our lives when we lose touch with those who hold us near and dear. Sometimes it is because they have moved away from us, literally and figuratively. More often it is because we have lost our perspective.

During the depression of the 1930s a lecturer spoke to a businessmen's group. He took a sheet of white paper, pinned it to the wall, then with a pencil put a black spot in the middle of the paper.

He asked, "What do you see?"

A man in the front row squinted and said, "A black spot."

Then the speaker said, "That's the trouble with us. We see the black spot, and we fail to see the great white field of opportunity surrounding it."

When the twelve spies went to survey the promised land of Canaan, ten of them saw only the walled cities and the giants. Two, Caleb and Joshua, saw the grapes and the pomegranates, the milk and honey.

So often in life, even though we have been called by the gospel to belong to the family of God, we fail to see the great blessings we have in that family. We see only the black spot of sorrow, of suffering, of work, of aggravation, of trouble. We see the walls and mountains of life, which seem so unscalable, the giants of opposition and difficulty. Focusing on the dark spots, we lose sight of the great white area of God's boundless love. We miss the fruit, the milk and honey of peace, pleasure and power that God has set before us.

Having entered God's family through faith in Christ, let us accept the blessings he sends us as evidence of the Father's love. Christ has made us God's children and we rejoice over every gift that comes from our Father's hand. For with each new blessing our heavenly Father reminds us, "I want you!" Keeping that thought uppermost in our minds will help us to focus not on the little black spot but on the glorious expanse of God's love.

Lord, keep reminding us how much you care for us and want us. Amen.

Pray continually; give thanks in all circumstances, for this is God's will for you in Christ Jesus. (1 Thessalonians 5:17,18)

OUR PRAYERS—COMPLAINTS OR THANKSGIVING?

The snowplow came around the corner, and with a giant "swoosh" the entrance to the driveway was blocked with wet, sticky snow from the street. Tommy and his father had shoveled the heavy stuff for over an hour, and now it was like starting all over again.

Impatiently Tommy demanded, "Why did God make this snow so heavy? Why couldn't it be the light fluffy kind?"

"If that were the case," said Tommy's father, "you'd be missing something. Look around you. This snow sticks to the trees. It's like God has begun decorating for Christmas. And it packs really well—just right for making a snowman."

That night during the family prayer everyone was surprised to hear Tommy pray, "Thank you, God, for heavy snow."

We are all a little like Tommy, aren't we? We often tend to dwell so much on the negative side of things that we fail to see God's goodness working in our lives. Our old Adam is a true pessimist. He even changes good encouragements from our Lord, like "pray continually," into hopelessly heavy burdens.

There is a way, however, to keep our sinful pessimism in check. It's to think like a saint and not like a sinner. It's to let God's positive promises outweigh our negative doubts. It's to have faith that a gracious God, who loves us in Jesus Christ, "in all things works for the good of those who love him."

That's right. In all things God works for our good. Even when it looks bad, it will turn out for good. The bloodstained cross and the empty tomb prove that.

Therefore Paul can say, "Give thanks in all circumstances." That's one way of following the encouragement to "pray continually." Simply change the complaint list into a thanksgiving list. It's bound to result in more of our thoughts rising to our Father's throne.

Positive, praying faith comes in only one way—by having God continually remind us that we are "in Christ Jesus." We are in his family through Christ, and he as our Father is eager to listen.

Wait for your Savior by praying — praying continually. Thank God for your "heavy snow." Even the burdens he sends are for our good.

Dear Father, teach us to thank you for all things. Even under life's burdens may your love draw us closer to the Savior, whom we eagerly await. In his name we pray. Amen.

Do not be anxious about anything, but in everything, by prayer and petition, with thanksgiving, present your requests to God. (Philippians 4:6)

PRAYER—SOLUTION FOR WORRY

Have you ever found yourself sitting in a hospital waiting room, anticipating a doctor's report on a biopsy? Those are anxious moments to be sure. You think of Paul's words: "Do not be anxious about anything." You believe those words, but that doesn't make it any easier to practice them, or so it seems anyway. "Do not be anxious about anything" doesn't mean to be foolhardy, but rather, don't be bothered or troubled.

Now the doctor may tell you not to worry about your condition, but you can't just tune out your problem and forget about it. It just doesn't happen that easily. You can try all kinds of things to get your mind off that biopsy report, but it doesn't go away by itself. You can deaden the pain, or superficially or artificially block out the tension, but that won't remove the cause of the problem.

Paul has a genuine solution for worry-free joy—PRAYER. One of our hymns tells us:

Oh, what peace we often forfeit,
Oh, what needless pain we bear,

All because we do not carry
Everything to God in prayer.

And isn't that true? St. Peter writes, "Cast all your anxiety on him because he cares for you." Getting rid of our worries before they worry us—that would be real joy.

And that is exactly what Paul suggests, "But in everything by prayer and petition, with thanksgiving, present your requests to God." Certainly God knows our needs even before we ask, yet he wants us to ask and promises to answer our prayers. James tells us in his Epistle, "You do not have because you do not ask God."

Our requests are to be made known to the Lord. In what better hands can any troubles or needs rest than in the hands of God! That's the way to beat worry. Paul's words contain the assurance that God will attend to all we ask or even think. And don't forget, this is done with thanksgiving. Our thanks will naturally be included in our prayers. A thankful heart is also a joyful heart.

Heavenly Father, remind us often to bring our cares to you. Help us to find joy in the assurance of your gracious help. Amen.

Now to him who is able to do immeasurably more than all we ask or imagine, according to his power that is at work within us, to him be glory in the church and in Christ Jesus throughout all generations, for ever and ever! Amen. (Ephesians 3:20,21)

STORM THE GATES OF HEAVEN WITH YOUR PRAYERS

When Samuel Morse invented the telegraph and proceeded to demonstrate the device on a test line that was strung between Washington's Capitol Building and Baltimore, the message he sent over the wires was "What God hath wrought!" It was a "miracle of communications." Man suddenly found himself able to send information across many miles with the speed of electricity.

Even more reason do we Christians have to marvel at the wondrous things that God has wrought for us spiritually and to praise him for them. God sent his Son to deliver us from death and hell. And he sent his Holy Spirit to work that faith in our hearts by which we apprehend our salvation. What a miracle God has wrought—a miracle even greater than that which God did when he parted the Red Sea or when he caused the sun to stand still in the sky.

Having reminded the "saints" at Ephesus of all that God had done for them, Paul closes this section of his letter with a stirring song of praise. In it he glorifies God for his power to do exceedingly more than we ask or think. Because of what God has wrought, and because of what he will continue to do through Christ until the end of time, all glory belongs to him alone.

What an incentive Paul's words are for Christians today! They are an incentive to "think big" when it comes to asking things of the Lord. We have a great and powerful God, who is able to deliver us from every evil and to preserve us unto his heavenly kingdom. We have a Lord who time and time again has demonstrated that he "is able to do immeasurably more than all we ask or imagine." We have a God who also invites us to come to him with all the boldness and confidence of a little child approaching his father.

Maybe you have a particular sin that keeps popping up, one that you find extremely difficult to overcome. It seems that with that sin Satan has found the chink in your armor. Should you despair? No! Rather, repent and believe that God has forgiven your sins for Jesus' sake. Storm the gates of heaven with petitions for help to improve your behavior. And know that your heavenly Father, who wants you to ask for deliverance from temptation, will surely answer your pleas and permit you to marvel at "what God hath wrought."

Dear Lord Jesus, increase our trust and confidence in you. Amen.

**Three times I pleaded with the Lord to take it away from me.
(2 Corinthians 12:8)**

TAKE IT TO THE LORD IN PRAYER

"**C**all upon me in the day of trouble; I will deliver you, and you will honor me." What a tremendously reassuring invitation and promise we have in this psalm verse. And what a comfort it is to us when life turns sour and we are overwhelmed with problems for which there seems to be no earthly relief. This is an invitation and a promise that comes from one who not only sees our troubles but has the power to do something about them. This is almighty God speaking by whose "word the heavens were made; who spoke, and it came to be; who commanded, and it stood firm," with whom nothing is impossible. This is the Lord who is in control of the universe, and certainly in control of our lives. His almighty power knows no limits.

But we pray not only to a God of might and power; we pray also to a God of love and mercy, of goodness and deep concern for our well-being. It was his unsurpassed love for the sinner that moved him to give his one and only Son as the atoning sacrifice for our sins. So Paul exclaimed, "He who did not spare his own Son, but gave him up for us all —how will he not also, along with him, graciously give us all things?" His love is not withdrawn in our tribulation. God's Son suffered affliction in greater degree than any human being has been called upon to endure, yet in that affliction he remained his Father's Son, the object of his love. There is his promise to us all, "For a brief moment I abandoned you, but with deep compassion I will bring you back. . . . I hid my face from you for a moment, but with everlasting kindness I will have compassion on you."

It is also a God of wisdom to whom we pray. He always knows what is best for us, far better than we ourselves know. We can always trust in him to deal with us according to his wise counsel.

The Apostle Paul didn't really have to think about what he should do about the "thorn in his flesh." There was no doubt in his mind about God's ability to heal him. There was no question about his Lord's love for him. He had confidence in the absolute wisdom of God. He pleaded with God, not once, but three times, to take his affliction away.

Calling upon God in our troubles is not a last resort—something we do when we have exhausted all other sources of help. No, it is the first thing we do.

Heavenly Father, we bless you for the privilege of prayer. Amen.

. . . Having been kept by the Holy Spirit from preaching the word in the province of Asia. When they came to the border of Mysia, they tried to enter Bithynia, but the Spirit of Jesus would not allow them to. (Acts 16:6,7)

GOD'S NO!

Mark Twain once said, "Most people are bothered by those passages in Scripture which they cannot understand; but I always noticed that the passages which troubled me most are those which I do understand." We all get his point, but the fact remains that the ways of God can be a little hard to understand sometimes. Our text for today gives us a good example of that.

Paul had been called by God to preach the gospel to the Gentiles. But when he wanted to minister to the people in Asia, God said, "No." When he wanted to enter Bithynia, God said, "No." It just didn't make any sense to Paul. It must have been a very frustrating experience.

But life is often like that. God warned us about this too when he said through the prophet Isaiah, "For my thoughts are not your thoughts, neither are your ways my ways."

There is only One who is omniscient, and that is God. He operates with a wisdom that is far greater than ours. He never makes mistakes in the ways that he deals with his children. Our text once again serves as a good example of that.

God had a good reason for saying No to Paul and not allowing him to enter Asia or Bithynia at this time. There was a more urgent need in Macedonia. There was a field white for the harvest that required his immediate attention. Once Paul started working there, he understood full well why God had said No to him earlier.

Unfortunately it doesn't always work out that way. There are times we cannot understand why God says No to us. Our loved one is stricken with an incurable disease. We pray with all the confidence we can muster that God will perform a miracle and heal that person. But the answer that comes back to us is No, and we end up shedding our tears at the funeral.

That could be a very bitter pill to swallow. It could fill our hearts with all sorts of doubts about the love of God for us. But when we think of Jesus Christ nailed to the cross and dying for our sins, how can we possibly doubt his love for us? Blessed with wisdom from above, we will continue to put our trust in God even when we can't understand when he says, "No."

O Lord, we believe; help to overcome our unbelief. Amen.

Always giving thanks to God the Father for everything, in the name of our Lord Jesus Christ. (Ephesians 5:20)

GIVE THANKS FOR EVERYTHING

Isn't Paul going a bit far when he encourages the Ephesian Christians—and us as well—to give thanks to God "always"? How can anyone always be thankful? Thankful for loss of a job? Thankful for crop failure? Thankful for the accident that happened on the way to work?

"Yes," Paul adds emphatically, "for everything." Everything? Even for that chronic illness which hinders my effectiveness at work, which is a burden to others, which I ask God frequently and fervently to take away? "Yes, for that too," is Paul's reply.

"But what did I ever do to deserve having all these things go against me?" Paul reminds us that he also "was given a thorn in the flesh." He pleaded with the Lord to take it away. The Lord answered Paul's prayer by showing him that in human weakness God's power would prevail. God's grace was sufficient for all things. To realize that truth was more important than anything else. It brought Paul closer to God than ever before.

That is why Paul reminds us here that "God the Father," is the source of every good and perfect gift. We are to thank him "in the name of our Lord Jesus Christ," who became poor, so that we through his poverty might become rich.

We sinners deserve nothing. Because of our many sins a just God has every right to banish us forever from his holy presence. But this same God in his love took pity on us and gave his only Son as a sacrifice for our sins so that we might live with him forever in heaven.

Knowing this, we also "know that in all things God works for the good of those who love him" and that nothing "in all creation will be able to separate us from the love of God that is in Christ Jesus our Lord" (Romans 8:38,39). No, not even those things that seem to be great misfortunes. We can always give thanks to God for everything!

We see how the wise Christian is, above all, the thankful Christian. The Spirit of thankfulness is the basis for his attitude toward all things in life, also those which bring despair to others. It determines his relationship with his God. It influences his actions toward others. It gives him courage to face problems in spite of disappointments and gives him everlasting hope in the face of death.

Lord, help me always to give thanks for everything. Amen.

Cast all your anxiety on him because he cares for you. (1 Peter 5:7)

CAST ALL YOUR CARE ON HIM IN PRAYER

"Don't worry!" That's easy to say. But what if you're taking off down the runway on your first airplane trip or facing the first day on a new job or visiting a doctor for a crucial examination? The human tendency is to fill your mind with anxious thoughts. Yet Peter's counsel to us is: "Don't worry!"

Every care and worry we have, every possible anxiety, can be cast on our gracious Father in heaven. Thus it is foolish for Christians to worry. Peter had experienced this on the Sea of Galilee. When worried about high waves that swamped his boat, he and the other disciples had called out, "Lord, save us!" And Jesus calmed the troubled sea as well as their troubled minds. When he was sinking in the turbulent waves of that same sea, Peter experienced the strong and gracious hand of the Lord, lifting him out of danger.

The Lord invites us to cast all our anxiety on him. But in our human weakness we sometimes insist on clinging to some of these cares. We try to work out by ourselves, or sometimes with another's help, such things as illness, financial difficulty, problems at school, approaching old age, etc. When we insist on carrying some of these burdens ourselves, we forget that the Lord has volunteered to care for us in every need.

In his Sermon on the Mount Jesus cautions us, "Therefore do not worry about tomorrow, for tomorrow will worry about itself. Each day has enough trouble of its own." We are to take one day at a time and rely on the Lord for sufficient strength to see us through that day and entrust the future to his gracious wisdom.

Peter's piece of divine counsel for today is a gracious invitation to pray to God and at the same time a promise that God will hear and answer our prayers. Why worry, when you can pray? We who have learned to know God as a loving father ought to cast our anxieties on him in prayer.

We have a God who cares about us so much that he allowed his own Son to shed his lifeblood to atone for our sins. God cares. He cares about our spiritual needs, and he also cares about our physical needs. We ought to trust steadfastly in his gracious care.

**I am trusting Thee, Lord Jesus;
Never let me fall.
I am trusting Thee forever
And for all. Amen.**

Because you are sons, God sent the Spirit of his Son into our hearts, the Spirit who calls out, *"Abba*, Father." (Galatians 4:6)

YOU CAN NEVER CALL TOO OFTEN

"**G**ive a gift that keeps on giving." That's how years ago a large company urged its customers to buy its appliances. It was a catchy slogan. And it made sense to a lot of people. Why buy flowers that soon die, while a blender, iron or toaster could be used day after day. But the truth of the matter is many of us have thrown some of those electrical appliances into the trash. Eventually they gave out and stopped giving.

But our heavenly Father gave us the gift which keeps on giving. Jesus our Redeemer made it possible for us to be adopted into God's family. God then "sent the Spirit of his Son into our hearts, the Spirit who calls out, 'Abba, Father.' " Hebrew children called their fathers "Abba," as American children might call their father "Dad" or "Daddy." With the Holy Spirit in our hearts, we Christians have the continuous assurance that God is our Father and we are his children. And so the Holy Spirit in our hearts teaches us to pray, "Abba, Father."

"*Abba*, I need a drink of water," the Hebrew child might call out at night, fully confident that his loving father would answer his request. "*Abba*, hold my hand," the frightened child might say when he needed the firm and loving clasp of his father's hand. Such comfort and confidence belong to every redeemed child of our heavenly Father every day. When the Apostle John thought about this he exclaimed, "How great is the love the Father has lavished on us, that we should be called children of God! And that is what we are!"

What a difference our Redeemer makes in everyday life! If today you face all kinds of anxiety at work, remember Abba. If school days are difficult, you aren't alone. Abba cares. If there are family problems that don't seem to get better, Abba is near. If you are alone, if you are ill, if you need any reassurance today at all, call to Abba. You can never call too often. You can never ask too much. The Father sent us his Son so that he might keep on giving us his love.

I have called Thee Abba, Father!
I have stayed my heart on Thee.
Storms may howl, and clouds may gather,
All must work for good to me. Amen.

Cast all your anxiety on him because he cares for you. (1 Peter 5:7)

YOU CAN NEVER ASK TOO MUCH

Everyone has his problems. Until we get to know someone quite well, we may not be aware of his worries and concerns. But we may be sure that he has them hidden away somewhere. A completely carefree life is perhaps never found in this vale of tears. Sin and God's chastening curse upon a sinful world have sown thorns and thistles in everyone's life.

Some of our problems are easily solved. Others are solved with great difficulty. Still others can not be solved at all. It is this last group that brings frustration, fear and unspeakable woe into our lives. As nagging worries, they lodge in our souls and allow us no peace. When they do not occupy our full attention, they churn about in the back of our minds.

Some well-meaning people recommend that we forget our woes. That is easier said than done.

St. Peter has better advice, and he speaks by the Holy Spirit. He says, "Throw your worries on God."

There are two good reasons for heeding his advice. Peter mentions one of them when he says, "He cares for you." While some people care about us more or less, and others, as we say, "couldn't care less," God cares. The other reason for handing our problems over to God is that God is able to cope with difficulties that are too much for us. With God all things are possible.

But Peter has mentioned the reason that is more important for our consideration. It is the one we are most apt to forget. We get caught up in the gloom of our own sinfulness and find it hard to imagine that God could really care about us. That he takes a personal and powerful interest in our woes is almost too much to believe.

Let's take another look at our God. His care for us is so genuine and complete, so wholehearted and sincere, that he gave his only-begotten Son for us, delivering him up to death for our sins. Then he raised him again from the dead, so that we might be sure that Jesus' sacrifice was acceptable. And Jesus himself has promised to come again and to receive us to himself.

Such Good News contradicts all doubt about God's concern for us. God loves me with his whole, infinite Being. He invites me to unload my worries on him. Yes, he commands me to do so, and it is only right that I do.

Lord God, to Thee my ways belong,
Take fear and care away;
Place in my heart salvation's song—
Thy mercy's bright, strong ray. Amen.

I always thank God for you because of his grace given you in Christ Jesus. (1 Corinthians 1:4)

ALWAYS THANKFUL FOR GRACE

Learning to say "Thank you" is an important step in growing up. Learning to thank God, to see and appreciate his grace, is important in growing as a Christian.

The Apostle Paul gave thanks for the grace God gave to the church at Corinth. But if you read further in this letter to Corinth, this thankful praise seems surprising. Serious problems had occurred in this church. The people had fallen into quarreling, immorality, drunkenness and envy. How could Paul always thank God for Christians like those?

Paul hadn't closed his eyes to their sin. As their shepherd, he gave them stern warnings to change their attitude and ways. Yet Paul was sincere in his thankful praise. The grace God had given them in Christ Jesus was the key to Paul's thankfulness. He knew that this love of God had triumphed over sin— even for those Christians at Corinth. In his own life Paul had seen how grace can change a blaspheming enemy of the church into a faithful servant of God.

Grace is the key to new life and thankfulness to God for us also. No one is without sin. God's holy law condemns us all as sinners. But thank God for his grace! He judges each one of us to be righteous and innocent because of what his Son has done for us. Jesus' holy life and sacrifice for us will always be the breath of life for our souls. His work as our Savior is the sure promise of peace with him forever.

Can we really always be thankful for what God does? The Bible shows us God's great love. He is our Savior and the source of everything good in our lives. He guides all the events of history as well as each moment of our day to serve our best interests. Even those things which cause us trouble and sorrow happen in harmony with his wisdom and love for us. Even the sting of sin and death fades when we see his grace and remember the perfect life and joy Jesus is coming to give us.

Remember God's grace and you will be "always thankful." Paul learned to see life from this point of view and so can we. Being thankful moves us to serve God and those around us. It reminds us that both joy and sorrow for a Christian are only different colors in the rainbow of God's love. And the best is yet to come!

Lord, fill my heart with thankfulness and my life with your love. Amen.

In keeping with God's promise we are looking forward to a new heaven and a new earth, the home of righteousness. (2 Peter 3:13)

A FEARLESS FUTURE

What will happen to us on judgment day? The Apostle Peter answered that very simply. "In keeping with God's promise we are looking forward to a new heaven and a new earth, the home of righteousness." On judgment day we will inherit a home of righteousness. That's good news. It is even better news when considered in contrast to what we have deserved.

When you woke up this morning, what was the first thing on your mind, "Today is Thursday; it's laundry day," or, "I only have an hour to get to work," or, "I wonder if it rained last night"? If you are like me, the morning's first efforts involve clearing the cobwebs from the brain and routinely mulling over the day's upcoming activities. Tomorrow morning let's try something different. Let's turn our attention to spiritual matters, "Where do I stand in relation to my God?"

If we take a look at ourselves in the mirror of God's perfect standards, the thought of standing before God isn't all that pleasant. He is holy; we are not. By the sin we are born with, by the wrong we do, and by the right we don't do, we deserve the worst. Our worries, doubts, greed, envy and anger have separated us from God's love. By all rights we have earned hell.

Thankfully, God is as merciful and forgiving as he is holy and just. He loaded onto his Son all our wrongs and transferred to us Jesus' perfection. Because of Jesus we won't get what we deserved; we will get what he earned. Now that is a truth worth holding onto as we begin each day. That is a truth worth holding onto every day, even to the end.

So what will happen to people on judgment day? When Christ Jesus appears in all his glory on that day, all the dead will be raised and brought before him with all the living. Those who have rejected God's mercy will be condemned, body and soul, to the eternal pain of hellfire and eternal separation from God's love. In the same moment, believers in Jesus will have their bodies glorified, and body and soul they will be with the Lord forever. As you sit on the edge of your bed tomorrow morning, ask yourself, "Where do I stand in relation to God? What will happen to me on judgment day?" Then think of the Savior, Jesus. He has prepared for us a home of righteousness. Therefore encourage each other with these words.

**Abide, O faithful Savior,
Among us with your love;
Grant steadfastness and help us
To reach our home above. Amen.**

If I am to go on living in the body, this will mean fruitful labor for me. Yet what shall I choose? I do not know! I am torn between the two: I desire to depart and be with Christ, which is better by far; but it is more necessary for you that I remain in the body. (Philippians 1:22-24)

COMMIT YOUR FUTURE INTO GOD'S HANDS

St. Paul was unsure of what kind of future he should wish for. What a blessing it would be if he would die and be with his Savior in heaven! On the other hand, what a joy it was to do the work of the Lord on this earth! Which should he choose? Which should he wish for?

Paul knew better than to try to make a decision on his own. He chose to leave the matter of his future in the Lord's hands. To do otherwise would be to play God. To decide for himself whether his life should continue or whether it should end would be playing God. Only the Giver of life also has the privilege of taking life.

We all know that millions of people today are trying to play God. Millions are trying to decide when life should come to an end. Thousands of suicides are committed yearly in our own land, many by teens and young adults. Millions of unborn children are being put to death by those who promote elective abortion. Some are also supporting euthanasia or "happy death," the ending of life prematurely to avoid the suffering and pain which may come with illness.

In every case individuals are playing God. They are taking from the Giver of life the privilege of determining when that life should come to an end. Our lifetime on this earth is so precious. It is the only opportunity we have to learn of our Savior's love. Dare we shorten that opportunity? The last few moments of life may be the ones in which a lost sinner finally learns of the Savior's love and forgiveness.

With St. Paul we commit our future into the loving hands of God. He knows what is best for us. If we have continued opportunity for fruitful labor in the Lord's vineyard, to God be the glory. If the God-appointed end of our life is drawing near and if we will soon be with our Savior in heaven, to God be the glory. What shall we hope for in the future? A difficult decision indeed. One we cannot make on our own. We commit our future into the hands of our loving and caring heavenly Father. He will make the correct decision for us. He will direct our life and our death for our eternal good.

Heavenly Father, into your loving hands I commit my future. May I serve you in love during my lifetime on this earth, and may I rejoice with you eternally in the next. In the Savior's name. Amen.

And we eagerly await a Savior from there, the Lord Jesus Christ, who, by the power that enables him to bring everything under his control, will transform our lowly bodies so that they will be like his glorious body. (Philippians 3:20, 21)

LOOK FORWARD TO CHRIST'S RETURN

We live now in a world that wallows in sin and is opposed to God's Word. And it is a constant vexation to us, as it was to righteous Lot while he lived in Sodom. But, like Sodom, our world and society will one day come to a crashing halt. And Christ, the great King and Judge, will appear. He will deal righteously with a sinful and rebellious mankind. And only those will escape who have washed their robes in the blood of the Lamb, that is, who believe in him as God's appointed sacrifice for their sins.

To us and all believers Jesus will appear, not as a fearful Judge, but as our Savior and glorious Lord. He will rescue us from this world; he will take us with him to that land which we have never seen but which is nonetheless our homeland.

And his will be a complete deliverance—not only from the evil influences of this world, but also from its evil effects. Each day we remain here we feel those effects: the quarreling and strife, the disappointments and frustrations, the worries and fears, the sickness and pain and weakness.

But when Jesus comes to deliver us, all that will be changed. The final episode in his plan of salvation will be to bring us out of this place into a marvelous place of joy, happiness and glory. Even our bodies will be changed for our new life there. Our present bodies corrupted by sin will be glorified at our resurrection, even as Jesus' body was at his resurrection. They will be cleansed from all weakness, from all sinful inclinations and from all death.

But for the present we are still on earth. And God has a reason for keeping us here for a while. It is our time of grace, during which God has graciously called us to a life of repentance and faith. It is also a time of opportunity—to bring that same gospel invitation to those still in darkness. But while we work and wait here, let us also turn our thoughts heavenward, to our homeland and to the one who will bring us there.

Our faithful God, through the gospel continue to assure us of our deliverance. Keep us faithful to our heavenly citizenship while here, that we may realize it there forever. Amen.

Therefore you do not lack any spiritual gift as you eagerly wait for our Lord Jesus Christ to be revealed. (1 Corinthians 1:7)

CALLED TO EXPECTANCY

When Mt. Vesuvius erupted, it completely destroyed the city of Pompeii. Many people were buried in the ruins under the hot lava and ashes. Many years later when excavations were begun, bodies were found in various places and postures. Some were found in the streets, as if they had been running to escape. Some were found in deep holes in the ground, as if they had gone there to hide. Where did they find the Roman sentinel? They found him standing at the city gate, where he had been placed by his captain, his hand still grasping his weapon. He had remained at his post—watchful and ready.

When the great day of judgment comes, will you and I be found watchful and ready?

God had made the Corinthians ready for that great day. By God's grace they did not lack any spiritual gift. God had done for them what he does for all Christians. He had graciously blessed them with everything they needed: the knowledge of their sin and its dreadful consequences; the good news of their complete pardon for Jesus' sake; and the needed information concerning judgment day, the resurrection from the dead and heaven.

The Christians in Corinth knew that they were completely forgiven. They knew that they had been declared righteous for Jesus' sake. They were certain that they had a home in heaven ready and waiting for them. With joyful anticipation and eagerness they could look to Jesus' coming.

So can you and I—and for the same reasons! "We wait for the blessed hope—the glorious appearing of our great God and Savior, Jesus Christ, who gave himself for us to redeem us." That day is going to be wonderful! It will be the first day of eternal bliss in heaven. Just imagine! We will be with Jesus in the special place he has prepared for us. It is all tremendously exciting. Like the Corinthians we also are filled with eager expectation as we "wait for our Lord Jesus Christ to be revealed."

The best way to spend our time until that day is, as Jesus put it, to be about our Father's business. That means using the talents and abilities God has entrusted to us for him and his kingdom. That means searching the Scriptures and continuing in prayer.

O blessed Redeemer, thank you for providing everything necessary to watch for your coming on judgment day. Fill me with joy and eager expectation as I wait for your return. Amen.

The Spirit himself testifies with our spirit that we are God's children. Now if we are children, then we are heirs—heirs of God and co-heirs with Christ, if indeed we share in his sufferings in order that we may also share in his glory. (Romans 8:16,17)

THE JOY OF HEAVEN

What a comfort it is for us to know that we are God's children through Christ's wonderful work of redemption! To this Paul adds for our eternal hope and joy, "Now if we are children, then we are heirs—heirs of God and co-heirs with Christ."

To what are we heirs? What is the inheritance of which Paul speaks? This inheritance is heaven which Jesus earned for us by his suffering, death and resurrection. And who of us is not interested in heaven? Who does not have a loved one in heaven? With the poet we say, "I'm but a stranger here; heaven is my home."

While the Bible does not tell us everything we might like to know about heaven, yet it does lift a corner of the veil to give us a glimpse of the glory that someday will be ours. In Psalm 16:11 we are told, "You will fill me with joy in your presence, with eternal pleasures at your right hand." St. Paul informs us in Philippians 3:21, ". . . the Lord Jesus will transform our lowly bodies so that they will be like his glorious body." St. Paul also gives us this picture: He [God] will wipe every tear from their eyes. There will be no more death or mourning or crying or pain, for the old order of things has passed away."

With our limited, human minds we are unable to picture fully the glory and beauty that some day will be ours. Nor do we have anything beautiful enough, or magnificent enough, or vast enough with which to compare it. Paul writes, "No eye has seen, no ear has heard, no mind has conceived what God has prepared for those who love him."

Furthermore, the joy and glories of heaven are eternal. In this world nothing remains. Great nations and kingdoms have arisen and fallen again. Even forests do not remain. They can be destroyed by fire or hewn down with an axe. But heaven and its joys are eternal.

The joy of heaven! This is the powerful and eternal message of the gospel. This is the message which pastors and teachers offer daily to their hearers.

Lord of Harvest, let there be
Joy and strength to work for Thee
Till the nations far and near
See Thy light and learn Thy fear. Amen.

And now, dear children, continue in him, so that when he appears we may be confident and unashamed before him at his coming. (1 John 2:28)

EAGERLY AWAIT CHRIST'S COMING

Jesus is coming. Are you ready? The thought of Jesus' second coming fills the unbeliever with terror. St. John saw a picture of that terror, and he recorded it for us in the book of Revelation. He wrote, "Then the kings of the earth, the princes the generals, the rich, the mighty and every slave and every free man hid in caves and among the rocks of the mountains. They called to the mountains and the rocks, 'Fall on us and hide us from the face of him who sits on the throne and from the wrath of the Lamb! For the great day of their wrath has come, and who can stand?' " (Revelation 6:15-17)

The unbeliever is right in fearing the coming judgment. What about us? Does the thought of judgment day make us uneasy? It does, because we are sinful human beings. We have violated God's will in thought, word and deed. We deserve nothing but God's wrath and punishment.

Yet, listen to the words of John in our text, "Continue in him, so that when he appears we may be confident and unashamed before him at his coming." We are God's children. Through faith in Jesus we possess the forgiveness of all our sins. The Lord has told us, "I, even I, am he who blots out your transgressions, for my own sake, and remembers your sins no more" (Isaiah 43:25).

When the Lord summons us to stand before him for judgment, our sins will not rise up to condemn us. Jesus paid for all of them by his death on the cross. We will not be ashamed to stand before God on that day, for we will be arrayed in the righteousness of our Savior.

It is no wonder that John tells us we may be confident and unashamed before Christ at his coming. Our confidence is not based on anything we have done. Our confidence is based on all that our God has done for us.

Jesus said, "I am coming soon" (Revelation 22:20). Are you ready? By the grace of God we are. We believe in Christ. We are God's children, clothed in Christ's righteousness. We pray, "Come, Lord Jesus."

Jesus, Thy blood and righteousness
My beauty are, my glorious dress;
Midst flaming worlds, in these arrayed
With joy shall I lift up my head. Amen.

We are confident, I say, and would prefer to be away from the body and at home with the Lord. (2 Corinthians 5:8)

FAITH PREFERS OUR HEAVENLY HOME

As seasons make their sweeping changes across the face of America, we often feel a stir of excitement within us. Feeling the warm summer sun, I can hardly wait to make my escape to a wonderful little vacation spot I've been dreaming about for a long, long time; a placid little glade nestled in the Adirondack Mountains of upstate New York. Perhaps you feel that way about a place where you long to be. I know St. Paul did.

Throughout the seasonal changes of his long and illustrious career, St. Paul longed to travel to the best vacation spot of all. St. Paul preferred his heavenly home. And by faith in Christ, he knew it had all been arranged. His flight was already booked.

The Apostle Paul was not suicidal. Nor did he despair of living because of the corruption of the world around him or because of his own sinfulness. Quite the contrary. St. Paul realized the importance of life as God's time of grace given to mankind to come to know Jesus as the Savior and escape God's wrath against sin. Being a messenger of God's grace, Paul wrote, "If I am to go on living in the body, this will mean fruitful labor for me."

Nonetheless, St. Paul did not regret that he would die. In fact, he looked forward to it. He longed to enter heaven and to enjoy to the full God's restored image of innocence, knowledge and righteousness. Like a little boy in a candy shop who wants to unwrap each piece, confident of its sweet taste, St. Paul wanted to shed his sinful nature in death, confident of Christ's forgiveness and the sweet taste of heaven which Jesus promised.

With the same confidence about Christ's forgiveness of our sins as St. Paul, based on the resurrection of our Savior, we too need not regret death or fear it. Even though death, the actual cessation of life in our bodies, is a mystery to us, we need not fear the outcome of death. Our departure has all been arranged by our loving God who sent his Son to die for us. By faith our flight has been logged into the Book of Life, taking us to an eternal vacation spot to be with our Lord Jesus Christ in our heavenly home.

Give me a faith full of divine confidence, dear Father, trusting in Christ's sacrifice for my sins, and opening heaven's door in death to an eternal paradise with my Savior. Amen.

When Christ, who is your life, appears, then you also will appear with him in glory. (Colossians 3:4)

TAKE THE HOPE THAT JESUS OFFERS

A young couple promised their four-year-old son that they would take him to the zoo. They did not set a specific time or date for the big event. Every day for the next week the little boy asked his parents if they would go to the zoo. Each time he was told, "Not today." Another week passed, then a month. As time went on the boy asked the question less frequently. He had almost given up all hope of going to the zoo when his father announced one sunny Saturday morning, "We are going to the zoo today." You can imagine the excitement of the little boy. His parents were finally making good on their promise.

The believers in the early Christian church waited anxiously for Jesus to return. They expected him to come in their lifetime. What joy filled the hearts of these people as they waited for the day Jesus would come! But Jesus did not come, in their time or the generations which followed. It was like the little boy and the promise that his parents made about going to the zoo. At first he was very excited about it, but when he did not see an immediate fulfillment, he began to place that promise in the background of his many other activities.

Now that almost two thousand years have elapsed since Jesus made his promise to return, our anticipation and excitement over his coming may have diminished. Therefore it's time to rekindle the comfort and joy in our hearts which his promise brings.

What a spectacular day that will be! Jesus will appear in all his glory to take his own to be with him in glory. Paul describes this event for us: "For the Lord himself will come down from heaven, with a loud command, with the voice of the archangel and with the trumpet call of God, and the dead in Christ will rise first. After that, we who are still alive and are left will be caught up with them in the clouds to meet the Lord in the air. And so we will be with the Lord forever. Therefore encourage each other with these words."

Are you suffering from illness or the loss of a loved one? Then take the hope that Christ offers and live. Depressed and worried about the economy and the future? Cling to Jesus' promise, and look forward to the eternal joy which he has won for you.

Savior, you have promised, "Because I live, you also will live." Make that promise a central theme in my life. Let me look forward to the day when this promise becomes a reality, and in the meantime help me to live a life of faith to your glory. Amen.

After that, we who are still alive and are left will be caught up with them in the clouds to meet the Lord in the air. (1 Thessalonians 4:17)

MEETING THE LORD IN THE AIR

Whenever some important dignitary arrives in our country, a grand welcoming party goes out to meet him. That will be the scene when our Lord comes on the clouds of heaven. The believers will meet their Lord in the air in welcome and join his triumphal descent. When that happens, they will be in the presence of the God who made them and redeemed them for himself.

Believers of the past longed to see their God face to face as he really is. Moses once made that request of God. But God told Moses, "You cannot see my face, for no one may see me and live." Believers of the present also long to see their Lord face to face, and they shall. For he has promised, "We shall see him as he is." But that will not become a reality until Jesus comes again and "will transform our lowly bodies so that they will be like his glorious body."

Right now our sinfulness prevents us from seeing God as he really is. But after the victorious Conqueror of death and hell appears on the clouds of heaven and his triumphant shout will have reached the dead in their graves and the believers will have come forth with their glorified bodies, the believers whom the Lord has left alive in the flesh at his coming will also experience his transforming power in their bodies. Then all the believers together will meet their Lord in his descent to punish his enemies and to grant his believers salvation in the new heavens and new earth.

Are we looking forward to that beautiful moment with eagerness and joyful anticipation when we shall be changed in the twinkling of an eye and meet the Lord in the air? Or do we lack enthusiasm to meet him because our conduct in word and action is not quite in keeping with the expectations of our coming Judge? Are we, as Adam and Eve were, afraid and more concerned about hiding than running to greet him with an enthusiastic welcome?

If our desire to meet him is somewhat less than fervent, let us remember just who it is we will meet. It is Jesus our righteous Judge through whom God has put away our sin and declared us fit to meet him. Yes, we are going to meet a Judge, but one who is loving, merciful and faithful. What a grand meeting we await!

Lord, let us look forward to meeting you with joy and faith. Amen.

God, who has called you into fellowship with his Son Jesus Christ our Lord, is faithful. (1 Corinthians 1:9)

GOD IS FAITHFUL

The movie ends and the credits glide by, a long list of all the people and activities involved in making the film. But in the story of our salvation there is only one credit, one name. All our hopes for this life and the next depend upon our Savior alone. He promises us, "I am trustworthy."

For this reason Paul always thanked God when he thought of the Christians at Corinth. Despite enemies outside and inside, the church would survive because God is faithful. His grace and reliability are the sure guarantee that all he has promised us will come to be.

Remember this simple truth: God is faithful! It comforts us because often we are not faithful to him. Our best intentions to trust and obey can crumble when we are threatened, unhappy or under pressure and temptation. Our love and patience with others may be shallow and weak. Even together as a church, we are sometimes slow to put into practice the very things we have united to say and do. The world we live in also makes it increasingly hard to follow Jesus and keep our consciences clear from sin.

If our hope of forgiveness and eternal life depended in any way upon us and our faithfulness, there simply would be no hope. But God is faithful! Through baptism and his message he has created new life in our hearts and minds. He called us into fellowship with his Son, making us members of his family, citizens of his kingdom of grace. God cares for us and leads us with his Word and Spirit as our Good Shepherd, our heavenly Father. The fellowship we have with God's Son and with all other believers in him is for our blessing and joy. Together we are ready and waiting for the coming of our Lord.

Just as the rainbow reminded Noah of God's faithfulness, God's Word will stand forever as proof that we can rely on him as our Savior. Do not take his promise lightly. God is also a faithful Judge, who will not be mocked by those who turn away. When Christ returns, he will be relentless in his judgment against those who do not believe. But by grace we are not among them. There is now no condemnation for those who are in Christ, who rely upon his work for our salvation. Our Savior is faithful.

When you are troubled by your sins and the evil of the world around you, take heart in this great promise: God is faithful!

Savior, thank you for your sure grace to us in Christ. Amen.

I can do everything through him who gives me strength. (Philippians 4:13)

COPING WITH LIFE—GOD'S WAY

Jesus once said, "If you have faith as small as a mustard seed, you can say to this mountain, 'Move from here to there' and it will move. Nothing will be impossible for you." Some people have mistakenly interpreted this verse and the above statement written by St. Paul to mean that if you set your mind to it, you can literally do anything. But God is not promising that we will be granted the magic power to do anything at all. He is speaking figuratively of the power of faith. Neither was Paul kidding himself into believing that he was omnipotent. But he was confident that through Christ he had the power to face whatever circumstances came along.

Some try to face life by being self-sufficient. They try to make contentment a human achievement. Paul's way—the Christian way—is to accept contentment as a divine gift and learn to be God-sufficient. Trusting in God's power rather than his own, Paul was able to face everything life could throw at him—hard work, imprisonment, floggings and beatings, threats of death and stonings, shipwreck, danger from all sides, lack of sleep, hunger, thirst, being cold and naked and the daily pressures of his concern for all the churches.

Without prayer and daily resting upon Christ's promises, St. Paul would not have been able to do it. Neither can we face the hardships of life without receiving the strength to endure from our God. We may not have the faith of a Paul or Luther, but even a weak faith is a true faith and a saving faith. And it becomes stronger with exercise.

With faith we can accomplish things that no unbeliever can ever hope to do. We can move God to grant our requests, providing they are in agreement with his will. As we bring the gospel to others we are instruments of the Holy Spirit, as he achieves the seemingly impossible conversion of unbelievers. In our own life we can overcome great obstacles. For whether we have little or much, at all times we have Jesus Christ. Walking with him and living in him we can be patient and hopeful in all things.

When my foolish heart asks why, quiet me with your words, "Be still, and know that I am God." Amen.

To keep me from becoming conceited because of these surpassingly great revelations, there was given me a thorn in my flesh, a messenger of Satan, to torment me. Three times I pleaded with the Lord to take it away from me. But he said to me, "My grace is sufficient for you, for my power is made perfect in weakness." Therefore I will boast all the more gladly about my weaknesses, so that Christ's power may rest on me. (2 Corinthians 12:7-9)

RELY ON THE LORD

This passage is quite often used together with that of Christ's prayer in Gethsemane to show that not all requests we bring to God in prayer are granted. Yet we must not lose sight of the truth that every Christian prayer is heard and answered by the Lord.

Paul asked the Lord for the removal of a nagging ailment, which he felt was impairing the spread of the Gospel. It seemed to Paul as if Satan were a boxer standing in his path and raining punches on his face. Paul could not make the progress he wanted to make.

Yet this "thorn in the flesh" served a good purpose in keeping Paul from becoming proud over the visions and revelations he had received. God simply could have told Paul that he had no right to question divine wisdom in this matter. But when Paul asked for relief, the Lord uncovered a truth that has become a well of encouragement for Christians ever since. God answered: "My grace is sufficient for you, for my power is made perfect in weakness." The ultimate purpose in all Christian suffering is that we may from experience develop a full, deep knowledge of our need to rely on the Lord and on his grace alone.

It is easy enough to say, "Oh, I depend on God for everything." But when all the props under us suddenly give way and we feel weak and helpless, then we learn from experience how much we really depend on God's grace alone in Christ.

We do not know what Paul's thorn in the flesh was. If he had wanted us to know, he would have told us. The fact that he simply calls it a "thorn in the flesh" makes it possible for us to compare it to our infirmities, whatever they may be. And the fact that he calls it a thorn "in the flesh" teaches us not to worry. God may permit the thorns to stick in our flesh for our good, but he will not let them touch our soul.

Dear Lord, help us to trust completely in your all-sufficient grace, realizing that it becomes most apparent in our weakness. Amen.

When he would not be dissuaded, we gave up and said, "The Lord's will be done." (Acts 21:14)

HIS WILL BE DONE

What Paul really needed from his friends was not their fretting and weeping, but encouragement. Instead of urging him to run from danger, they should have been strengthening him for the ordeal he faced. They could have reminded Paul that the Lord Jesus was directing his life and had promised to be with him always—no matter what.

Instead, it was Paul who strengthened them. The will of his Lord held no terrors for Paul. He knew Jesus loved him so much he had given his own life to rescue him from hell. Paul had experienced long years of Jesus' love and care for him. He, in turn, devoted all of his energies to telling people what Jesus had done to rescue all men from the certain disaster of hell. Paul was even ready to die for such a Lord.

When his friends saw they could not change Paul's mind, they fell silent and learned from his example of joyful acceptance to say, "The will of the Lord be done." After that, no more was said. No more needed to be said. Although at first they had been anxious about Paul's safety, they finally committed their hearts with confidence to their loving Lord. In faithful obedience, they submitted to his will. That settled it.

These Christians did not reluctantly give in to an unavoidable decree of God. They did not say with a fatalistic sigh, "Whatever will be, will be." They said, "The will of the Lord be done." Their acceptance of his will was not a surrender to fate, but an exercise of their faith. When they could not clearly see the good that God might do, they trusted that he still would do it. They believed, without knowing how, that whatever the Lord had decided should happen to Paul would be for the best. "In all things, God works for the good of those who love him" (Romans 8:28). Paul was not afraid of what might happen. And now, neither were his friends.

When we pray, "Thy will be done," we are to be ready to accept, as Paul did, whatever God may send our way. We too have seen God's faithful love for us, and we are sure that his will can bring nothing but good to us. Whether he sends pleasure or trials or even death, like Paul we should gladly accept it. It all comes from the same Lord. He is not punishing us. He only seeks our good.

His will be done!

**My God, my Father, make me strong,
When tasks of life seem hard and long,
To greet them with this triumph song:
Thy will be done. Amen.**

And we know that in all things God works for the good of those who love him, who have been called according to his purpose. (Romans 8:28)

GOD IS ON OUR SIDE

How can ill health, suffering, loss of possessions and other kinds of disaster possibly work together for good? Well, they don't work together for good for everyone. They only work for the good of those who love God. That makes the big difference.

The unbeliever simply cannot understand this. He can't understand how calamities in life can serve to draw one closer to God and to refine one's faith. He can't understand how afflictions, or what he would be inclined to call bad luck, can draw one away from the world and lead one to a richer prayer life and a stronger reliance on God. He can't possibly understand how trials and temptations uncover the evils in one's heart and at the same time make the faithfulness of a loving and gracious God stand out like the sun in a clear sky.

The child of God, on the other hand, understands all this very well. He has complete confidence in what his Savior tells him: "Are not two sparrows sold for a penny? Yet not one of them will fall to the ground apart from the will of your Father, and even the very hairs of your head are all numbered. So don't be afraid; you are worth more than many sparrows."

In view of this and with Christ's redeeming sacrifice as the perfect background, it would be strange indeed if we could not share Paul's complete confidence: "And we know that in all things God works for the good of those who love him." It is this confidence which not only makes life bearable for us but also provides us with a cheerful outlook. After all, God is on our side. Our hopes here and hereafter have a solid basis. Their fulfillment does not depend on our feeble, groping, spasmodic efforts. God himself has taken the matter in hand. We are secure no matter what. Listen to the Lord as he asks and answers the questions in the book of Joshua: "Have I not commanded you? Be strong and courageous. Do not be terrified; do not be discouraged, for the LORD your God will be with you wherever you go."

Ye fearful saints, fresh courage take;
The clouds ye so much dread
Are big with mercy and shall break
In blessings on your head.

Dear Lord, keep us secure even in affliction. Amen.

I have great sorrow and unceasing anguish in my heart. (Romans 9:2)

IN THE HOUR OF SORROW

Ever since the advent of sin, sorrow, disappointment, unceasing anguish and heartache have all been a part of life. Man has apparently realized this and has tried unsuccessfully to deal with the problem of sorrow and pain. The first way of dealing with sorrow is the way of the pleasure-seeker who says, "Avoid it." The second is the way of the stoic who says, "Grin and bear it." The third is the way of the person who says, "Deny it."

But there is a better way, and that is God's way. Through the Bible we come to the realization that nothing happens to us without God's permission. We must understand that despite sorrow and unceasing anguish we are still God's people through faith in Christ who gained for us complete pardon for our sins. We must remember that God reaches down from heaven and puts his everlasting arms beneath us to keep us from falling, to keep us on the way that leads past all our sorrow, pain and anguish into eternal life.

Sorrow is not a sign that God does not care for us, but rather it is a mark of his affection. The Bible states, "The Lord disciplines those he loves." We must realize that sometimes our sorrows will continue, and for this God may have a special purpose in mind. After all God did not remove all of the Apostle Paul's anguish. He proved that through this troubled man he could turn the world upside down. St. Paul was given the glorious chance to preach Christ crucified.

God does not always let us have our way. He leads us into his paths to make us into devout believers who rely solely on his grace. Our sorrow and anguish may be a time of testing, in which it becomes clear that we are sincere when we profess our complete dependence and trust in him.

It is easy to walk with God when he comforts and gladdens every step. But when he begins to discipline us and the road of life becomes a little bumpy, we might quickly discover that what we called faith was more satisfaction with our happy circumstances than trust in God. So one of the reasons God allows sorrow and anguish to come into our lives, is to strengthen and refine our faith. In the hour of sorrow we learn to rely on him more completely and cling to him more firmly.

Lord, I would clasp Thy hand in mine,
Nor ever murmur or repine:
Content, whatever lot I see,
Since 'tis my God that leadeth me. Amen.

For I am convinced that neither death nor life, neither angels nor demons, neither the present nor the future, nor any powers, neither height nor depth, nor anything else in all creation, will be able to separate us from the love of God that is in Christ Jesus our Lord. (Romans 8:38,39)

OUR ANCHOR IN THE STORMS OF LIFE

While at the shore of a lake on a stormy day, I noticed a sailboat anchored about a hundred yards offshore. The wind blew and the waves beat against that boat, threatening to dash it into pieces on the jagged rocks that lined the shore. But the sailboat, held tightly by the anchor and rope, survived the storm. Soon the storm was over.

As Christians, I am certain that there have been many times when we have felt very much like that sailboat. The storms of life can be pretty fierce. We seem like such a tiny craft in the midst of such a big and cruel lake. The wind and the waves beat against us, threatening to smash us to pieces.

At times like that it is good for us to remember the words of assurance which the Apostle Paul offers us in our text today. He reminds us of the fact that as long as God is with us, there is no power on earth and no power in hell that can ever tear us away from him. We have the strongest possible anchor. The storms will still come, but we have the assurance that God will help us ride out those storms. Our boat will never sink, since God is with us always.

This is the same God who has promised us, "I give them eternal life, and they shall never perish; no one can snatch them out of my hand." The only way to get out of God's hand is if we jump out. No one, nothing can ever tear us away from God. Someone once compared life to a trip across the ocean on a slow-moving ship. We go from good weather to bad again and again. God pilots us through stormy seas until we finally reach the safe harbor of heaven where there will be no more storms to bother us.

No one is forcing God to do this, nor do we deserve his protection. He loves us so much that he wants to help us. If he loved us enough to send his Son to die for us, he certainly loves us enough to keep us safe from every earthly storm. Bonds of love tie us, anchor us to him — bonds which will never be broken.

In ev'ry high and stormy gale
My anchor holds within the veil.
On Christ, the solid Rock, I stand;
All other ground is sinking sand.

Lord, always keep us in your love. Amen.

In this you greatly rejoice, though now for a little while you may have had to suffer grief in all kinds of trials. These have come so that your faith—of greater worth than gold, which perishes even though refined by fire—may be proved genuine and may result in praise, glory and honor when Jesus Christ is revealed. (1 Peter 1:6,7)

ENCOURAGEMENT FOR EVERY TRIAL OF LIFE

Not long ago an American rock and roll star died. One of his fans said that she no longer had any reason to live. Idolaters lose everything when their idols perish. But it is not so with believers in Christ. We have become heirs of eternal life. In every trouble our faith "shines through the gloom and points us to the skies."

This portrait of Peter takes us far from the Sea of Galilee. He is a prisoner for the Lord in Rome not long before his execution under Nero. It is Peter's final exam in the school of faith. His faith in Jesus enables Peter to face death. The memory of Jesus' revelation at the Sea of Galilee enables Peter to encourage other believers. Peter holds out to them the hope that is ours in Christ's empty grave and beyond our grave: "an inheritance that can never perish, spoil or fade—kept in heaven for you"(1 Peter 1:4). Our faith may be tried in different ways. We may be in our own prison hospitalized with an incurable disease or awaiting the outcome of major surgery. Peter teaches us to see the divine purpose in every trial of faith. That hymn we sang in church on a Sunday may come to us in our present circumstance with fuller meaning and greater comfort:

The clouds ye so much dread
Are big with mercy and shall break
In blessings on your head.

(TLH 514:3)

Luther wrote, "If God disposes that you must suffer, accept it, console yourself with bliss that is eternal, not temporal. . . . Peter likens the gold that is tested by fire to the testing of faith by temptation and suffering. . . . Thus God imposes the cross on all Christians to purge them that faith may remain pure, as the Word is, so that one adheres to the Word alone and relies on nothing else. For we really need such purging every day because of the Old Adam."

May Peter's faith while a prisoner of the Lord show us the divine purpose in every trial of faith, that we, also, receive the end of our faith, the salvation of our souls!

Heavenly Father, may we learn from our Savior, as Peter did, that in every trial our faith is more precious than gold in your sight. Amen.

For when I am weak, then I am strong. (2 Corinthians 12:10)

STRENGTH IN WEAKNESS

Strength is an admirable quality. Everyone wants to be strong; no one wants to be weak. The physically strong always have an advantage over the physically weak. The world relies on such strength. Nations vie with each other for military might. They depend on the strength of arms to secure supremacy in the world and often use their strength to suppress the weak. Athletes train strenuously to develop strength, because the strong are the winners; the weak the losers.

What could Paul possibly mean when he says, "When I am weak, then I am strong"? How are these two opposites compatible? It is another of Paul's profound paradoxes. Just as he found joy in his sufferings, so he finds strength in his weakness. What an amazing display of God's grace!

It is the grace of God that makes us forget whatever human strength we may have and depend entirely upon the strength supplied by the Lord. The strong think they have no need of help and do not seek it. The weak know their need and lay hold of the Almighty's strength.

The accomplishments of the great heroes of faith were not the result of the human strengths these individuals possessed. Moses could only point to his weaknesses, the abilities he lacked when the Lord called upon him to lead his people out of Egypt. Never did Moses say, "I have led you out of slavery." It was always, "The Lord with his strength, with his mighty hand has brought us out of Egypt."

The gospel did not prevail because it originated in the great powers of the first century, in the learning of Greece and in the strength of Rome. It originated in the weakness of Palestine and Galilee. As Paul declared, "God chose the weak things of the world to shame the strong." The weakness of God is stronger than man's strength. In the weakness of his sufferings the strength of Christ was made perfect. His cross is the strength of Christianity.

The Lord manifests his strength in our weaknesses, too. The trials we endure, the sufferings we experience, the crosses we are called upon to bear display the grace of him who invites us, "Come to me, all you who are weary and burdened, and I will give you rest." May we cast all our anxiety upon him because he cares for us, and when we suffer according to his will, commit ourselves to our faithful Creator and continue to do good. Then in our weaknesses we are strong.

Strengthen my faith, O Lord, so that I may always see your grace in my afflictions and live in the strength that you supply. Amen.

But he said to me, "My grace is sufficient for you, for my power is made perfect in weakness." (2 Corinthians 12:9)

LOOK FOR GOD'S ANSWER

Often when we ask a question, we anticipate the answer. We already have in mind what the response to our question should be. But it happens very often, too, that the answer we receive isn't at all what we were looking for. Obviously, when we ask for something, we expect to receive what we are asking for. That's the reason we make the request, isn't it? So when we address our prayers to God and plead with him to help us in our need, we know how we want him to answer our prayer. We want him to remove the trouble that afflicts us. That's the answer we are looking for. Isn't that what it means to pray confidently, trusting in God's almighty power and in the assurance of his loving concern for our well-being? It certainly is. But remember, God answers our prayer according to his divine wisdom and not necessarily according to our wishes, no matter how frequently and fervently we plead with him to grant the answer we are looking for.

We can never say, then, that God isn't listening or that he doesn't care. His plans for us may just be different from what we think they should be. It is not for us to prescribe the time when he should help nor the manner in which he does. Sometimes we may be so determined that our way is the only way that we don't recognize God's answer when he gives it!

We certainly can learn from Paul's example. God did not give the answer Paul was looking for. But God did answer Paul's prayer—according to his own purpose and plan. "My grace is sufficient for you," he told Paul. He was reminding Paul that we are completely dependent on God's grace. By God's grace Paul was an apostle, and the effectiveness of his work as a chosen messenger of the gospel was not going to be diminished by his continuing to bear the thorn in his flesh. Paul's preaching of the Word would succeed because it is God who gives it success, and not because Paul was physically strong and healthy. God's power is all the more evident when he accomplishes his purpose in the weakness of the human instrument he has chosen to carry out his work.

Never forget that we are the objects of God's grace, just as Paul was. It is by his grace that we are his children and have the privilege of addressing him as our dear Father and placing our petitions before him. He will answer according to his grace and purpose.

We thank you, Lord, for every answer to our prayers. Amen.

And the God of all grace, who called you to his eternal glory in Christ, after you have suffered a little while, will himself restore you and make you strong, firm and steadfast. (1 Peter 5:10)

LOOK TO GOD FOR STRENGTH

As we look to the future, we must realize that our strength and our hope are entirely dependent on God's grace, the undeserved love he shows us. By grace God has sent his own Son to die for our sins. By grace God has called us into his kingdom. By grace through faith in Christ we can look forward to eternal glory.

We need to look to God for strength. That is Peter's God-inspired counsel to us. Without God we can accomplish nothing. It would be ridiculous for a mountain climber to try to scale a lofty peak without a rope or for an explorer to head down a river in a canoe without a paddle. Likewise it is foolish for anyone to think that he can face the rigors of life on his own without the strength and help God gives.

Peter directs us to the God of grace who will help us endure the sufferings of this life that will last for a short time when considered in the context of eternity. We can see the concern Peter has for the suffering Christians of his day who were sorely tested in their faith. But note how he again assures them that their sufferings are only for "a little while."

We need to have the proper attitude toward sufferings. We must realize that when we have to pass through God's refinery, it is his intent to purify the gold of our faith. Whatever draws us closer to God, however hard to bear at the moment, is a hidden blessing for which we should be eternally thankful. God had one Son without sin. He has no sons without suffering. It may be a cross for us now, but it will be a crown in the hereafter. We take heart from the words of the Apostle Paul, "And we know that in all things God works for the good of those who love him, who have been called according to his purpose."

God has promised to equip us with all that we need to endure suffering. He can restore us to oneness with him. He can keep us firm in true faith. He can make us steadfast in our allegiance to his Word. The God of all grace and power promises to guide us safely through to eternal glory. What a blessed assurance that is!

Rock of ages, cleft for me,
Let me hide myself in thee.

God of grace, make us strong, firm and steadfast in Christ. Amen.

To the praise of his glorious grace, which he has freely given us in the One he loves. (Ephesians 1:6)

AMAZING GRACE

What is grace? To some it is the name of a pretty girl they know. To others grace is what you say before you eat. To still others grace is good manners, or the action of a performer in a ballet. To the sinner, grace is the unmerited mercy of an all-loving God.

Grace is an amazing thing. It is hard to define. It is love, but more than love. It is undeserved love. This grace has been freely given to us by God.

God's grace flows freely, daily, bountifully. It is not a slow drip, drip, drip from the faucet of his love. It is grace sufficient to cover all our sins, no matter how bad they are or how often they have been repeated. It is grace in abundance for every day of our lives. It greets us in the morning, fills our days with the sunshine of God's love, and covers us warmly through the night.

God's grace flows freely in another sense. It is ours without price. A good thing, for we could never begin to pay for our forgiveness. The national debt exceeds billions of dollars. Even if we laid all of this money at the feet of the Almighty, it would not be sufficient to purchase forgiveness for a single sin. But what we could not earn or buy, God gives to us freely "in the One he loves."

Not that this grace is cheap. It has been paid for by the tremendous price of the suffering and death of the holy Son of God, the "One he loves." Twice God declared his love for his Son. At Jesus' baptism God called from heaven in a loud voice, "This is my Son, whom I love." On the Mount of Transfiguration the disciples heard the voice from the cloud proclaim, "This is my Son, whom I love." God's grace flows freely in his beloved Son, Jesus Christ.

It is this Savior whose perfect life, mighty death in payment for sins and victorious resurrection on the third day purchased our forgiveness. Thus God provided a fountain of forgiveness and mercy for all people of all generations. This free-flowing grace of God deserves our praises now and throughout eternity.

Lord God, heavenly Father, we praise you for the glorious grace that purchased our eternal forgiveness. We confess that what we could not pay for or earn has been freely given us in our Savior, the One you love, and the One we love. Amen.

Who has known the mind of the Lord? (Romans 11:34)

KNOWING THE MIND OF THE LORD

What an amazing creation of God is the human mind! However, most attention these days is given to computers. How much information can the computer store? How fast can it operate? We often tend to forget that each of us has a mind which puts even the most powerful computers to shame.

It has been said we use only a small portion of our brains. Even at that our minds are capable of some astounding things. Consider the speed of the brain in eye-hand coordination. The eye sees a ball speeding our way and in an instant sends a message to the brain which in turn sends a message to the hand to reach up to catch it. We think a home computer is more than adequate if it has a memory capacity of 128K, but just consider the memory capacity of the human brain. It has been said that everything we have ever known or experienced is in our minds somewhere. Consider the human mind's ability to reason and to make decisions. Show me a computer which can do these things as well, or do them at all for that matter. Even though more is being learned about the human mind all the time, we still don't understand its many-faceted complexities, intricacies and abilities.

How then can we expect to understand the mind of the Lord? How can we ever hope to investigate the mind of him who knows absolutely everything? How can we whose minds are corrupted by sin expect to comprehend the mind of the holy and righteous God? Isn't that completely presumptuous? Yes, for man by nature it is.

"But we have the mind of Christ," Paul says in 1 Corinthians 2:16. That means that by God's Word the Spirit reveals the mind of the Lord to us. As believers we know that God thinks thoughts of love and kindness toward us in Christ Jesus. We learn that because of Christ's death on the cross there is no longer in God's mind any wrath or hatred toward us. We understand that God has only our best interests in mind, that he wants only what is best for us in our lives now, and that he wants us with him in heaven forever. In God's Word we come to know the mind of the Lord in another sense. We understand the way God wants us to think and speak and live.

"Who has known the mind of the Lord?" No computer ever built will be able to know God's mind. The greatest minds of men have never nor will they ever discover the mind of the Lord by their own powers. Only believers know the mind of God because he has revealed it to them in his Word.

Lord, help me to know your mind ever better through the daily study of your Word. Amen.

We have not received the spirit of the world but the Spirit who is from God, that we may understand what God has freely given us. (1 Corinthians 2:12)

COUNTLESS BLESSINGS OF FAITH

By means of human reasoning we cannot bring ourselves into the Christian faith, just as we cannot use worldly wisdom to argue anyone else into believing. Dr. Martin Luther understood this well when he wrote in his Small Catechism, "I cannot by my own thinking or choosing believe in Jesus Christ, my Lord, or come to Him."

By nature we have neither the strength nor wisdom to believe. For we are spiritually dead. And a spiritually dead person can no more enable himself to believe in Jesus, than a physically dead person can make himself alive again. He needs someone outside himself to do that for him. God has done it for us.

This is why the Apostle Paul declared that he spoke not by the spirit of the world but rather by God's Spirit. Through the Holy Ghost Paul knew God's wonderful wisdom. This is also the only way anyone will ever know that wisdom.

The Holy Spirit comes to us as infants through God's Word and Holy Baptism, "the washing of regeneration and renewing of the Holy Ghost." Older ones hear God's Word, and by his grace the Holy Spirit works faith in Christ in their hearts. Paul tells us that "no man can say that Jesus is the Lord, but by the Holy Ghost." He also says that faith in Christ is a gift of God: "For it is by grace you have been saved, through faith—and this is not from yourselves, it is the gift of God—not by works, so that no one can boast."

The Holy Spirit revealed many blessings to us when he brought us to faith in Jesus Christ. We now trust in Jesus as our Savior. We know our sins are fully and completely forgiven for Jesus' sake. We are at peace with God. We can pray to our dear heavenly Father "as dear children ask their dear father." We know that when we die our soul will be with the Lord in heaven. We know that our body will be resurrected a glorious body and reunited with our souls on the Last Day. We know we will spend eternity in our Father's magnificent mansions above in heaven. This is God's glorious promise to us through Jesus Christ our Lord.

These are some of the countless blessings that come with a Spirit-worked faith. Surely God has been gracious to us! May our hearts be filled with thankfulness—now and forever.

Into Christ baptized,
Grant that we may be
Day and night, dear Spirit,
Perfected by Thee. Amen.

73

As the Scripture says, "Anyone who trusts in him will never be put to shame." For there is no difference between Jew and Gentile—the same Lord is Lord of all and richly blesses all who call on him. (Romans 10:11,12)

NO MATTER WHO YOU ARE!

Whose Son is he? The people who know the answer to this question are a most privileged people!

This wonderful privilege, though, is not reserved for a select few. This wonderful privilege is freely offered to all. God will have all people to come to know the truths about his Son, Jesus Christ.

God is no respecter of persons. He does not practice discrimination on the basis of age, sex, race, or social status. He knows that there is no difference. He knows that all have sinned. He knows that all need a Savior. There are no exceptions. Both Cain and Abel needed a Savior. Both Pharaoh and Moses needed a Savior. Both Saul and David needed a Savior. Both Mary Magdalene and Mary, the mother of Jesus, needed a Savior. Both John and Judas needed a Savior. Both the prodigal son and his elder brother needed a Savior. Both you and I need a Savior. The need is universal, and God met that need.

The Bible reveals that God loved the world . . . that he gave his only-begotten Son for the world . . . and that he invites the world to come to know and believe in his Son. Thus, "the Scripture says, 'Whosoever believeth on him shall not be ashamed.'"(KJV) The word "whosoever" is all-inclusive. Richard Baxter, a noted preacher in Scotland, claimed that he could not thank God enough for the word "whosoever." It meant more to him, he said, than if the Holy Spirit had put his own name into the Bible. He declared, "If God had said that there was mercy for Richard Baxter, I would have thought that he must have meant another Richard Baxter. However, when he says 'whosoever,' I know that he means me!"

Not one of us is outside the circle of God's love. The love of God is not exclusive. It is all-inclusive. Whosoever we are, we are invited to learn the saving truths about Jesus Christ. However, what we know of Jesus Christ literally must be taken to heart. It is possible, you see, to miss God's promise of forgiveness and life by sixteen inches. That, by the way, is the distance between the head and the heart. It is not enough to know Jesus intellectually with our minds. We must also know him intimately with our hearts.

Lord, whosoever we are, may we always embrace you with all of our mind and heart. Amen.

Those he (God) called, he also justified. (Romans 8:30)

GOD'S GRACE COMES TO OUR RESCUE

A frightened man enters the courtroom and nervously faces the judge and jury. He is charged with first degree murder. The death penalty is his sentence, should he be found guilty. The physical evidence seems to be irrefutable. Yet he pleads not guilty.

The accused man is hoping that his lawyer can suppress the damaging evidence. Maybe the investigating officer made a technical mistake in searching the scene of the crime. Maybe the arresting officer failed in properly reading him his rights. Maybe some of the jurors can be swayed with emotional appeals so that the verdict will be guilty of manslaughter or even a lesser crime. Maybe, just maybe, he can get out of the charge completely. But it may take months or years as the case works its way through appeal after appeal. How agonizing this process is for the accused, not to mention the continuing burden of guilt on his conscience.

Then what is it going to be like to stand before the judgment seat of God? The evidence is absolutely irrefutable. We are sinners many times over. No earthly testimony or human argumentation can lessen the guilt. Justice demands the eternal death penalty. That means never-ending suffering in the fires of hell. The situation is hopeless.

Such is our rightful condition before the eternal tribunal of the Lord. But once again in his grace our God comes to the rescue. With the absolute judicial power he possesses, he simply declares us not guilty. He announces that all convicting evidence has been removed and that all charges have been dropped. He proclaims that we are justified, that is, righteous in his sight.

How can God do this and still be a holy and just God? Simple. With love for us sinners he planned for our justification by sending his Son to be our Redeemer. The blood of Jesus blots out the mountains of evidence against us. Not only has Jesus sacrificed himself for us, but he also pleads our case before the Father. For his sake our sins are forgiven. "All . . . are justified freely by his grace through the redemption that came by Christ Jesus" (Romans 3:24). And we don't have to wait in agony for the verdict. We are justified here and now. Once again our Lord has done it all.

O Lord, it is because of your amazing grace alone that you forgive a sinner such as me. Help me to serve you with my life, for Jesus' sake. Amen.

Oh, the depth of the riches of the wisdom and knowledge of God! (Romans 11:33)

PLUMBING THE DEPTHS OF GOD'S GRACE

Most of man's knowledge about the sea bottom has been gained over the years by the use of special instruments. For many years the depth of water was measured with a sounding lead. A ball of lead was attached to a wire rope. The lead was dropped into the ocean, and the rope was let out until the lead touched the bottom. The rope went over a wheel which measured the length of rope paid out. Sometimes it took several hours to make one sounding in deep water.

In recent years a new method called sonic sounding has been developed. Some waves sent down from the ship are reflected from the bottom, so that an accurate measurement of the depth becomes possible. In this way it has been learned, for example, that the Pacific Ocean off Mindanao is over six and a half miles deep!

How does one plumb the depths of God? Is there a wire long enough to measure the greatness of God? Can we somehow measure reflected sound waves to learn about God? How does one begin to fathom the knowledge of One who knows absolutely everything there is to know? How does one measure infinite wisdom? Can the creature plumb the depths of the Creator? The fact is that if all the greatest minds in the history of the world were to use their combined intelligence and learning they still could not even begin to plumb the depths of God's wisdom.

That does not mean that we are totally ignorant of God's wisdom and knowledge. The works of God all around us—the universe, the earth, the creatures, our own bodies—lead us to join the psalmist in saying, "In wisdom you made them all" (Psalm 104:24).

Paul certainly was aware of the greatness of the wisdom of God revealed in the creation. But in our text Paul sings a song praising the greatness of God's wisdom revealed to us in the gospel of Christ. From eternity God determined to send his Son into the world to die on the cross for the sins of all mankind. No human being ever conceived such a wise plan. In fact, to the mind of sinful man it seems like nothing but foolishness. Only to the one in whom the Spirit has worked is it true wisdom. "Oh, the depth of the riches of the wisdom and knowledge of God!" Let us join Paul in falling on our knees in worshiping the God of our salvation.

Lord, help me always to realize that knowing you as my Savior is true wisdom. Amen.

For from him and through him and to him are all things. (Romans 11:36)

GOD'S BLANK CHECK

Charles Steinmetz, the great electrical engineer and inventor, never received a fixed salary from those who sponsored him. From time to time his backers would give him a book of blank checks. Whatever he needed, great or small, he only had to fill in the amount on a check, sign his name and present it to the bank.

Not too bad an arrangement! It surely would help at bill-paying time if one never had to worry about the checkbook balance.

Steinmetz's backers could eventually have run out of money, however. Surely Steinmetz's friends were helpless in keeping him from getting sick. They couldn't give him the strength, knowledge and ability he needed to do his work.

We have an infinitely better arrangement with God. God provides for the needs of all people. God is the origin of all things. From his creating hand came the universe, the earth and all creatures. From him comes all we need for our bodies and lives. Rain, sunshine, crops, food, drink and shelter all come from God. If God were to withdraw his sustaining hand for even an instant we would have nothing and we could not live.

Through him you and I and all creatures continue to exist. "In him we live and move and have our being" (Acts 17:28). We couldn't take a breath; our hearts couldn't beat; we couldn't put one foot in front of another if it weren't for God. He is not only present in our world but in our very beings.

From him alone also comes our salvation. It is all the work of his grace in Christ Jesus. Through him alone come all our spiritual blessings.

In a sense God has given us a blank check. It is made out to us, and it is signed in Jesus' blood. We can fill in the amount. Do we desire a stronger faith? We can write it in, and he will give it. Do we wish to see more fruits of faith in our lives? They are ours. Are there things we need for our bodies and lives? We can fill them in, and he will give them to us as he knows best. "From him and through him are all things."

Also "to him are all things." He is the final goal of the universe and all created things. All have been created to give praise and glory to his name.

Lord, help me remember that everything I am and everything I need comes from you. Help me praise you with my whole being. Amen.

For in him you have been enriched in every way—in all your speaking and in all your knowledge. (1 Corinthians 1:5)

THE BEST LIFE HAS TO OFFER

Grandpa reached into his pocket and brought out two coins for Lois and her little sister. Lois and Grandpa smiled at each other; this was their special joke. Grandpa held up the coins for the youngest to see and asked her, "Now, which one would you like, this big nickel or this little dime?" She quickly took the nickel, and Grandpa laughed as he gave Lois the dime. Little sister always took the nickel!

Our idea of what is best, of what offers us the greatest worth, is not always so good. Someone who knows better must teach us the true value of things. We need to learn where and how to find life's treasures.

Paul thanked God for teaching these things to the Christians at Corinth and for blessing them. They had become rich in every way. How? Paul says, "*In him* you have been enriched," that is, in Jesus. Even unbelievers benefit from God's creation, the physical wealth of this world. But only in Jesus Christ can a person become rich, rich in every way—physically, spiritually and eternally.

In Christ, we not only have all we need for our bodies and life, but also rich spiritual gifts. Love, joy, peace and hope are all ours through his Holy Spirit. We also have the precious promise that Jesus is coming again. We will be free forever from sin, death and sadness. The priceless treasure of an eternal inheritance with the Lord is ours already, set aside for us until Jesus returns.

The grace of God had enriched the Corinthians with a clear understanding of these riches in Christ. They had received both the desire and the skill to share the good news about their Savior with others. Joy in a new life with Christ, a change of heart about sin, an eager anticipation of Christ's return—all these blessings shone forth in their thinking and speaking. They were rich. Even the problems of this church could not dim the gleam of the treasures the believers shared.

Where do you look for the best life has to offer? Money, a fine house and expensive entertainment are wonderful things, yet they often disappoint us. And it's no secret that these things do not last. The prophet Isaiah gave us this map to better riches: "[The Lord] will be the sure foundation for your times, a rich store of salvation, wisdom and knowledge; the fear of the Lord is the key to this treasure." Look to the Savior for the best life has to offer. In him, we are rich in every way.

Lord, give us also the best riches life offers. Amen.

Grace and peace to you from God our Father and the Lord Jesus Christ. (1 Corinthians 1:3)

GRACE AND PEACE IN CHRIST

Each star in the night sky has a wonderful secret. What we see as only a twinkle of light is actually the blaze of a brilliant, distant sun. Consider what that tiny sparkle really is, and you will appreciate a star's true majesty and power.

Our Bible verse is just a brief thought. But it's like a star. Although this verse is small, it has a wonderful message. Consider what these words are saying, and you will appreciate the true majesty and power of our Savior's love for us.

The Gentiles once greeted one another with a Greek word that resembled "grace." The Jews said and still say, "Shalom," meaning "Peace." The Holy Spirit guided Paul to join these two thoughts as a special greeting in his New Testament letters. For Christians of all time, these words are like a diamond ring on a bride's finger. They remind us of love and faithfulness, the Father's love-in-action for us in Christ.

Grace points to the way God feels about us and treats us. Grace is kindness, generosity and love shown even to those who do not deserve them. Because we are all sinners, we deserved punishment. But God gives us love. We often forget to thank him. We often live as though he isn't even there and as though he will never return. But the Lord cares for us. He has forgiven our sins through Jesus. He watches over us and blesses us. God shows us grace.

Grace brings us peace with God. This peace does not come from us. It isn't just how we feel or something we must make for God. Jesus created this peace for us. He did this by keeping his Father's law perfectly for us and by suffering on the cross the punishment for our sins. The Holy Spirit reminds us of what Jesus has done. Through God's Word, the peace we have moves us to trust the Lord more and more. It moves us to live thankful lives in harmony with God's Word.

Trouble, worry and our own sinful weakness often bring a shadow over this peace. But they can never overcome it. How can we be sure? God our Father and his Son our Lord have created grace and peace for us. The cross guarantees this gift forever. We are thus ready and waiting for Christ's return.

What a wonderful message is in this one little verse! Whenever you hear these words, remember God's great gift of love to you!

Lord, may my life be a thankful answer to your grace and peace. Amen.

And he gave orders to stop the chariot. Then both Philip and the eunuch went down into the water and Philip baptized him. When they came up out of the water, the Spirit of the Lord suddenly took Philip away, and the eunuch did not see him again, but went on his way rejoicing. (Acts 8:38,39)

GOD'S GRACE IN BAPTISM

After it was all over, it must have seemed like a dream to the Ethiopian. What kind of man was this, who came to him, explained God's word to him, baptized him and then vanished! But the Ethiopian knew it was real. He now knew that Jesus Christ was the Lamb in Isaiah's prophecy, his Savior; he had been baptized; he really had an answer to the questions of his heart. And he was glad. As he continued his journey, he continued to rejoice.

This is perhaps one of the most unusual baptisms in history, but it is basically no different from yours and mine. Every Christian baptism is the same. It is a means by which God gives us the forgiveness of sins. No wonder the Ethiopian was happy! Through his baptism he was firmly established in his newly-received faith in Jesus. He was beginning to discover what many other Christians have experienced through their baptisms.

Baptism means life! Life with God. By baptism we have been born again so that we can live in God . . . live by God . . . live for God. Baptism has broken the chains of sin, death and hell. Baptism has set us free in Christ; and it gives us boldness to go into battle against temptation. Baptism delivers the victory of Jesus' death and resurrection to us. As St. Paul says in his letter to the Romans (6:4): "We were therefore buried with him through baptism into death in order that, just as Christ was raised from the dead through the glory of the Father, we too may live a new life."

Is it any surprise that the Ethiopian went on his way home rejoicing? That is the same joy we have available to us in our baptism. In our baptism we find new power to love and to live with God. In baptism God has lavished on us the joy of forgiveness and has given us a panoramic view of heaven. No matter how many years have passed since you were baptized, your baptism is still and will always be valid. It is a solid rock and source of spiritual refreshment and renewal. In a world burdened with many and daily troubles, in a life beset by many and powerful temptations, that is good news—the very Good News of the gospel of Christ.

O Lord, how good and faithful you are in spite of my sinfulness and unfaithfulness. As your baptized child, I return to you for forgiveness and for a renewed zeal to do your will; in Jesus' name. Amen.

Who though faith are shielded by God's power until the coming of the salvation that is ready to be revealed in the last time. (1 Peter 1:5)

THANK GOD YOU'RE SAFE

Yes, it's great to be alive—spiritually alive in Christ, filled with a living hope as heirs of God. Yet being a Christian in this world is not a "piece of cake." In fact, without the grace of God it would be impossible to remain a Christian.

The fact that we are alive, born again children of God, means that our life will be a struggle, a daily battle. The unholy three, the devil, the sinful world and our sinful flesh, gang up on us. They work hard to weaken and destroy our faith and our spiritual life.

"Our struggle," Paul wrote, "is not against flesh and blood, but against the rulers, against the authorities, against the powers of this dark world and against the spiritual forces of evil in the heavenly realms." Indeed, the devil's schemes can sometimes make us wonder whether it is so great to be alive. The fierce temptations we face, the sins we struggle against make us wonder, "How can I ever win? How can I hope to remain a believing child of God against such odds?"

One thing is sure—if it came down to us against Satan, if it were only up to us and our own strength and will, the battle would be lost. Peter, for one, discovered that we cannot rely on our own powers.

But Peter himself here encourages us to know and to trust that we are safe. The unholy three—devil, world and flesh—cannot win the battle and steal our salvation from us. "Through faith you are shielded by God's power," Peter tells us, from the present moment until the time when Jesus comes again to give us our inheritance of eternal glory.

Thank God for his mercy! It really is great to be alive in Christ, to know that our gracious God will not allow us to fall back into the hands of Satan and into spiritual and eternal death. He will shield us, guard and keep us till the last day.

But let's be sure that we don't miss two important words, "through faith." God's promise does not give us the right to fall asleep and to neglect our faith and spiritual life. God keeps us in faith by his Spirit through the preaching of the gospel and the sacrament of the altar. As we faithfully use them, he keeps us; we will be safe.

Heavenly Father, guard and keep us so that the unholy three may not deceive us or lead us into false belief, despair and other great and shameful sins; and though we are tempted by them, enable us to overcome and win the victory, through our Lord Jesus Christ. Amen.

In this way, love is made complete among us so that we will have confidence on the day of judgment, because in this world we are like him. (1 John 4:17)

BUILD YOUR PRESENT ON THE FUTURE

An evangelism approach used by some congregations opens with the question, "If you were to die tonight, do you know for certain where you'd be?" People who look at themselves and their lives for the answer don't know for sure—and are afraid of the question. People who look to God's love in the death and resurrection of Jesus Christ know certainly that their death will mark the beginning of eternal life with their Lord. God's love in Christ offers us that wonderful assurance. And in love God proposed that we might be able to approach the great day of judgment boldly.

But isn't it very cocky and presumptuous to say we know that our eternal destiny with Jesus is sure? No! To say anything less would be a doubting denial of what Jesus accomplished on the cross. St. John says that we have been made like Jesus, even though we are still in the world. That is not to say we have reached perfection here, but that we are now the adopted sons and daughters of God. We are the objects of our Father's love, as Christ was loved by his Father. We have been credited with the perfectly righteous life Jesus lived for us. He has paid for and removed our sins, which would otherwise have banished us forever from God's presence. So even though we are still on this side of judgment day, we who in baptism have "put on Christ" (Galatians 3:27) face that day with boldness.

But how is it that we should be bold? Doesn't the Bible tell us to be meek and humble? It tells us to be all of these at once: meek and humble as we evaluate ourselves and our miserable works, which are all tainted by sin; but bold and confident as we see the grand and glorious works of Christ and his righteousness, all of which belong to us by faith.

Our Christian hope is not some vague wish for the future. It is the eager anticipation of an assured future that fills our present with meaning. We are not to build our future upon the present, but our present upon the future. The empty cross points to our crown of glory in heaven. It gives us new courage. It lifts up our drooping spirits. And it brightens up our gloomy faces with the sure message that Christ is our Savior, God is our Father, and heaven is our home.

Fix our eyes on the crown of eternal glory your love has secured for us, dear Savior, that we may live boldly for you in our time of grace. Amen.

In this you greatly rejoice, though now for a little while you may have had to suffer grief in all kinds of trials. (1 Peter 1:6)

HOPE OUTLASTS TROUBLE

There was a time when the prophet Elijah was so overwhelmed by the difficulties of his work that he simply gave up and prayed to die. It is a feeling many since Elijah's day have shared. Life is indeed difficult. At times it may seem unbearable. For many, suicide seems the only answer, the easy way out.

"To end it all. To be rid of my suffering. To put my treatments behind me." How simple it all seems.

A man once said, "When you say a situation or a person is hopeless, you are slamming the door in the face of God." Yes, it's not easy to lie in a hospital bed day after day. Nor is it fun to come home when somebody in the family believes the only answer to life comes out of a bottle. But even these problems are not too big for God. If you give up on them, if you give up on life, you are really giving up on God.

How can you give up on God when he brought you into life? How can you give up on God when he gave his one and only Son to be your Savior? How can you give up on God when he has been with you with his word on the pages of the Bible?

Do not give up on him who has promised, "Never will I leave you; never will I forsake you." God will not give up on you.

We simply need to remember that every problem in life is only temporary. We can outlast it. God may well bring our difficulties to a close with the new dawn. In this we can greatly rejoice.

But what of the person who has been told his illness is terminal? How can we call that temporary? If we will just look to the garden where a man by the name of Joseph of Arimathea owned a burial site, we will note that the grave previously occupied now stands empty. Christ has conquered death. And we now have the hope of life in heaven. In Christ we can outlast any problem, even death.

When Elijah prayed that God would let him die, God instead patiently listened to his troubles and then renewed his hope in the promises of the Lord. God is listening to you. Talk to him in prayer. Listen to him through his Word. And then conquer each day with hope in a God who truly cares for you.

O my Savior, help me to endure my griefs and to sing your praises. Amen.

So that through endurance and the encouragement of the Scriptures we might have hope. (Romans 15:4)

THERE'S ALWAYS HOPE FOR TOMORROW

"The sun'll come out tomorrow," Little Orphan Annie sang in the movie. Anytime she got depressed and began to feel hopeless, she'd sing that song. Suddenly she felt better; she had hope for a brighter future. She also sang this song for others. And no matter how depressed they were, she got them to have hope for tomorrow.

All of us want to have hope. Sometimes little gimmicks help to get us out of the dumps. There's an ice cream cone for a little leaguer who struck out four times in the game. How about a kiss for a little girl who scraped her knee rollerskating? Mother who has had the worst day of her life gets taken out for dinner.

But even the best gimmick will let us down. The hurt may be just too painful for a kiss to take it away. The tragedy may be just too devastating for an ice cream cone or even dinner out to make us feel better. Things can get so bad sometimes that there doesn't seem to be any hope, and no cute song from an adorable little girl will make us feel better. But even then, there is hope.

In the Scriptures we learn that there's always hope for tomorrow.

These were written "so that through endurance and the encouragement of the Scriptures we might have hope." Endurance is the ability to stand up under heavy pressure and hold on, like a weight lifter who raises a barbell and holds it over his head. Endurance is our ability to put up with difficulties and come through. And this endurance in faith and life comes from the Bible.

As we read the Bible, God talks to us. He encourages us. He gives us the strength to endure. He gives us examples of how he has delivered his people in the past. He says, "I still have the same power and the same love to help you today."

When things look hopeless, look to the Bible, and find hope. Do you need help? God can provide it. Do you need forgiveness? God will give it. Do you need peace of mind? God has promised it and will give it to you. When things look hopeless, turn to the Scriptures, which give you encouragement and endurance. For with the Word of God, there's always hope for tomorrow.

Holy Spirit, turn me to your Word and fill me with the endurance and encouragement that only your Word can give. In this way give me hope for all my tomorrows. Amen.

The creation waits in eager expectation for the sons of God to be revealed. (Romans 8:19)

A WORD ABOUT THE FUTURE

The young and the young at heart often find it difficult to wait. It might be a party, a reunion with a friend, or some other big event that they are looking forward to. Anticipation fills their whole being. They just can't wait until the big day comes. If you have ever experienced that kind of anticipation, then you will certainly be able to understand our word about life for today.

In this verse we are told that the creation is on pins and needles as it waits for the completion of God's promises to his people. The creation waits with anticipation for the formation of the new heavens and earth, for the day when the resurrected and glorified saints will stand face to face with their God in glory. What a great day that will be!

Some people live their lives fearing their past, others are filled with doubts about the present and many are totally uncertain about the future. A few have hope that the future will be better but have no valid grounds on which to base that hope.

To live in fear, to live in doubt or to live with a groundless hope are not necessary evils in life. Jesus Christ calms fear, cancels doubt and supplies firm ground for a certain hope. Fear is calmed because, thanks to Jesus, all is right between sinful mortals and God. Doubt is canceled because, "If God is for us, who can be against us?" Hope is firmly established since Jesus declared, "Because I live, you also will live."

By God's grace we can look forward to each succeeding day. We can look forward with hope, peace and joy. Life is not a joke—with us as its target. In Christ, life is a wonderful blessing to be lived in the sure hope of ever better things to come.

Each day brings us closer to glory. With each passing day, the anticipation builds also in the creature world as the time for the revealing of God's sons draws near. "Dear friends, now we are children of God, and what we will be has not yet been made known. But we know that when he appears, we shall be like him, for we shall see him as he is."

"Forever with the Lord!"
O Father, 'tis Thy will.
The promise of that faithful word
E'en here to me fulfill. Amen.

In his great mercy he (God) has given us new birth into a living hope through the resurrection of Jesus Christ from the dead. (1 Peter 1:3)

THE CHRISTIAN'S LIVING HOPE

A very important part of every person's life is hope. There is scarcely a day when we do not indicate in some way or another that we are hoping for something. "I hope that package comes in today's mail." "I hope the dentist does not find any cavities in my teeth." "I hope we have meat loaf for dinner."

Very often this word "hope" expresses nothing more than a fond wish. Even though the sky may be overcast with dark, threatening clouds, you may say, "I hope it doesn't rain today." You may say that even though you are reconciled to the fact that rain is almost inevitable.

The Bible uses this word "hope" in a different way. It uses it in the sense of a sure hope or a certain hope. When we speak about our hope for eternal life, this is more than just a vague wish that some day we are going to dwell in the mansions of heaven. This is a confident hope. We live with the marvelous certainty that after we leave this earth we shall dwell with all fellow believers in the presence of God's glory.

Peter thus speaks of a living hope. He writes that the God and Father of our Lord Jesus Christ "has given us new birth into a living hope through the resurrection of Jesus Christ from the dead." Our living hope is very closely connected with the resurrection of Jesus. On the cross Jesus died. He was dead. But on that glorious first Easter morning he rose from the dead. He now lives. He is our living Savior who promises, "Because I live, you also will live."

Likewise we also were once dead, spiritually dead. When we came into this world we were dead in trespasses and sins. But through our new birth we are now spiritually alive. We have a living hope, a hope that is alive. We have a hope that will never fail. This gives us complete confidence that some day we shall follow our Savior in rising from the grave. How rich we are to be blessed with a living hope!

My hope is built on nothing less
Than Jesus' blood and righteousness;
I dare not trust the sweetest frame,
But wholly lean on Jesus' name.
On Christ, the solid Rock, I stand;
All other ground is sinking sand. Amen.

And I have the same hope in God as these men, that there will be a resurrection of both the righteous and the wicked. (Acts 24:15)

STAND UP WITH HOPE

To say the least, St. Paul's situation was precarious. He had been arrested and imprisoned. With the aid of a smooth-talking lawyer, the enemy had brought some very serious charges against the Apostle. Governor Felix could sentence Paul to a lengthy prison term. He could order Paul's death.

But in spite of the danger which he faced, Paul was undaunted and unafraid. Without worry or care, he boldly defended himself and his work in Felix's court.

What was the source of Paul's fearlessness and courage? In his defense before Felix Paul points to the reason for his confidence. He declares that he has "hope in God." He is sure that "there will be a resurrection of both the righteous and the wicked." So what if he must languish in prison for awhile! So what if enemies put an end to his life! Paul was confident that Jesus would raise his body from the dead and would bring him to the glory of eternal life.

In this world we too must face danger and hardship. Some people may actually threaten to kill us. Others may try to hurt our feelings, to destroy our family happiness, or to ruin us financially. Then there are the ever-present dangers of a tragic accident, a serious illness, being laid off of work, a flood, a tornado and other natural disasters.

But no matter how great the danger may be, we need not be frightened or upset, if we hold fast to Jesus in faith. Come disaster, pain or death, still we shall be "more than conquerors" through him that loved us. Jesus fills our hearts with hope. In his Word he assures us that all things, including the gravest danger and deepest sorrow, must work together for good to them that love God. Even when we "pass through the valley of the shadow of death," we need not fear any evil. Jesus will bring us safely to the other side. And we shall dwell in the house of the Lord forevermore.

In every peril and danger, let us stand up for Jesus boldly and courageously. For we have the sure hope that Jesus is at our side to defend us and to deliver us.

Lord Jesus, forgive our fears and weakness of faith. Fix our eyes on the hope of glory which you have pledged to us. Help us to stand up for you with boldness and courage. Amen.

Praise be to the God and Father of our Lord Jesus Christ! In his great mercy he has given us new birth into a living hope through the resurrection of Jesus Christ from the dead. (1 Peter 1:3)

A LIVING HOPE

"**I**'m sorry, Mrs. Lansing, there was nothing we could do." It was the evening of Christmas Day. Daniel Lansing had gone to church alone that morning while his wife and his children's families slept late. The whole family had come home for the holidays. They had eaten and talked and laughed together. And then after that evening's good-byes, Daniel sat down in his easy chair—and died.

At the funeral home, Mrs. Cheryl Lansing wrestled with the urge to cry each time someone expressed his sympathies. Yet she listened as they filed by and said, "If there's anything we can do." "He looks so natural." "We'll miss him too."

All well meaning, surely, but the pain wasn't truly lessened until— "Remember, God not only gave us Christmas, Cheryl, he also gave us Easter." Linda Danson, a neighbor from her husband's church, had come. What was that she said? "He also gave us Easter."

These words lingered long after the funeral. Rather than mailing the thank-you to Linda, Cheryl decided to walk over to her neighbor's and drop it off personally. In the middle of shoveling her front steps, Linda puffed that it was time for a break anyway. She insisted that Cheryl come in for tea or coffee. After some small talk, Cheryl asked, "What did you mean, 'He also gave us Easter'?" Linda stared at the steam rising from her cup. She was looking for divine guidance on what to say.

Linda told Cheryl of the Savior, told her how the Jesus of Christmas was the same person who later died on a cross near Jerusalem. This same Jesus actually rose from the dead on the first Easter morning. He promised an eternal life of joy in heaven to all who believe in him—as Daniel had believed.

Oh, Cheryl had heard it all before from her husband. But this time the words seemed somehow different. God was using the calling home of her husband to call her home in a different way. He reclaimed Cheryl as part of his flock through the power of his word. And now Cheryl had something she had thought during this past week she would never have again. She had hope, a living hope. Because Daniel's Savior lived—no, because THEIR Savior lived, Daniel hadn't really died. And neither would she.

My Savior, help me ever cling to the hope of the resurrection. Amen.

What we will be has not yet been made known. (1 John 3:2)

THERE IS MORE IN STORE

When we begin to add up all the blessings we enjoy as the people of God, the list just keeps on growing. We're simply overwhelmed by God's graciousness. In explaining the First Article of the Creed, Luther makes a list of blessings from God: "clothing and shoes, meat and drink, house and home, wife and children, land and cattle, and all my goods and all that I need for my body and life." And then in the Second Article Luther points to the greatest blessing: "[He] has redeemed me a lost and condemned creature."

But there is still more to come! Our text for today says that "what we shall be has not yet been made known." Doesn't that whet your appetite as to what God has in mind for us in glory?

When we consider these words of our God, a growing anticipation of glory ought to develop within us. If a father tells his child, "I have a surprise for you on Friday," can't you imagine how the youngster will grow in anticipation of what the surprise might be?

Our heavenly Father does much the same thing. He tells us that we shall live with him in glory, but he doesn't tell us much what that glory will be like. He does tell us enough to know that it is going to be most pleasant and happy.

What effect should this have on our living in this world? For one thing, it ought to be a constant reminder that in this life we occupy only temporary quarters. Our permanent home is with God in heaven. Keeping this in mind helps us maintain a proper attitude toward this world and the things of this world.

What a terrific hedge this future hope is against depression or despondency! Satan would like nothing better than to get us long-faced and feeling sorry for ourselves over the loss of some earthly possession, or over our health problems, or over personal relationships. Obviously the problems of life aren't pleasant, but neither do they snuff out our hope. This hope rests upon the promises of God, and he in no way lies or deceives. There is more in store, much more. We have God's Word on it.

Dear Lord, you have done all things right. Your creation was without flaw. Your redemption of all men is perfect and complete. And beyond this you hold before us a promise of even more blessings to come. Keep us living in faith and trust through all the trials of this life. Help us to realize that the sufferings of today cannot diminish the beauty and joy of what you have in store for us. We ask this through your Son, Jesus Christ, our Lord. Amen.

Dear friends, now we are children of God, and what we will be has not yet been made known. But we know that when he appears, we shall be like him, for we shall see him as he is. (1 John 3:2)

ANTICIPATING HEAVENLY JOY

What will heaven be like? From what Scripture tells us, heaven is a place of perfect joy and happiness. It is interesting to note, however, that Scripture often speaks of heaven in terms of what will not be there. This is because we are sinful human beings living in a sinful world. We have not experienced perfect joy and happiness, and we cannot imagine what that will be like. Scripture speaks in terms of sin with all its sorrows being absent from heaven. This gives us a picture of what our heavenly existence will be.

St. John received a revelation of the new heaven and the new earth. He described it as a place where all sin is removed. Death, mourning, crying and pain will be things of the past. Believers will live eternally in the presence of their loving Savior. John said of those in heaven, "They are before the throne of God and serve him day and night in his temple; and he who sits on the throne will spread his tent over them. Never again will they hunger; never again will they thirst. The sun will not beat upon them, nor any scorching heat. For the Lamb at the center of the throne will be their shepherd; he will lead them to springs of living water. And God will wipe away every tear from their eyes" (Revelation 7:15-17).

In heaven we will be confirmed in holiness, freed from the corruption of sin so we may serve our Lord forever in righteousness. We shall have the same bodies, but they will be glorified, patterned after the glorious resurrection body of Jesus.

What glory we have to look forward to! What joy will be ours! Yet, this joy also serves us now. In this life our eyes are often clouded with tears. Because we live in a world corrupted by sin, we experience pain and heartache. When we become burdened by the problems of this life, we need to remember the words of John, "Dear friends, now we are children of God . . . But when he appears, we shall be like him." We have joy that makes life worth living. We have hope that takes the fear out of dying. Praise the God of our salvation for the hope he has given us!

O sweet and blessed country, the home of God's elect!
O sweet and blessed country that eager hearts expect!
Jesus, in mercy bring us to that dear land of rest,
Who art, with God the Father and Spirit, ever blest. Amen.

And we know that in all things God works for the good of those who love him, who have been called according to his purpose. For those God foreknew he also predestined to be conformed to the likeness of his Son, that he might be the firstborn among many brothers. And those he predestined, he also called; those he called, he also justified; those he justified, he also glorified. (Romans 8:28-30)

I'M SURE!

"**G**eorge, if you should die today, will you go to heaven?" "Yes," replied George. "You can't be absolutely sure, can you?" asked his friend. "I'm sure! and I'll tell you why I'm so very sure."

God invited me to be his child. He did this through the good news of the Gospel which tells me of my salvation in Jesus. He has seen to it that I have not only heard but have also accepted his invitation. He has caused my heart and mind to accept the invitation. In this way faith that trusts in Jesus for salvation was created in me. Because of this faith, God is no longer angry with me over sin. My God-given faith takes the righteousness of Christ and makes me holy and just in God's eyes. That's how I was made his child.

As his child I'm sure that everything that happens to me will serve for my good and lead me yet closer to the Lord. You see, God will let no harm come to any of his children. In fact, it has to be this way. Before time began, God knew me and decided that I was to become his child. Therefore he provided a way for my salvation in Jesus. He saw to it that I was invited and called to be his child through his holy Word. He moved my heart to accept and believe the invitation. He is actually keeping me in faith right now through his Word. That's why I have faith that trusts in Jesus' blood and righteousness. That's why I am his child. That's why I have a sacred promise from him.

Our gracious Lord, who made me his child through faith in Jesus, has made me a sacred promise. He has promised that he will glorify me, that is, make and keep me perfect for heaven. So it's just a matter of time until he will also give me the perfect reason for his inviting and calling me. In heaven his promise will be kept.

"Yes, dear friend, I'm sure I will go to heaven when I die. God has taken the whole matter out of my hands and has given me the gift of eternal life. Oh, how he loves me! You're his child by faith in Jesus. You too can be sure," encouraged George, as he was taken to the operating room where God kept his sacred promise to him.

O Lord, truly you have loved us. Amen.

Not only so, but we also rejoice in our sufferings, because we know that suffering produces perseverance; perseverance, character; and character, hope. And hope does not disappoint us, because God has poured out his love into our hearts by the Holy Spirit, whom he has given us. (Romans 5:3-5)

OUR JOY AMID TRIBULATION

In this sin-cursed world in which we live, things don't always turn out the way we plan. As a result our hearts are often filled with sorrow, disappointment and fear. But what a comfort it is to know that we have a Savior who can say, "I know exactly how you feel. I faced those same hardships during my life on earth." It's with a full personal understanding of all our problems that our Savior graciously invites us, "Come to me, all you who are weary and burdened, and I will give you rest."

But we've never seen Jesus. We've never actually heard him speak to us. How can we receive strength and comfort from someone whom we've never seen or heard? That's the work and function of the Holy Ghost. The Holy Ghost comforts us in all our tribulations by directing our attention to the loving concern which Jesus has expressed for us in his Word.

Are you a young person who sometimes wonders, "Could Jesus possibly know and understand how I feel?" Remember the rich young ruler? The Bible shows that Jesus understood that young man better than that young man understood himself. Are you growing old and feeling concerned that you're becoming a burden to your loved ones? Jesus can understand this concern. Didn't he appoint John to care for his mother so that she wouldn't feel unloved and unwanted in her twilight years! Have you lost a loved one in death? Jesus knows the feeling. He wept at the grave of Lazarus. Jesus knows the feeling of being so completely exhausted from work that one can barely keep one's eyes open. He knows the feeling of pain. Yes, he even knows what it feels like to die, for remember, he died for our sin.

It was the Holy Spirit who inspired the apostles to record all these feelings of Jesus in the Scriptures, in order to assure us that Jesus knows what we feel and is able to meet our needs. By bringing us the good news about Jesus' great love for us, the Holy Spirit fills our hearts with the strength needed to face all our problems with patience, hope and joy.

Above all, Jesus took our sins away. He removed that which would make our tribulations unbearable. That's how much he loved us!

Holy Spirit, in all my tribulations comfort me with the good news of Jesus' love for me. Amen.

If we have been united with him like this in his death, we will certainly also be united with him in his resurrection. (Romans 6:5)

CERTAIN TO RISE

What is certain in this life of ours? "Death and taxes," the cynic replies. "Everything else changes." Families grow up. Cities sprout suburbs. Bulldozers level houses for parking lots. Idled factories become upscale condominiums. A lot of people don't even know where their next meal is coming from. What is certain?

For the Christian it is not only death that is certain. We can be certain to rise on the last day to everlasting life. That is because we have been united with Christ. By faith God has completely joined the life of his Son and our lives together.

When a gardener grafts a branch to the tree, he expects that graft to take hold and receive its nourishment through the tree. If the tree suffers damage in either its trunk or root system, the graft will also suffer. The graft shares the life of the tree.

Or consider a hot-air balloon. The basket in which the balloonist rides does not soar through the sky without the balloon. If the balloon plunges to the ground, certainly the basket will also follow. One destiny awaits both.

Jesus Christ is the tree to which we have been grafted by God's grace through faith. Whatever Jesus experiences, we will experience. The same destiny is ours.

Jesus really died on the cross to take our sins away. It is historical fact. We are sure it happened. Easter is another historical fact. We believe that Jesus rose from the dead. Because he rose, we will rise. Jesus promised. His promises are sure.

Our certainty can be just that, and not wishful thinking. We base our hopes not upon the changing nature of this world or upon the fickle people who fill this world. We base our hopes upon our eternal and unchanging Lord Jesus Christ. We have been united with him in his death by faith. We will certainly also be united with him in life everlasting.

Heavenly Father, give me the certainty that, just as my Savior Jesus rose from the dead, I too will rise on the last day and spend eternity with you in heaven. Amen.

For I am convinced that (nothing) . . . will be able to separate us from the love of God that is in Christ Jesus our Lord. (Romans 8:38,39)

A FRIEND ON OUR SIDE

Let's pretend that I am a small child. I am not gifted with a great amount of natural ability or physical strength. Now, let's pretend that right down the street from me there live three other children. They are the neighborhood bullies. They are big, and they are strong. They have also told me that they are not particularly fond of me. In fact, they have told me that the next time they see me downtown, they are going to pick a fight.

Now let's pretend that one day my mother asks me to go to the store for her. How would I feel? Probably not very good, right? I would want to do what my mother asks, and yet I am afraid because of the threats I have received. I am not sure if I can overcome that problem by myself.

But then, just when things seem to be at their worst, my uncle comes to visit. He is big, and he is strong. Nothing frightens him. He looks at me and says, "Come on, I'll go along with you to the store." How would I feel then? Not so frightened anymore, right?

Why not? Because I have a big, strong, powerful friend right beside me. I know that as long as he is there, none of the bullies will bother me. So I walk down the street with a definite feeling of security, with a newfound sense of confidence. I have nothing to fear. I am convinced of that.

Have you ever felt that way in the course of your lifetime? Sometimes the problems, the pains and the persecutions of this life seem to squeeze us so tightly. We seem so terribly weak and powerless. We are frightened. We don't think that we can overcome those bullies by ourselves. And we are probably correct. By ourselves we cannot.

But fortunately for us as Christians we don't have to overcome them by ourselves. We have a big, strong, powerful ally and friend. He does the fighting for us. And he is not just someone who visits us every now and then. He is with us every day of our lives. This is his promise. We can now be secure with nothing to fear. We, like Paul, are convinced of that fact.

Heavenly Father, be with us and give us courage to face and to overcome any problems that plague us. Amen.

Though you have not seen him, you love him; and even though you do not see him now, you believe In him. (1 Peter 1:8)

THANK GOD YOU BELIEVE

"We would like to see Jesus," some Greeks said to Philip the disciple. They wanted to see and meet personally this man of whom they had heard such wonderful things.

Every Christian has the same longing—to see Jesus. Perhaps it is in our most difficult moments that we most wish we could see Jesus. The sight of our glorified Savior would do so much for us, we think.

Maybe sometimes we envy those women, those disciples, even Thomas, the doubter, who were privileged to see the risen Lord with their own eyes. How much stronger we'd be if we could have the same opportunity!

But that's really not necessary, is it? The marvelous thing about faith is that it clings to the unseen. The disciples saw Jesus because they were to be the eyewitnesses who would pass on what they had seen to others, including us. Not all need to see him. But everyone needs to hear about him.

Remember what our Savior said to Thomas, "Blessed are those who have not seen and yet have be-

lieved." Certainly Peter had that in mind as he wrote the words of to-day's text. He knew that sight is not necessary for faith. Faith in God and in Christ can exist perfectly well without seeing. "Faith is being sure of what we hope for and certain of what we do not see," the writer to the Hebrews reminds us. We should also remember that there were many, like the scribes and Pharisees, who did see Jesus on earth but still refused to believe in him.

Though we have not seen our Savior with our own eyes, we love him, for we have heard about his love and sacrifice for us. Even though we don't see him, we still believe in him, for by God's Word and Spirit we have received the gift of faith.

We would indeed like to see Jesus. And one day we will. But until then we can thank and praise our God that we believe without seeing, that we know our Savior as well and love him as the disciples who followed him during his ministry. Until we do see him, we are confident that:

Blessed are they that have not seen
And yet whose faith hath constant been;
In life eternal they shall reign.

Lord Jesus, our crucified and risen Redeemer, accept our thanks and praise for faith, life and salvation. Keep us in that faith until we see you with our own eyes in glory. Amen.

We . . . rejoice in God through our Lord Jesus Christ, through whom we have now received reconciliation. (Romans 5:11)

LOVE BRINGS TRUE JOY

Happiness, it is said, is a state of mind. Some days that state of mind is nowhere to be found. Observe the faces of those who pass you on the sidewalk. Some look as if they had eaten ground glass for breakfast. Even at a funeral you won't see faces that long.

Perhaps it's understandable. Our economic picture doesn't always promote happiness. Homeowners live under the burden of having to pay one bill after another. A river of depressing news threatens to drown us each day: the soaring crime rate, child abuse, political scandal, illegal drugs, marital unfaithfulness, energy and environmental crises—all add heavy weights to the strains under which we live. No wonder ours deserves to be dubbed the aspirin age.

In times like these even Christians are prone to depression, lured to seek relief in shallow, worldly cures. The final words of our lesson, however, are an invitation to find true joy in our God and his Word. Still, this joy is hard to feel. Why?

When we sense that someone is holding something against us, we go on the defensive and are even tempted to become hostile. This is even more true of our relationship with God. If things are not going well, if illness or financial setbacks or other personal problems are threatening us, we are tempted to think that God is punishing us for our sins. But that is not the case with God's children. As Paul tells us, "God was reconciling the world to himself in Christ, not counting men's sins against them." God does not hold our sins against us anymore. So complete is our reconciliation in Christ that God feels nothing but the warmest love for us. He gives us his peace, the strength to rejoice even in trials, the secure hope of salvation.

Only the knowledge of this love of God can quiet the Christian's heart when it is troubled. When a lake is deep, storms may ruffle the surface waters, but below all is calm. Life will test our spirits too, but if we immerse our thoughts in the depths of God's love, we will still rejoice, even when we must weep. "Though you have not seen him, you love him; and even though you do not see him now, you believe in him and are filled with an inexpressible and glorious joy, for you are receiving the goal of your faith, the salvation of your souls" (1 Peter 1:8,9).

Dear Lord, we rejoice in you. Give us power to express that joy in the way that we live. Hear us, for Jesus' sake. Amen..

And do not grieve the Holy Spirit of God, with whom you were sealed for the day of redemption. (Ephesians 4:30)

SEALED WITH THE HOLY SPIRIT

These inspired words of the sacred writer are some of the most comforting words in Scripture. We are "sealed" with the Holy Spirit "for the day of redemption." Sealed is a legal term. The seal makes valid the statement of a person. The seal guarantees it. Probably for the majority of us Christians, this sealing occurred already in our baptism when as babies we were brought into God's family. For others it may have occurred later, when they came to faith as adults. In either event, the Lord assures us that this seal will stand to the last great day, when we will be freed from sin and death and be his forever in heaven.

Because we have this seal, this assurance of God that we are his no matter what, he will be with us and keep us to the very last day. What a tremendously powerful defense this knowledge is against temptations and against the attacks of Satan, who wants us to think that our faith is uncertain and our future shaky.

Regardless of what happens, we can be sure we are God's. He has sealed us as his own in the Spirit. That is the most wonderful knowledge, and we need to hang on to it.

When we get up in the morning, when we are about the business of the day, when we are lying down at night, we know that we are in God's hands because he has sealed us to be his own. He is by our side with his gracious will and his almighty power. The Bible assures us that "the Lord knows those who are his." He knows us and keeps us in his love.

What a surge of joy, power, gratitude and praise is ours, as we understand that we are sealed for the day of redemption! The burden of feeling that the future of our faith depends on our own strength is lifted. We know our own strength is not dependable. But the Spirit of God works through the means of grace with his almighty power. In that we can feel safe and secure!

God does not want us to use this feeling of security in our faith to become indifferent toward sin. Rather, he wants to provide comfort amid times of helplessness and feelings of despair. And he gives us motivation when he assures us that we are sealed by the Spirit. Knowing that we belong to God, we will want to live as his children.

Dear Holy Spirit, I am so happy in the knowledge that you have sealed me. You have assured me that it is your almighty power that will keep me in the faith to the last day. For this I praise you. Amen.

He cares for you. (1 Peter 5:7)

GOD CARES

Every once in a while something may happen to make us wonder whether anyone really is concerned about us or not. Do we mean anything to anyone? Or are we just numbers on a charge card, a license plate, a social security card?

It is not unusual suddenly to discover that there are more people who have a real concern for us than we ever imagined. But it is also true that there is no one who has a greater interest in us and a greater concern for us than God does.

It should hardly be necessary for Peter to write as he does and to say: "He cares for you." For isn't this apparent from personal experience? When day after day God supplies, not only what we need, but far more; when we find joy in our work and God crowns our labors with a measure of success; when in the morning we arise from a refreshing sleep and when in the evening we return home safely; doesn't all of this say simply but eloquently: "He cares for you." And then we look back over our past and see how God has watched over us and led us to this very hour. Perhaps now we can see to an extent how he is able to bring good out of those times of suffering and sorrow. Once again we are reminded that God cares about us.

More important than all of these things, God has also given us his Word. There we learn how God in love chose us from all eternity to be his own, and how, to make this a blessed reality, he sent his own Son to be our Savior, to give his life for us. At the cross of Calvary, more than anywhere else, we see God's matchless love—a love that forgives, a love that restores to us eternal life.

Because of what Jesus has done for us, God is no longer angry with us. He is pleased to send his holy angels to watch over us. He guides the flow of history so that men will not be able to rob us of our salvation. He restrains the power of Satan, closes the gates of hell and opens the gates of heaven for us.

No, it should not have been necessary for Peter to write as he did. But that we might not doubt it even in our darkest hour, God had him say it once more: "He cares for you."

My spirit on Thy care,
Blest Savior, I recline;
Thou wilt not leave me to despair,
For Thou art Love divine. Amen.

Who shall separate us from the love of Christ? (Romans 8:35)

CHRIST'S LOVE IS OUR SECURITY

We need security, but so often we feel very insecure. We hang our need for security on some very thin wires at times. Take our health, for example. People who have that wide, vertical, zipper-like scar down the middle of their chests are living proof that we are all only a pulse beat this side away from that side. Something as tiny as a blood clot, smaller, much smaller than a pea, if lodged in the wrong place, can suddenly turn our speech into a slur and reduce our steps to a shuffle or less.

We hang the heavy need for security on the thin wire of our possessions. We know better, but we still do it. Materialistic to the core, we convince ourselves that life does consist in the abundance of the things we possess, that contentment is not limited to food and clothing, that birds of the air and lilies of the field don't know what they're missing without all these creature comforts. Enter layoffs and medical bills and unexpected expenses. Exit the comfortable savings account and the financial plan. Snap goes the wire on our security.

Or the thin wire may be familiarity and predictability. We feel secure with the same job, the same house, the same school, the same family, and on and on. Enter the corporation take-over, graduation, a new political regime. Snap goes the wire. All the above have their good places in our life, but they don't give us what we ultimately need.

"Who shall separate us from the love of Christ?" asks the Apostle Paul. His answer is clearly implied. No one and and no thing. God's love shown to us in Christ is the sturdy cable on which we can hang our need for security.

Christ's love is universal. "God so loved the world." There is no need for us to fear that we are excepted from this love.

Christ's love is unchanging. "Jesus Christ is the same yesterday and today and forever." There is no need to fear that his love will disappear at some future time.

Christ's love is unconditional. "While we were still sinners, Christ died for us." We can reject Christ's love, but never destroy it. It is there for us always. It offers us forgiveness and life, as well as the security we long for and need to have.

O Lord Jesus, we thank you for your love which is given to us and never taken from us. Help us rely upon it always. Amen.

My message and my preaching were not with wise and persuasive words, but with a demonstration of the Spirit's power, so that your faith might not rest on men's wisdom, but on God's power. (1 Corinthians 2:4,5)

RELYING ON GOD'S POWER

At times Paul presented a rather negative picture of himself as he preached at Corinth. Recall what he said of himself: "I did not come with eloquence or superior wisdom. . . . I came to you in weakness and fear, and with much trembling. My message and my preaching were not with wise and persuasive words." From just this description of his preaching we might expect to learn that all his hearers were disappointed, bored and totally turned off.

But they were not. The book of Acts tells us, "Many of the Corinthians who heard him believed and were baptized." Why? Was it because they were so impressed with the man Paul? Obviously not. It doesn't seem there was much in his appearance, style or vocabulary to be impressed about. Only because of the power of God did the Corinthians know of their salvation in Christ after hearing Paul preach.

From A to Z our salvation is the powerful work of God. He planned it. He worked it out at the cross by his Son. His inspired Word tells us of it and invites us to receive it. By the power of his Spirit we are led to accept the great news of our forgiveness and are kept in the saving faith. That's why we can be positive of our salvation. It is based 100 percent on God's power. What confidence that marvelous fact gives!

Faith that relies on people can sometimes disappoint us. We may have had the rug pulled out from under us when we thought we could trust someone. A friend who sends us a valentine one day might disappoint us the next.

It could even happen that the pastor from whom we learned the Word of God might later reject God's Word. Certainly that would shock us and disappoint us. But it would not place our salvation in jeopardy. Our faith does not rest on men, "but on God's power."

Rely on your faithful God's power, and you have every reason to be certain of your salvation. He cannot disappoint.

Thank you, Lord, for the assurance that from beginning to end my salvation is your powerful work. Now I may serve you in confidence and tonight rest secure through Jesus Christ our Lord. Amen.

LaVergne, TN USA
19 May 2010
183282LV00003B/3/P